The
Hank Adams
Reader

An Exemplary Native Activist and the Unleashing of Indigenous Sovereignty

Edited by David E. Wilkins

FULCRUM
GOLDEN, COLORADO

Library of Congress Cataloging-in-Publication Data

The Hank Adams reader : an exemplary native activist and the unleashing of indigenous sovereignty / edited by David E. Wilkins.
    p. cm.
  Includes bibliographical references and index.
  ISBN 978-1-55591-447-9 (pbk.)
  1. Adams, Henry, 1944- 2. Indian activists--United States--Biography.
3. Indians of North America--Civil rights. 4. Indians of North
America--Claims. 5. Indians of North America--Politics and government.
6. Trail of Broken Treaties, 1972. 7. Wounded Knee
(S.D.)--History--Indian occupation, 1973. 8. American Indian
Movement--History. 9. Self-determination, National--United States. 10.
United States--Race relations. 11. United States--Politics and
government. I. Wilkins, David E. (David Eugene), 1954-
  E90.A26H36 2011
  970.004'97--dc22
  [B]
                         2011006043

Printed in the United States of America
0 9 8 7 6 5 4 3 2 1

Design by Jack Lenzo

Fulcrum Publishing
4690 Table Mountain Drive, Suite 100
Golden, Colorado 80403
800-992-2908 • 303-277-1623
www.fulcrumbooks.com

Contents

Acknowledgments

I am, as always, grateful to my family for their unstinting love and support: Evelyn, Sion, Niltooli, and Nazhone. And thanks to Sam Scinta for his staunch belief in this project. The librarians and archivists at several outstanding libraries and historical societies provided the bulk of the papers presented in this collection: the Seeley G. Mudd Manuscript Library at Princeton University; the Center for Southwest Research at the University of New Mexico; the Minnesota Historical Society; and the Special Collections Library at the University of Washington. And to Daniel Cobb, who was kind enough to share some of his own research with me that featured the early years of the National Indian Youth Council.

My deep appreciation also extends to my two gifted mentors, George Whitewolf (Monacan) and Vine Deloria Jr. (Standing Rock Sioux). George devoted his life to resuscitating and sustaining the lifeways of both eastern and western Native peoples, while Vine did the same and was the first person to bring Hank's name to my attention in 1980. Vine and Hank shared a common love for the peoples, the lands, and the cultures of the Northwest Coast and admired them for, among other things, their dedication to the perpetuation and enhancement of treaty rights.

A hearty thanks also to Nicole Gruhot of the University of Minnesota, who skillfully typed the entire manuscript, and in her spare time no less. I am also deeply appreciative of Carolyn Sobczak, whose excellent editorial skills helped clarify and strengthen the book.

Of course, this work exists only because Hank Adams has spent his entire adult life exercising his personal sovereignty to help enhance the collective sovereignty of Native peoples in the northwest corner of the United States. But Hank's brilliant writings, testimonies, and diplomatic skills have influenced indigenous peoples and their intergovernmental relations throughout North America and parts of Central America as well.

Foreword

Billy Frank

Hank Adams has been my good friend for more than fifty years.

I first met the skinny Indian kid with black-rimmed glasses at small intertribal meetings in the early 1960s. We were trying to figure out what we were going to do about the state prohibiting us from selling our steelhead, which they classified as a game fish. He was with the Quinaults and wasn't much more than a teenager at the time, but you could tell he was smart.

Months later, I was out on Nisqually Cutoff Road one day when he stopped to ask me for directions to Franks Landing, my family's home for many years. He was there to organize the fight for treaty fishing rights. It was the beginning of a long journey for us and our families. In the years that followed, he became a brother to me.

We've been through a lot together: getting beaten up, arrested, and jailed. Those were hard times, but we laughed a lot. I started calling Hank Fearless Fos—from the character in the *Li'l Abner* cartoon strip—after he got shot while tending a net on the river. I still call him Fearless today, because that's what Hank is. He's fearless.

It was Hank who kept us going throughout the long struggle for treaty fishing rights that led to the Boldt decision, in 1974. He has always been there for us. Even after he was drafted into the army, he found ways to keep on helping us, coordinating our efforts, building support from elected officials, and finding a little money to keep us all going. I'm not sure that we could have done it without Hank. He was everywhere, all at once, organizing, strategizing, and communicating.

Hank is one of the great thinkers in Indian Country. He remains a trusted adviser to many. I talk to him every day, because the fight continues every day and will never be over.

Hank's whole life has been dedicated to helping Indian people, but he has really helped all citizens of the United States. He is not just a champion of treaty rights. He is a champion of civil rights for all people.

He could have been many things: a lawyer, a professor, a politician. But those jobs would have just tied him down.

Hank shoots for the stars, and that's what he's been doing for his whole lifetime. We're just tagging along.

Introduction

Social movements, like the struggle for women's rights, the unemployment workmen's movement, the environmental movement, the Black Power movement, and others, ripen when a series of unpredictable forces coalesce, signaling that there is an opportunity for change. This need for change or, better yet, transformation is sometimes precipitated by a significant event—the death of a key person, the enactment of a particular law or court decision, or a natural catastrophe—that then combines with a mixture of forces that may be fed by anxiety, stress, ideology, excitement, or raw power imbalances.

Frances Fox Piven and Richard A. Cloward, in their classic study *Poor People's Movements: Why They Succeed, How They Fail*, emphasize that "the emergence of a protest movement entails a transformation both of consciousness and of behavior."[1] The transformation of consciousness, they argue, has three aspects. First, the established system is viewed as having lost legitimacy. Second, the members of the protest group, who had previously accepted the status quo, now begin to demand rights. And finally, the people come to believe that they have the power to change conditions for the better.[2]

The transformation in behavior is also remarkable and typically involves two features. First, "masses of people become defiant: they violate the traditions and law to which they ordinarily acquiesce, and they flout the authorities to whom they ordinarily defer. And second, their defiance is acted out collectively, as members of a group, and not as isolated individuals."[3]

While social movements may have multiple causes, their goals often include multiple desired changes—incremental, reformative, and sometimes radical—that are designed to improve the lives, respect the rights, or protect and enhance the resources of a group's members.

A critical element in nearly all effective social movements is leadership. For it is through smart, persistent, and authoritative leaders that a movement generates the appropriate concepts and language that capture the frustration, anger, or fear of the group's members and places responsibility where it is warranted. The group's leaders are also usually adept at clearly identifying the goals, desires, and aspirations of the members while being able to artfully explain to the majority group how they, too, may also benefit from the changes being sought by the disenchanted group. Finally, the leader is able to facilitate and manipulate the media in a way that augments the members needs. Imagine, for instance, the women's rights movement without

Elizabeth Cady Stanton or Gloria Steinem; or the Chicano movement without César Chávez; or the Black Power movement without two of its most distinctive leaders, Martin Luther King Jr. and Malcolm X.

For the Native nations in the United States, still staggering economically in the recent wake of World War II, the early 1950s were a particularly volatile, depressing, and frustrating period. They were facing the horror of political and legal termination at the hands of the US Congress,[4] the imposition by several states of criminal and civil jurisdiction via Public Law (P.L.) 83-280,[5] and forced relocation into urban areas. Unlike women, African Americans, or Latinos, the established Native nations, numbering more than 560 and each with its own unique government and history and separate political relationship with the federal and state government, experienced a demographic diversity and political distinctiveness that made it implausible for any single Native leader to emerge who would have persuasive ability, substantive knowledge, or the necessary skills to transcend all or even most indigenous national ideologies.

Despite this enormous set of complicating factors, several Native leaders who would eventually gain a measure of national status did, in fact, rise to the occasion in the early 1960s; and by their principled actions, brilliant intellect, visionary leadership, powerful oratory, and remarkable writing skills, they were able to lead both an individual nation and international indigenous renaissance that continues to the present.

Various scholarly works[6] have chronicled the emergence of and critical roles played by individuals such as Clyde Warrior (Ponca), Mel Thom (Walker River Paiute), Bruce Wilkie (Makah), Billy Frank Jr. (Nisqually), Vine Deloria Jr. (Standing Rock Sioux), Richard Oakes (Mohawk), Tillie Walker (Mandan-Hidatsa), Helen Peterson (Northern Cheyenne/Lakota), Robert K. Thomas (Cherokee), and Helen M. Scheirbeck (Lumbee). These individuals came of age in the 1950s and 1960s and fought tenaciously to resurrect and stabilize the sovereign status of both their individual nations and Native nations in general, and they focused their attention on addressing the issues both internal (education, poverty, housing) and external (lack of treaty enforcement, state taxation attempts, voting violations) that were bedeviling indigenous peoples at this decisive historical juncture.

Each of these individuals warrant serious attention for the distinctive voice and methods they employed—individually, organizationally, and collectively—in motivating their peoples and in challenging the institutional and perceptual status quo of the larger society. But there is another Native individual whose name must be added to this list of indigenous luminaries—that person is Henry "Hank" Lyle Adams, an Assiniboine-Sioux.

Hank Adams: "The Most Important Indian"

In August 1972, Vine Deloria Jr., already a widely recognized Native intellectual, was invited to give an address at Alfred University in New York.

Deloria responded by saying he had other obligations and would not be able to participate, but he encouraged university officials to invite Hank Adams instead. Adams, Deloria said, had not received much notoriety because he was "slight of build, very quiet, and remains on the rivers fighting the game wardens." But, Deloria went on to say, "in my mind histories written a generation from now will say that he was the only significant figure to emerge in the postwar period of Indian history."[7]

Two years later, Deloria followed up these brief laudatory comments with a full-length article about Adams that he boldly titled "The Most Important Indian."[8] Why would Deloria, already the author of several best-selling books and numerous articles, a former director of the National Congress of American Indians (NCAI), and possessed of one of the most brilliant and incisive minds of anyone, credit Adams, and not himself, with being the most important Indian?

In part, Deloria's title reflects his own inherent intellectual modesty. Deloria was well aware in 1974 that he, too, had acquired a significant measure of national attention because of his work with NCAI (he was executive director from 1964 to 1967) and his paradigm-shifting books *Custer Died for Your Sins*; *We Talk, You Listen*; and *God Is Red*. But as an intense, astute, and well-read student of indigenous/state affairs, treaty rights, and intercultural relations, Deloria understood more clearly than anyone at the time that Hank Adams had already accomplished much in just the first three decades of his life and that he was far too self-effacing an individual to ever trumpet his already considerable achievements as an indigenous political strategist.

A few choice quotes from Deloria's honorific essay explain very clearly why he felt so strongly about Adams's personality and talents and clarifies why Adams deserves our attention now.

> Adams is best known for his work in the fishing rights struggle in the Pacific Northwest...but for the record he was not only present but handled most of the planning and press releases. If there was a clear message coming from the early fish-ins, it was because Adams was able to gather sufficient resources together to get the protests under way, and the relatively sparse information on his presence there testifies to his commitment to getting the job done rather than gathering headlines.[9]

> Over the past decade, Adams has become the leading theoretician on the Indian side of the question and has never abandoned his original contentions about the scope of the Indian fishing right.[10]

> When Hank came into the fishing rights struggle the Indians were disheartened, disorganized, and certainly demoralized. In the decade in which he has been active, the situation has completely reversed. The right to fish guaranteed in the 1854–1855 treaties has been upheld in the Supreme Court and lesser

federal courts and the tribes now have a fishing commission, with Hank as the new fish commissioner, to supervise their recently reaffirmed right to fish.[11]

In less than a year, then, Hank Adams has been highly instrumental in resolving two major and bitter confrontations between Indians and the federal government [The 1972 occupation of the Bureau of Indian Affairs (BIA), and the 1973 occupation of Wounded Knee on Pine Ridge Indian Reservation].[12]

Eventually Hank won his [legal] points at least with the experts on the Indian side, and while many of the people hated to admit it, they had to conclude that Hank, a layman with no legal training, knew more about Indian treaty law than almost any of the lawyers working in the field.[13]

Three decades after Deloria wrote his article, *Indian Country Today* (*ICT*), the leading national Native newspaper, bestowed its first American Indian Visionary Award, in 2004, on a close friend of Adams's, Billy Frank Jr. (Nisqually). Frank is a dedicated warrior who battled local, state, and federal officials for years in a relentless effort to secure and exercise his and his nation's treaty-reserved right to fish. The next two recipients of this prestigious annual award were, not coincidentally, Vine Deloria Jr. (2005) and Hank Adams (2006). This dynamic trio of men, in the words of Jerry Reynolds,

would be a triumvirate of titans, giants who walked the earth to set people an example for centuries to come. In the contemporary West, one could imagine a telling focused on organizational effectiveness and the skill sets, neatly divided into practical activist (that would be Frank), intellectual strategist (Deloria), and far-sighted visionary (enter Hank Adams), that are required to accomplish the most complex and difficult tasks.[14]

The descriptions *self-effacing* and *far-sighted visionary* are only rarely attributed to the same person, but in Hank Adams's case they are symbiotic, nearly organic characterizations of this shy, reclusive man, a person described by one writer as "tireless, fiery, chain-smoking, lights-out brilliant, and soul-deep loyal to a sacred undertaking."[15]

As part of the festivities associated with the award, a number of friends and associates wrote short articles lauding the newspaper's choice of Adams as the recipient. The editors, for example, who decide the recipient, noted that while the award was given in recognition of Adams's vision, courage, discipline, and commitment, it was his "quiet modesty or natural humility that was found most admirable."[16] And they concluded the column by noting that "Adams is universally credited by those in the know—among those who were there—with finding peaceful solutions that saved lives in dangerous confrontations, with rescuing important historical and legal documents under great stress, and with becoming perhaps the most trusted Indian activist-intellectual formulating strategies and policy during the formative and often dangerous period of the American Indian Movement for rights and resources."[17]

Suzan Shown Harjo, another leading Native activist, who has known Adams for years, had this to say about him in her essay: "Adams, like Deloria, was an intellectual who never set himself above the people. Unlike Deloria, who was highly educated and credentialed, Adams has a high school diploma and is largely self-taught."[18] And she noted that one of Adams's real strengths during the fishing rights wars was his ability "to explain to large and small audiences the similarities and differences between civil rights and treaty rights, and how the laudable goal of 'equal rights' for women and people of color was a catchphrase used against Indians by treaty abrogationists to candy coat their objective of ending Indian rights and resources."[19]

Jim Adams, an *ICT* reporter, described in his column the breadth of Adams's intellectual activism: his efforts as a teen protesting Washington State's extension of jurisdiction on the Quinault Reservation under P.L. 280; his work on voting and fishing rights with the National Indian Youth Council in the 1960s–1970s; his critical role in 1972's Trail of Broken Treaties; his efforts to return the confiscated BIA documents; his brilliant negotiating skills in mediating a peaceful end to the 1973 siege at Wounded Knee; his travels to Nicaragua in the 1980s to express solidarity with the Miskito people; his engagement with Congress to have established the Little Bighorn National Monument (1980s–1990s); and finally, his battles in the 1990s with Washington State over the gaming initiative he felt was not in the best interest of the Native nations.[20] Adams has lived a spirited life that has benefitted countless thousands of people.

Adams: A Personal History

Adams, an Assiniboine-Sioux, was born on May 16, 1943, on the Fort Peck Reservation, in Poplar, Montana. Early in his youth, his family moved to the Quinault Reservation, in Washington State. Before and during his high school years (he graduated with honors from Moclips High School in 1961), Adams, never averse to hard work, labored a quarter of the year as a migrant laborer, mill worker, clam harvester, and salmon fisherman to supplement his large family's meager income.

In 1957, at the tender age of fourteen, Adams was exposed to one of the most pressing political issues of the day, the federal government's unilateral grant to Washington of criminal and some civil jurisdiction over Indian Country in the state, including the Quinault Reservation via P.L. 280. He attended a meeting where Quinault members bitterly complained about the joint federal and state action to impose state jurisdiction without tribal consent.[21] This undemocratic affront to Quinault sovereignty compelled Adams to act, and it set him on the path to challenge many other indigenous indignities and violations that he would learn about as he matured.

After graduating from high school, Adams enrolled at the University of Washington, where he studied for nearly two years. But his intellectual fervor and need to feel socially, morally, and politically engaged in the multitude of issues confronting Native peoples obliged him to abandon collegiate studies so that he could, in his words, "work full time on Indian community problems and concerns, and their study, which seemed both more immediately compelling and challenging than continuation of college."[22]

Adams continued to immerse himself in the treaty and statutory law of Native nations and the state and federal government as applied in the state of Washington, and he soon came to realize the need for lobbying, communication, and the development of position papers that outlined strategies he believed were required to confront the harsh conditions that were negatively impacting indigenous peoples. Soon, an unpredictable confluence of events would culminate in 1963 with Adams joining up with the recently established National Indian Youth Council (NIYC), under the leadership of Clyde Warrior and Melvin D. Thom. NIYC had been established in 1961 in the wake of the American Indian Chicago Conference. The organization consisted largely of Native college students, and it was designed to be a more vocal advocacy and service organization than the senior national Indian organization, the NCAI.[23]

Adams was hired as the special projects director and he undertook a number of assignments in several states, including his home state, focusing especially on treaty-based fishing rights and Native self-governance. Within the next two years, Adams also got involved with the NCAI, which was led by Vine Deloria Jr. from 1964 to 1967, for whom he worked as a research secretary from 1964 to 1965. He also served as a staff student assistant in 1965 for the Tillie Walker–led United Scholarship Service (USS), an organization that provided financial assistance to Native students.

It was during this hectic period that Adams would become familiar with yet another Native interest organization, the Survival of American Indians Association (SAIA), which organized a demonstration and march on the Washington State Capitol, in Olympia, in December 1963 to protest the harassment, violence, and treaty violations that Native fishermen were experiencing at the hands of local whites and state game officials.[24]

By the mid-1960s, Adams was deftly juggling multiple jobs. In March 1964, he, along with Clyde Warrior and Bruce Wilkie, led over two thousand protesters in another major demonstration in Olympia challenging that state's frequent assaults on Native fishers. But Adams did more than organize the march. Using all his skills, he plotted out a brilliant legal, public relations, and communication strategy that set the tone for the next decade of fishing rights and other sovereignty-based initiatives.

He enticed Charles Kuralt to bring out his CBS show to cover the saga at Frank's Landing. He brought in [Marlon] Brando. He instigated and facilitated three stirring film documentaries: *In the Shadow of the Evil*; *Treaties Made, Treaties Broken*; and, especially, Carol Burns' *As Long As the Rivers Run*. He helped to conceive and to secure the funding for publication of *Uncommon Controversy*, a report sponsored by the AFSC [American Friends Service Committee] on the Washington fishing rights controversy.[25]

More importantly, Adams made what would be the first of many visits to Washington, DC, in an effort to convince bureaucrats and lawmakers of the need to introduce legislation and improve regulations to protect Native fishing rights, as well as raise other issues.[26] In fact, he moved to DC in 1965 and spent most of his time there for the next three years.

Adams, like many other young men at the time, received his draft notice for the army in 1964. He initially refused to be inducted, protesting the way the United States was violating Native treaty rights and declaring that "I owe and swear first allegiance to the sovereignty of my tribes and my people."[27] He later relented and honorably served from 1965 to 1967. While he was stationed at Fort Belvoir, Virginia, he served as the editor of the post newspaper, the *Belvoir Castle*, sharpening his already substantial writing and editorial skills. During his three-year military stint, besides his service duties, he also befriended Ralph Nader, made extensive contacts with key congressional committee members and their staffers with regards to indigenous issues, analyzed the Elementary and Secondary Education Act in an effort to see how this law could be amended to better serve the educational needs of Native youth in Indian Country, found time to serve as director of the Quileute Nation's Community Action Program, and continued to provide leadership on the fishing rights struggle in Washington State.

In addition, he, along with others, carefully researched the status of Frank's Landing, a six-acre tract of land in Washington State, proving that this important fishing site was a legally constituted part of the Nisqually Reservation. And he was a member of the National Indian Advisory Board and the Office of Economic Opportunity's Upward Bound program.

Adams, SAIA, and Beyond

Nineteen sixty-eight was a watershed year for Adams. He returned to the West Coast and ratcheted up his involvement in local, regional, tribal, and national affairs. First, he became executive director of the SAIA, the nonprofit organization devoted to the development of Native community and broader public awareness of indigenous rights, particularly treaty rights. Second, he served as a consultant to the staff of Senator Robert F. Kennedy and the Senate's Select Committee on Indian Education. Third, he was a member of the national steering committee for the Poor People's Campaign, chaired first by Martin Luther King Jr., and then by Ralph D. Abernathy after King's assassination.

When Adams was interviewed on July 3, 1968, about his and other Indians' involvement in the Poor People's Campaign, he said that while Natives had not achieved their immediate goals—passage of Senator George McGovern's new Indian policy and an overhaul of the BIA—they had sparked a "responsible revolution" in the United States. He went on to say that a "committee of 10,000" had been formed to put pressure on federal officials to improve conditions for Native peoples. Adams, all of twenty-five years old, said that he was even considering running for Congress.[28]

In fact, he ran for Congress twice, in 1968 and 1972, as a Republican. He was defeated both times, but in the 1972 race, after having spent only one hundred dollars more than the filing fee, he garnered nearly 40 percent of the vote for the Republican nomination for US Representative in the third congressional district.[29]

But it was the US Supreme Court's 1968 fishing rights decision, *Puyallup Tribe v. Department of Game*,[30] that propelled Adams even further in his battle for treaty rights. In this case, the Court unanimously held that the state of Washington had jurisdiction over Nisqually and Puyallup fishers who had been convicted of exercising their rights to fish outside the reservation but at their "usual and accustomed places" in accordance with explicit treaty provisions.

Washington State had asserted that its prohibition of Native fishing outside the reservations had been spurred by conservation concerns, not because of racism or anti-treaty arguments. The state's rationale, however, was not accepted by Adams or his colleagues in the struggle, Janet McCloud, Al and Maiselle Bridges, and others.[31] In fact, the empirical evidence showed that while there were less than a thousand Native fishers in the entire state, there were more than 140,000 non-Indian fishers and more than 4,500 non-Indian commercial fishing enterprises. The commercial fishermen were taking about 80 percent of the salmon in Puget Sound and offshore before the meager number of Native fishermen even had a chance to fish.[32]

Adams, who was still residing in DC because of his part in the Poor People's Campaign, led a large multiracial group of marchers toward the Supreme Court on May 29, 1968, to protest the *Puyallup* decision. When they were confronted by the Metropolitan Police Force, Adams was able to convince the officials to allow a small group of the protesters inside so they could deliver their petition to court personnel, requesting that the Court reconsider its ruling. The petition read, in part, "The fishing rights were not granted to the Tribes—they already possess them—but rather were retained by the Indians in their treaty agreements, and were guaranteed the protection of the US in their exercise."[33]

After Robert Kennedy's assassination, Adams returned to Washington State, where he fought valiantly to secure for Native nations their ancestral and treaty-based rights to fish. He was arrested and jailed numerous times, and in January 1971 he was shot in the stomach while maintaining vigilance over a set net for some friends.[34] Adams said two white men had done the deed. The police, however, challenged his account. His assailants were never apprehended.

Meanwhile, the federal government had finally intervened as coplaintiff in the fishing rights battle with the state of Washington in September 1970 when it filed *United States v. Washington* on behalf of what would eventually be fourteen tribal coplaintiffs. But the tribes initially had little confidence in the lawsuit and worried that they might possibly lose all their treaty rights. Their fears seemed justified when George H. Boldt, a conservative Tacoma US district court judge, was assigned the case. Alvin Ziontz, one of the tribes' attorneys, says that Adams was so concerned about the case that he went to Washington, DC, "to ask the government to drop the lawsuit, believing it did not represent the best interests of the Indians."[35]

In an address to the Young Lawyers Section of the Bar Association on November 2, 1971, Adams identified several specific concerns about the way the federal government was handling the case. He said, for instance, that one of the government's lawyers, within a month after the case had been filed in September of 1970, had filed motions for intervention on behalf of several tribes "who he had never before met with, and with whom he has since refused to meet to discuss that action or other actions where the tribes could use legal assistance." He also said that the United States was refusing to "defend the tribes' rights to regulate their fishing activities off the reservations, except within the limits allowed by the state," something it had done previously.[36]

Despite Adams's initial concerns, it was clear as the case developed that the Native nations and the United States had a powerful legal, moral, and strategic position vis-à-vis the state. Besides having Adams, who, even without a law degree, was granted legal representative status to appear on behalf of individual Nisqually Indians, the federal government also enlisted the expert witness help of Dr. Barbara Lane, an anthropologist. She was already widely recognized as one of the leading authorities on the Native nations of the Pacific Northwest and on indigenous treaty rights in general.[37]

This combination of talented individuals, buttressed by overwhelming historical and legal evidence, won the day for the nations, although the decision enraged thousands of non-Indian fishers and the state of Washington: the 1974 landmark ruling held that treaty Indians were entitled to 50 percent of the commercially harvested catch in Washington State.[38] Once the Boldt decision had been delivered, Adams then easily segued into the equally difficult task of setting up the administrative network necessary to implement the decision. He served as interim coordinator in 1974 of the intertribal Northwest Indian Fisheries Commission (NIFC), which provided the staff and resources for the five treaty areas and the twenty tribes involved in the daily comanagement of the fisheries throughout western Washington. And he also served as the fisheries management coordinator for the Puyallup Tribe from 1974 to 1975. In that capacity he sought technical assistance and federal funding for the tribe's fishery programs. He also "envisioned a corps of Native American fishery biologists and enforcement officers to regulate the fisheries."[39]

Despite his lack of formal legal training, Adams already had nearly a decade of experience in legal research and judicial proceedings involving Indian tribal and individual treaty, statutory, constitutional, and other legal matters. He had represented himself and other Indian parties (including Native governments) in several state and federal courts on civil, criminal, and treaty matters.

As one example, in 1968 he had been arrested and appeared in Thurston County Superior Court as a result of activities during a series of demonstrations in support of Indian fishing rights, allegedly in violation of state regulatory salmon-fishing statutes. During the trial, Adams appeared pro se (for himself), waived jury trial, and was found guilty by the court. He appealed the judgment to the Court of Appeals in 1971. In *State v. Adams*[40] he admitted to using a set net, but declared that his "only purpose was to demonstrate the irrationality of the statutes prohibiting the use of set nets," and he therefore contended "that his action was 'symbolic speech' protected by the First Amendment to the US Constitution."[41] The court, however, was not swayed by Adams's arguments and upheld his conviction.

Also in 1971, Adams was invited by an agency within the North Vietnamese government to lead a five-person indigenous delegation to Hanoi. Adams wrote that "we go to Vietnam as 'pro-American' Indian people, holding, however, a judgment that America has been predominantly wrong in its roles in Vietnam."[42] The trip did not take place, however, because of local developments in Washington State and the war's prosecution. Adams continued to work privately with the families of several Americans held in Vietnam as prisoners of war or who were missing in action.

Like his good friend Vine Deloria Jr., Adams was also convinced that churches needed to be actively involved in correcting and adjusting their own policies and attitudes with regard to Native peoples. Between 1968 and1971, he served as a member of the Presiding Bishops Ad hoc Committee on More Indian Involvement for the National Episcopal Church, and he served on the Screening and Review Committee for the Episcopal Church, which reviewed grant applications to its General Convention Special Programs and its Northwest Region General Convention youth program.

In 1971, Adams chaired an ad hoc committee for new Indian politics and in his capacity developed a fifteen-point program for what the group was calling a New National Indian Policy that would "remove the human needs and aspirations of Indian tribes and Indian peoples from the workings of the general American political system and…reinstate a system of bilateral relationships between Indian tribes and the federal government."[43] This brilliant proposal, reprinted on page 89 of this volume, called for renewed treaty making, a constitutional amendment devoted to Native rights, and a permanent indigenous land base of 105 million acres. The gist of this proposal was reprised the next year during the Trail of Broken Treaties, when Adams masterfully crafted what has since become known simply as the Twenty-Point Proposal.

Finally, in May 1971, Adams was chosen by the National Indian Education Associaton (NIEA) to receive one of the organization's Abraham Lincoln Awards for his "courageous action in pursuit of equal opportunities." Adams was touted for his work with SAIA and his decadelong battle to have Native treaty rights upheld and tribal sovereignty recognized and supported.[44]

Broken Treaties, Wounded Knees, and Other Infirmities

By 1972, Adams was well known in Native circles as a gifted political, legal, and media strategist, as well as a savvy mediator. And he had amassed a wealth of experience and expertise on a number of hot-button topics: treaty-based fishing rights, criminal and civil jurisdiction, taxation matters, tribal sovereignty, and Indian land tenure, among others. Thus it came as no surprise that he would play a leading, if underappreciated, role in two of the major events in 1972–1973, the Trail of Broken Treaties Caravan/BIA takeover and the occupation of Wounded Knee.

The Trail of Broken Treaties Caravan, organized during the summer of 1972, started simultaneously in three cities: Los Angeles, San Francisco, and Seattle. The activists, fueled by deep frustration and anger over ongoing treaty violations, the murders of Native individuals like Raymond Yellow Thunder, Leroy Shenandoah, and Wesley Bad Heart Bull, and a sense of betrayal by both tribal governments and federal officials, motored their separate automobile caravans on a meandering course across the country. The plan was to rendezvous in St. Paul, Minnesota, where they would finalize their strategy and develop specific goals before heading on to Washington, DC, where they planned to arrive on the eve of the national election in the hopes of securing the attention of the nation and the presidential candidates, President Richard Nixon and Senator George McGovern.

When the three groups converged in St. Paul, numbering more than three hundred individuals, they divided into small working groups to draft out their major concerns. Topics that surfaced included a call for treaty renewal, closer scrutiny of tribal government officials, and the role of the federal courts, as well as land rights, international law, hunting and fishing rights, and more. Once the groups had completed their assignments, all the data was delivered to Adams, who then isolated himself in a hotel room. In the course of the next forty-eight hours, he drafted one of the most comprehensive indigenous policy proposals ever devised, titled simply "The Twenty Points." The proposal, building upon the fifteen-point one he had drafted the year before, "emphasized a return to bilateral treaty relations, restoration of

100 million acres of land, full tribal control of the reservation, religious and cultural freedom, and abolition of the BIA."[45]

The Twenty-Point Proposal was so far-reaching in its scope that the existing structures and personnel of both tribal governments and the United States had profound difficulty comprehending its meaning. Russell Means notes in his autobiography that he learned at that time that Adams was "a genius at analyzing problems and interpreting the Indian outlook vis-à-vis the Eurocentric male worldview."[46]

The story of what unfolded over the next several months once the caravan participants arrived in Washington, DC, including their eventual six-day takeover of the BIA, have been chronicled by a number of commentators.[47] Adams had not been in the BIA at the critical takeover moment, but once the standoff began and federal marshals began to threaten the Indian occupants, he offered his services as mediator "in hopes of preventing bloodshed and violence."[48] For three days, he patiently and carefully negotiated a truce with the White House Task Force. As a result, the occupation ended without bloodshed, with the federal government offering travel money, some $66,650, to the demonstrators and declaring that they would study the activists' Twenty-Point Proposal.

But when the Indians left the bureau, some of them were ferrying out hundreds of thousands of documents taken from the bureau's files, some of which were classified. When the federal government realized what had transpired, they began a nationwide search in an effort to recover the documents. Once again, Adams stepped up and offered his services to help recover the documents. He was convinced that the capture of the papers by the Indians was undermining their cause.[49]

At Adams's insistence, the documents began to be returned sporadically to his apartment in Washington, DC. When he would receive a batch, he would contact the FBI and have them picked up. By this time, Adams, who had forged a close bond with Jack Anderson and Les Whitten, two well-known investigative reporters, had contacted Whitten about the latest set of documents that had been returned, and together they planned to deliver three boxes of documents to the FBI on January 31, 1973. But as they and Anita Collins, a Paiute, were loading the boxes into Whitten's car, a team of FBI agents surprised them and quickly arrested the three individuals. They were separately charged with having unlawfully received and concealed the documents "with intent to convert the said property to [their] own use and gain," despite the fact that it was Adams who had been dutifully returning the documents to the FBI. Adams, Whitten, and Collins pled not guilty. The charges against them were serious: they each faced up to ten years in prison and a $10,000 fine.[50]

The government's case against the three quickly fell apart, however, when BIA officials had to admit that Adams had scheduled an appointment with them the same morning they were arrested, and Adams's lawyer brought forth a receipt for documents from Adams that was signed by the very FBI agent whose name and number were inscribed on the latest boxes of BIA papers—verifying that Adams had already returned some documents to the government.

Two weeks after the arrests, a federal grand jury refused to indict the three and concluded that far from receiving and possessing stolen property for their own use, Adams and Collins had "recovered the documents as a public service and were in the act of returning them to the government when arrested, while Whitten was merely covering the news event as a reporter."[51] The government quickly dropped all charges.[52]

Jack Anderson, who wrote a widely syndicated column at the time, had these laudatory, if slightly romanticized, things to say about Adams during this troubling episode: "Hank has a quiet dignity not at once apparent in his rumpled, careless appearance. He could fade into a casual crowd as easily as his forbears faded into the rolling prairie. He speaks as softly, too, as the Sioux once trod...His gentle manner, nonetheless, was but the moss on a character of granite. There is a nobility in his character that is missing in his features."[53]

As the Trail of Broken Treaties Caravan members made their way home, a complicated confluence of events—interpretations of the 1868 Lakota-US treaty, tribal government corruption, police brutality, a conflict between Russell Means and Pine Ridge's tribal chairman, Dick Wilson, and substantial land-leasing problems—were mushrooming on the Pine Ridge Reservation, in South Dakota, that would culminate in a seventy-two-day occupation, popularly known as Wounded Knee II. Once again, Hank Adams played the pivotal role as the crucial liaison who negotiated a peaceful resolution of this nationally known event. Adams served at the request of Leonard Garment, counsel to President Nixon, and at the request of the Oglala people. According to Deloria, "the major point of contention in the settlement was the promise of the White House to send out a team of negotiators to meet with the traditional chiefs and medicine man of the Oglala Sioux on the treaty of 1868."[54]

The indigenous resurgence occurring throughout the nation compelled some in the US Congress, at tribal insistence, to consider the creation of a bipartisan commission to closely examine Native issues and intergovernmental relations. Adams, not surprisingly, was also involved in these discussions, and once the American Indian Policy Review Commission was established in 1975, he was charged with leading the task force on Indian treaties and the trust relationship.

Although Adams's national profile became less visible after the late 1970s, he continued to be involved in a number of domestic and international affairs. At the national level, he remained active in the fishing rights affairs of the Northwest Native nations. He has also been involved in negotiating water rights accords between some Northwest Native peoples and non-Indian governments. He also fought to get the federal government to authorize, fund, and construct the Little Bighorn Battlefield National Monument Indian Memorial.[55]

In the mid-1980s, Adams, along with Russell Means and Glenn Morris, went on a monthlong fact-finding mission to Nicaragua to express their solidarity with the Miskito people of that state, who were in rebellion against the Sandinista government.[56]

While those familiar with Adams will recall his considerable work on fishing rights and major social movement events like the Trail of Broken Treaties, the scholarship and documents in this volume reveal a man with far greater interests and concerns than just those two important topics. Adams's brilliance is evident in the bevy of writings, speeches, and testimonies on topics that also include civil rights, media and literature, trust and land issues, the American Indian Policy Review Commission, and taxation and economic concerns, as well as in his incisive critiques of federal, state, and indigenous agencies. But the sheer number of Adams's works necessarily meant that I had to be selective in choosing which of his many writings to include, which to elide, and which to print in full. Space constraints required omitting a majority of the documents, but several of his particularly incisive and path-breaking works in fishing rights, the Trail of Broken Treaties, and several other areas are printed in full so readers can grasp the full weight and force of his intellect.

Adams has shown a nearly inexhaustible desire, leavened with an equal amount of sheer talent—five decades' worth and counting—in an unrelenting effort to stabilize, strengthen, and improve the standing of indigenous peoples, minority groups, and the larger society as well. He is an exemplary Native activist, indeed.

Notes

1. Francis Fox Piven and Richard A. Cloward, *Poor People's Movements: Why They Succeed, How They Fail* (New York: Vintage Books, 1979), 3.
2. Ibid., 3–4.
3. Ibid., 4.
4. House Concurrent Resolution 108 (August 1, 1953), the infamous termination resolution, also euphemistically called the Indian Emancipation Proclamation, was the federal government's official policy from 1953 until the mid-1960s. "Termination" entailed the legislative severing of federal benefits and support services to a number of Native nations, including the Menominee and Klamath.
5. P.L. 83-280 (August 15, 1953) delegated to five states—Washington, Oregon, Minnesota, California, and Nebraska (with a few reservation exemptions)—full criminal and some civil jurisdiction over Indian reservations and their residents within their borders and allowed other states to assume such jurisdiction if they chose to do so and fulfilled certain constitutional requirements.

6. See, e.g., Vine Deloria Jr., *Custer Died for Your Sins: An Indian Manifesto*, rpt. ed. (Norman: Univ. of Oklahoma Press, 1988) and *Behind the Trail of Broken Treaties: An Indian Declaration of Independence*, rpt. ed. (Austin: Univ. of Texas Press, 1985); Alvin Josephy Jr., *Red Power: The American Indians' Fight for Freedom* (Lincoln: Univ. of Nebraska Press, 1971); Stan Steiner, *The New Indians* (New York: Delta Books, 1968); Adam Fortunate Eagle, *Heart of the Rock: The Indian Invasion of Alcatraz* (Norman: Univ. of Oklahoma Press, 2002); and Daniel M. Cobb, *Native Activism in Cold War America: The Struggle for Sovereignty* (Lawrence: Univ. Press of Kansas, 2008).

7. Vine Deloria Jr., letter to Gary S. Horowitz of Alfred University, September 7, 1972.

8. Vine Deloria Jr., "The Most Important Indian," *Race Relations Reporter* 5, no. 21 (November 1974): 26–28.

9. Ibid., 26.

10. Ibid.

11. Ibid., 27.

12. Ibid., 28.

13. Ibid., 27.

14. Jerry Reynolds, "Honoring Hank Adams," *Indian Country Today* (January 6, 2006).

15. Charles Wilkinson, *Messages from Frank's Landing: A Story of Salmon, Treaties, and the Indian Way* (Seattle: Univ. of Washington Press, 2000), 44.

16. Editor's Report, "Hank Adams: 2006 American Indian Visionary," *Indian Country Today* (January 6, 2006).

17. Ibid.

18. Suzan Shown Harjo, "Hank Adams: An Unassuming Visionary," *Indian Country Today* (January 6, 2006).

19. Ibid.

20. Jim Adams, "Hank Adams: American Indian Visionary 2006," *Indian Country Today* (January 6, 2006).

21. Charles Wilkinson, *Blood Struggle: The Rise of Modern Indian Nations* (New York: W.W. Norton & Company, 2005), 110.

22. Hank Adams, "Personal Vitae," author's possession.

23. S. James Anaya, "NIYC," in *Native America in the Twentieth Century: An Encyclopedia*, ed. Mary B. Davis, 373–374 (New York: Garland, 1996).

24. Fay G. Cohen, *Treaties on Trial: The Continuing Controversy over Northwest Indian Fishing Rights* (Seattle: Univ. of Washington Press, 1986), 69.

25. Wilkinson, *Messages from Frank's Landing*, 44.

26. Vine Deloria Jr., *Indians of the Pacific Northwest: From the Coming of the White Man to the Present Day* (Garden City, NY: Doubleday, 1977), 162.

27. "Won't Answer If Drafted, Says Adams," *Aberdeen World* (Aberdeen, WA), March 18, 1964 .

28. "March of the Poor Held Failure for Indians," *The New York Times*, July 4, 1968. Adams did run for Congress twice—in 1968 and 1972. He was defeated each time, although in the 1972 Republican primary he won more votes than his competitor in the largest counties.

29. "Indians Love Election Bids in Washington State Primary," Frederick T. Haley Papers, Box 81, Folder 1, 1. (hereafter, Haley Papers).

30. 391 U.S. 392 (1968).

31. Cobb, *Native Activism*, 178–179.

32. Deloria, *Indians of the Pacific Northwest*, 165.

33. Cobb, *Native Activism*, 181.

34. Cohen, *Treaties on Trial*, 81. And see Deloria, *Indians of the Pacific Northwest*, 193–194.

35. Alvin J. Ziontz, *A Lawyer in Indian Country: A Memoir* (Seattle: Univ. of Washington Press, 2009), 95.

36. Haley Papers, Box 81, Folder 10, 3–4.

37. Deloria, *Indians of the Pacific Northwest*, 166.
38. 384 F. Supp. 312.
39. Sharon Malinowski, "Hank Adams," in *Notable Native Americans*, ed. Sharon Malinowski and George H. J. Abrams, 3 (New York: Gale, 1995).
40. 3 Wash. App. 849 (1971).
41. Ibid., 850.
42. Haley Papers, Box 80, Folder 8, 1.
43. Alvin Josephy, "What the Indians Want: Wounded Knee and All That," *The New York Times*, March 18, 1973.
44. Haley Papers, Box 81, Folder 2, 1.
45. Wilkinson, *Blood Struggle*, 141.
46. Russell Means with Marvin J. Wolf, *Where White Men Fear to Tread: The Autobiography of Russell Means* (New York: St. Martin's, 1995), 227.
47. See, e.g., Deloria's *Behind the Trail of Broken Treaties* and Joane Nagel's *American Indian Ethnic Renewal: Red Power and the Resurgence of Identity and Culture* (New York: Oxford Univ. Press, 1996).
48. Vine Deloria Jr., "Old Indian Refrain: Treachery on the Potomac," *The New York Times*, February 8, 1973.
49. Mark Feldstein, "The Jailing of a Journalist: Prosecuting the Press for Receiving Stolen Documents," *Commonwealth Law and Policy* 10 (Spring 2005): 147.
50. Feldstein, "The Jailing," 148.
51. Jack Anderson, *The Anderson Papers* (New York: Random House, 1973), 173.
52. "Reporter Freed in Indian-Data Case," *The New York Times*, February 16, 1973.
53. Anderson, *The Anderson Papers*, 179.
54. Deloria, *Behind the Trail of Broken Treaties*, 79.
55. Adams, "Hank Adams: American Indian Visionary 2006."
56. Stephen Kinzer, "US Indians Enlist in the Miskito Cause," *The New York Times*, November 11, 1985.

Fishing Rights

Hunting and fishing have long been of critical importance to indigenous peoples since both enterprises provide life-sustaining food as well as contribute to the distinctive cultural identities and socioeconomic systems of Native nations. In the Northwest, fishing, particularly for anadromous fish (those that swim up a river from the sea to spawn) like the many species of salmon, was as vital as the land itself for survival and independence. But as non-Indian settlers began to arrive in droves in the middle of the nineteenth century, it inevitably led to serious conflicts and the establishment by the State of Washington of many rules and regulations that profoundly and unjustly constrained the rights of Native fishers, who had explicit treaty guarantees to fish and gather established in 1854 and 1855.

This is the singular issue and the sundry related topics—what does tribal sovereignty mean; what happens when treaty rights butt heads with state's rights; how does a Native nation's on-reservation rights comport with its off-reservation rights—that introduced the world to the determination and talents of Hank Adams as he galvanized the treaty and nontreaty tribal nations to restore and exercise their distinctive reserved rights, civil rights, and human rights.

The documents that ensue reveal Adams's sheer brilliance. He set out to frame this critical topic in a way that eventually culminated in a series of federal court rulings that finally acknowledged the treaty rights of many Native nations to fish at all their "usual and accustomed places" and to have a crucial partnership role in the protection, oversight, and sustainability of managing human relations with the various fish species.

Telegram

To: President Lyndon B. Johnson (June 26, 1968)
The White House
Washington, DC

Urge your immediate personal intervention to secure release and dismissal of criminal charges against Sergeant Richard Sohappy, 20, US Army, 101st Airborne Division, now on recuperative furlough at Skamania County Jail, Stevenson, Washington. Sergeant Sohappy holds 4 purple hearts, a silver star, a bronze star, and army commendation medals as record of his first two duty tours in Vietnam. Has been arrested three times since June 14th on criminal charge of "Fishing with a Set Net," while in fact exercising a legitimate "Right of Taking Fish in all Usual and Accustomed Grounds" under the Yakima Treaty of 1855.

While Richard meets what is demanded of him in service to his country, this nation denies him his right to meet the needs of his family—to provide food and income to sustain the twenty-five members of two Sohappy families.

Salmon fishing is prohibited only in those areas where Indian rights exist. While Indian families are denied their constitutional and treaty-sustained fishing rights, white sports fishermen have been taking more than a million salmon, and white commercial fisherman catching more than 100 million pounds of salmon, annually.

Request immediate action and full force of Federal Government to give life to the law of the constitution and these treaties. Request immediate intervention in Richard Sohappy's case and investigation in all other cases of arrest related to Indian fishing. Request complete record and results of any investigations made publicly available to us. Request US attorney General's opinion detailing responsibilities and obligations of the Bureau of Indian Affairs to protect Indian tribes and individuals from the type of harassment, intimidation, and violence, including continuous and forcible seizure of properties, carried against us by the state of Washington, and to defend the Indian interest and rights from depredations, denial, and destruction.

Immediate intervention required for Richard Sohappy since due process shall be denied him, and probable disposition of his case be forfeiture of $1,750 in bails, with his return to Vietnam on July 4th.

He may not return. Other Indian fisherman have not. Let him know now that it is not a "Crime" to love his family and people, to seek to provide for them, to set forth to defend their rights and interests, and to bring respect and security to our basic way of life. We urge your immediate action.

Most Respectfully,
Hank Adams, Director

Memorandum

Survival of American Indians Association, Inc.
(Indian Contingent National Poor People's Campaign)
November 1970
Memorandum on Court Cases Affecting Indians' Treaty-Secured Right of
    Taking Fish
To: Indian Tribes & Fishermen
Attn: Attorneys Representing Indians
From: Hank Adams, Survival of American Indians Association

Over the past seven years, the Survival of American Indians Association (SAIA) has maintained certain constant and consistent positions regarding the "right of taking fish" secured to Indians under the Treaty of Medicine Creek and other treaties. Activities to sustain these positions in actual practice and by support of judicial decrees in the courts have centered upon the Nisqually and Puyallup Rivers. There has undoubtedly been major misunderstanding regarding the viewpoints and positions of SAIA as relate to the treaty right itself, Indian fishermen, and Indian Tribes. This memorandum attempts to state and clarify our stand.

What rights are secured under the treaties? The Medicine Creek Treaty states: "The right of taking fish at all usual and accustomed grounds and stations is further secured to said Indians in common with all citizens of the Territory..." The Preamble of the treaty identifies the contracted Indians, "who, for the purpose of this treaty, are to be regarded as one nation..." Article 2 of the treaty provides for the reservation of several land tracts to which the Indians agreed to remove themselves to and settle upon—these not in every case being located upon or immediately adjacent to the 'usual and accustomed fishing areas' secured in Article 3; and Article 6 provides for the contingent extinguishment of the specified reservation in favor of any future removals and consolidation of Indian populations that might be determined in their best interests. Isaac Stevens' letter transmitting the treaty to Washington, DC, explains the purpose of the treaty provisions as understood by the government's principal representative in negotiations.

The more significant passages from that statement of purposes and intent include:

...[A]s to reserves, it was proposed to admit as few reservations as possible, with the view of finally concentrating them in one...I was highly gratified by the result, as in the first instance they desired more reserves and larger reserves...I would estimate the numbers of the tribes at 682...Referring to the provisions of the Treaty it will be seen that they cede their title to all their lands...they retain for present use and occupation three small reserves of two sections each...These reserves have been so selected as not to interfere with existing claims, or with the progress of settlements, and yet at such points and would enable the Indians to catch salmon, gather roots and berries, pasture their animals on unclaimed land and participate, as heretofore, in the labor of the Sound. These rights, with restrictions, are secured in Article 3d of the Treaty...I estimate the cession made by them includes 4,000 square miles or 2,560,000 acres...It will be seen that Article 6th gives authority to the President to remove these Indians to other reserves or to consolidate them with friendly tribes in a single reserve...They catch most of our fish, supplying not only our people with clams and oysters but salmon to those who cure and export it...It may be here observed that their mode of taking fish differs so essentially from that of the whites that it will not interfere with the latter...It is not believed that the pasturage in common with whites on unclaimed land will lead to difficulty...The reserves provided for in this Treaty are now being surveyed and marked out, on the completion of which I shall give pubic notice that they are Indian reserves and not subject to the action of the Donation Law...The next Treaty–tribes have a population of 2223, own 425 canoes...Every effort will be made to establish them on a single reservation. The Tribes on the Straits and Western Shore of the Sound, numbering 982 persons, owning 256 canoes...will then be taken in hand and, if practicable, placed also on a single reservation. Should we succeed in this, there will be no difficulty it is believed, hereafter to transfer the tribes included in the present treaty to one of these reservations. The provisions of the Treaty now submitted for approval will form the basis of treaties with Indians of similar habits—that is those of the Sound, of the Coast, and of the Lower Columbia.

Letter

December 30, 1854, at Olympia.
Sir Isaac I. Stevens

Our position is that the Treaty, particularly Article 3, was designed and intended to "reserve a way of life" to the Indian people and was drafted with "strict reference" to the conditions of that way of life. The geographic definition of "usual and accustomed grounds and stations" was the only restriction placed upon the "right of taking fish (salmon)," except that the taking of shell fish was prohibited in "any beds staked or cultivated by citizens"; this latter, in effect, being the only restriction prescribed, the former being declaratory of a geographically-defined fishing area (or zone) to which the Indians' unrestricted fishing rights should both extend and be limited. The treaty-secured fishing rights exist only within the bounds of this geographically defined fishing area, and do not exist outside it. Where the treaty sought to place restrictions upon rights or privileges, the treaty explicitly included them....

Thus, it was only the extended fishing right that was given security and stability under the treaty, without reference to the reservations of lands to relate to—there being the hope that the Indians would not remain on the reservations specified by the treaty, but would be removed to consolidated reservations and then be required to remain thereon (by the Treaties'—Omaha and Medicine Creek—Articles 6 and Article 2), except when leaving to fish or to be occupied in fishing activities and labor. There was design to extinguish land reservations; yet design to secure the fishing right against any consequences associated with disposition of land reservations or settlements. There was clear intent to reserve and secure to the Indians their traditional fishing areas, against any exclusion or restriction by the future settlement of those areas as contemplated and then occurring.

The treaty phrase "in common with all citizens" has both practical and legal meaning. In practical sense, it means that the future presence of non-Indian citizens in traditional fishing areas would not act or operate to exclude Indians from those areas or preclude their fishing activities or extinguish their rights in those geographically-defined, treaty-secured areas. In other words, the Indian fishing rights were to endure against any shared presence of Indians and citizens in the areas, and these fishing rights were to stand against any claims that might be made on these specific areas by non-Indian citizens. Such reading contemplates fishing to some extent and degree by non-Indian citizens in those areas, and does not preserve the rights of Indians or citizens at the expense of the rights of the other, or the extinguishment of the rights of either. The legal meaning of "in common with all citizens" has no particularly relevant reference to mode, methods or times of fishing—it is more significant to the nature of the rights secured and the element of "equal protection" that Justice Douglas in *Puyallup Tribe v. Department of Game of*

Washington determined to be "implicit" in terms meaning. (Remember the Stevens' supposition that there would be no difficulties because of different modes of fishing.)

What, then, are the fishing rights secured in the Treaty? They are by the language of the Treaty those rights secured to "said Indians" "who...are to be regarded as one nation" and (in common) to all citizens of the Territory. In practical sense, the term "all citizens" can only relate to the government of those citizens, or all citizens as represented by their government, and explicitly does not confine itself only to those citizen who happen to be fishermen or who will fish. This is to say that the nature of the rights secured to Indians are in the nature of the rights secured to all citizens or the State. This is consistent with the historic relationships between a people or nation and the fish and game within their sovereign domain.

Particularly relevant to this conceptual understanding are the decisions rendered in *Geer v. Connecticut* (1896), in which Justice White wrote:

> The wild game within a state belongs to the people in their collective sovereign capacity. It is not the subject of private ownership except in so far as the people may elect to make it so; and they may, if they see fit, absolutely prohibit the taking of it, or the traffic and commerce in it, if it is deemed necessary for the protection or preservation of the public good...

The rights secured to the Indians, or nation, within the traditional fishing areas, geographically-defined (extended and limited), in our view are in the nature of rights held by all citizens, or the State, within their territorial waters—including those within Indians' "usual and accustomed" fishing grounds not included within or reserved to the exclusive use of Indians. Which is to say, that the Indian tribes or nations have and possess the right and power to control the game and fishery resources within these traditional waters (off-reservation), held concurrently with an equal right and power of all citizens, i.e., the State.

If the rights secured to Indians (as one nation) were equal to those rights secured in common with, and not denied to, all citizens, then they were those rights secured to all citizens in their collective sovereign capacity (territorial and state); in fact, as already held by the Indians in their own sovereign capacity. The sovereign capacity of the tribes had already been judicially established and sustained by the US Supreme Court in *Worcester v. Georgia* (1832), and was observed in the process and by the fact of making a treaty with the United States. The judicial doctrine that the sovereign capacity incorporated the regulatory rights or power to control fisheries within their domain has most recently been affirmed and chronicled in its history by the case of *Menominee Tribe v. United States* (1968) before the United States Supreme Court. That the Tribes' relationship to the fish and game resources are not dissimilar to those of States or all citizens thereof is supported by a host of judicial decisions. There is nothing in the Treaty of Medicine Creek or the purposes and intent detailed by Isaac Stevens to suggest that the Treaty sought to diminish, modify or extinguish the Indians' rights and relationship to the fishery resources within their usual and accustomed fishing domain. On the contrary, the evidence clearly supports a position that there was desire to maintain the rights held in the Indians' collective sovereign capacity and to preserve those rights already held within their domain of usual and accustomed fishing areas—although limiting its exclusivity or exclusive authority to reservations to be established (not then yet established). The rights to the resources, including the power to control, secured to the Indians were those rights possessed prior to the treaty, maintained after the treaty, and possessed prior to the establishment of any reservations some several years after the treaty was negotiated. (The treaty terms gave continuity and stability only to the fishing rights and the geographically-defined "Usual and accustomed fishing grounds," something not afforded the proposed and ultimately established reservations or residential land tracts.

The construction of the Treaty indicates that the "nation's" sovereign rights over the resources were reserved or secured against any relinquishment or cession of those rights, as seen in the following:

ARTICLE 1: The said tribes and bands of Indians hereby cede, relinquish, and convey to the United States all their right, title, and interest in and to the lands and country occupied by them, bounded and described as follows...

ARTICLE 2: There is, however, reserved for the present use and occupation of the said tribes and bands the following tracts of land, viz:...all which tracts shall be set apart and, so far as necessary, surveyed and marked out for their exclusive use...

ARTICLE 3: The right of taking fish at all usual and accustomed grounds and stations is further secured to said Indians in common with all citizens of the Territory,...

ARTICLE 4: In consideration of the above cession, the United States agree to pay to the said tribes and bands...

The clear implication is that the fishing rights at all usual and accustomed grounds and stations, as well as the tentatively scheduled reservations of land tracts were "however reserved" and further secured" against any cession, relinquishment and conveyance made in the Treaty's first article. The consideration made or provided for in Article 4 implicitly acknowledges the Article 2 & 3 exceptions to the cession and relinquishment of "all their right, title and interest" made in Article 1.

Essentially, what we are saying, is that the "right of taking fish" is equivalent to the right and "power to control" the taking of fish, to control the resource for its good and for the common good of the people, and to control the people within the sovereign authority of the government and people in their relationship to the resource, its management, its harvest, its preservation, its development, and its conservation. The tribes have the right of regulating their people and the management of the fishery resources throughout their usual and accustomed fishing areas; exclusively on reservations, and with equal authority as the State in the limited off-reservation waters. A concurrent jurisdiction exists in usual and accustomed waters off the reservations, which may express itself in mutually-agreed-upon regulations for both Indians and citizens, or different regulations drawn by separate tribal and state authorities for each citizens and Indians. The tribes and State might either exercise their respective "power to control" separately as equals or as equals together in mutual agreements.

A different reading to the treaty might be obtained if the treaty had secured a right of taking fish 'in common with any citizens,' instead of all citizens as it did. The commonality is the collective sovereign capacity of the Indian people of the contracted nation and of all citizens of the territory/state, and their respective "powers to control" their people and the taking of fish and the general resources. Our interpretation is consistent with the sovereign capacity and authorities possessed by the Indian tribes at the time of and prior to the making of the treaty; and consistent with the form and nature of rights by which "all citizens" relate to the fish and game resources under the laws of the State and its constitution...

Our interpretation places treaty Indian fishermen beyond the scope and jurisdiction of the State in regulating upon fishery resources and fishermen as a matter of course or within the normal exercise of their police power within off-reservation usual and accustomed fishing areas. It does not deprive them (all citizens or the state) of resources to a harmful Indian fishery detrimental to a rational conservation or management program, or Indian fishery threatening a condition of harm or destruction to those fishery resources. As well, our interpretation does not deprive Indian tribes nor Indian individuals of their recourse to any program of mismanagement of fishery resources undertaken by State agencies, but enhances the Indian position for ensuring rational management and utilization of resources.

Our interpretation recognizes a twenty-four hour, every-day, every-year, forever relationship between Indians and the fishery resources in all areas where the rights are secured. We do not confine this relationship to several days a week, or those hours prescribed by the State of Washington; nor relate only to the benefits of taking fish from the waters. Rather we recognize for Indian people the larger responsibilities that must be sustained in proclaiming a "right and power to control the taking of fish"—the responsibilities observed in favor of the fishery resources and the responsibilities sustain for the common good of all the people.

We reject the notion that our only relationship to the resource is that of drawing upon it under a doctrine of "fair share" or "fair allocation" administered to or controlled by the State of Washington. We refuse to be treated as just another class or classification of fishermen who happen to be Indian. If the State must deal with us, let them deal with us in our collective sovereign capacity, as Nations of Indian People; and let us maintain our relationship to the fishery resources in that capacity. Only in that capacity can we maintain our responsibilities to the resources and all our people for all time; only in that capacity can we fulfill contract with our children, born and unborn, our own contract to their future.

This interpretation is contrary to the ruling made in the so-called *Sohappy* case, or decisions of Judge Belloni of the federal district court of Oregon. It is, consequently, contrary or at variance with the suit or complaint brought by US Attorney Stan Pitkin in the case of *United States v. State of Washington* in Seattle's federal district court for Western Washington. It is considerably different from the positions taken by the US Government in the *Puyallup* case on remand from the US Supreme Court in Pierce County Superior Court. Their positions embrace the ruling of Judge Belloni that the State, not the federal government nor the Indians, have the sole right of regulating Indians' fishing activities off-reservations. We renounce and reject that ruling.

In the past, both the federal government and the State have rejected that position. In 1886, the United States Government dispatched federal troops to Indian off-reservation fishing sites in Western Washington to protect Indian fishermen and curing shelters from molestation and destruction by non-Indian citizens. Between 1915 and 1921, the State of Washington's fishing laws recognized a 5-mile perimeter or area away from Indian reservations in which Indian fishermen were not subject to the State laws—the perimeter being a recognition that the fishing rights extended beyond the reservation boundaries and out at distance into the "usual and accustomed" fishing areas. When the people of Washington State enacted the fishing laws by Initiative (77) in 1935, they included the specific disclaimer of jurisdiction over Indian fishing, expressed in Section 9 as follows: "The provisions of this Act do not apply to fishing by Indians under Federal regulation..."

This, we believe, is the only valid law relating to Indian fishing that has been placed upon the books in this century—and it is the only time that the citizens of the State have expressed themselves directly by law-making and regulation since the right of taking fish was secured to Indian tribes in common with all citizens, who, as Indians, in their collective sovereign capacity have ownership of the fishery resources within their domain.

Our position has been that the fishing rights are essentially a tribal property right which is subject initially to the original jurisdiction, control and regulation of the resident tribal authority throughout their usual and accustomed fishing areas; and, being in the nature of secured property and a property right, can not be infringed or encroached upon by the State of Washington unless there is a prior court or judicial determination that the

State warrants a remedy or recourse to a harmful Indian fishery or Indian fishery that demonstrably threatens the resources, or when sufficient cause or reason established or given that restrictions beyond tribal regulations are required for the benefit of the fishery resources. We believe that the Doctrine of Eminent Domain provides a source of authority and supplies the recourse and procedures to the State for protecting itself and the resources against a detrimental or destructive Indian fishery. In this respect, we believe that the treaty fishing rights are property and property rights private to the respective tribes to which they are secured, or essentially private property, that are subjected to doctrine of eminent domain (or a larger public good) by the shared ownership of resources by the tribes and all citizens in off-reservation customary fishing waters, and which are likewise afforded its limitations and protections. Consequently, we believe that the State is limited from acting against Indians' treaty fishing activity or against the tribes' powers to control (their fishermen and their resources off reservations), by their State Constitution's Article 1, Section 16, except "...Whenever an attempt is made to take private property for a use alleged to be public, the question whether the contemplated use be really public shall be a judicial question, and determined as such, without regard to any legislative assertion that the use is public..." Thus, the only appropriate procedure for limiting upon Indians' regulatory and fishing rights off-reservation is through civil court action, timely brought to secure a judicial pre-determination if any restrictions might be imposed upon a tribe's regulatory framework or provisions, or upon their fishing activity for some prescribed time period or for some specific duration. In other words, we consider injunctive relief, temporary or permanent through some specified time period, as the proper recourse and remedy available to the State for acting to control a detrimental or harmful Indian fishery. We consider the decision by the US Supreme Court in the *Puyallup* case as doing little more than deciding that civil injunction were appropriate remedy and course of action open to the State. It affirmed the validity of injunctive relief—it did not mandate or establish authority for the State to regulate Indian fisheries as a matter of course or as a normal occupation for State's agencies...

Memorandum

March 2, 1971
Survival of American Indians Association
Statement of Hank Adams, Executive Director

We have this week requested the US Departments of the Interior and Justice to withdraw their complaint in the forthcoming federal suit, *United States v. Washington*, or seek declaration of a non-suit, and to relieve US Attorney Stan Pitkin and (Interior) Assistant Regional Solicitor George Dysart of further responsibilities and involvement in the conduct of any federal suit in which Indian treaty fishing rights are at issue.

On Thursday, in Tacoma Federal District Court, we shall petition Judge Boldt to dismiss the fishing rights case, *United States v. Washington*, in appropriate manner to allow its refiling or reinstitution at some near future date. We believe that our petition must be granted in the interest of justice and for the purpose that vital treaty rights may be removed from the serious jeopardy in which the Messrs. Pitkin and Dysart have placed them by the processes of surrender they have engaged.

We have requested the new Secretary of the Interior, Rogers Morton, to undertake an immediate intensive review of federal positions and the nature of the federal complaint before this matter proceeds to trial. We have recommended that the Interior and Justice Departments assign a joint special legal team to work on the revision, preparation, processing and conduct of this important case—once new steps have been taken to ensure that it will be handled properly, fairly and justly.

Blatant mismanagement of *United States v. Washington* has already occurred, initiating with formulation of the complaint and its subsequent filing without consultation or consent of the treaty tribes it professes to act in behalf of—sufficiently to constitute a blundering betrayal of the government's trust responsibilities to the Indian people involved and who shall be directly affected by its outcome.

Clearly, the case does not seek to affirm Indian treaty rights or to define their particular nature, but rather attempts to secure judicial validation of temporary federal positions and policies—and reduces the nature of Indian rights to whatever definition is given them at any given time by such positions and policies, or any federal spokesman in official capacity, however lowly, and whatever his disposition, proper or improper.

Unfortunately, the offices of Stan Pitkin and George Dysart apparently view Indian treaty rights within the same dimensions and distortions as they regard their own roles as federal protectors of Indians. In such roles, they have effectively reduced their responsibilities to those of protecting Indians "from themselves," "from each other," and "from their rights—tribal or treaty." Tragically, they have proceeded to give extravagant exercises to their "limited responsibility." For example, they have not seen need to protect Puyallup tribal funds, but they have seen need to protect Puyallup Indians from the elected tribal government—and imposing a government of their own choosing, see a need to protect individual Puyallup Indians from the qualified Constitutional Bill of Rights, as extended to Indians for the first time in 1968, in order to maintain that government. They see no need to protect Indian fishermen from white vigilantes, unlawful state police actions, and wrongful prosecutions, or upon their own lands—but see need to protect Indians from their legal and lawful rights would bring. They fail to see that, most importantly.

We need protection from George Dysart and Stan Pitkin!

With minor exception, several of the salmon species do not strike at lures in the estuaries and fresh waters of the south Sound in the latter stages of their migration and normal development cycles. The salmon preserves and, for all practical purposes, their prohibitions have continued in force to the present date and effectively deprived most Indian families all source of salmon supply for commercial use and personal consumption purposes.

When the citizen voters of the State enacted fishing regulations by Initiative 77 in 1934 for some succeeding years, their measure provided that the State law would not apply to Indians fishing under federal regulation. The Washington administrative agencies applied this exception, however, to mean simply that they would not enter the reservations they recognized to enforce State law and the prohibitions of the salmon preserves.

The State and its white citizens doubtlessly always had 'justifiable' reasons to give for denying the Indian tribes their primeval fishing rights. There can be no serious claim that there ever prevailed conformance and compliance with the treaty contract by non-Indians or State government.

The rationalizations and reasons for non-compliance and treaty violations by the State, ranging from 'conservation necessary' to 'equal application of reasonable law,' are absent claim of validity when measured against the facts.

The comparative catch impact by the several user groups is fairly, although roughly, reflected by the percentages: Non-Indian Commercial, 80%; Non-Indian Sports, 15%; and Indian Commercial, 5%.

The average annual commercial catch for the 25-year period between 1935 and 1960 of 6,433,806 salmon of all species would fairly represent an average commercial catch for the past 50 years—although major portions of those averages are comprised of large Pink Salmon catches, made only in odd-numbered years. The record salmon sports catch of 1.31 million is more a reflection of future sports fishery impact upon the resources than it is representative of past catch levels. The Indian share of the commercial salmon catch has ranged between 2% and 8% of the total salmon catch. But these figures are misleading, as are many others.

Since 1950, the highest level of Indian commercial catch numbered 815,290 salmon of all species in 1963, of which 546,244 were pink salmon.

The total State commercial catch that year was 9,310,920. Yet note that Muckleshoot Indians caught only 724 salmon of all species in 1963!

Other treaty tribes were restricted in 1963, and remain restricted, from catching any fish at all. Breakdown of the total Indian percentages indicate that most the Indian-caught fish are taken by a few tribes whose resources are almost fully contained or secured within their reservation boundaries, such as on the 150,000-acre Quinault Reservation with its multi-stream production. Identical rights and comparable resource, however, had been secured to all the treaty tribes by the several treaties.

During the last fifty years the Muckleshoot Indians were prohibited from fishing their traditional grounds on the Green Rivers system—always a major producer of salmon and steelhead—several million salmon escaped into the river without harvest. Additional to wild-run escapements and spawn, more than a million Chinook and silver salmon have reached the Green River hatchery since 1935. In the period 1938–1969, the count of hatchery arrivals were 601,156 silvers and 292,692 chinook, total. These figures represent an unwarranted deprivation of Indian rights, coupled with an under-utilization of fish resources, surplus spawn escapements, and wasted production.

The Muckleshoot White River fishery, if not reflecting some catches actually taken from covert Green River fishing, has generally numbered from less than a thousand to several thousand fish of all species since the late 1930s. Their largest catch prior to 1970 was 19,880 in 1952, mostly silver salmon. The inland and upstream location of their forced fishery, however, has frequently left them with catches of salmon that have deteriorated to their lowest commercial value as a saleable food commodity. Some are in their last moments of survival, and others are the sturdiest or smallest fish which have escaped past Puyallup Indian fisheries downstream.

The Puyallup Indian fisheries have been among the most seriously maligned by incomplete, distorted, and misleading figures relating to any fishery in the State. Re-establishing their fishery in the early 1950s after decades of prohibition, they have been accused of nearly destroying or depleting the salmon and steelhead resources of their river—particularly in 1963, when their catch total reached 75,218 salmon. But 53,425 of that total were pink salmon, not reared in the hatcheries, and for which the State determined there had been adequate to excellent spawning escapement. This was not an inordinate catch for that year, when 5,671,717 pink salmon were taken commercially in the Straits and northern Puget sound.

The 1963 low returns of chinook and silver salmon to the Puyallup River hatchery were the general basis for the charge of depletion, but the Puyallup Indian catches of those species were comparable to previous years catches. However, the chinook catch among the non-Indian commercial fishery in the northern Sound had nearly doubled over the 1962 catch—obviously as incident to the liberalization of regulations for maximizing the harvest of the nearly 6 million pink salmon, which run concurrently to some extent with the chinook runs.

Some of the lowest chinook returns to the Puyallup hatchery have occurred in those years when Puyallup Indians have not been fishing at all. Only exceptionally has the chinook return to the hatchery exceeded a thousand fish, and then in as many years when Puyallup Indians were fishing as when they were not fishing at all.

There may well have been excessive fishing of silver salmon in 1963, but by all fisheries in the State having impact upon a run declined to 800,967 in catches, considerably below the 1.1 million average for the 1935–1960 period. But adequate escapement, rather than excessive harvest, is represented by the return cycle in 1966, when the total catch reached 1,681,454 silvers, being the highest catch of the previous decade. In lodging charges against Puyallup Indian fishing, the State has consistently failed to relate to the natural run stocks and their escapements.

The best evidence of adequate escapements past Puyallup Indians' nets on their river is demonstrated by the figures relating to steelhead catches, where the sports fishery is located predominantly upstream from the tribal fishery. The Puyallup steelhead fishery in the ten years between 1952 and 1962, never caught more than 3,552 steelhead by nets, and generally substantially less. The non-Indian steelheaders upstream caught in the range of 4,144 to 18,496 steelhead, with catches in excess of 10,000 steelhead for five of those years.

The Nisqually Indian fishery represents the only Indian fishery on the southern Puget Sound which has operated continuously throughout the past half century, the tribe having had recourse to reservation lands. There is no hatchery located on it, and plants have been made in it only in recent years. It fairly represents the methods of Indian river fishing.

The catch records on the Nisqually River reflect nothing less than a stability of all resources on its system, and is demonstrating progressive and sustained increases in the steelhead, pink and chum salmon species. The Nisqually chum have thrived while most other rivers along the Pacific Coast have experienced sharp declines, and hatchery facilities experienced a general lack of success in their artificial rearing.

This newspaper recently reported that a large percentage of the Nisqually catches of 1969 were the result of state hatchery plants, financed by white fisherman dollars. Of the 20,225 salmon of all species caught that year, 17,217 were chum salmon which including no hatchery plants. The misfortune of the Nisqually has been that past State and federal policies have caused a disregard of its potential as a producer and a failure to develop its remarkable potential or to take advantage of it.

An irony of present State policy to 'provide' extended off-reservation fishing seasons on the Nisqually has been that the 'special seasons' have been established for the lowest volume resources on the river. When the highest volume chum resources are running concurrent with the steelhead—the secondary highest volume resource on the Nisqually—no off-reservation fisheries are permitted and the Washington Fisheries Department abandons all its claimed management responsibilities for salmon resources.

The several 'special off-reservation seasons' established by the State in the past several years must be regarded as more a legal maneuver and political ploy than as practices representing conscientious management of fish resources.

As a general rule, with respect to the types of Indian fisheries conducted upon the rivers, the catches are a fair indicator of the escapement beyond the nets. When large volumes are being caught, many are escaping. When the numbers are low, fishing activity should be curtailed.

There are numerous factors affecting the effectiveness of the small gillnets used in the Indian fisheries: seasonal conditions, water levels and flows, water clarity, degree of darkness and lightness, location of placement in the channel, structuring of channels, patterns of movement of the different species, and so on. In large measure, the salmon and steelheads' own physical senses and sensitivities are their best protection against being caught in a gillnet—as, when in their feeding stages, they contribute to their vulnerability of being caught by hook-and-line.

State citation of unrelated surveys on the Fraser and Columbia Rivers involving non-Indian gillnet fisheries to evidence a threat presented by every Indian net, or asking consideration only of the most extreme possibilities, while totally disregarding or ignoring the actual fishery experience and practices of the Indian fishermen in this State, has imposed an unfairness and injustice which contributes only to increased public ignorance and animosity, while contributing nothing toward remedy to controversy and toward rational management of valuable resources.

What was the intent of the Medicine Creek Treaty respecting Indian rights? The State Supreme Court presently is considering a position claim of the State that the treaty intended only that Indians should be allowed to continue fishing until Indian populations had concluded a process of becoming "civilized" and then be able to "advance" into different pursuits and occupations.

Commercial fishermen were paid $41 million for their fish commodities in the State last year. Is that the "uncivilized" economic state that the treaty sought to spare its Indian beneficiaries from? Did it really intend that the people of traditional fishing societies should cease being fishermen in favor of an increasing non-Indian population that would also have hundreds of thousands of its members embracing sportfishing as a vital part of their lives, if not an integral part of their developing culture? Hardly.

The Medicine Creek Treaty does not suffer a fault of ambiguity, nor succumb in the decay of antiquity. The right secured to "said Indians" in the treaty, as with the right secured to "all citizens of the Territory," was not subject to a need to prescribe all the conditions of its subsequent exercise, inasmuch as the character of the fishing right had already been among the most well-defined rights in the history of Anglo-Saxon law for centuries. Even in the absence of an Indian population in this State, or absent the controverted treaties, that ancient law would control the definition of the right of taking fish for the State of Washington and its non-Indian people.

The already established rule was that the fish and game within a nation or state belong to the people in their collective sovereign capacity, with all property rights in the resources being in the sovereign for the use and benefit of the people, and with their taking being subject to absolute governmental control for the good of the resources and the common good of the people. There is no private right in the citizen (or tribal member) to take fish or game, except as expressly given or inferentially suffered by their State (or tribal) government—or the people in their collective sovereign capacity.

The sovereignty of the Indian people was recognized by the treaty in its making, as was their ownerships of the fish and game resources. The only cession and conveyance of rights and interests from the Indian treaty nations were made to the United States, and the "right of taking fish" was secured against such cession. The term "said Indian" has reference only to the tribes and bands which the treaty had previously described or designated as "one nation."

The equivalent or equal right in the fish resources, however, was secured in common with "all citizens of the Territory," in their collective sovereign capacity. The word "all" itself is a collective term and, consistent with previous construction of the treaty, clearly indicates that Article 3 does not relate to Indian fishermen and citizen fishermen as such, but rather to the sovereign entities which could possess and control the right.

The State of Washington could only succeed to the right and interest in the fish resources as was conferred upon "all citizens of the Territory" in their collective sovereign capacity. The fish and game statutes of Washington, embodied in RCW Chapters 75 and 77, represent nothing less and nothing more than the collective sovereign expression and capacity of "all citizens" of the State. The Laws of Washington can not subordinate nor subject the comparable sovereign right of tribal Indian people in the fish resources, or their tribal sovereignty, to an overriding control of "all citizens" of the State, if there is to be any compliance with the treaty and its securing of a common, identical, equal and equivalent right.

To interpret the treaty provision in anything other than the respected sovereign terms which were applied would represent an extreme departure from all Anglo and American law which preceded the treaty's negotiation, and from the ancient law embraced by the State of Washington in characterizing the right and relationship to the fish resources when emerging to full sovereignty in 1889.

It's somewhat ironic that such intense conflict between Indians and non-Indians should develop over fishing rights and fish resources, insomuch as the concept of common ownership and absence of private title in the resources represents a commonality in property values shared by the Indian people and the immigrant Europeans which did not extend to most other forms of property, such as land.

The basic limitation against anyone destroying the resources flows from the inherent responsibility and mandatory obligation of the sovereign entities and authority to control their taking for the good of the resources and the common good of the people. The treaty secured the Indian nations this positive sovereign power and right to be exercised over all Indian persons over whom sovereignty was and is held—or from whom sovereignty derives.

Application of the right at this time means that Indian tribes may regulate all fishing activities of Indian people within their sovereign authority throughout the extent of their customary fishing domains. Again, the treaty right does not exist elsewhere. The State may do likewise with its citizens, as well as non-residents of the State. Hopefully, the State and tribes shall cooperate in their respective controls upon common activities in the exercise of their comparable equal rights.

Only through such recognition of rights and responsibilities shall either the State and tribes be able to offer the resources, as well as their respective citizenries, the benefits of rational management and productive development. By having the full flexibility of their sovereign control restored to them, the tribes would again have capacity to locate their fisheries in the most appropriate places and be able to conduct their harvests at the most appropriate times. For Muckleshoot, Puyallup, and Nisqually Indians, this could allow fewer fish to bring them much greater economic value than has been true of the past.

Unnecessary harvests in the salmon nurseries and nearby spawning grounds could be abandoned, in some cases in favor of developmental activities, and transferred to more appropriate harvest and utilization sites. Return to some marina areas could allow a more balanced harvest upon certain low volume species of particular rivers, by relieving impact upon them there and making up any necessary differences in catch level from available stocks passing through the Sound and being surplus to the needs of other home streams, creeks or rivers.

If the State of Washington had been secured only the customary fishing domains as were secured to the tribes of southern Puget Sound, it is quite likely that its management expertise would demand that its fisheries not be limited to and located on the Muckleshoot or Nisqually Indian Reservation, but be placed elsewhere within the secured domain, at least for certain species. Importantly, the treaties secured the tribal fishing right to prescribed geographic water areas, rather than in relationship to reservation locations. Irrespective of the establishment of reservations, the fishing right was retained and secured—and afterward, reservations were established in some cases, and frequently away from water areas altogether.

Few forces are working for an equitable resolution of this controversy on the basis of recognition and respect for established sovereign rights, the rational management of valued natural resources, and for serving the larger public interest and good of both Indians and non-Indians before satisfying the aggressive demands of self-interested user groups. The United States' lawsuit against Washington State aggravates the irrationality by engaging a numbers game that merely demands more fish and more days for fewer Indian fishermen, fishing in the wrong places.

Apparently, the commonality of Indian and non-Indian property values in the fish and wildlife resources, drawn and joined from diverse histories and experience, is only myth. For white citizens, it perhaps stands only as a vacant theoretical value in much the same respect as the theoretical constitutional constraints which are supposed to protect Indian treaty rights from State interference and extinguishment.

While some anadromous fish species near extinction in some streams, the white banner again goes up to claim a white ownership in nature's fish when reared in public hatcheries—or anywhere. With premeditation of future injury, hatcheries displace Indian sovereignty, and all citizens fail to recognize and protect the aesthetic value of a salmon, naturally privileged to make distant journeys among the seas with an inerrant return to place of birth, spawning unmolested within its natural habitat in waters not piped in and undisturbed by civilized wastes or destructive industrial operations. Meanwhile, the architects and defenders of the real white values—sometimes lawmakers and political administrators, frequently newspaper writers and editors—applaud it all in their forums and on their typewriters, oblivious to the devastation of natural resources and to the travesty of human rights and values.

Letter

March 22, 1971
Survival of American Indians Association
Mr. Smith Troy, Prosecuting Attorney
Olympia, Washington 98501

Dear Mr. Troy:

We respectfully submit that your office may now serve a vital and significant public service by making a conscientious review of policies and practices
relating to the arrests and prosecutions of treaty Indians exercising their fishing rights under the Treaty of Medicine Creek of 1854, when in direct conflict
with State laws and regulations, and then adopting and declaring a public policy for your Office which will sustain your obligations under the law to both
the constitutional and statute laws of the State, as well as to the federal treaty
law. A public policy statement issued at this time could help to lessen conflicts
inherent to the controversy and could help tremendously to give direction
toward a resolution of problems by courageously assuming responsibility of
pointing out where basic responsibilities have been abandoned.

You are doubtlessly aware that various measures introduced into the
Washington Legislature would have varied impact upon the fishing rights controversy—none would necessarily act in favor of Indian rights, but measures
requested by the Executive Branch of state government would have effect of
confining the controversy to civil process with remedies of civil injunctions or
declaratory judgements or both. Other measures would have effect of relying
upon criminal prosecution of Indians with design of eliminating any 'burden
of proof' the state might otherwise be obligated to assume for 'providing' its
regulations against off-reservation fishing as being reasonable and necessary.

We would be hopeful that any statement you might issue would clearly
favor one process over the other, and in such statement demonstrate that
evasions of responsibilities by federal and state officials, rather than resolving the problems, complicate them and create a chaotic situation rendering
resolution more difficult.

Additionally, I personally would want to request that your office move
the Superior Court for an execution of sentence against myself to begin on
July 1, 1971. This would allow myself sufficient time to complete various
legal matters and proceedings, and to wind up certain other affairs, personal
and organizational in nature. At this time, it seems likely that I will not
be able to conform to the conditions for suspension of 5 months of the six
months sentence (that of paying any money to the County or State), and if
not, I would reasonably expect your office to move for vacation of the suspension of sentence. In order to satisfy the hungry public, you might make
reference to this in any public statement.

In order that you may understand our own views upon what would constitute an appropriate form of statement from your office, or any conscientious public official in consequential capacity, we are preparing a draft of substantial positions for your consideration. We are also attaching various position statements we have made in our attempts to resolve these issues, responsibly and with minimal injury to anyone's obligations and legitimate interests.

We sincerely appreciate your every consideration in this matter.

Respectfully,
Hank Adams, Director

Letter

April 12, 1971
Survival of American Indians Association
Mr. Brad Patterson
Presidential Assistant
Attn: Office of Leonard Garment
The White House
Washington, DC

Dear Mr. Patterson:

Enclosed are copies of a brief comparative analysis of the differing federal and Indian positions as generally being pursed in the federal suit, *United States v. Washington*, along with our own proposed complaint and memoranda in support of our intervention in that suit. It must be clearly understood that the United States has opposed and continues to oppose our own intervention as individuals in this action.

Clearly, the result of our positions being considered and sustained before the courts would have effect of demanding that the various federal, state and Indian governments sustain a greater level of responsibility toward the good of the fishery resources, as well as the good of the respective Indian and non-Indian peoples, than has ever been contemplated before. Our position requires a more effective and appropriate disciplining of demands placed upon these vital and valuable resources by all people having rights and interests in them than has ever been sustained before. In its construction and philosophy, our position introduces and necessitates a sustaining level of integrity, good conscience and good faith in the relationship between Indian people and "all citizens," or the State of Washington, and the relationship with anadromous fish resources of common interest, which, in being almost totally absent before, has never been relied upon or invoked for resolving these difficult problems of a century's standing.

I am providing you with a list of other plaintiffs' attorneys in this case in order that you may consult with them regarding their views and attitudes toward the federal positions, their positions, and our own. I think you shall probably find a general consensus that the federal government could have, and should have handled this case much differently and better. We believe that it remains the legal obligation and moral responsibility of the United States to alter and improve its standing and positions in *United States v. Washington* before it proceeds to trial.

We are thoroughly convinced that failure to resolve these matters appropriately in the courts at this time will serve not to resolve them at all. What is now an uncomfortable-to-explosive situation, could only become much worse.

We shall sincerely appreciate your every consideration and action for

securing an appropriate governmental response to the requests and information we've directed to you.

Most respectfully,
Hank Adams, Executive Director

Comparative Analysis of Merits of Complaints in *United States v. Washington*

US Complaint provides:
A. That the State may regulate Indian fishing as normal function of State
    government; providing
    (1) fair share of harvest assured;
    (2) regulations non-discriminatory.
B. The State must provide 'special' Indian fisheries, designating Indian fish-
    ing as a subject matter distinct from other fisheries, and allow prior hear-
    ings for setting Indian seasons.
C. When regulations have been promulgated, after hearings for Indians, the
    state may enforce their regulations against Indians through arrests and
    prosecutions and criminal penalties for Indian violators.
D. Off-reservation fishing rights are principle focus of federal suit, with the
    question of the State's relationship to off-reservation fishing areas of Tribes
    subject to determination by the action, with off-reservation rights being
    considered in adjunct to on-reservation rights and fishery resources.
E. Primary reliance for accommodating treaty fishing rights should be
    placed upon the reservation fishery, with off-reservation fisheries being
    operative only when reservation fisheries do not fully accommodate the
    Indian people having fishing rights.

Individual & Other Indians Claims:
A. Indian Tribes, or Treaty Nations, have reserved sovereign authority to
    regulate and manage Indian fisheries, Indian fishing, throughout cus-
    tomary fishing domain, without regard to whatever on or off reservations.
B. Unless Indian fishery is demonstrably harmful to resources, their sus-
    tained levels and propagation, the State requires no restrictions, limita-
    tion upon or recourse to a tribally-regulated Indian fishery.
C. Criminal process is improper for application to treaty Indian fishing. If
    a harmful tribal fishery is operating or threatening, the State may seek
    remedy and recourse by appropriate civil action in courts of competent
    jurisdiction.
  C.a. Criminal process violates federal and state constitutional prohibitions
    against *ex post facto* law; and

C.b. Criminal process wrongly relies upon unqualified legislative and administrative assertions that laws are 'reasonable and necessary,' contrary to constitutional principle that taking of property shall be a judicial question and its justification determined as such.

D. Treaty fishing rights have singular or uniform characteristics, whether on or off reservations; on reservation, tribes have exclusive control and ownership of resources and their management; in other areas of customary fishing domain, there is shared ownership of resources with all citizens, or the State, with Indian persons remaining under sovereign control of tribes.

E. Tribes should time and place their fisheries in those areas their customary fishing domain as will provide for taking of fish, in whatever allowable levels of catch, where the fish are at their highest quality level as a food and saleable commodity, and their value the greatest—by methods and means in such places as the catch levels or take is controllable or subject to limitation for maintaining fishery management needs.

Comparative Analysis: Complaints in *United States v. Washington*

US Complaint provides:

F. Only enrolled members of organized tribes have a right to fish.

G. The Indians' "right of taking fish" is satisfied by dealing only with those Indians who are fishermen, or who constitute an 'Indian class of fishermen' among all classes of fishermen of the State—i.e., the non-Indian classes os sports & commercial fishermen.

H. "All citizens" may regulate the fishing activity of those citizens who are fishermen or who take fish; "all citizens" likewise may regulate those Indians who are fishermen or who take fish.

Consequences and Results of Federal Position

United States places a premium upon drawing clear distinctions between Indians and citizens—as fishermen—deriving their 'rights' of being fishermen from expressly different authorities and origin—without seeking any substantially new protections fro Indian rights or situational relationships between Indians and citizen fishermen, or between Indians and resources secured to the tribes in geographically defined and limited areas by treaty.

The anticipated result of the federal suit is merely that of assuring a few more days of catching fish in off-reservation waters with assent of the State drawn via perfunctory hearings and repetitious court reviews of regulations adequacy.

Such result is totally unacceptable to considerable numbers of Indians who have been obligated to challenge the existing system of state laws and regulations—such result will not resolve either the problems or the continuing controversy.

Individual and Other Indians Claims:

F. Indian persons descendant from tribes contracted by the treaties, who have maintained relations with an Indian community, shall not be deprived their right to fish, even if their name had not been placed upon a tribal enrollment.

G. All Indian people of a tribe or Treaty Nation own the fishery resources in their collective sovereign capacity—as "in common with all citizens" of the State—all Indians, whether fishermen or non-fishermen, have constant and continuous right in and relationship to the "right of taking fish" or the related fishery resources.

H. State statutes and regulations are expressive of the collective sovereign capacity and authority of "all citizens" by which some or any citizens may be controlled in their taking of fish: All Indians of a Tribe may likewise control Indians under their authority in taking of fish by an equivalent exercise of sovereign authority.

Results Sought by Indian Claims and Positions:

Indians treat fishery resources and geographic area where secured by treaty as a viable economic base, reflective of full time relationships and responsibilities in management, conservation, development, and utilization. Attempts to create situation protective of sovereign rights and authorities, whereby even a designated or sustained level of Indian fish catches in the near future may allow the development of a related-and-extended job structure in the management, development and economic utilization of managed and available harvestable resources. A clear possibility is that of fishing to a controlled economic structure (not sought by federal positions) as a first remedy, instead of having to fish for as many numbers of fish in order to secure a near decent level of income. Local control and self-government by Indians in their treaty secured waters, would focus major responsibilities for protection of the resources in the watershed areas where the needs for protection are greatest—and impose a requirement for assured escapement levels upon both State and Indians before any harvesting is allowed anywhere.

Testimonial

August 5, 1971

Statement of Hank Adams: Relating to Complaint Seeking Damages Totaling
$20,000,000 against certain members of the Tacoma Police Department
and the State Departments of Fisheries and Game

The extreme seriousness of the allegations made in my complaint should not be cause for refusing to take them seriously. They are not frivolous. They are extremely serious. I have complete confidence that sufficient proof shall be supplied in the courtroom.

To the extent that any of the defendants have been instruments of public policy or prevailing public attitudes, one regrets their individual involvement totally. To the extent that public indifference may create a realm in which an individual's personal prejudices, hatreds, ignorance or bigotry may become uniformed and operate in the guise of performing the public will in service of a public trust, one can only regret that the public would care so little for their own police officers as to allow such indifference and such operations.

The central issues raised relate to responsibilities rather than regrets, however. The laws under which my suit is brought were designed to protect against abandonments and assumptions of public responsibilities on purely discretionary bases. But in larger perspective—when one sees police officers commanded to herd some people around the countryside; and apparently called upon to abandon other people on riverbanks, while other people are left to roam the countryside at liberty to impose or enforce their own laws, one wonders, "Who is responsible?" (Do you try to answer or to understand with reference to a Leschi; or a Centralia Massacre; or a Seattle of 1854 or a Seattle of 1919, to find an answer in an understanding of society as confined in time as it is in geography, both given to a tradition of violence under a doctrine whereby those responsible are not responsible?)

I would have preferred to have claimed damages in amount of $1 against each defendant and still endeavored to fulfill the task of meeting the tremendous burden of proof this suit requires—which would have sustained certain principles involved, and which would have been in conformance with a "poverty oath" taken by myself nearly four years ago, dictating that I should not gain property or wealth or more than subsistence or sustenance from my work or activities. However, there have been real and substantial damages done. And these damages arise from an extremely unfortunate situation in which many Indian people find no protections existing for them under the law (whether treaty, federal or state) or rendered by public law enforcement agencies; a situation where it appears the only protection that may be secured is that which may evolve from enforcing an understanding against public officials and police officers of the liabilities which may attach to a failure to act, or a failure to act lawfully, or from unlawfully acting. In order that there be no misunderstanding, I choose now to declare that any damages which shall be received (or may be) in this case will be directed to other people's control and use for any of the following purposes:

1. Medicine Creek Treaty Indians for any inter-tribal cooperative fisheries development plans or projects such tribes may devise;

2. A state police agency for use in professional police training activity, including instruction relating to rights of Indians;

3. Financial aid to Indians attempting to become lawyers or policemen;

4. Survival of American Indians Association for purposes devised by it.

Additionally, it should be known that I've never engaged a dialogue against police or enforcement officers of any agency as being "pigs", or made use of other such derogatory terms. For must police officers and policemen, I have maintained the highest regard and respect; not only to those who I may relate to impersonally, but to a number who have contributed valuably to my experience.

Other than a forthcoming statement relating to the prominent New York attorney who will prosecute my suit for me, I will be making no further public comments relating to this action prior to and except in the course of court proceedings.

Hank Adams

Essay

January 14, 1972
Survival of American Indians Association

(Franks Landing)—There has been no dishonoring of deals with the Thurston County Prosecutor or Sheriff for arranging my surrender into their custody—because I made no deals with either of them. I had declared my intention to enter their jail for execution of the sentence imposed against myself on Dec. 4, 1968, and shall do so.

The State and County have acted to place myself in jail for reasons of (1) stopping my visit to North Vietnam; (2) stopping Indian resistance to the unlawful actions of the State Game Department on the Nisqually River; and (3) to prevent timely review in the federal and state courts of the Game and Fisheries Department and the assistance rendered them by the US Army at Fort Lewis. A related or underlying reason for their action at this time derived from our announced and developing plans to work to ensure that US Senator Henry M. Jackson would not be presented to the American people as either a presidential or vice-presidential candidate.

Again we must point out that a six-month sentence was imposed at my trial, notwithstanding any conditions for suspension of any portion of it—since in my first communication with Mr. Smith Troy in 1970 declared I would not meet any such conditions. Mr. Troy has no discretionary or lawful authority to modify the six-month sentence or shorten it by his public statements. To us, six months is no more objectionable than thirty days or one day for being illegally placed in jail. Our basic objection, however, relates to the procedure that the State has employed of continuously changing their rules, disregarding the supreme treaty law consistently, and ignoring State law when necessary, to maintain its policy against any exercise of treaty fishing rights and to coerce and intimidate Indians for making such exercise by repeated arrests, trials, and 30-day sentences.

My trial examined my alleged violation of regulations of the Fisheries Department—regulations which were subsequently invalidated by the State Supreme Court. The Court of Appeals however substituted a statute as basis for reaffirming my conviction and refused to examine the regulations involved. The statute, which prohibits use of set nets in any waters of Washington, remains on the books, while the Fisheries Department violates both treaty and state law with the special "Indian Fishing seasons" for river set net fishing. The Court of Appeals also ruled that a State law which required that my case be heard by a jury, instead of solely a judge, was without force and no more than an expressions of concern. If it were any more than that, they reasoned, they would have had to reverse my conviction. So at this point, the conviction and Smith Troy's sentence have no relationship whatsoever with my actions of September 6, 1968, at Capitol Lake or to my trial in December of that year and its results.

It is less interesting that five non-Indians arrested with me in 1968 were acquitted than it is that no white men have been forced to defend their fishing activities to protest Indian net fishing since the fall of 1968—and federal District Judge George Boldt sanctioned more fishing activity than I intended or engaged in at Capitol Lake—and for which Suzette Mills still faces criminal charges and trial for. If the Fisheries Department is correct in violating the State law in declaring special Indian fishing seasons, one can only wonder why they do not provide for seasons on the Nisqually River when the Chum Salmon are running in January and February—why they claim no management responsibilities for the major salmon resource of this river, certainly as important as any others resource of the river, and warranting greater protective attention than the salmon which could not have been caught at Capitol Lake in September of 1968.

Neither the actions of the Game or Fisheries Department can be sustained against impartial and fair judicial review of the facts and the laws involved. If the Fisheries Department acted with any consistency on the Nisqually River, the Game Department would be left without any allegation of authority to continue its attacks on Indian fishermen, men and women. The Game Patrol would have to stop beating Indians in January and February—and there is no political popularity in this County or State for such restraints.

Washington State should be proud, by its standards, in having a unique mercenary force of enforcement agents—a Game Patrol Riot Squad that has no other purpose, function, or responsibility than to attack Indian people, lives and property. Perhaps the public pride in their Indian attack squad shall be sufficiently pronounced that the Game Patrol may parade their units in public view, fully armed and righteously uniformed, and out from the cover of darkness and Walter Neubrech's lies.

Our suit in federal court, filed earlier this month to secure relief against the US involvement on the Nisqually River, was intended to demonstrate to the Justice Department what facts it should be considering and the laws it should be attempting to uphold in relation to Indian fishing on the Nisqually. The Justice Department and the US District Court unfortunately operated together to delay that action in order that the relief requested would not be timely and would cease to be important. We were attempting to reactivate Mr. Stan Pitkin's interest in his case, *United States* v. *Washington*, and to force him to begin acting again to secure appropriate actions and proceedings in it. If Mr. Pitkin fails yet to act in this matter, he shall share full responsibilities for any consequences of State actions on the Nisqually in coming days.

By taking me to jail at this time, the State and its departments and officials shall achieve none of their aims. They shall not restrict our travel, and they shall not defeat us on the rivers. We shall be vindicated in all our actions, even if we must be vindicated by sitting in your jails. We shall be vindicated in our lives and activities of fishing on the rivers. We don't have to make any deals to do it—political prisoners, like Smith Troy and Henry Jackson, may have to spurn conscience and make deals to survive—we don't have to. We stand accountable for all our actions and are prepared to handle or receive the consequences of them. We shall be vindicated and we shall be free.

Letter

June 21, 1972
Survival of American Indians Association
Mr. Les Whitten
Jack Anderson Associates
Washington, DC 20006

Dear Les:

Please read the enclosures, or review them with care. Again the central issue relates to treaty-secured tribal fishing rights. The critical concern is that all the Indian tribes of the Pacific Northwest shall be dispossessed of their most valuable rights and interest in the salmon and steel head resources by the actions of the United States Justice Department, Interior Department and the State of Washington by pending legal actions. It is impossible for us to alert the various Tribes to the danger of imminent loss because the United States attorneys are both advising and representing the Tribes or treaty nations, and independent intervening actions are being represented in behalf of a dozen tribes by just a couple attorney combines who, although displeased with federal attitudes, are doing nothing contrary to the United States positioning and plans.

It's a damn complicated situation, involving damn complicated issues. It may be difficult for anyone to appropriately comprehend—but we appeal to you to try in order that the Anderson column might generate the influence for corrective action—which we clearly lack. We have not been able to secure appropriate response or inquiry from congressional members (1) because of the routine method of simply routing protests and letters to the concerned agencies for comment, and (2) because the congressional members who would be most inclined to grab onto the issues presented are too closely tied in with the BIA's "New Team" to either give credence to our statements, or withhold our information from Senators while feeding them safer and easier issues (That is, staff level.). The same problem exists with reporters who generally handle "Indian issues" for the *Washington Post, Evening Star,* and the *New York Times.*

Any suggestion that the matter be handled in a book will be taken to heart—but the problem will remain of having the right actions taken with regard to the issue on a timely basis. Also the credibility problem remains for the Indian author. Should that be me, one should consider the political and judicial careers are maintained and built, at least enhanced, in this part of the country by addressing attacks against myself for the benefit of the local citizenry.

I'll attempt to piece together a report with annotated exhibits to communicate the wrongness and injury inflicted by the government agencies and officials. These are fishing societies being threatened with virtual destructions. If one cannot comprehend how these particular Indian people would be without their fish, I don't know how one might explain it. Perhaps—if one could imagine America without its bombs? But please review the attached.

Best wishes,
Hank Adams

Memorandum

June 21, 1972
Hank Adams, Executive Director
Survival of American Indians Association
An Analysis Report of Actions & Positions of the US in Federal Court &
In Its Department & Agencies Regarding Nisqually & Puyallup Indians,
Their Treaty Fishing Rights, Relationships to Governmental Units, &
Franks Landing

Last week, United States Attorney Stan Pitkin filed a Motion to Dismiss a lawsuit brought against the Secretary of Defense, Director of the Selective Service System, and the Commanding General of Fort Lewis (*Matheson v. Laird*), which was filed in federal district court on January 13, 1971, by several Indian persons related to the Nisqually and Puyallup Tribes of Indians. The Indian plaintiffs notified the court that they did not resist nor object to dismissal primarily because the two Indians whose situations raised the issues of forced draft or service in the US Army indicated decision to no longer be involved in the matter—and because of an unworkable political mess in the Puyallup Tribe.

However, a number of exhibits and affidavits were entered with the US motion which both further verified the involvement of the United States Army in the actions of the State of Washington to extinguish and eliminate Nisqually Indian fishing rights and activities on the Nisqually River outside of the reservation boundaries. Additionally, evidence was offered in statements and documents which indicates that the positions of the united States on the issues of tribal fishing rights secured in the Medicine Creek Treaty remain precisely as were outlined by the Secretary of the Interior in 1962, have not been altered in any federal presentations before the courts, and only briefly were subject to limited policy exception for a two-year period between 1966 and 1968. The reasons that the United States Attorney and the Department of Justice and Interior objected so strenuously to individual Indian intervention in the lawsuit in which they represent the five Indian treaty nation groups, and define their positions (*United States v. Washington*), become even more obvious.

US Army Involvement on the Nisqually River:

Shortly after our legal action was filed against military authorities, an Associated Press writer from the Seattle Bureau, Elias Castillo, filed a story of interviews with former Army intelligence agents Alan G. Gibbs and Ralph Stein. The AP dispatch (appearing February 4, 1971, in the *Seattle Times*), related that Indian fishing activities were maintained under constant surveillance by the Army and information supplied to its Counterintelligence Analysis Detachment (C.I.A.D.), particularly when Dick Gregory was involved at

Franks Landing in 1967 and when University of Washington students joined us in the fall of 1968. Agents covered our involvement in the 1968 Poor People's Campaign as well, myself being one of the dozen member of the PPC National Steering Committee organized by the late Martin Luther King. The quoted reason: "if there was violence it could conceivably involve the use of troops from Fort Lewis. We would be the ears of the Army if troops were called in."

An unverified report received by us stated that Army units at Fort Lewis were on standby alert status for the State-Tacoma raid on the Puyallup Indian encampment on Puyallup tribal trust lands on September 9, 1970. The US Departments of Justice and Interior had offered advices to local officials in support of the police attack—then reached a contrary conclusion six months afterward, issuing an Opinion from Washington, DC, that the United States held the lands in trust, that state and local officials and enforcement agents lacked jurisdiction there, and that the invasion was doubtlessly an unlawful exercise of state authority—rather, police power. (The Solicitor's Memorandum Opinion of March 26, 1971, did not itself deal with these questions nor make these specific assertions. However, federal officials publicly declared them as conclusions following from its import and implications.) (A subsequent opinion strengthened the claims.)

The exhibits presented last week in response to our complaint that persons who supported or sympathized with our activities were subject to extortion and intimidations to prevent their support or involvement give additional verification to the allegation. The affidavit of James M. Greenhalgh, Education Services Officer, Army Education Center at Fort Lewis (dated March 9, 1971) states:

As part of my duties, I coordinate arrangements for on-post classes conducted by personnel from the University of Puget Sound. Dr. Earl LeRoy Annis, a professor with the University of Puget Sound, was scheduled to teach military personnel at Fort Lewis beginning in January 1971. His presence on Fort Lewis was deemed not to be in the best interest of this military community because of his widely publicized support for dissident and militant organizations, his public disrespect for the American flag at a Kiwanis breakfast last summer, and his arrest (and subsequent conviction) for defying a police order to disperse at a demonstration by Indians on the Puyallup River last fall.

Dr. Annis is associated with the American Friends Service Committee and is presently State Secretary for the Washington American Civil Liberties Union. Having no prior relationship with Puyallup Encampment, he was sent there when the raid commenced to observe whatever might happen. When blocked by police guards and snipers, he found it necessary to enter the area by swimming the river. If his jury might have had the same bearing as Mr. Greenhalgh, it would have mattered little whatever the details. Mr.

Greenhalgh's judgements were enforced, however, before the court jury hear his case...

Military personnel have been directly involved against Indian persons and with State enforcement officers from the Washington Departments of Fisheries and of Game on the banks of the Nisqually River—and independently at Fort Lawton as well. In their June 12th Memorandum, the US government claims that Indians have not been held in Stockades, nor ordered away from Fort Lewis, nor subjected to prosecution for entry upon lands under the Fort Lewis military jurisdiction. In march of 1970 more than one hundred different Indian persons were held for as much as a day in the stockade at Fort Lawton (in three separate occasions, involving more than 50 on the first, 75 on the second, and 80 on the third)....Even after part of Fort Lawton was leased to Indian groups in agreements and ratification were concluded in the final months of 1971 and early this year, 1972, lists of Indians' names were being maintained at the Fort Lewis Military District installations—and Indians were barred from the posts even to join the celebration of the lease in public and traditional ceremonies.

The direct involvement of military personnel is further illustrated by photographs...[They] show military policemen fighting with Valerie Bridges, approximately two months before her death in 1970. A month before that in February 1970, Valerie was viciously attacked by three State Game Patrolmen at Franks Landing when, by herself, she attempted to defend her fishing net set within her grandfather's property boundaries from the game wardens who motored across the river from Fort Lewis. She was subdued by them, taken in their boat, returned to Fort Lewis, and then taken from Pierce County to the Thurston County Jail in Olympia. More than thirty attacks by State fish and game wardens were made against Franks Landing from the Fort Lewis side of the Nisqually River between 1963 and 1970—with nets, boats and motors, and Indian persons being seized and removed from the area by way of the Fort Lewis approach and departure. (Violent raids by fish and game officers from the Fort Lewis—Pierce county—side of the river are depicted in the McGraw-Hill film feature "Treaties Made—Treaties Broken" and in the SAIA film "As Long As The Rivers Run." The police use of clubs, leather-encased-metal saps, two-foot-long flashlights (in the daytime), and other weapons are shown—together with officials stating that their men were "unarmed.") In other instances, military personnel accompanied State agents to prevent entry of other persons, Indian and non-Indian, military and non-military, into the public access areas where the State officers were acting against Indian fishermen and their gear and properties....The army members then stood by while, without making any arrests, the State agents pulled Maiselle and Norma's net from the water, then dragged the two Indian women from their boat, and proceeded to drag them over the rugged terrain of roots, rocks, gravel and caked dirt for a considerable distance. When a Thurston County Sheriff's

Deputy arrived, I directed that he assist me in make a "citizen's arrest" of the State officers if they commenced to drag the women any further in an assault against them. When he confirmed that he would have to comply with my request, the fisheries agents only then stopped dragging the women and placed them under arrest for "unlawful fishing," only then taking them into custody and to jail. The United States Attorney in its memorandum of June 12th, instant, declares: "The allegation that the military defendants have provided facilities for the use of State law enforcement officials in harassment of Indian is without foundation in fact." The use of military facilities and the involvement and presence of military personnel in the State enforcement activities had been previously acknowledged in letters from the Department of the Army and from the Fort Lewis Commanding General. The character of the "facts" presented is not drawn from that acknowledged use and presence, but from the explanations for them.

Acknowledgment with explanation is provided in a Telex of 18 March 1969 to US Senator Warren G. Magnuson, stating:

> Concerning the allegation that military personnel supported State officers at Franks Landing on 16 January 1969, the military police were notified by the State of Washington Fish and Game Department that violations of State fish and game codes were observed at Franks Landing on the Nisqually River adjacent to Fort Lewis, and that they were going to apprehend the violators and use the Fort Lewis approach for this purpose. The Military Police were present during this apprehension for the purpose of protecting military property from destruction or unlawful entrance. At no time did the military police leave the military reservation or become involved with any activity off the military reservation. The state fisheries department was allowed to launch their boats from the military reservation in accordance with Army Regulations. There were no incidents involving military personnel at any time during this period, and the actions by the Military Police in the performance of their duties were strictly in accordance with the provisions of Section 2671, Title 10, United States Code (10 USC 2671) and Army Regulations...

On March 17, 1969, the Commanding General of Fort Lewis wrote myself with a statement nearly identical to that sent Senator Magnuson the next day. When advised that the explanation was unsatisfactory in failing to explain other instances and incidents of involvement, Major General William W. Beverly covered those items he couldn't explain in his response....

Washington State Fish and Game officials are authorized under provisions of the United States Code and Army Regulations to have access to the military reservation. The State Game Department has a license to use and occupy the boat ramp and access roads leading to the Nisqually River from the Federal reservation adjacent to Franks Landing. Neither Indians nor other citizens are prohibited from fishing the Nisqually River from the Fort Lewis reservation, providing they abide by the state law and Army regulations.

The military police are responsible for the protection of military property from destruction and to apprehend violators of state laws or Army regulations on the military reservation. Assistance rendered to the Washington State Fish and Game Department is no more than that rendered to any other civilian law enforcement agency. The area referred to is of concurrent jurisdiction, and the Washington State Fish and Game Department is not obligated to notify the military police when they enter this portion of the reservation. However, normally a courtesy call is given to military police authorities. No formal record is kept of these calls...

Army & Courts & Prevailing Federal Positions: 1962–1972
In the United States Attorney's response to our lawsuit against military and defense authorities, filed in federal court law week, Stan Pitkin and his assistant Charles W. Billinghurst argued that any court examination of treaty rights issue relating to fishing activities was "barred by the doctrine of *res adjudicata*." In moving for dismissal of our action, the United States argued in conclusion:

It appears from the Complaint, the Affidavit of Lt. Colonel Ray W. Berry, Provost Marshal, Fort Lewis, Washington, and previous litigation by plaintiffs and other Indians in *Puyallup Tribe v. Department of Game of Washington* (1968) that plaintiffs have had a lengthy dispute with the State of Washington regarding their fishing rights under the Treaty of Medicine Creek. In *Puyallup, supra*, the Tribe in which plaintiffs claim membership contended that conservation measures imposed by the State of Washington unlawfully infringed on fishing rights granted the Indians under the Treaty. The Supreme Court of the United States held that the State of Washington had the authority to regulate fishing within the State for the purpose of conservation notwithstanding the Treaty...To the extent that plaintiffs complaint concerning the cooperation between the State and the defendants in enforcing State fish and game regulations, those matters are barred by the doctrine of res adjudicata.

When we were complaining of the military involvement with state agents in 1969, Assistant Secretary of the Interior Harrison Loesch responded for the Department and for President Nixon with statements very similar to the filings of the US Attorney as stated above. In a letter of April 29, 1969, Mr. Loesch explained:

The controversy over off-reservation Indian treaty fishing rights has been going on for many years with the Indians usually claiming that they are exempt from any form of state regulation, and the States contending that the Indians are subject to all of the regular State laws and regulations applicable to citizens of the State generally...In 1942 the United States Supreme Court rejected both of these views in the case of *Tulee v. Washington* (1942), a case involving the right of the State to require a treaty Indian to purchase a state fishing license. However, this decision did not resolve the controversy and the matter again reached the Supreme Court in 1968 in the case of *Puyallup*, et al. (1968). In that case the Court reaffirmed its earlier view that off-reservation Indian fishing was subject to State regulation....

A most significant fact is that the Nisqually river, which forms the boundary line between Pierce and Thurston Counties, meanders in and adjacent to the Fort Lewis Military Reservation through more than ten sections of land, or for a distance of more than ten miles along the lower reaches of the river. That these are "usual and accustomed" fishing waters secured under the Medicine Creek Treaty has never been seriously questioned by anyone.

Military officials have continuously justified their actions and those of the Washington State agencies by invoking the authority and provisions of Public Law 86-797 (approved September 15, 1960) and Section 2671, Title 10, United States Code (10 U.S.C. 2761, 72 Stat. 29, P.L. 85-337, approved February 28, 1958)....

If the federal statutes and code sections said nothing more, there could be no question but that the Fort Lewis and Defense Department officials have been acting only as authorized and directed by the Congress of the United States. However, although the military authorities have been silent with respect to the validity and enforceability of the Indian rights under the treaty (both in their formulation of the Cooperative Plan and their defenses of it), the Congress and the federal laws are not silent upon the matter of Indian rights!....

Of the more than 100 arrests of Indians by State fish and game officers on the Nisqually River, Franks Landing, and Fort Lewis, between 1962 and 1972, not one conviction has been sustained against any Indian having rights under the Medicine Creek Treaty and making claim of them. Convictions entered have been overturned or dismissed on appeal; there have been numerous acquittals. (Six Indians served 30-day sentences in 1964, but on summary contempt of court citations, and without examination into the lawfulness or unlawfulness of their fishing activity.) Not one boat or motor or net among hundreds seized in that period has been returned to the Indian owners by the State. However, the arrest actions continue—with the support of the Departments of Defense and of the Interior, which continue to ignore both the applicable federal statutory provisions and the Medicine Creek Treaty, and rights of Indians, which are recognized to be controlling as their constitutional supremacy warrants.

Application of the 1963 Cooperative Plan covering Fort Lewis and major areas of the Nisqually River, directing and allowing an enforcement of State fish and game laws against all persons including Indians, and the administrative dismissal of Indian complaints throughout the past decade, can be viewed in better perspective when one examines the policies and positions of the Department of the Interior during that period. A letter to Senator Warren G. Magnuson from former Secretary of the Interior Stewart Udall on April 16, 1962, makes it exceedingly clear that the United States agencies entered the 1963 Cooperative agreement with the position that no exceptions should be made for the Treaty of Medicine Creek in the application and enforcement of State fish and game laws against treaty Indians fishing in waters outside of Indian reservation boundaries.

(When a copy of the April 16, 1962, was sent me at my request earlier this year, the Department of the Interior carefully blocked out the names and organizational affiliations of the white citizens of Washington State who had promoted the statement of departmental position at that time. The identifying deletions indicated that the response was to protests and demands of various sportsmen's and steelheader's associations in the State. A principal figure at that time was the late Cliff Harrison, who was an officer of statewide sportsmen organizations, as well as being fish and game editor for the highly influential *Seattle Post-Intelligencer*. His name and affiliations are among those blocked out in the copy in its release to me this year.) The pertinent parts of the 1962 Udall letter state:

> To my knowledge, little of the ill will between the Indians and the sportsman has arisen because of Indian fishing within the boundaries of their reservations. Rather, it largely derives from the fact that some Indians are fishing commercially at sites outside reservations which are only described in the treaties as "usual and accustomed grounds and stations...
>
> Despite the fact that the US Supreme Court in the *Tulee* case and, more recently, in the case of *Kake v. Egan*, has declared that Indian off-reservation fishing may be regulated in the interests of conservation, many Washington state officials (pending a decision by the State Supreme court in the appeal of the McCoy case) feel that they are helpless to prevent netting in the Skagit, Green and other rivers and that the only recourse is for the Federal Government to "buy out" the Indian fishing right.
>
> I should like to point out that this Department represents both the Indians and the fishermen of this country and intends to do its best to help them work out their differences. However, in its actions, it must be guided by what is, or appears to be, the law. At present, it is clear that the treaty Indians of the State of Washington enjoy an exclusive right to fish within their reservation boundaries in the manner and according to the season of their choice...

The basic position and attitude expressed by Interior Secretary Udall in 1962 is essentially the same as that stated by Assistant Secretary Harrison Loesch in his letter of April 29, 1969, except that *Puyallup* (1968) is cited in place of *Kake v. Egan* as reaffirming the *Tulee* case of 1942 "that off-reservation Indian fishing was subject to State regulation." When United States Attorney Stan Pitkin in his June 12, 1972, Memorandum states that "the Supreme Court of the United States held that the State of Washington had the authority to regulate fishing within the State for the purpose of conservation notwithstanding the Treaty," in defense of the military involvement on the Nisqually River, and that the fishing issues "are barred by the doctrine of *res adjudicata*" from further judicial examination, he is embracing the position stated in 1962. Additionally, the positions taken by the United States in its federal lawsuit in behalf of the several treaty groups of tribes in Western Washington coincide in all respects with the Udall statement—seeking nothing more than that advocated then.

The central issues of the "treaty rights dispute" are settled in the form expressed by Udall, Loesch, and Pitkin, because the Department of the Interior and Justice Department attorneys have not opened them to any other examination, nor never presented them in any other form or in light of any other asserted interpretation within the courts. It has been obvious that the federal government resisted and opposed our intervention in *United States v. Washington*, because we were prepared to point out that the Interior Department has established itself as a 'Court of First Judgement' on the rights of Indians, and by that self-appointed standing had invoked a supposed 'doctrine of res adjudicata' with the judgement issuing Secretary Udall in 1962— not within the actual judiciary system.

The exception to the Federal Policy 1962–1972 is notable—and drastically different from the Udall-Pitkin approach. However, it evolved not from the Department of the Interior, but from the highest levels of the Justice Department. Edwin L. Weisl, Jr., Assistant Attorney General of the United States, was the architect of the temporary policy which partially operated between 1966 and 1968. A brief statement of that policy was addressed to myself and the National Indian Youth Council in 1966:

The Department of Justice is determined to defend the treaty rights of the Indian tribes, since federal treaties are solemn obligations of the government, whether they are with foreign nations, or Indian tribes. Thus, in the case of Indian fishing, it is our policy to defend, on request, individual Indians, who fish in accordance with the treaty and tribal regulations, in the event they are charged, by a state, with violation of its fish and game laws. We plan to use other legal avenues to insure that the various tribes are able to pursue their treaty fishing from outside interference.

o o o

Ironically, most Indian tribes of Western Washington were intensely angered by the construction of the case and issues in *Puyallup*, and the consequent decision issuing from it. It was primarily that anger and their opposition to the *Puyallup* ruling which caused the various tribes to welcome the representation of the federal government and its attorneys in *United States v. Washington*, filed September 18, 1970, and tentatively slated for trial in federal district court around April 1973. The tribes have not been informed by the federal attorneys that the United States takes the position that *Puyallup* settled all issues regarding regulatory rights, and that the US position seeks to impose the *Puyallup* decision solidly against all the treaty tribes of the area. A most revealing illustration of the federal posture in the pending litigation was presented in a pretrial Conference Hearing in federal court at Tacoma on May 25, 1972, where the US attorneys succeeded in securing a ruling against individual Indian intervention in the case. When we stated a position that the treaties secured an equivalent and equal right to the tribes as is presently held by the State of Washington and that the tribes were vested with a sovereign shield of authority for controlling the fishing activities of related treaty Indians and for providing protection against outside interferences, the federal judge expressed a personal agreement with our positions. However, he took option of ruling in favor of every opposing argument presented by the federal attorneys, who held tightly to the 1942–1972 federal posture of the *Puyallup-Tulee*-Pitkin-Loesch-Dysart-Pittle-Udall "doctrines," "*dictum*," and decreed determination on the character and application of the treaty rights secured—virtually eliminating any need to go to trial, while denying our absolute right to.

Federal Policies Toward Franks Landing & Its Resident Indian People:
In another of the affidavits filed by the United States Attorney in federal court last week, the Fort Lewis Provost Marshal Ray W. Berry declares: "In fact, the only area adjacent to the Fort Lewis reservation that I am aware of in which there has been any difficulty between State officials and Indians is that in the so-called Frank's Landing." The government's Exhibit Number One is a memorandum from the 'court of first (and frequently final) judgement' for Indian matters, the Portland Area office of the Bureau of Indian Affairs. It is addressed to the Regional Interior Solicitor and carries a certification from George Dysart in the Solicitor's Office, with an apparent attempt to indicate some standing of 'legal opinion.' However, it lists its origin in the BIA Tribal Operations division, although it is signed by the BIA Community Services section. In regard to the question of whether the US Army and the State Departments of Fisheries and Game are using portions of Franks Landing on the Fort Lewis side of the River to attack the remaining portions of Franks Landing together with Indian fishermen on the Nisqually River, the memorandum states:…"You will note from the attached map that much of the land from this parcel had been eroded by river action. It is probable that the north bank of the river may now be inside the original boundary of the tract." Oddly, the map referred to was eliminated from the Exhibit when filed in the

federal district court. It would have helped to substantiate our claims and complaints. In addition, the BIA offers the following information and opinion:

This land was purchased for Willie Frank Sr. in 1919 with proceeds from the disposition of his trust allotment in the Fort Lewis taking. Copy of the deed is attached. It is our understanding that the purchase of this land was pursuant to the plenary powers of the Secretary of the Interior since there is no specific federal statute which authorized this purchase. We are unable to conclude that the land was secured to them "under authority of the treaty."

On September 2, 1970, a Thurston County judge ruled that Franks Landing was and is treaty-protected land outside the jurisdiction of the State of Washington. (Franks Landing is predominantly located in Thurston County. The BIA memorandum quoted above states that it is "located in Pierce County, Washington," but then attempts to claim that it is not on that side of the river with Fort Lewis.)

Ever since the 1970 local court ruling, Washington State officials have publicly declared that they regard Franks Landing as being outside their jurisdiction, unless some contrary court decision might henceforth be issued. A State Supreme Court Judge has suggested that Franks Landing "may be one of the most unique tracts of Indian land" in the United States, in one instance of restraining enforcement of fish and game laws there and granting recognition to its treaty protection status. When US District Judge Alfred Goodwin of Oregon (now of the Ninth Circuit Court of Appeals) last year issued restraining order against Washington tax laws against Franks Landing, Indian persons residing there and their commercial business and sales, the State proceeded to position claim that Franks Landing is a part of the Nisqually Indian Reservation, although located several miles from it, and should be subject to State taxing laws "consented to" by the Nisqually Tribal Council. Later in the same case (March 1972), US Judge William N. Goodwin of the Western Washington District termed Franks Landing as an "Indian country refuge" in accepting a State stipulation that it would not act against persons or property at the Landing instead of issuing an injunction against previously threatened actions by the State.

The Bureau of Indian Affairs, its Portland Area Office and its Western Washington Agency, have adopted and sustained an extremely hostile attitude toward Franks Landing and its Indian residents. It has consistently sided with the Washington Departments of Fisheries and of Game, other local enforcement officers, and the US Army in their attacks and raids. Repeatedly, the State Attorney General's Office and county prosecutors have introduced into court evidence a statement issued by the Acting BIA Area Director, A.W. Galbraith, on October 23, 1968, which declared: "Franks Landing on the Nisqually River is not under Federal jurisdiction. The State has full law enforcement jurisdiction there as elsewhere outside an Indian Reservation.... It does not lack any jurisdiction over that area."

Agency Superintendent George M. Felshaw, additionally, has liberally issued commissions as "Special Officers" of the Bureau of Indian Affairs to state and county enforcement officers, who flash their card certificates of federal authority whenever they come upon Franks Landing. (Our informing them that federal commissions are not a vesting authority or jurisdiction over State matters or alleged offenses has always seemed beyond their comprehension. It is simply regarded as license for any action taken.) Now that we have been informed of the provisions of the 1963 Cooperative Plan between the US Army and the State Departments of Fisheries and Game, we can realize that the Interior Department and Defense Department have purported to "authorize" enforcement of State laws on the total stretch of the Nisqually Rivers, and the BIA commissions would operate to remove even those limitations that may have appeared to exist, notwithstanding any designation of an area as being under "concurrent" or "exclusive" jurisdiction.

The approximate six acres of Franks Landing was secured for Willie Frank in 1919 in replacement and in lieu of a 205-acres restricted allotment on the Nisqually Reservation in 1918. The local United States Attorney of this district at that time arranged for the uncontested condemnation of 3,300 acre of Nisqually lands—despite actions of the Interior Department's efforts to prevent the condemnation and to arrange for a leasing arrangement with the War Department. The lands were taken by Pierce County and title to them transferred to the United States for use in the enlargement of Fort Lewis.

Although the BIA states that it is "unable to conclude that the land was secured to them 'under authority of the treaty,'" it is simply apparent that the United States government has not reviewed the records it holds on file relating to the actions of the 1917–1919 period. The federal and local state courts have both determined (although not issuing a final judgement) that virtually no other conclusion is possible....

In these matters, the BIA and federal officials in other governmental units have assumed the freedom to ignore records and facts, treaties and federal laws, court decisions and Congressional intents. Their unfounded "conclusions" and arbitrary policy positions are given supremacy above all other considerations.

The hostility of the Bureau of Indian Affairs to the Indian people in the families at Franks Landing has been demonstrated in additional matters. The BIA Area Office and Western Washington Agencies have each refused to provide documents and information to Nisqually and Puyallup Indians to use in defense against State prosecutions for fishing—while providing the same or other documents to the Washington Department of Game and of Fisheries to base both arrests and prosecutions upon. The 1966 Nisqually Tribal Enrollment has been provided to the State agencies, while refused to tribal members and other Indians by the BIA.

The Udall plans and policies outlined in his April 16, 1962, to define tribal memberships "so that persons who are not entitled to treaty privileges can be prevented from claiming them" resulted in a 1966 Nisqually enroll-ment that has been used most damagingly against Nisqually Indians who were not included in it, and particularly against Nisqually Indians at Franks Landing. The qualifications for "Nisqually" enrollment did not require that persons be of Nisqually blood, but only that they be of "Indian blood" and be born on the reservation or have been resident on the reduced Nisqually Reservation and included in its resident census of July 1, 1945.

Herman John, Jr., was not included on the Nisqually enrollment, although his grandparents were allotted on the original Nisqually Reserva-tion, and his grandmother Lizzie John was full-blood Nisqually. His father, Herman Klaber John, was listed on the 1919 Nisqually Census, but not the 1945 census—because he was killed in combat during World War II in 1944. The Army-supported attacks against Franks Landing by State enforcement officers have at times been against his children and grandchildren.

Alvin Bridges was not included in the Nisqually enrollment, although his great-grandparents were allocated on the original Nisqually Indian Res-ervation. His return to the area after or during World War II, when he served in the Army, was not rapid enough to place him on the 1945 Census. His Nisqually great-grandfather would be the great-great-grandfather of the pres-ent Nisqually Council Chairman and the great-grandfather of the two imme-diate Council Chairmen, sisters Mildred Ikebe and Zelma McCloud. Mrs. Ikebe and Mrs. McCloud's mother was enrolled as a Puyallup Indian (as is Alvin Bridges' mother), and their father was enrolled in the Warm Springs (Oregon) Tribes (Wasco) and allotted there. However, their father fell heir to lands on the reduced Nisqually Reservation that was not condemned, and their family maintained continuous reservation residence after 1919, which qualified them for enrollment under the 1945 census and the 1966 approval by the Secretary of the Interior. On the other hand, Alvin Bridges Nisqually-Puyallup-Duwamish Indian is not on any enrollment approved by the Secre-tary—and is refused entry upon the Nisqually roll.

Prior to declaration and implementation of the 1962 Udall doctrine on Indian fishing rights, Al Bridges was regarded as a Nisqually and was issued Nisqually Indian tribal identification for use in his fishing activities. His dif-ficulties initiated when he was acquitted in a state prosecution for fishing on a finding that he was a bloodline Nisqually Indian; however, Indian in-laws of the tribal chairman and spouses of other tribal members were con-victed because they were without Nisqually Indian blood. Judge Shackleford affirmed his right to fish away from the Nisqually Reservation in a written statement, while instructing the other Indians to remain on the Reservation to fish or face State prosecution. The BIA and the Tribe have both continued to allow the major fishing activity on the Nisqually river to be conducted by these non-Nisqually-blood Indians (as well as non-Indians) within the reservation boundaries during the past decade—while joining the State fish and game agencies in attacking Al Bridges and other Nisqually Indians in off-reservation areas.

The State Fisheries and Game Departments, the Bureau of Indian Affairs, and the Nisqually Community Council, have all been aware that non-Nisqually have been catching some of the largest annual amounts of fish on the Nisqually River—under their protection—while joining forces to attack the families of Alvin Bridges, Herman John, Bill Frank, Sr. (the only surviving full-blood Nisqually) and Jr., with the support of the US Army facility and personnel of Fort Lewis. The present Nisqually Chairman, Harold Ikebe, son of Mildred Ikebe, and less Indian and less Nisqually then any of the Bridges, Johns, or Franks, publicly calls for the attacks, while heading a basketball team sponsored by the State Department of Fisheries.

On June 1, 1970, attorney George Dysart wrote a three-page memorandum to members of the Nisqually Council for the Office of the Regional Interior Solicitor in apology for United States involvement in an appeal of a State prosecution against Al Bridges—and apologizing for not challenging the trial court's finding that Al is a "descendant of a member of the Nisqually Indian Tribe." In its decision invalidating the State fishing regulations for the period between 1965 and 1969, the State Supreme Court (its highest) on October 1, 1970 (No. 40871), restated the fact which all courts have consistently found or accepted: Alvin Bridges has direct "relationship to the Nisqually Indian Tribe" and is "a beneficiary of the 1854 Treaty of Medicine Creek."

In sum, the Udall doctrine of 1962 has operated to deprive more treaty Indians of their treaty rights than to make any Indians rights secure. The BIA and Interior officials have persisted in attacking all those who disagree with them, and the 1962–1972 policy, as "dissidents" who are owed protection in no quarter, nor from any source. Assistant Regional Interior Solicitor George Dysart has been the most callous offender—believing that the full power of the federal and state governments should be brought against any Indians who do not follow his advices or conform to his views. He has directed the oppositions against Alvin Bridges and Herman Johns and their families; he has been consistently wrong on the status of the Puyallup Indian Reservation lands and upon Franks Landing; he led the fight to prevent intervention by Indian individuals in the pending case of *United States v. Washington*.

While associated with the United States Attorneys Office in the US District Court of Western Washington in *United States v. Washington* in behalf of five different treaty groups of Indian tribes, Mr. Dysart on March 30, 1972, sat in assistance to the US Army Corps of Engineers' counsel in opposing Indian treaty tribes and Indian fishermen who were seeking to prevent premature flooding of fishing grounds on the Columbia River. The Oregon US Judge nevertheless granted the Indians' petition for an injunction against the Corps. In a related matter, after Dysart accused Indian residents of the "Cooks Landing In-lieu Fishing Site" of having a "mutinous attitude" against the BIA and the Yakima Tribal Council, he drafted revisions in federal regulations governing their home sites—prohibiting the maintenance of permanent homes (already constructed) and declaring that "Facilities for camping on the sites hall be limited to tents, tepees, campers and mobile trailers." In enforcement, the February 15, 1969, regulations provided: Any structures erected or maintained in violation of this section may be removed, demolished, or otherwise disposed of, with or without prior notice, as determined by the Area Director, and the cost of such dispositions shall be assessed against the person responsible for the structure." When evictions notices were issued, Mr. Dysart answered protests with expressions of sympathy, but explained that he was powerless because the "regulations" (which he drafted) "require" removal or destruction of the homes. Interior backed down only after a statement of the move was published in *Playboy Magazine*, and did not renew its attempts (until the March 30, 1972, federal court hearing on the Corps of Engineers' plans) in the face of strong funding support for "Cooks Landing" by US Rep. Julia Butler Hansen. In that case, however, there again was federal law which should have been controlling. The Act of March 2, 1945, which provided for acquisition of the "in-lieu sites "to replace Indian fishing grounds submerged or destroyed as a result of the construction of Bonneville Dam," provided "That such lands and facilities shall be transferred to the Secretary of the Interior for the use and benefit of the Indians, and shall be subject to the same conditions, safeguards, and protections as the treaty fishing grounds submerged or destroyed."

The Flooding & Erosion of Franks Landing:
In a title report of 1925, the BIA noted that Franks Landing has periodically been reported to be located in both Pierce and Thurston counties from time to time. A 1967 'tract diagram' purports to show river erosion for the ten preceding years, and oddly diagrams a "Boundary—Future Channel" for the Nisqually River, running directly, diagonally through the middle of Franks Landing. If such a channel were dug, the diagram might serve some future date in correctness. However, since 1968, the river has been helped on the opposite bank to dig its won channel on the Franks Landing side. The consequence will still be to run the river through the area shown on the 1967 diagram—but in such a manner as to leave none of the lands of Franks Landing remaining on either side.

On May 29, 1968, the *Daily Olympian* reported that the US Army and State Game Department were completing a cooperative program of rip-rapping the opposite bank of the Nisqually River. Additional work was done upstream. Since fall of 1968, the west side of the Nisqually River has moved almost 300 feet inland, eating into the upriver half of Franks Landing. The erosion was aggravated by the 1968 Army-State Game labors, and has accelerated in succeeding winters. If no remedy is acted upon this summer, most of Franks Landing could be lost in the 1972–1973 high waters and flooding of the Nisqually. Early this year, all the remaining trees between 20 and 60 years in age on the upper property were taken out by the river, together with other vegetation and housing facilities.

In 1968, the BIA came to examine the damage and merely took photographs. No response was offered the following year; but in 1970, the BIA answered our appeals for assistance by sending us the developed photographs of the pictures taken earlier. At request of the Governor's Office this year, the BIA did come on the scene while hundreds of non-Indian students and members of Chicano organizations worked to sandbag the area to prevent further washout. The BIA did reimburse us for some expenses paid to other groups for gravel, sandbags, and rip-rapping materials, but only on the most minimal scale. Since then, nothing has been done by the BIA, although an inquiry was made to the Army authorities at Fort Lewis to determine whether there might be some surplus military land available to replace that lost at Franks Landing or to be used for our needs. The Army responded that there was none.

The photographs show the relocated channel of the Nisqually River, with its current running downstream directly into Franks Landing, almost to its interior boundary, then flowing in a 90-degree angle around the landing toward the rip-rapped land licensed by the Army at no-cost to the State Game Department. A relocation of the channel would probably be the cheapest means of protecting the property, but the Army Corps of Engineers has reported that the costs of any corrective action would not be justified in terms of the minor value of the lands threatened. State agencies proudly proclaim the Nisqually River as being one of the best flood-controlled rivers. They are probably correct. In the fifty miles of river, from its source at Mount Rainier to its mouth on Puget Sound, Franks Landing was the only land area damaged by floods this year and in the several previous year. The "flood-control" project obviously has been able to pinpoint its target while eliminating damage in peripheral areas.

Concluding Statement on Issues:
The combined actions of the US Department of Interior, its Bureau of Indian Affairs, the US Army in relation to Indians residing along the Nisqually River or fighting for treaty fishing rights, and the State of Washington Fisheries and Game Departments' actions against Indians and their rights, were the basis for the Puyallup Tribe Ordinance of 1970, prohibiting forced service or duty in the US military by Puyallup Indians....Rather than deal with the issues raised by that Ordinance here, we simply state our belief that the situation faced by Indian people on the Nisqually and Puyallup Rivers justifies actions by Indian men and youths under the Puyallup Ordinance. It is not fitting that 93-year-old Willie Frank should be compelled repeatedly to appear

in State and Federal courts to protect his rights and properties—and his grandchildren from State criminal charges for fishing, as well as testifying in my behalf—and be thrown out of court by the United States Attorneys in an attempt to resolve these issues in *United States v. Washington*—yet find his grandchildren dragged off by the United States to serve in its military, or, to be faced with lengthy sentences in military stockades as his grandson Mike McCloud is now faced, once he might be taken into custody.

As well, the actions and positions of the United States in its lawsuit against the State of Washington is not structured to resolve the controversy or dispute between Indians and citizens, or their tribes and the State. Rather, it simply seeks to vindicate the never-abandoned policy adopted by Interior Secretary Udall in 1962 in response to white citizens' complaints. White citizens are satisfied with the federal action because it represents their interests, not the tribes nor the fish resources. Federal and state fisheries biologists have expressed clear support this year for the positions taken by Indians, as reflected by the "Comparative Analysis of merits of Complaints in *United States v. Washington*" as prepared for Mr. Brad Patterson of the White House in Washington, DC, but never responded to again after its submittal to him. The artificial nature of the issues raised against Indians, and to the tribes' prejudice, are presented more fully in the attached article series written at request of the University of Washington *Daily* earlier this year.

Finally, it should be noted that the interests of Indian people are being represented, in essence, by just three different attorney combines, including federal attorneys, acting in behalf of Western Washington Tribes. Although several of the attorneys involved would love nothing better than to have their own private views imposed upon all Indian people and fishing tribes, and question why any Indians might not be satisfied, it seems that there is a pervasive lack of conscientiousness, honesty, or courage on the part of private and organizational attorneys in reporting to the tribes on the case of *United States v. Washington* in the federal courts. The federal position taken on behalf of the tribes has been seriously questioned by rulings of the Supreme Courts of Idaho, Michigan, and California during the past fifteen months—as well as by University of Washington Law Professor Ralph W. Johnson in the *Washington Law Review* this year—yet multi-tribal attorneys have expressed no concern or alarm over the United States positioning and posturing in the tribes' "behalf" in the present case. If the Udall-Loesch-Pitkin-Dysart-Pittle doctrine of 1962-1972 is now affirmed by the federal court system, the Indian tribes will have allowed "their" attorneys to betray their treaty and the future of their tribes and children—without even having had an "Indian treaty rights position" presented before the courts, as noted by Professor Johnson in regard to the *Puyallup* case before the US Supreme Court, and reaffirmed by Edwin Weisl in his statement that the "government badly mismanaged the case." The Indians' stakes are much higher now—involving the lives of virtually all Indians of Western Washington, their properties and fish resources, and their sovereign treaties and necessary rights. It is not a time for foregoing examination of actions or for allowing betrayals.

Letter

August 14, 1973
Survival of American Indians Association
The Hon. Elliot Richardson,
Attorney General of the US
The Hon. Rogers C. B. Morton,
US Secretary of the Interior
RE: Federal Mishandling of *United States v. Washington* (Civ. 9213)

Dear Sirs:

We respectfully urge your immediate review of actions being taken in behalf of Indian Tribes of western Washington by federal attorneys in the case of *United States v. Washington*, filed in Tacoma US District Court in September 1970, and now scheduled for trial beginning August 27th. Particularly, we request that the United States request delay in the issuance of the imminent "pre-trial order"—which shall be controlling upon the conduct and outcome of this extremely important trial—until the United States has acted to change its position to adequately represent the rights and legitimate interests of the affected tribes.

If this lawsuit proceeds with the United States adhering to the positions that it presently maintains, unwarranted and grievous injury shall be done to these valuable treaty rights.

o o o

The primary problem created by federal attorneys in their construction of the case and definition of issues is that of denying at the outset any Indian or tribal right to regulate and manage their fisheries throughout the customary fishing areas where they have secured the right under the treaties.

o o o

In recent years, both the Departments of the Interior and of Justice have made extravagant claims of commitment to uphold and defend the constitutional, treaty, civil and other legal rights of Indian people. The federal actions in this case constitute an effective refutation of such claims and an effectual disclaimer of any such commitment....When *United States v. Washington* was filed nearly three years ago, the complaint was drawn without consultation with the several treaty tribes on whose behalf the federal government, as trustee and fiduciary, purported to be acting. The different tribes were invited and encouraged to independently enter the case as interveners—while attempt by individual treaty Indians to intervene were vigorously, and successfully, resisted by the United States.

o o o

Our judgment has to be that *United States v. Washington* can not resolve the central issues in the treaty fishing rights dispute, but will more likely create battle lines which will carry this dispute to its greatest intensity by sanctioning the most brutal and vicious actions against Indians by the State....Is due process satisfied in depriving a people of their property rights, or robbing those rights of their essential character, simply because the deprivation and the robbery occur in court by federal representations in behalf of the Indian victims? Will you examine and review this matter conscientiously—or shall you again assume the propriety and correctness of your own actions and, thus, direct us to look forward to the inevitability of our own further loss, which again you shall not share nor suffer?

We shall appreciate your most immediate responses.

Respectfully yours,

Hank Adams, SAIA National Director; in behalf of Suzette & Sid Mills,
    approving for themselves & for Powhatan & Wahelute
Ramona Bennett (Puyallup Tribal Chairman); for herself & Teresa Bridges
    (Vice-Chairman)
William Frank, Jr., for himself & Willie, Sr.; & Reggie Wells; Rena Wells.

Letter

August 15, 1974
Survival of American Indians Association
Messrs. Leonard Garment & Brad Patterson
Special Assistants to the President
The White House
Washington, DC 20050

Dear Len and Brad:

Enclosed is a copy of a draft for a proposed executive order for presidential chartering of the Indian Fisheries Commission,* as discussed during the July meeting with the interim Commission members.

This draft has been reviewed by the different tribal representatives, Commission members, and various of the tribes' legal counsel. The suggested changes are noted on page 3 of the draft. Tribal attorneys indicated that they would study the proposed order and advise of any additional suggestions for changes.

Otherwise, the Commission has authorized myself to work on attempts to secure appropriate (presidential) action for this issuance of such an Executive Order, essentially through yourselves and other concerned federal officials.

I'm forwarding copies to Interior Solicitor Kent Frizell and Assistant Attorney General Wally Johnson with copies of this letter in order that they may offer their response on the proposal as quickly as possible. The purposes to be served by the order are generally stated in the draft. However, there are additional justifications and these can be communicated when your offices present us an initial response and address us with any questions you would need us to answer.

Please respond directly to Forrest Kinley, Chairman, Indian Fisheries Commission, PO Box 309, Marietta, WA 98268; with copies to myself. We sincerely appreciate your every consideration and action on this matter.

Respectfully yours,
Hank Adams, SAIA
National Director

* The Northwest Indian Fisheries Commission was formally established in 1974. It has helped the treaty tribes in carrying out biologically sound fisheries policies and provides the member tribes a unified voice on fisheries management and conservation issues when dealing with the state and the federal government.—Ed.

Executive Order
No. _____
September ___, 1974; F.R.
__Establishing and Chartering an Indian Fisheries Commission__
__(Pacific Northwest)__

WHEREAS the United States has entered into and maintained contracts with the several Indian tribes, bands, and nations as are parties to the treaties of Medicine Creek, Quinault, Point Elliott, Makah, and Point No Point, respectively, under which the separate Indian populations retained certain autonomous rights and authorities for governing their communities and for controlling the extensive fish resources secured to them; and

WHEREAS these Indian people uniformly own or possess a "right of taking fish," exclusively within the boundaries of their designated reservations, and "in common with all citizens" in their other customary tribal fishing areas, as reserved against relinquishment in the language of the several treaties; and

WHEREAS it is the declared policy of the United States "to help develop and utilize Indian resources, both physical and human, to a point where the Indians will fully exercise responsibility for the utilization and management of their own resources and where they will enjoy a standard of living from their own productive efforts comparable to that enjoyed by non-Indian"; and

WHEREAS there exist significant modern opportunities for fulfilling basic beneficent policy and program objectives for Indian people while satisfying the promising ideas, initiatives, plans and hopes of numerous Indian tribes and communities; and

WHEREAS the separately held treaty rights and resources of these Indian tribes are substantially interrelated for such reasons as major migratory fish resources are involved and being affected by actions of unrelated tribal entities at distance as well as by authorities of mixed jurisdictions in joint use areas, additional to the impact and diverse interests of non-Indian user groups and agencies operating under the responsibilities or claims of state, national, and inter-national governmental bodies; and

WHEREAS the treaties leave the President with authority to implement their provisions in safeguarding the independent interests and established rights of the respective Indian tribes, or to recognize common needs among the separate Indian communities in acting to advance their common welfare and unique opportunities:

NOW, THEREFORE, by virtue of the authority vested in me as President of the United States, it is ordered as follows:

Section 1. Establishment of Commission. There is hereby established the Indian Fisheries Commission of the Pacific Northwest (hereinafter referred to as the "Commission"). The Commission shall be subordinate to, and shall act as an inter-tribal governmental agency in behalf of Indian tribes under the respective treaties of Medicine Creek, Quinault, Point Elliott, Makah, and Point No Point, whose recognized tribal governments are hereby granted charter and authorization to devise and adopt a constitution and bylaws providing for the organization and operation of the Commission. In the designation of any board or body of commissioners for the Commission, the Indian people possessing tribal fishing rights under each particular treaty shall be represented by at least one (1) commissioner for the combined area or tribes covered by that treaty.

(a) The Commission may exercise any power or authority possessed by any member Indian tribe, or member treaty nation, to whatever extent such powers or authorities are assigned the Commission by the member tribes, collectively or individually, and assented to by any individual Indian tribe affected by their exercise. Any member tribe, or combination of tribes, may contract with the Commission to permit it to exercise any assigned authorities, to provide any services, or to conduct any approved programs.

(b) The commission is authorized, subject to direction form the tribes, to receive and expend funds from both public and private sources, and, accordingly, may seek authorizations and appropriations from the Congress in support of the functions of the Commission, or in support of the activities and programs of the member tribes, collectively or individually. The commission is further authorized, consistent with any existing law and its constitution and bylaws, to contract with Federal agencies for the administration or delivery of any funds, programs, or services, which would otherwise be provided by such agencies to the same Indian tribes or people.

Section 2. Functions of the Commission. The Commission shall:

(a) Formulate general Indian treaty fisheries policies and programs to promote, coordinate, or enhance the management and conversation practices of member Indian tribes, and to generate broad utilization of the collective information and experience available through the combined Indian populations.

(b) Assist in providing technical advice or training services from available or developed sources for member tribes as needed in their independent, coordinated, or cooperative fishery management efforts.

(c) Aid in the gathering, exchange or dissemination of report, statistical or other information for use by the tribes, state and federal agencies, and international commissions, in the operation, regulation, or evaluation of their anadromous fish management programs and related activities.

(d) Coordinate with tribal, state, federal and related agencies in the development of program plans or priorities, budgeting processes, conduct of fish harvests, maintenance or rehabilitation of fish resources, and in the development of future public policies for the care and utilization of these resources, while representing the specific Indian interests in such matters.

(e) Assist in public information and education projects, including any meetings or exchanges with non-Indian commercial or sports fishery interests and user groups, for minimizing conflicts and developing good will in attitudes, and for addressing the environmental, ecological, and conservation concerns of the Indian and general public.

(f) Assist the member tribes in planning or programming for fisheries related industries or economic enterprises, management related job structures, and the training or education of qualified industrial, technical or professional personnel from among the Indian population for advancing tribal objectives.

(g) Recommend amendments to this Order, or other acts which may be taken under 25 U.S.C. 9, for effecting or furthering the purposes of this Order.

Section 3. Establishment of Planning Council. There is hereby established, for purposes of advancing the efforts and objectives of the Commission, a federal Indian Fisheries Policy and Planning Council (hereinafter referred to as the "Planning Council"). The Planning Council shall have membership as follows: The Secretary of the Interior who shall be the chairman of the Planning Council, and the two Assistant Interior Secretaries having primary administrative responsibilities for each the subject matter of Indian Affairs and of Fish and Wildlife; the Assistant Secretary of Commerce having primary administrative responsibility over the National Marine Fisheries Service; the Assistant Secretary of State having primary administrative responsibility for international fisheries policies and problems; the Associate Director of the Office of Management and Budget having primary responsibility over budget matters relating to Indian people and programs; and five commissioners from the Commission as shall represent it and each Indian treaty area included under the Commission.

Section 4. Compensation and per diem. Members of the Planning Council who are officers of the Federal government shall receive no additional compensation by reason of this order. Other members of the Planning Council shall be entitled to receive compensation and travel expenses, including per diem in lieu of subsistence, as authorized by law for persons in the government service employed intermittently (5 U.S.C. §§ 3109, 5703).

Section 5. Assistant to the Council and Commission.

(a) Each Federal department and agency represented on the Planning Council shall furnish such necessary assistance to the Planning Council and to the Commission as may be authorized by section 214 of the Act of May 3, 1945, 59 Stat. 134 (31 U.S.C., 691), or other law. The Department of the Interior shall furnish necessary administrative services for the Planning Council.

(b) Any staff of the Planning Council which may be necessary, shall be assigned by the departments and agencies represented on the Planning Council, and may be detailed or assigned as necessary to work for designated periods with the staff of the Commission.

(c) The chairmen of each the Planning Council and the Commission shall periodically submit timely reports and budget recommendations to the Director, Office of Management and Budget (OMB) as appropriate (86 Stat. 770).

Section 6. Meetings. The Planning Council shall meet on the call of the chairman and at least once semi-annually. The Commission shall meet at times prescribed in its constitution and bylaws.

President
The White House
September _____, 1974.

Testimonial

US Senate. Hearing Before the Committee on Interior and Insular Affairs and the Committee on Commerce, 93rd Cong., 2nd Sess., September 20, 1974 (Washington, DC: Government Printing Office, 1975).
Statement of Hank Adams, Northwest Indian Fisheries Commission:

Mr. Adams. Yes, in the statement that we have submitted for the record, including a background statement on makeup of the Northwest Indian Fisheries Commission and the member tribes, we do take the position that we are not opposing Lynn Greenwalt's nomination, but that we strenuously object to plans and policies to which personnel in the Department of the Interior have committed themselves and apparently it wouldn't matter who was the director of the Fish and Wildlife Service.

I think that the Fish and Wildlife Service are failing to understand their own rule in relationship to Indians and failing to understand the Indians' relationship to the resources that the tribes retained under the several treaties in the Pacific Northwest.

I have here a copy of the Department of the Interior's Department Manual, part 501, chapter 2, which spells out the relationship between the Fish and Wildlife Service and the Bureau of Indian Affairs. It says that the Fish and Wildlife Service shall be the technical assistants to the Bureau of Indian Affairs in carrying out its trust responsibilities to the Indian tribes and their resources.

It does make reference to—I mean, for instance, off-reservation treaty fishing rights. It doesn't exclude the Fish and Wildlife Service from having a direct relationship to Indians and their resources but at this point they are asserting that they are wholly independent of their trust responsibilities that the Department of the Interior and the whole of the US Government has to Indian tribes.

I think that if Mr. Greenwalt is confirmed and he has been in the office for some time already, that he should review that departmental manual and more or less clear up in his own mind what his role and responsibilities for Indians and Indian resources are.

For the committee file, I would like to submit a map prepared by the Department of the Interior which does show the various treaty areas in the extensive amounts of resources that are still possessed by Indian tribes in the State of Washington and its vast water areas, its substantial land areas, and its considerable amounts and numbers of fish resources.

Senator Metcalf. While you have the map up there would you point out that area that Mr. McMinds suggested was covered by the *Boldt* decision.

Mr. Adams. Mr. McMinds will point it out.

Mr. Guy R. McMinds. This area here. [Indicating green and yellow area.] It includes Grays Harbor. This area here. Puget Sound and Olympic Peninsula.

Senator Metcalf. And the area that you traced up there, is that the Columbia River?

Mr. McMinds. The Columbia is here. Grays Harbor is here, just south of the colors, into the center of the mountains back over following the International Boundary out to—

Senator Metcalf. Along Puget Sound and along the coast down to Grays Harbor, there.

Mr. Adams. There is another case of the United States versus the State of Oregon involving the Columbia River and part of the $690,000 was requested to service the Columbia River tribes, a budget amount of $140,000 was requested to provide the management services to eastern Washington and some Oregon tribes.

So, that is affected as well because, in fact, the tribes do have considerable fish and water resources, both under their exclusive control and under their shared control.

We cannot understand how the US Fish and Wildlife Service or any of the sister agencies like National Marine Fisheries Sciences Services can ignore these major resources. They have created a vacuum of responsibility when it comes to the Indian-related resources, when I don't think this Congress should tolerate that and I don't think the Government of the United States can tolerate it.

In the matter of the funds and the processes that have brought us here today, I will go through a chronology of what happened in the request for the funds and the ultimate plan to divert them away from those original purposes to the State agencies.

The initiation was the Judge Boldt decision and he said that the tribes had to have their own management, professional, technical services available to them, or under their own staffing, in order that they could implement it and carry out its decision free from State inferences negating the benefits of the *Boldt* decision and advancing the plans and objective of the Indian tribes.

So the Bureau of Indian Affairs and the US Fish and Wildlife Service did prepare a statement of request based upon an identification of existing needs among the tribes themselves. On March 29, there was an interdepartmental briefing here in Washington, DC, in which these amounts, these figures, about $1.9 million was stated by the Bureau of Indian Affairs as the amount needed to help the tribes in their development of their governmental capacity and the US Fish and Wildlife Service identified this $690,000 as the amount needed to service the technical assistance, biological needs.

Now, these funding amounts were then carried to the Office of Management and Budget and to the White House. They were pared down on the Indian BIA area to $1.5 million and that request was sent over here to Congress. The $690,000 was determined by the Office of Management and Budget as the amount being bare-boned already and couldn't be cut. So they submitted the request over here for $690,000 for the technical services funds.

Senator Metcalf. May I interrupt for a moment?

So the budget came up and you had the $690,000 from the Office of Management and Budget and it went to the various appropriation committees to the House and Senate. Now, did you participate in discussions or preparation of material before those appropriation committees?

Mr. Adams. Yes. A number of tribes did work on the preparation and this is the key point, Senator. Mr. Nat Reed sat here this morning and told the Senators that he didn't know what the State planned to do with the money, what the basis of their requests were, and he told us at the White House Monday that they have not submitted any justifications or statements identifying the needs they were supposedly trying to meet.

The tribes, working with the Northwest Fisheries Program Office have made repeatedly detailed plans for programing funds and serving the existing needs.

And though we have made plans time and time again, and we made the basic outline for the $690,000, now we are told that we got to come in with a plan on Monday, that is what they are waiting for. Actually, they have made a commitment only to a meeting for Indians and, in this chronology. I can indicate where they have made real commitments for the money to the State agencies.

So, this is the only commitment Mr. Reeds has made and Mr. Greenwalt's service, at this point, now that the money has been secured by the administration by the tribes through the responsiveness of the appropriations committee and the Congress. Now the only thing we are left with is a commitment to a meeting and they are left with commitments for the funds.

But I would make reference to a letter of August 23, 1974, from Frank G. Zarb, Associate Director of the Executive Office of the President, Office of Management and Budget, addressed to myself, informing me.

I must apologize for taking so long to acknowledge the telegram for the general financing of Indian fishing rights. As you probably know, we asked the Congress for an additional $2.49 million in 1975 to implement Judge Boldt's decision. We feel that this amount is sufficient to accomplish the objectives, given the resources already available within the Department of the Interior. We expect this amount to be appropriated. Most of it was appropriated, and we did not ask for additional money for the regional solicitor in Portland because we believe that for implementing of Judge Boldt's decision should be either within the existing totals or should be provided by priority. Sincerely, F. Zare.

So the Office of Management and Budget thought we were asking the Congress for these moneys that we were talking about when we took the request to them and had set the figures back in the chronology of what happened is the State of Washington's Game and Fish agencies did the inter-requests to the Department of Interior and probably Members of Congress, undoubtedly Members of Congress, for additional funding for themselves to do something.

One justification that I saw, it asked for 21 law enforcement protectors, enforcement officers. On another, the same justification from the Department of Game asked for one helicopter. But anyhow, they did make these requests and they found out that we were processing it, the Department of Interior, Bureau of Indian Affairs, and Fish and Wildlife Service, were processing $690,000 as a request to the Congress to implement the Boldt Decision, so they came in with similar requests.

They asked for $692,000 for Department of Game and $612,000 for the Department of Fisheries and then they asked for meetings with the Department of Interior. They asked for meetings with the Secretary of Interior Rogers Morton, and Carl Krause, State Director of Game, flew to Washington, DC, to meet with Secretary Morton, but that was deferred to a later meeting in Washington State which took place on June 24. This is where the machinations, the political motivations, come into play, in that meeting on June 24th in Olympia where the Secretary flew in without any public notice and met with the Department of Fisheries and Game and with—

Senator Metcalf. When you say "Secretary," was that Secretary Morton or Secretary Reed?

Mr. Adams. That was Secretary of the Interior Rogers Morton.

Senator Metcalf. We talk about Assistant Secretaries and Under Secretaries—that's why I asked you to make that identification.

Mr. Adams. No; this was Mr. Morton, himself, and the State noted its objections to the Boldt decision and said it was unfair. They stated their objections to Indian tribes exercising any management role whatsoever and they stated their objections to any additional federally operated or Indian-operated fish hatcheries and in the Fish and Wildlife Service's description or memorandum report of that meeting, Secretary Morton did make commitments to them and did accede to every one of their objections.

The people who were in the room including Kahler Martinson, the regional director of fish and wildlife services, and some other departmental personnel, and they immediately gave a report at the meeting to Mr. Greenwalt so he would know what the commitments were on the question of hatcheries.

Now, about 2 years ago, a number of tribes asked the Fish and Wildlife Service for a feasibility study for a hatchery in southern Puget Sound and that because of some very decent, good comprehensive work that the Fish and Wildlife Service had done previously for the tribes, that we would get a good report.

Now, after the Secretary Morton meeting with Fish and Game, where they said, "We don't want any more Indian-related hatcheries." They finalized their report and they left out the bulk of two years' work that the Fish and Wildlife Service put in there. In place of that, they just submitted their conclusions, the objections of the State Game Department and State Fisheries Department, saying "We are opposed to any Federal fish hatcheries for Indians."

So that the quality of the work of the US Fish and Wildlife Service has been severely affected by the recent development of close relationships between Secretary Morton and the Fish and Game Departments of the State.

Secretary Morton, in that meeting with them, said, "Yes, I must agree that multiple management never works and that we will do what we can through contracting of finances to the State in order that we can keep the management responsibility where it belongs, with the State."

Now, this, as far as the fact that the State itself has multiple management systems besides the tribes in existence already. In this case area, there is the Canadian-American Management System and there is the Federal management system outside the 3-mile limit.

So, this is an artificial issue. It is designed to prevent the tribes from ever getting out from under the thumb of the State and managing their resources without State interferences. But that June 24 meeting with the State was crucial and he did make commitments.

Mr. Martinson, at the regional level, accepted those statements at that meeting as the policy and commitment of the Department of the Interior and that is why the information was immediately communicated to Mr. Greenwalt.

As we indicate in our statement, Mr. Morton thinks a lot of Mr. Greenwalt, but promised the State that they would get to work on him to make certain that he was going in the right direction and that he knew what his position had to be in the State and so then, at that point, OMB actually had not formally requested the money at that time. The Interior appropriations bill had not been processed through the Congress and when it was finally processed, OMB, in the last minutes of the appropriation process, did get the request over here and the Congress did commit the $690,000 plus $1.3 million for the tribal BIA matters, apart from the direct fishery management question.

After the Congress acted, you were still talking about statements of needs from the state plus the Indians' $690,000, but the only money that was appropriated by this Congress was the Indians' money. So, when you were talking about who gets what, we were talking about who gets the Indians money. Now, there was another meeting set up scheduled for August 27 in Portland, Oreg. And this was between the US Fish and Wildlife Service and the State Departments of Fisheries and Game and the purpose of that meeting was to divide up the moneys which it seemed certain the $690,000, and Indians were not invited to that meeting and, in fact, what happened—some field staff people, who had been working directly with the tribes refused to participate in that process or in that meeting of dividing up the Indians' funds without even divulging it to the Indians.

Also, we were able to point this out to the White House and the White House said, "You had better be with the Indians" and so that means the meeting was canceled and this meeting for next Monday, September 23, was set up to meet with Indians and the two State agencies and Fish and Wildlife Service.

Again, as I say, it's demanded that the tribes come in with specifics and a new plan, a detailed plan, on what the tribes are going to do with the money, but that's how the money was generated to the plans that were already prepared. The State has prepared no plans. As I say, the only commitment we have left at this moment is a commitment to meet with us in a meeting that we forced to come about.

There is no commitment for funds if it remains under the departmental control.

Senator Metcalf. Is that meeting in Washington?

Mr. Adams. It's in Washington State, in Olympia.

Senator Metcalf. Are you going to be there, Mr. Adams?

Mr. Adams. Yes; we are.

Senator Metcalf. You are all going to be there?

Mr. Adams. But even at that meeting the Regional Director, Mr. Martinson, who says as Mr. Greenwalt says, this morning, that he has the decision-making authority to decide what is done with that money. He tried to beg out of the meeting when we met with him previously. He said, "Do I have to be there?"

They weren't even going to put their decision makers in that meeting with us, except that we insisted "If you are going to make a commitment to a meeting, you at least ought to come to it."

So, this is what we are dealing with. Now, we do have serious questions about what is going on in the Department of Interior. We know, as Mr. Greenwalt states in a memorandum, that "We are dealing with a hot issue here. There is a lot of political pressure. There are a lot of non-Indian sports fishermen in this country. There is almost a million within the State of Washington, itself." There is some problem in making the readjustments that Judge Boldt has decreed that the treaties commanded.

But, somebody is going to have to suffer those readjustments and what the Department is saying at this point and many people who have an interest in these matters, is that we just have to readjust our politics and readjust the law in order that Judge Boldt's decision will never be implemented. So this is what we are dealing with and we don't have the power, really, to protect ourselves. This is why I took the United States coming in to help us in this case because we have been fighting it for almost a century already. We have written a full record of Indian-white relations in Washington State, in the US Supreme Court from 1905 up through last year, because each element of the right and each element of activity on the part of the Indians is challenged by the State.

Just one other thing. Not through your committee file or anything, before I close, I do think I should point out some of the things that the State departments and agencies have done with the moneys that they have had before, in the past.

Now, in talking about the Nisqually and Puyallup Rivers in the State of Washington, the State has said that they need these Federal funds and they do already have a lot of Federal funds, there is $17.4 million is fish funds this year's appropriations, There is an additional special $300,000 in anadromous fish appropriation through Fish and Wildlife Service and so they are not talking about a single source like we are. This is our only available source of funds, that $690,000.

One of the things they are saying is that we need to put together a lot of new data and we are starting from a zero base on fisheries data on a lot of these rivers. This is true. This is true of the Puyallup River. This is true of the Nisqually River.

This notebook here shows where they have been collecting data. This is alphabetized. In that alphabet is every member of the Nisqually Indian Tribe, complete with pictures, arrest records, and all kinds of information that they have been digging out on Indian families.

They have information showing that the 44 Nisqually fishermen in 1963 averaged out an income of $533 from the fishery resources in a year, that non-Indians took over 13 million salmon and 11 million in commercial fisheries and almost 2 million in sports fisheries and yet one tribe was only getting $533, but the State game department, the department which is asking money to put together figures now, not only dug that out from their fish records, they went to the employers of every Indian to see how much money they were earning.

At Fort Lewis, the Department of the Army provided them the incomes, mostly part time, earned by the Nisqually Indians. There is welfare statistics in here that the State game department went out and sought out on every Nisqually Indian.

There is social security information provided by the Federal Government, and there are also statements that the Bureau of Indian Affairs provided as to the money in individual Indian trust accounts.

This is what they have been wasting their money on in the past and we don't think, you know, that they should have just a blind commitment for new moneys to fight Indians in the future and certainly without justifying it to everyone.

We had to justify that $690,000 to the Congress. They don't even have to justify it to the Fish and Wildlife Service and they get a commitment to have some of it.

This here is a more exhaustive study on the Puyallup Tribe. Now, they are starting from a zero base on the fish resources on the Puyallup River system. That's why they say they need the money. Now, this goes through 55 Puyallup Indians and it goes into reports on how much food the families have in their cupboards, how dirty their houses are, how clean they might be. It examines which of the Indian children are legitimate or illegitimate. It goes to say how much the families are spending on fuel oil and where they purchase their fuel oil. It goes through the same sources to put together this information and again it is alphabetized and it is part of the reason why the tribes don't have any justifiable trust in the agencies which are about to get their money, to get the Indian's money.

I wish, you know, that some Senators would look at some of this information. It's the type of information that have brought governments down. It's—it goes on with the Indians; by who does it—

Senator Metcalf. How did you get this information, Mr. Adams?

Mr. Adams. We have been in court for 10 years.

Senator Metcalf. You got it by court order?

Mr. Adams. We got it by a discovery process.

Senator Metcalf. A discovery process in court?

Mr. Adams. No

Senator Metcalf. Would you mind leaving that so that some of us can examine it with the assurance that it will be returned to you in its entirety without any missing pages?

Mr. Adams. Yes; I would be glad to do that, Senator, and I would, perhaps, like to put some paperclips on a few choice pages.

Senator Metcalf. Very well. If you would call our attention to some of the items.

Mr. Adams. Because it does have also an expression of the attitude of these agencies saying that these Indians are like wild animals in the jungle, they don't deserve much of anything.

Senator Metcalf. I am just directing the staff that, after you have left it here, next week, I hope, it will be called to my attention and some of us will be permitted to look through it. It's the kind of thing that maybe Senator Ervin, in his right of privacy bill, has been complaining and objecting about for a long, long time and it is something that should be a matter of grave concern. I don't know whether it is a matter of concern with respect to Mr. Greenwalt's confirmation or not, but it's a matter of concern for us that this sort of material is being compiled and this procedure going on.

Mr. Adams. Yes, OK. We would appreciate it.

Senator Metcalf. If you want to put some tabs in or some paperclips, or something, that would be helpful.

Mr. Adams. OK. Well, I think I will check to see if any of the other Commission members have additional remarks and then I am fairly well through. I would make two more submittals to the record and one is a letter from the Puyallup Tribe to the regional director dated August 21, dealing with those questions of the hatchery , the feasibility study, and then an article that was carried by the Seattle P.I. a few weeks ago relating to State actions in the implementation of the *Boldt* decision.

Senator Metcalf. And those will be incorporated into the file, unless we find that excerpts are necessary for the completion and the understanding of the entire record and in that case they will be incorporated.

Mr. Charles Peterson. I don't think we have anything else, Senator Metcalf, and we wish to thank you very much for the time your Commission has given to us to present our problems here before you.

Senator Metcalf. We are delighted to have you here. We are always glad to have Mr. Adams here. He has been before the committee before and his usual articulate and eloquent presentation is appreciated.

Mr. Adams. Thank you, Senator.

Senator Metcalf. Thank you, again.

Letter

Northwest Indian Fisheries Commission
October 8, 1974
The Hon. Rogers C.B. Morton,
US Secretary of the Interior,
Department of the Interior
Washington, DC 20242

Dear Secretary Morton:

Enclosed is an Northwest Indian Fisheries Commission (NWIFC) position paper regarding the uses of the $690,000 appropriated to the US Fish & Wildlife Service (USF&WS) for the purpose of aiding Indian tribes in their management of extensive anadromous fish resources, and in their implementing the requirements of the Boldt Decision, by services supplied through the USF&WS Northwest Fisheries Program. Copies of related correspondence are also enclosed.

We believe the record in this matter firmly establishes that these funds were secured for prescribed services to the tribes involved in the Boldt and Belloni Decisions. Although we sincerely hope that such procedures shall not become necessary, the NWIFC has authorized legal action to prevent any misallocation or misuse of these funds in manners oppositional to established Indian interests and rights—and the mandates of the federal court decisions.

At their recent conference in Spokane, the Affiliated Tribes of Northwest Indians adopted a resolution joining in our general position.

We would note that the Washington Department of Fisheries (WDF) has expressed its view that these USF&WS funds should not be fragmented into small chunks which would end up accomplishing little or nothing for everyone. In our most recent session with WDF and the Game Department, the Fisheries Department indicated its preference for seeking its desired funds from the US F&WS Anadromous Fisher Conservation Act funds ($110,000). The Game Department continues to insist that these funds (the $690,000) were secured solely on the request of Director Carl Crouse, without anyone's assist, and the WDG money demands ought to be met immediately from them. The premise is demonstrably untrue—although some Interior officials continue to encourage Mr. Crouse in his unfounded views.

The different tribes and their officials are genuinely displeased, and justifiably angered, by departmental and USF&WS maneuvers in this matter. A clear and unmistakable statement of Interior Department policies and plans for conscientiously acting to implement the Boldt decision is definitely needed immediately. The delays and indecision, if not underhanded dealings, regarding the assistance needed by the tribes, not only injure the interests of the affected Indian people, but demonstrate a blatant disregard for the proper management of considerable fish resources—and the time schedules naturally imposed upon their useful study, research, inventory and analysis.

The tribes of the Pacific Northwest have uniformly requested that the available USF&WS funds be committed to the Northwest Fisheries Program, with any necessary additional staffing, to carry out obligations placed with the United States and the tribes under the Boldt rulings. As well, the tribes strongly oppose any attempts to break up the NWIFC into several unrelated, disjointed and uncoordinated units under supervision of the USF&WS Regional Office—or to otherwise gut the service capacity of the Northwest Fisheries Program, and to fail to adequately staff its operations under the direction of its Tumwater, Washington, headquarters.

In our positions paper, we refer to an effort to blunt the effects of the Boldt decision and to actively limit tribal authorities in management of fish resources and utilization of related opportunities. As well, we express view that the integrity and reputations of USF&WS personnel are now subject to being corrupted or fouled by the imposition of the discernible political design within the Interior Department.

If the tribes can not expect a decent standard of honesty from the Regional Directorship, or other levels of the Fish & Wildlife Service, in their dealings on Indian issues and programs, both the Indian people and the general public reasonably should be able to expect the removal or replacement of the offending personnel or appointees. At the moment, frankly, we do not fully know who is responsible for the various decisions which have placed us in position of lodging these and other complaints.

Recent actions of the Fish and Wildlife Service do cause us to believe that several attempts to sabotage tribal plans and resources development programs have been sufficiently serious in the misuse and waste of governmental resources and personnel as to warrant congressional inquiry and examination for misfeasance and maladministration in that agency. We will forward you copies of any congressional correspondence relating to these matters in order that your office might consider independent or alternatively appropriate actions.

Again, we want to impress upon you the importance of acting immediately to commit the appropriated $690,000 to the Northwest Fisheries Program—or to inform us of any contrary decision. Personnel and hiring actions are crucially affected by decisions relating to funding uses. Equally important is the management capacity over present and progeny cycles of the fish resources which shall be enhanced by timely utilization of these funds— or which may be diminished to harmful extent by failure or needless delay.

We shall appreciate your attention to this matter.

Respectfully yours,
Hank Adams, Commission Coordinator for Forrest Kinley, Chairman

Testimonial

Billy Frank and Hank Adams Testimony Before the Subcommittee of the Committee on Appropriations for 1979, House of Representatives, 95th Cong., 2nd Sess: Part 9 (Washington, DC: Government Printing Office, 1978).

Mr. Frank. Thank you.

I am on the Council, and I am the Fish Manager for the Nisqually Tribe, and the past chairman of the Northwest Indian Fisheries Commission.

I have here today Mr. Hank Adams, a volunteer consultant, and of course, Cathy Douglas could not make it today. But in order to utilize my time I would like to have Mr. Adams make my statement, and I will be available for questioning or anything.

Thank you.

Mr. Yates. Please proceed, Mr. Adams.

Mr. Adams. We would like to offer these other things for the committee file in support.

Mr. Yates. They may be received for our files.

Mr. Adams. We have statements relating to support, and justification for the funding request that the Nisqually Tribe is making now for a fish hatchery on the Nisqually Reservation and a rearing station also on the Nisqually Reservation in amounts of $3 million for the hatchery and $5000,000 for the rearing station.

This would be requested from the Bureau of Indian Affairs, and additional $1 million from the engineering and studies relating to the development of an additional hatchery on the Nisqually Reservation which has been proposed for ownership by the Tribe, for contracted operation by the Washington Department of Fisheries.

Mr. Yates. Do you have an agreement with the Washington Department of Fisheries?

Mr. Adams. Yes. The agreement that has been formulated between the tribe and the Washington Department of Fisheries is contained in this document.

The other document that is presented is a report that has been made to the Federal Fisheries Task Force on Washington Fisheries, and it includes these projects and a regional team of that Presidential task force has approved and recommended funding of these projects that we speak of.

What in total we are talking about is approximately a half dozen different enhancement projects that would be integrated into a cooperative management program between the Nisqually Tribe and the Washington Department of Fisheries. This is designed to restore and rehabilitate resources of the Nisqually River drainage in the southernmost portion of Puget Sound, and which would satisfy both the needs of Indian people in Southern Puget

Sounds as well as the growing needs of the non-Indian commercial and sports fisheries in the region.

One of the concerns or reasons why the tribe has come back at this time is because there is on line for funding, both by the State and the Federal Government, some $15 million worth of the salmon enhancement programs in this coming year. Approximately $33 million in State funded projects, some 42 projects or 31 projects, and two main projects for Makah and Tulalip under the BIA and US Fish and Wildlife Service budget has been requested by the Administration.

Now, the Nisqually River and resources come at the end of a very intense impact cycle upon salmon resources in the Pacific Northwest. There has been no enhancement facilities in that area, and yet the Nisqually River has contributed to a range of Indian fisheries, the Canadian fisheries, the foreign fisheries, as well as troll, persinger, and gill net fisheries of the non-Indian population as wells as additionally the support fisheries.

One of the problems here is that this new production in other areas is going to intensify harvest impacts upon a rather vulnerable resource that exists in Southern Puget Sound.

Mr. Yates. In what way?

Mr. Adams. When you produce greater amounts of fish in the more northern areas in Puget Sound, it is for the purpose of allowing additional harvest impacts. The Nisqually resources being anadromous fish, have to pass through all of those intercepting fisheries, and the Nisqually resources are unaided.

What the Federal Task Force and tribe and States have proposed for the Nisqually is about $15 million worth of enhancement projects, but we think and the Fisheries Department agrees, that it does not make sense to wait for $15 million when the more sensible use of funds is to proceed on some fo the planning that is needed, and on the projects that could sustain some of the additional impacts that will be generated by these new production facilities of others.

Mr. Yates. Mr. Dicks, did you have a questions ?

Mr. Dicks. Thank you, Mr. Chairman.

I just want to congratulate the gentleman on a very excellent statement.

I think the point you make is very well taken.

The fish, as they come back into the Strait of Juan de Fuea and into Puget Sound, are fished by all the various user groups you mention, so any project like this contributes to the entire area, and I think you make a very cogent argument.

I also was impressed that you have gone beyond one option, which was to build a large monolithic hatchery, and are focusing on the smaller projects. I think this is probably a better way to utilize the water and to utilize precious dollar resources, and I think it will aid your project.

I think it has been a very wise and prudent decision, and I commend the gentleman.

Mr. Adams. Just these two projects, and the minimal production projections would produce a quarter of a million adult salmon to harvest by all commercial interests and an additional 35,000 by sports fisheries on the valuations of salmon both for determining cost effectiveness as well as the return to fishermen would be on the first return cycle of adult production, would be worth a little more than $3 million, and we are asking $3.5 million for those.

Mr. Yates. Mr. Duncan, did you have a question?

Mr. Robert B. Duncan. No questions.

Mr. Dicks. How long would it take to get these projects planned and started?

Mr. Adams. There are a lot of preliminaries that have to be done. The State developed the project for Muck Creek, and we have developed in the context some trout assistance, the plans for the reservation, so construction could be completed and we could be utilizing returns, egg kegs from this fishery, so next year.

Mr. Dicks. You could really start up next year?

Mr. Adams. Yes, and this is ready to go.

Mr. Dicks. Good.

Thank you very much.

Mr. Yates. Thank you very much, Mr. Adams and Mr. Frank.

Trail of Broken Treaties
and Wounded Knee II

The two events featured in this section were part of a much larger and longer era, popularly known as "Red Power," which roughly ran from the Alcatraz takeover in 1969 to the Longest Walk, which culminated in Washington, DC, in 1978. Vine Deloria Jr., while still the executive director of the National Congress of American Indians, is said to have coined the term in a 1966 speech at the organization's annual meeting.

Deloria, Adams, and many others were part of a new group of young Native activists committed to improving the lot of indigenous peoples on every level and to transforming indigenous/white relations in a manner that reflected the vitality of Native sovereignty, the importance of treaty rights, and the need for more honest and realistic intergovernmental relations.

The selected documents that follow reflect the depth of Adams's knowledge about Native peoples, social movement dynamics, and democratic theory. His policy ideas and skilled analysis of the benefits, personalities, and cause and effects of these two intense and dramatic events in contemporary Native and American history provide a personal, detailed, unabridged, yet panoramic view of these singular moments in indigenous/white affairs.

Press Release

Ad Hoc Committee for New Indian Politics
Hank Adams, Chairman
PRESS STATEMENT: December 2–5, 1971

A national "ad hoc Committee for New Indian Politics" was established during the week of November 14–20 in Reno, Nevada, to conduct the campaign outlined in the attached release of Survival of American Indians Association, issued Nov. 12–14. The participating active membership of the ad hoc Committee shall remain unnamed or unpublicized until after mid-January 1972.

Political Purpose: The basic purpose of this effort shall be to remove the human needs and aspirations of Indian tribes and Indian people from the workings of the general American political system and structures and to reinstate a system of bilateral relationships between Indian tribes and the federal government—as well as to create a positive basis for bilateral dealings between tribes and state governments.

We seek simply to develop a state of independence for Indian people by July 4, 1976. There's no need to declare independent states or nations to secure this. There is primary need to restore the fundamental relationship between the American government and Indian people as provided in formulation of the Constitution of the United States—a legal relationship which has steadily deteriorated into a condition of adverse dependency upon the government by Indians and a subjecting of Indian people to near-total non-Indian control. After two centuries of national independence, this Nation can now afford to allow Indian people to return to our own state of independence, and to be fully-equipped with the rights for community self-determination and creative community development. The most meritorious proposals for advancing Indian interests, rights, and welfare have been lost to the power processes of the American political systems. We face increasing demands to totally emerge ourselves—our 200,000 potential voters—into these political processes and systems merely to secure position to advocate that we be granted hearing for an advocacy of our desires—not to determine outcomes or ultimate results—while we have not yet been allowed to be involved with our own lives by the fundamental standards of consent and control, or consent to external control.

Platform Proposals: The following are among the interrelated proposals we shall seek support for among the various political presidential candidates

---

* Inadequate and decrepit housing has been a major issue in Indian Country since the late 1800s. In 1996 Congress enacted the Native American Housing Assistance and Self-Determination Act, which took all of the Department of Housing and Urban Development's Indian-related housing programs and provided Native nations with the opportunity to apply for block grants.—Ed.

and separate political parties and conventions:

1. A national commitment by constitutional amendment, statutory enactments, and executive or administrative implementation, to restore a permanent non-diminishing Native American land base of not less than 105 million acres by July 4, 1976, which lands shall be perpetually non-taxable and which may never again be alienated from Native American or Indian ownership;

2. A national referendum to be held among all tribally-related Indian in the nation, prior to July 1974, to render decision by majority vote whether or not the Bureau of Indian Affairs (BIA) shall be abolished in apparatus and functions by July 4, 1976;

3. A statutory commitment and authorization for a continuing appropriation of not less than $1,000,000,000.00 annually for each of the next twenty-five years—not including service costs or claims settlements payments to Alaskan Natives or other Indian claims payments—for direct federal assistance to reservation Indian tribes, communities, organizations and individuals, including indigenous institutions and service facilities, if BIA is abolished;

4. A commitment that an additional continuing annual appropriation, not less than 15% the amount committed to reservation communities, shall be allocated for direct federal assistance to non-reservation and urban Indians or native people;

5. Establishment of a National Indian Housing & Construction Credit Authority with funding and authorizations to secure and guarantee long-term, low-interest loans and credits in an initial amount of One Billion Dollars, which may be satisfied in interest payments, repayments of principal, or any redemption of bonds issued, from other continuing Indian appropriations (item 3 above), with a directed obligation of providing for the construction of 50,000 new homes* on or adjacent to Indian reservations for Indian families, as well as providing for any necessary electrical utilities, water sources and systems, and sanitation and sewage facilities, as minimal objective within the first five years after establishment of the Authority;

6. Designate a priority and declare a policy of first consideration for funding such community-economic development projects which shall substantially contribute to an objective of creating an average of 15,000 new, permanent jobs or occupations for reservation Indian annually for the next ten years, including projects and economic enterprises which rely upon regional or inter-tribal consolidations of useable natural and economic resources, or community cooperative ventures, and management of harvestable, renewable natural resources;

7. Repeal of federal statutes and nullification of state enactments inconsistent with statehood enabling acts or constitutions of states which disclaim jurisdiction and taxing authority over Indian lands and people in order that civil and criminal jurisdictions shall be restored to the autonomous tribes, together with total Indian immunity to state taxing authority;

8. A statutory enactment providing that complete taxing authority upon properties, use of properties and incomes derived therefrom, and business activities within the exterior boundaries of Indian reservations, as well as commerce between reservations, shall be vested with the Indian tribal governments or their appropriate subdivisions;

9. Granting consent from the United States to the several states to recognize Indian tribes as being governmental units and public bodies having positive power to govern their territory, rights agencies, institutions, and people and authorizing the States to grant positive standing within the structures of State governments, with additional authorization to exercise concurrent governing jurisdiction in any governmental measure consented to by the particular tribe or Indian people affected, whether by means of compact or contractual agreements and arrangements;

10. Recognize by statute that the internal sovereign authority of Indian tribes extends territorially beyond reservation boundaries to include any Indian rights, resources, or activities, and the management or control thereof, when such rights and resources and related activities have been secured to Indian tribes and Indian persons in particular or general off-reservation areas by treaty provisions;

11. By statute, enable individually-owned Indian lands to be placed in trust with the tribal governments particularly related to them, excepting non-reservation lands, if by majority consent a tribe approves a transfer of trust from the United States, and if a new tribal constitution is adopted by any such tribe to provide for management of such trust responsibilities over lands and resources—at any time after July 4, 1976;

12. Provide a federal interest-payment bonus to Indian tribes or federally chartered Indian corporations, who, have limiting investment opportunities within their own reservations or communities while having an availability of tribal or corporation investment funds, invest in economic or job development projects or new industries on other Indian reservations or in communities of other tribes, where investment capital is lacking or non-existent, but where business development and investment-return opportunities are viable and realistic—with such bonuses to be of sufficient amounts, either in relation to the principal investment or the duration of schedules of repayments or returns, to encourage such inter-tribal investments;

13. Provide for a schedule or scale of voluntarily-declared "excess income" for any publicly or privately employed Indian, or married Indian couple, who may divert such "excess income" for hiring or employment of other Indian persons working under tribal or community sponsored, controlled or directed projects or labor, in return for an appropriate schedule of federal income tax credits and exemptions. (Example: A single Indian who might declare income more than $8,000.00 as being "excess," might receive a total tax exemption if his "excess income" diverted toward the employment

of other Indians exceeded 25% of his income ceiling.);

14. The federal district courts, upon petition of an Indian tribe making claim of substantial injury to, or interference in the equitable exercise of, any rights, governing authority, or its utilization or preservation of resources, secured by treaty, should be directed by federal statute to grant immediate enjoinder or injunctive relief to the complaining tribe or tribal government against any non-Indian party, including state governments, agencies, or political subdivisions, alleged to be engaged in such injurious or interfering actions, until such time as the district court may be satisfied that a treaty violation is not being committed, or otherwise satisfied that the Indians' interests and rights, in equity and in law, are preserved and protected and secure from jeopardy;

15. Authorize selected Indian communities to develop demonstration, experimental, or alternative institutions in the fields of education and community health services—such as an 10-year accelerated elementary and secondary school system with accreditation for college entry or alternate occupational or job training—where assumption of control of existing facilities may be feasible, for developing qualified institutional models in such fields by July 4, 1976.

An Overview: The foregoing is not our complete political platform proposal, but reflects current areas of general agreement and advocacy among the ad hoc Committee. Clearly, we seek amnesty from the prisons of despair and release from the bars against a promising and productive future—a prison constructed by unresponsive politics and indifferent politicians of power. Our campaign is predicated upon a belief that a majority of conscientious Americans are appalled by the effects of the politically powerful constantly preying upon a politically powerless people—the first people of this country—and may now support our bid for freedom. If true, a first generation of Indian people may experience security in their lives—for the first time in the life of this Nation.

Press Release

1972
Survival of American Indians Association
Trail of Broken Treaties

Today a number of Indian people embark upon a journey across the American nation to its capitol in Washington, DC. Three separate caravans of Indian people, small in numbers, begin our journey today from Seattle, Los Angeles, and San Francisco. Possibly, a fourth caravan shall originate from Portland, Oregon. Officially, our route shall follow and be known as "The Trail of Broken Treaties." An itinerary map denoting our pace of travel is provided herewith.

As many names could have been given to our present campaign as there are reasons for our going. Yet the reasons are too numerous to recite. To seek common understanding may seem trite—but to establish a meaning for the unbroken chronicle of broken treaties, and unbreached infamy visited upon Indian people by unquestioning majorities of White America, taxes all abilities for rational understanding, even a capacity for imagination, beyond any realm of possible belief. Therefore, we begin our respective journeys with a question, posed by us, of, "Why, America?" and propose to return with answers of what must be done by ourselves and all others, and how the basic question might be resolved, firmly and finally, in order that our children might be ensured their future by our peoples' being, for the first time in 200 years, made secure.

Our numbers shall increase as we cross the country, and be multiplied as we carry the message of our accomplishment—or unjustified failure—upon our retraced route of return. We rely immediately upon the news and information media of this nation to announce our plans and progress as we proceed across our native soil. We acknowledge a paradox wherein we have already secured the support of the leadership in Christian churches at a national level and in statewide church organizations, while not knowing the level of support among local communities and the respective denominational laities—the paradox lying with the comparative situation wherein the officialdom of various Indian Tribes are being encouraged to denounce us and reject our undertaking by influential non-Indians, despite the evidence and expressed support of numerous Indian community members, not having personal positions or ambitions to sustain with requisite non-Indian approval or acceptance, reflective of the sole standards of accountability—or no accountability—imposed upon tribal officials and Indian governing structures.

Final positions on issues to be presented in Washington, DC, and the strategy of specific plans there, shall be decided during a five-day meeting in St. Paul, Minnesota, where the multiple caravans will converge on October 22, 1972; subject to revision among the total group of Indian people arriving in the National Capitol on November 1st. We are requesting Indian people to arrange to join us on either of those two dates, if for overriding reasons they are otherwise unable to travel with us now. Whatever the final number of Indian persons arriving and participating there, we fully expect that it shall be the largest number of Indian people ever participating in an endeavor of this kind and magnitude.

We are determined that our current effort shall be as disciplined as it is demanding, while being neither oppressively marshaled nor obtrusively militant. It shall be carefully controlled, while remaining subject to the best influences of creativity in action and thought generated among the Indian participants and our non-Indian support. We believe there can be a New Majority—a majority that is not content merely to confirm itself by superiority in numbers, but which by conscience is committed toward prevailing by ceasing wrongs and doing right. The Constitution of the United States and 371 treaties with Indian tribes would seem to command this of all—not just majorities—a simple commitment, not to changeable constitutions and ignorable treaties, but to universal and eternal human values. So we deport, and ask, "Why America?"

Memorandum

April 19, 1973

Survival of American Indians Association

To the US House of Representatives Subcommittee on Indian Affairs: The Honorable Lloyd Meeds, Chairman

Re: Summary of causes for events at Wounded Knee and on the Trail of Broken Treaties Caravan; Suggested actions and attitudes for preventing recurrence of incidents.

Mr. Chairman and Members of the Committee:

I appreciate the opportunity to clarify my viewpoints regarding the events at Wounded Knee and at the BIA Building last November, and to offer suggestions relating to alternative courses for securing change. Wounded Knee is related to and partly result of the federal failure and refusal to understand and appreciate the purposes and intents of the Trail of Broken Treaties caravan last fall. Before destruction and damage to the BIA Building, hundreds of Indian people rebuked by Administration actions which fully demonstrated that the caring and conscience of the American Nation has difficulty in rising above the level of an adversary relationship to Indian people—notwithstanding the constitutional and moral standards which would appear to dictate a better form of relationship. The mental mood and state of mind which prevails at Wounded Knee is one which seeks to restore legitimacy to relationships between the Indian and American nations—and, if it is to be strictly adversary, to reduce (or elevate) that relationship to its most "perfect" form; namely, a state, or acts, of war. If there shall be killing by Indians at Wounded Knee, the act or acts shall, within the peoples' minds, be in the nature of war. It would be a clear, if final, expression of "sovereignty" by a people who have been subjugated and injured by "beneficial" and unenforced laws -- a people denied their natural sovereignty and control at all levels of individual, community, and national life.

My relationship to the Trail of Broken Treaties Caravan, and more recently to Wounded Knee, has not been as a "leader," or organizer, or decision maker, but peripherally and on invitation as a resource or researcher, and as a concerned Indian person—interested in helping to achieve the central objectives sought through these activities, or shared is the attitudes and aims of Indian people generally across this nation.

To state that I am not, nor have never been, a member of the American Indian Movement (AIM) is not a statement—so some reporters have apparently construed—that AIM may not, or fails to, be a vital and valued force among Indian people in communities around the country today. It is not an attribution of blame to AIM for destruction of the BIA Building.

The documents I submitted for hearing record and transcript clearly indicate that Messrs. Harrison Loesch, former Assistant Interior Secretary for Public Land Management, and John O. Crowe, former deputy Commissioner of Indian Affairs, were principally responsible for the decisions which resulted in the damage to the BIA Building—not so much by chance or misjudgment, but by an intended self-rewarding design. The information that I prevented Indian security forces from interfering with Park Police Sgt. Ralph Smith in informing his superiors by radio that a decision had been "made to take over the BIA building"—more than an hour before Indians left St. Stephens Church to go to the BIA the morning of November 2—again was not a casting of blame upon AIM, but a further indication that Interior officials refused to respond appropriately to the situation. The Indian security men had simply responded to my instruction that "we came to Washington to get officials to assume their responsibilities and duties, so we should not interfere with the performance of this."

Most Indian persons within the BIA Building did not participate in any deliberate acts of destruction—although the first damage occurred in efforts to construct an effective defense against threatened police actions or attacks. The major levels of deliberate destruction came as if incidental to an unstated decision that, if the BIA Building should be valued by the government more than Indian people were valued, then the United States should not secure any victory or value by attempting another defeat of Indian people through violent and forcible eviction. The initial removal of artwork and handcrafts from the BIA Building were undertaken for the protection of these items from damage or destruction.

Most Indian people within the building did not approve, favor or participate in deliberate destruction of the facility—and are no more responsible for the damages done there than are members of this congressional committee—but were not possessed of the power or disposition to prevent it. A number of older women favored burning the building in order that the public not see the extensive damage "and think this is how we keep house."

(In personal involvement, I informed the White House and other officials that damages to the building were occurring only with each repeated threat of police action. I suggested the framework for a negotiated settlement. The government waited, however, until after the massive destruction of November 6, to respond affirmatively to suggestions for protecting the people and preserving the building. By that time, I could cease to care for the building and only continue to care for the Indian people within it. Then, I did stand ready to fight beside the others in any defense made. When a decision was announced for burning of the building at midnight, I urged that instead the action be initiated immediately (between 6 and 7 p.m.) Or delayed to the following (election) morning—in order that heavy motor vehicle traffic could be utilized to delay police and firefighting actions long enough to allow all people in the building to totally abandon it and move away to avoid direct confrontations or violent fights with police forces. Leading members of the

AIM argued against the immediate action and forced the delay. The agreement of the White House to meet with TBT representatives to negotiate an evacuation altered the situation later the same evening, and I was requested to become principle negotiator for the Trail of Broken Treaties Caravan with the White House.

The White House negotiations did not follow a form of presenting nonnegotiable demands, but rather one of attempting to establish processes by which legitimate issues could be dealt with and whereby there could be effectual compliance with the Order of the Circuit Court of Appeals which had prevented a police attack on November 6. Since the Circuit Court had directed the federal government to assume a financial obligation for resolving the situation, TBT argued that the obligation might take the form of transportation assistance for returning to the respective home communities. The Circuit Court introduced a grant of amnesty to Indian persons leaving the BIA Building by November 8th, so TBT argued that the White House could reasonably maintain a posture against prosecutions.

The Journey to Wounded Knee:
The hostile reaction to the Trail of Broken Treaties following the departure from Washington, DC, directed the eventual routing toward Wounded Knee. TBT participants dispersed toward their homes, while an opposition to them coalesced behind a demand for their punishment in any form possible. Canned editorials swept across the country to denounce "the harm done to the Indian cause" in newspapers which had never found the space to mention an "Indian cause" or note an Indian need upon their pages before; failing even then to devote the matter an original thought.

Under the direction of former Congressman Wayne Aspinall, this Committee demanded that any public official who had acted decently or with humane feeling during the first eight days of November come before it to apologize for their decency and considerate actions. On appearance, the highest officials explained that apologies were not required—since, in fact, they had not been decent at all, but rather deceitful and dishonest once again with the easily-duped American Indian people. The promises and commitments which had been made with the rebellious group, without hesitation they ensured, would be transformed into effective forms of future denial and punishment. Even the scheduled "responses" to the issues raised and proposals presented by the TBT would assuredly not be appreciated by the "rebels."

(The following week, Rep. Aspinall would meet with the sophisticated, 27-year-old Central Arizona Project Association in Phoenix, Arizona, to urge that Indian rights and demands for CAP water usage priorities be resisted aggressively. News reports of Interior Secretary Rogers C.B. Morton's appearance in Phoenix the next day carried the information and quotes: "We hope to give Arizona this project as a present for Christmas"; 'The Fort McDowell

Indian reservation, northeast of Scottsdale is in a special situation which must be rewarded, because it would be inundated by the Ores Dam water at the confluence of the Salt and Verde rivers. The CAP aqueduct also crosses near there'; Secretary Morton noted that this would constitute a 'major problem,' with a remedy, "Obviously, a new reservation must be found for them," he said.)

The punitive design of departmental officials developed into an Administration-wide attack against the Indian destructionists, but struck out haphazardly to victimize Indian people, tribes and organizations, who had never destroyed anything. "AIMs" and "urbans" simply replaced the words 'Indian people' or Indians in many bureaucrats' vocabularies and in such newsprint, both in a deliberate attempt to polarize the Indian community and to degrade against anything disagreeable or any dissent within it.

Federal funds were withdrawn from AIM-related activities—and from activities and Indian people mistakenly believed to be related to or controlled by AIM-related persons. Indian persons, such as Clyde Bellecourt, who had worked as hard as anyone to negotiate TBT's departure from the BIA building in November, and who had scrupulously informed audiences in advance and in addresses about his fourteen and one-half years in penal institutions in public forums for several years, had "their criminal backgrounds" 'revealed' in copyrighted news stories and media which suggested an impossibility of social and personal rehabilitation for any Indians, if not suggesting extreme punishment merely for having such a record—or alien deportation with dispatch. The financing and funding sources of the American Indian Movement (AIM) and other Indian organizations were repeatedly distorted by columnists or erroneously commingled in widely-distributed news reports to mislead the public and to establish a force to deny positive governmental actions.

Local police agencies and private citizens in numerous parts of the country joined in the attack with the encouragement of public officials and an assumption that Indian people and Indian rights had again become vulnerable, unprotected targets. In the Washington State Legislature, for example, persons associated with group vigilante actions against treaty Indian fishermen spoke openly of filling the rivers with Indian blood, if the State should act responsibly to recognize tribal fishing rights and to join in programs for rational management of shared fishery resources. US Army personnel from Fort Lewis joined the Washington Department of Game's "Indian Riot Squad," which has no functions or purpose for existence other than to act with its unpaid volunteers against Indian people as a race possessed of "intolerable" special rights. Additionally, the 540th Aviation Unit of the Washington National Guard anticipated the future, according to Captain Chris Lane, with mock combat training and war games against a Nisqually Indian community—under the direction of a Commanding Officer named Sullivan, who demanded "realism" to the point of providing details of the geographic landscape and of designating the names of Indians (actually living there) who should be "killed" in the mock exercise.

In California, the slayer of Mohawk Indian philosopher and fighter Richard Oakes, who had provided leadership and courage in the initial day of the Alcatraz occupation and in more difficult, yet more compellingly legitimate, pursuits of claims for California Indians, went to trial. The principal witness for the defense testified that the defendant had bragged about the murder with the statement that "It's open season on coons and Indians"; the jury was persuaded by the sentiment, and the murderer was quickly acquitted.

In Nebraska at Scottsbluff, as in numerous other small towns of the West and mid-West, police officers became abusive of Indians resident to and passing through the area, acting without any lodged complaints or any apparent reasons to evict Indians and Chicanos from their lodgings and to order their movement out-of-town. National news media ignored that confrontation and the consequent judicial prosecution of the Indians' and Chicanos' complaint, which resulted in the issuance of one of the most broad and significant retraining orders for protection of civil rights ever issued by a federal court outside of the South. The validity of the Native American grievances were given credence by the court order—and admitted by the State, county and city officials and police agencies, which had been restrained from violating civil rights in a variety of respects, and who concluded the action by entering a conciliation agreement promising corrective action and conscientious application of the communities' laws in the future. Remaining unchanged in Nebraska, however, was the "Indian bounty law" for Thurston County, which converts the arrest and jailing of Indians into a lucrative business for county jail administration, when budgets or costs advance beyond a certain level and a special state subsidy automatically becomes available on a per Indian head basis.

The national news media rejoined the "Indian struggle" at Custer, South Dakota, where the legal process surrounding the killing and killer of Wesley Bad Heart Bull had scarcely received press notice, but where the threatened armed confrontation between Indians and non-Indians, the burning of public and private buildings, and arrest actions or resistance carried Indian people back into a national media spotlight. Coverage was still available for concurrent or continuing confrontation politics in Rapid City, highlighted by the "liberation" of several downtown bars or taverns where local white citizens gather to reinforce their longstanding hatreds and racial prejudices against Indians.

Meanwhile, the nation remained oblivious to threatened armed resistance by Indian encampments in Western Washington to mercenary police oppression and attacks against Indian fishermen. (Arms were set aside and the encampments dissolved after Governor Daniel J. Evans established a moratorium against arrests and threatened killing of Indians by the Washington Game Department. This came after numerous appeals from many sources to his office; and after a declaration by the largest tribes and inter-tribal organizations in the State that state agencies could no longer attack the fishermen of any particular river without having Indians from all the Tribes joining in whatever necessary defense.) Also ignored, without special concern to the federal government, a local federal judge retaliated against Indian actions by declaring that the Puyallup Indian Reservation and that tribe's rights cease to exist; and state revenue and police agents increased activities of seizing and confiscating hundreds of thousands of dollars in Indian properties of Indian businesses at approximately a dozen different reservations.

Of special concern and a cause for increasing anger among Indian people in a number of States were the incidents in which Indians died or were killed by non-Indians—while local authorities were generally inclined to treat the matters as minor offenses; while inquest juries were reluctant to view acts against Indians as being crimes at all. At the same time, bails set for Indians charged with offenses reflected a first form of punishment by prosecutors and courts, being set at inordinately high levels no matter what the crime or circumstances related to alleged commission, and demonstrating great disparity in attitude and treatment accorded other citizens. In Billings, Montana, two dead Indian victims were tested for alcoholic levels in their blood streams, while the non-Indians responsible for their deaths were given no such tests—although they admitted in the two separate cases taken to inquests, where they were cleared from charges, that they had been drinking prior to their actions which resulted in Indian deaths. On two successive days in February, young Indian men were shot by Bureau of Indian Affairs (BIA) policemen on the Fort Hall Indian Reservation—where incidents of suicides among adolescents and young adults has been epidemic in the past decade, while the tribal government has only shown superficial concern. The BIA police killed the first Indian; but failed to kill the second, probably only because the young man's father come out of his house with a rifle and ordered the police to stop shooting after they had pumped six shots into his son. The Indian father was arrested for armed assault for his interference—and the BIA Agency and Tribal Council entered a resolution of request for higher-powered weapons so they would not need to use so many shots "to bring these Indians down," or to kill them.

The Indian people arrived at Wounded Knee with an attitude and determination that, if America would continue to allow its local non-Indian communities to kill Indians without anyone noticing or with impunity, then America could no longer hide its lack of human regard for Indian people, but would have to kill its next Indians before the eyes, and with the attention, of the entire world.

The Police State at Pine Ridge

One fact which has received virtually no attention is that the United States had already dispatched 100 US Marshals to the small town of Pine Ridge on the Pine Ridge Indian Reservation for around-the-clock duty a full two weeks before numbers of the Oglala Sioux Tribe invited AIM and other Indian people to, and joined in the occupation of, Wounded Knee. The federal marshals had already occupied Pine Ridge—taking over the Indian Agency building, school cafeteria facilities, and some local school dormitory space.

Wide-spread complaints of civil rights violations and abuses of police and governing authority on the Pine Ridge Indian Reservation had been voiced and were mounting steadily among the Oglala Sioux membership across the reservations since, at least, the previous fall. The BIA had allocated special new funding for hiring of a couple score of special police deputies to work under the auspices of the Agency Superintendent and the tribal president Richard Wilson in early November, additional to local Indian who had volunteered "services" to Wilson, and had maintained the heavy police presence in the subsequent months. Even before the Wounded Knee occupation was declared in the course of a meeting there, federal roadblocks had been set up on the roads leading away from the village, Persons leaving the meeting early found that the small town was already besieged by police forces. When others returned to Wounded Knee with information about the roadblocks, the full occupation was declared, and the trading post and other properties were immediately invaded for securing arms and supplies for defense and for maintaining the occupation and Indian people surrounded there.

Two days before the Wounded Knee occupation began, Russell Means was attacked and beaten, along with a man acting as his legal counsel, by five volunteer "security men" acting under the direction of tribal president Wilson. The assault occurred at a store in Pine Ridge. On November 10, 1972, the tribal president dictated, and the tribal court decreed, both that members of AIM should not be permitted on the Pine Ridge Indian Reservation and that Russell Means and other Oglala Sioux Indians would be prohibited from meeting with one another or joining in any assembly or speaking activities on the reservation. These actions were taken prior to Russell Means return to the reservation and his family's home at Porcupine after the dispersal and departure from Washington, DC, of the Trail of broken Treaties Caravan.

Members of this congressional committee have expressed their support and sympathy for Richard Wilson and his actions, indicating a view that the activities he controls are right, reasonable, rational and responsible. The calling of some Indian people, "gutter rats," does not suggest the need for the imprisonment stated as much as it appears to call for extermination or execution. When political leaders, public officials, and police powers almost uniformly declare and determine that Russell Means and other Indians have no rights nor place within either the American System or their own Indian society, the "Second Battle of Wounded Knee" evolves as a tragic answer to the question, "Where can they go?"

In fact, the support for Dick Wilson's 'natural human reaction' or 'reasonable and responsible' actions become an advocacy for an increase in and compounding of wrongs, violence, and injury to humans and to law, rather than support of their elimination or reduction by responsible actions in government and among the citizenry. The abuses of tribal governing authority and powers at Pine Ridge have not been directed solely at Russell Means and Indian members of AIM, but more generally and harmfully against other members of the Oglala Sioux Tribe—including other tribally elected Indian officials.

Dave Long, the longtime popularly-elected vice president of the Oglala Sioux Tribal Council and Executive Committee, was arbitrarily and, without doubt, unlawfully suspended from his offices by the tribal president in latter November—simply for communicating by letter and in person with other members of the Oglala Sioux Tribe, who did happen to be members of AIM, as well as being residents of the Pine Ridge Indian Reservation. Mr. Long repeatedly stated publicly that he did not support the AIM, but did support the Twenty-Point Proposal advanced by the TBT Caravan in Washington, DC, and that he would not be denied his rights of discussing or working for implementation of some of its ideas with other members of his community and tribe. (Most tribal councils and inter-tribal organizations in the United State have taken a similar position. The most recent position paper of the National Tribal Chairmans Association, presented to this Committee, drew upon the content of the TBT proposals in formulation of some of the present NTCA positions.) When Dave Long went with Russell Means to the United States Attorney in Rapid City for securing assistance in the protection of his civil liberties and political rights, he was turned away—while the US Government acted to increase the police powers and capabilities upon the reservation for enforcing the deprivation and denials of his rights.

Only if one chooses to completely ignore Dave Long and other elected officials, including reservation District Councilmen, can the actions at Wounded Knee be constructed to be an "illegitimate" or "extortive" challenge against "duly-constituted government and governing authority." When the representatives of tribal chairman Wilson complain to this committee that the Justice Department has suspended tribal authority "for dealing with the problem at Wounded Knee," they fail to provide the information that the tribal governing bodies have lacked the official quorum support and requirements for effecting any legal Council or Executive action since mid-February. The actions of the tribal court and judges—jumping into the vacuum of authority to provide interim "government by order and decrees"—does not introduce an element of legality to the activities presently being attributed to "duly-constituted government," notwithstanding the willingness and enthusiasm of BIA police agents and local volunteers to enforce the interim "authority" and lawless order.

There is broad support among the Oglala Sioux throughout the Pine Ridge Indian Reservation for the Indian people now in Wounded Knee (as well as a strong concurrent support and desire for a peaceful settlement of the present confrontation). That support does not represent a division between opposing majority and minority political groups, but is derived from growing resentment against the transformation of tribal government from an instrument of popular will or of the people into private seats of personal power for few individuals—fully supported by the United States with finance and with the exercise of police power. Each protest prior to Wounded Knee, instead of bringing about improvement or corrective action to command legitimate exercise of governing authority, brought forth more repressive acts and increased the measures of tribal-federal police oppression.

Last summer, for example, the Federal Bureau of Investigation (FBI) investigated a civil rights complaint relating to the arrest and jailing of an Indian school teacher, Dorene Bad Heart Bull, by BIA police officers on the Pine Ridge Reservation. They had broken her leg, or bones in one foot, and been brutal in other manners, then placed her in jail without treatment. The FBI concluded that a civil rights violation had probably occurred and could be successfully prosecuted. With as much significance, their report constituted a general indictment against the tribal court system, including practices of police and judges—noting that one judge arbitrarily dismissed all cases against persons arrested by particular police officers; that both judges and police officers demonstrated discriminatory partiality and bias against some Indians and in favor of others in decisions of whether or not to arrest or to prosecute in the matter of various offenses; among other abuses of authority or discretion. Nonetheless, Interior and Justice officials decided not to prosecute in the investigated case for the reason that a prosecution might aggravate the instability and inequities evidenced in the functioning of tribal government and its court and police agencies.

More recently, on April 4th and 5th, a BIA policeman arrested two of four young Indian men who, while untruthfully claiming to be members of AIM, fired into a car being driven or occupied by two non-Indian schoolteachers, from Scenic, South Dakota, and subsequently at a US mail delivery man, with a shotgun and .22 rifles. The two men were taken to the BIA-tribal jail at Pine Ridge. Within hours after their arrest, the two were dismissed from jail and charges by tribal judge Dorothy Richards—sister of one of two men arrested. This contrasted sharply with the handling of other cases in the same time period, when other Indian residents of the reservation were being held without charges, or in some cases being jailed for as long as a week without hearing by the tribal court. The BIA police officer involved in this particular case was angered by its handling, but, because Agency Superintendent Stanley Lyman and BIA Area Director Wyman Babby have consistently condoned such practices, he was left without recourse for processing a complaint. (He has stated his willingness to testify on the matter at an appropriate form of hearing.)

It is not uncommon to hear Oglala Sioux people of all ages beyond childhood speak of the reign of terror which exists, and has existed, on the Pine

Ridge Indian Reservation. The entry of US Marshals into Pine Ridge in mid-February was not viewed as a form of protection, but intensified the fears and feelings of threat. Respected local leaders frequently profess that now they "feel safe only in Wounded Knee" and complain that they can not enter.

Failures to End Confrontation at Wounded Knee:

A number of the Indian people in Wounded Knee, as across the Pine Ridge Indian Reservation, were not born as citizens of the United States—and did not become citizens until they received a land allotment under the control of the US Secretary of the Interior, or until a statutory grant of citizenship was extended to all Indians generally in 1924. A good number of others persons in Wounded Knee are American Indians who are but second-generation citizens of the United States. This is an important consideration in understanding the claims and statements being made in Wounded Knee, and among Indian people in others parts of the nation.

The 1868 Treaty of Fort Laramie continues to hold as much promises for the lives of Sioux Indian people or more than has been offered by or materialized from an approximate half-century of citizenship in this nation. What has developed into violent confrontation and the potential for greater violence at Wounded Knee evolves largely from the violence directed against the lives of Indian people through failures to enforce or apply existing laws. In much the same manner as the violence of unenforced regulatory, civil, and criminal laws has constructed slums and ghettoes around this country, the persistent and patterned failure to apply or enforce laws for the benefit of Indian people as Indians, or Indian people as citizens, has created and sustained a tormented and tortured existence for Indian communities across this land.

I do not believe that every individual has a right to interpret every law to his own favor, or to be governed only by those laws of one's liking or choosing. When Russell Means appeared before this Committee, he was not in violation of the 1868 Sioux and United States treaty as some members of the Committee suggested. He had delivered himself up to the authorities of the United States on their charges of "wrong-doing," although maintaining his innocence against those charges. He was here after being freed on bond.

If the Wounded Knee confrontation concludes peacefully, the Indian people in Wounded Knee have constantly stated their acceptance and expectation of liability for their actions. They have made no demands for "amnesty" (some say because a request for amnesty is an admission of jurisdiction which might legitimately be denied). Rather, they have simply demanded an application and enforcement of the existing law—including any valid treaty law. They have asked that neither the United States nor persons in tribal government be permitted to continue operating, acting, or exercising authority outside the law, or in violation of it. That has been the substance of their demands, and it constituted the particulars of the March 19th and April 1st proposals, which led to the negotiated agreement of April 5th.

There have been protested, however, demands imposed upon Indian people with respect to national treaty law which do not apply as demands upon non-Indian citizens with respect to other laws. Rather than reading the treaties and following its law or provisions, the United States, its agencies and non-Indian citizens, insist that treaty law first be litigated, or otherwise have the life drained from it, before it shall be applied upon the actions of non-Indians or in favor of Indian people. Neither the national nor state governments in their practices regard treaties as existing affirmative law—and Indians are constrained from following these laws as written, most frequently by the exercise of police power against even the most explicit treaty-sanctioned rights. National treaties which apply to all people of this country are reduced, therefore, from supreme law which Indian people might follow, as with other federal or lesser laws, to having the near-singular dimensions of being an uncertain defense which might be invoked after the treaty law has been attacked or denied by the police powers of other people.

"Indian sovereignty" at present is an anomaly or abominable distortion of an existing, legally-accepted fact. The present claims for restoration of Indian sovereignty is simply a call to rid the existing and recognized rights of the abnormalities and deviations which have developed and effectually denied Indian people the autonomous self-government that is integral to the Indian relationship with and to the federal government of the United States. This renewal or respect of Indian sovereignty is necessary, not to roll back the pages of history, but for allowing Indian people again to gain a foothold for having access to a promising future.

In the minds of Wounded Knee, that future is at stake. It can be forfeited at a personal level, if it might be secured for other Indian people, particularly for new and coming generations They have been prepared to die—and to kill defensively—because they desperately want that other Indian people and their own children may live in "more perfect" Indian nations than have previously been possible or permitted by the United States.

It is recognized that a peaceful settlement there can operate toward the same purposes, and contribute more substantially to them—but only if some change, positive in nature and revolutionary in scope, has occurred or become possible outside of Wounded Knee. There will be no peaceful settlement if the people there are convinced that prevailing attitudes deny that possibility or have only become more adverse and hostile.

A peaceful settlement was initially beyond reach because the federal departments refused to admit the existence of the larger problems, injustices and inequalities, prevailing upon the Pine Ridge Indian Reservation and operative beyond the constraints of law in the exercise of tribal governing authority; together with their refusal to treat the Wounded Knee situation as anything other than a police matter and action to be taken against criminals. When the Administration's attitude altered and began to address the concerns of the Indian people, the initiation of a settlement—immediate, for ending the armed confrontation; long-range, for dealing effectively with the discernible problems and expressed concerns—because possible and desired, and was provided for in the April 5th Agreement.

Inasmuch as ultimately it did not constitute a settlement, it perhaps does not matter much who broke or abandoned the April 5th Agreement. For the sake of future events which I will address, I should briefly discuss my own understanding of it. The substance of the agreement was formulated in verbal discussions in the DMZ teepee on March 31st, with federal representatives inviting a written proposal of provisions, which was prepared and presented on April 1st. Agreement was reached on most of the ten points on that date, and general agreement followed on remaining points the following day. On April 3rd, only specifics relating to a series of White House-level meetings with traditional Sioux headmen and chiefs regarding the operation of treaty commission—besides the precise language of a final agreement—remained unsettled. On that date, an immediate White House meeting was proposed for either Wounded Knee or Washington, DC, preliminary to one already agreed to for the third weak in May, and intended as a federal act of "good faith" for activating a final dispossession of arms and weaponry.

The senior federal negotiator resisted any agreement which required any pre-conditions for the dispossession of arms, or which constituted anything less than a simultaneous implementation of the agreement. The timing of a proposed phone call from a White House meeting was discussed, with the Wounded Knee side making reference to a previous federal proposal which called for a phone call immediately preceding commencement of a "high-level" meeting in Sioux Falls, and arguing that the same thing was being proposed except at a White House level. The federal negotiator objected to any trip to Washington until after a dispossession of arms had been affected. We argued that a simultaneous disbarment would begin preparing the actual plans for the final dispossession of arms immediately after signing, and that the actual final disbarment would be occurring as soon as an agreement was signed— that both sides would begin preparing the actual plans for the final dispossession of arms immediately after signing, and that the actual final disarmament would occur at the time of the arrival at the White House meeting and the receipt of a call at Wounded Knee that the meeting was ready to commence.

Although I did not attend the final two sessions of negotiations on April 4th and 5th, I was assured that the federal government had accepted those terms, except for proposing that the meeting be held at Rapid City; these assurances being provided me by federal representatives and Wounded Knee attorneys. Instead of the Rapid City site, Wounded Knee countered with a proposal that the meeting be held in Syracuse, New York, among the territory of the Six

Nations of the Iroquois Confederacy. Finally, I was advised that Washington, DC, had been accepted as the site, but not at the White House, and rather at the offices of the National Center for Dispute Settlement. There had been no indication of any changes in the basic terms of the agreement for the meeting and the immediately preceding call for activating the dispossession of arms—although I was aware of a federal insistence that it would accept no other terms.

Honestly, I do not believe there was a federal violation of the April 5th Agreement in Washington, DC. If any violation on the part of federal authorities occurred, it could only have happened in the course of federal arrest and judicial proceedings in Rapid City on the evening of April 5th—and there are certain reasons for believing that the spirit of the Agreement was violated there, but within the domain of local judicial authorities and beyond the direct control of federal officials directly involved in the negotiations or the implementation of the agreed upon terms. The Federal District Judge did reject the arrangements which had been made by the Justice Department for processing Russell Means through his bonding and release hearing in Rapid City, although that Judge did not preside over the hearing and was without any apparent reason for interfering in the arranged procedures—other than his previously demonstrated anger over the incidents in Wounded Knee.

I know as well that Wounded Knee attorneys and related persons had debated proposed language for the agreement at length, but I do not believe the Agreement, nor its essential terms, were betrayed by the language or words used within it, nor greatly affected by the words or language. The basic intents and commitments were clear and carried beyond the content of the Agreement.

The Forces Against a Settlement at Wounded Knee:
A number of Indian people—families and individuals—who I respect highly for their commitments to and work in behalf of the future of Indian people throughout the United States have been involved at times in Wounded Knee since the end of February. I have no doubt but that there are substantially more—in fact, countless—people outside Wounded Knee who do not want to see a peaceful conclusion and settlement to end the armed confrontation, than there are persons of similar mind, if any, in the village. There are some factors which encourage its continuation—and other crucial ones which make resolution difficult; including dishonesty and distrust.

Finally, the matter is not resolved merely by passing a simple judgement that the people in Wounded Knee are "wrong"—unless that were to be used as the basis for demanding they quit the village or otherwise be routed out or killed by heavy police action. Most of the people in Wounded Knee previously have never deliberately violated any laws in their lives. Yet they have experienced a world of wrongs committed against themselves or other Indian people, while not having any methods or means to cause the wrongs to cease or be corrected, or to cause right to be done.

There are wrongs occurring inside and outside of Wounded Knee—and all those who see wrongs on but one side, or fail to make conscientious and discriminating judgements on what constitutes real wrongs, make resolution more difficult. Those who have viewed the problem as being an internal Indian dispute on the reservation—and have chosen sides—make a settlement more difficult, if encouraging wrongs by the side of their choosing.

There is virtually no evidence that the actions at Wounded Knee has had any beneficial impact whatever upon the Department of the Interior and its Bureau of Indian Affairs. Their general attitudes toward most Indian people continue to grow worse and more punitive in nature. While being centrally responsible, in concord with Oglala Sioux tribal officials, for the development of the armed police confrontation, Interior and BIA officials have encouraged the wrongful and unlawful activities of Indian and non-Indian on the Pine Ridge Indian Reservation outside of Wounded Knee—which previously makes an appropriate and immediate settlement of the confrontation next to impossible.

At a time when I was possessed of the best capacity of personal influence for helping to effect an agreement for settlement within Wounded Knee, as well as being available to discuss with tribal president Richard Wilson and Special Assistant to the Secretary of the Interior Marvin Franklin their concerns and interests, BIA and Interior officials met with Wilson and informed him that I carried an outline for an agreement with some chance of bringing about a settlement. When I arrived on the Reservation, tribal authorities and BIA Police, in the company of Agency Superintendent Stanley Lyman, were waiting for me—refusing to meet with me and acting to make certain that I did not make entry into Wounded Knee. They missed my arrival, however, but, when finding out I was there, came into the BIA Agency Building, where I had commenced a meeting with two Assistant Attorney Generals of the United States and abducted me—across state lines and more than fifteen miles beyond the reservation boundaries into Nebraska.

Not giving up, a couple of days later I was able to reach by phone a former Executive Director of the National Congress of American Indians (NCAI), who works as an executive assistant to chairman Wilson, and who I thought might be able to favorably influence a decision allowing my re-entry to the Pine Ridge reservation. This took place on the day after a tribal councilman, Leo Wilcox, had been found dead in his burned-out car as a result of a freak accident occurring while he was drinking. (AIM was immediately being blamed for his "murder.") I mention this because the executive assistant is the same person who told this committee that "all our traditional chiefs are dead; they died in the last century." On that day, he informed me: "There can be no negotiations. They killed one of our chiefs. Now tradition takes over. Because they've killed one of ours, we're going to have to get together with his people and go on down into there and get a blood settlement. It'll probably be a bloodbath. I'm sorry its got to happen, Hank, goddam, but that's the way it has to be...."

Prominent national Indian organizations have also failed to aid in or utilize their influence for bringing about a peaceful settlement or an end to violent confrontations. The relationship of the National Congress of American Indians (NCAI) and the American Indian Press Association (AIPA) to the serious and dangerous situations on the Pine Ridge Reservation both followed an undisciplined form of a family affair. The sister of the NCAI Executive Director Charles Trimble works for tribal president Richard Wilson; Trimble succeeded Leo Vocu in NCAI, leaving the top executive post in AIPA. While NCAI went to Pine Ridge to assist Wilson in publicity and public relations efforts, AIPA staff writers remained in Washington, DC, to engage in an activity of calling a major newspaper office to personally berate and critically reprimand the reporters for writing of the issues on the Pine Ridge Indian Reservation in manners reflecting adversely upon the Wilson administration.

Issues relating to the preservation of tribal sovereignty can legitimately be raised before this Committee, by NCAI or others, but the conflict of relationships, if not of interest, represented by the NCAI role at Pine Ridge is important for understanding the total complex of issues involved. Both NCAI and the National Tribal Chairman's Association (NTCA) have taken positions in opposition to the application or implementation of the 1968 "Indian Bill of Rights"—which had purpose in enactment of protecting the interests and rights of Indian individuals from abuses of tribal governments and exercises of tribal governing authorities. Legal services organizations which specialize in Indian legal matter have adopted general policies against invoking the "Bill of Rights" authorities for protecting individual Indians from unlawful acts by tribal officials. Individual rights, more appropriate termed, "sovereignty of the individual," is not a concept alien to tribal sovereignty or balanced Indian societies, nor is it a contradiction or challenge to Indian self-government—indeed, being a precious part of it. But where, outside of Wounded Knee, does it have advocacy in the conduct of public policy; where, when demonstrably needed, does it have application as a matter of existing law?

Indian people can be encouraged that the general membership of this committee has shown strong interest in making conscientious examination of problems and issues, rather than attempting to pre-judge their merits and impose pre-exiting notions upon the lives of Indian people. However, the members of Congress can aggravate problems such as that at Wounded Knee by making blanket, non-discriminating judgements or condemnations of situations which are not wholly wrong or right; nor exclusively good or bad. Necessary change, and alternative means of securing it, will not occur or evolve, if congressional committees operate more as forces for controlling Indian thought than as responsive units of government, which are themselves affected or influenced by positive Indian thought and meritorious judgements that should be considered—not simply ratified or rejected in being.

Many publicly-reported statements of Indian officials regarding the occupation of both the BIA building and Wounded Knee have been made for the primary purpose of securing or maintaining approval or "good standing" with non-Indians, including members of Congress and Administration officials. White approval of behavior, actions, opinions and decisions has become an almost-frightening conditioning process for most Indian persons who become public figures or enter public life at whatever level. In the course of the December and April hearings, this Committee in general has probably given effectual approval and gracious ratification to as many wrongs, in government and among Indian people, as it chose verbally to condemn or criticize. After drawing first distinction or division among personalities, good and bad, wise and derelict, the wrongful actions of the "good" and the "wise," on the whole, have escaped scrutiny or critical judgement.

I have great discomfort in a national situation where so many Indian officials are able to maintain "impeccably good relations" with non-Indian public and political officials, while their relations with their own communities and Indian constituencies have deteriorated to such a state that incidents such as Wounded Knee occur—and threaten to become a common occurrence across the country. Indian sovereignty is seriously threatened when tribal governments need only satisfy the requirements of securing non-Indian approval—and secure it, while ceasing to be accountable continuously to the governed Indian population."

The choosing of sides on the Pine Ridge Indian Reservation by most people, who have cause to consider, or to become involved with, it, has created a void of people with sufficient moral influence to effect a decent settlement of the Wounded Knee occupation and to restore peace and order and an atmosphere of justice on the Pine Ridge Indian Reservation. For every Congressman who believes that the tribal president has acted reasonably and responsibly, there are a thousand white citizens who are willing to furnish guns and ammunition to Indians who they believe to be "right" in Wounded Knee. If the weaponry does not reach there, it will remain available for use— and likely be used—elsewhere, if Wounded Knee ends "wrongly" with Indians dying. There seems a general failure to realize just how serious the threat of violent confrontation and death is at Wounded Knee—and an equally serious failure to realize that Wounded Knee is not confined to Wounded Knee.

If one knows what the situation is on the Pine Ridge Indian Reservation and reads of the majority support or sympathy of the American public for "Indians at Wounded Knee," as reflected in the recent Harris Poll, one imagines that the public does not understand or know what it is among Indian people and Indian aims that they "support." Doubtless, as with the overwhelming support demonstrated for Indian positions at each the Republican and Democrat National Conventions last summer, it is an abstract support for abstract Indians which does not translate or transform effectively into concrete and constructive change in governmental policies and actions toward Indian people in conformance with general and specific community desires. A reading of such "public support" by involved Indians, nonetheless, becomes an encouragement to indefinite continuation of the confrontation at Wounded Knee, even if leading to a bloody conclusion by continuation, partly to demonstrate that the government does not respond to either the public or Indians—and partly to prove to both the American public and government that it is dealing with, not abstract storybook or history book "Indians," but real Indians—not of 1890, but of today.

I sincerely believe that various high-level officials in the US Justice Department have began to understand the situation they are faced with and the general reasons for its occurrence. Their dilemma is presently less one of not being able to control what happens in Wounded Knee than being one of not being able to control what happens outside of Wounded Knee, as well as being unable to make the decisions which should be made by the Department of the Interior and BIA. (It is almost repetitive of the grotesque application of responsibility which become apparent during the early stages of the BIA Building occupation. Then several government officials, possessed of the decision-making capacity to direct a police attack against the several hundred Indian people and perhaps kill all if necessary, claimed they did not have the authority to allow re-arrangement of tables in a CSA Building for Indian and federal authority to sit closer to one another for talks directed toward ending the occupation and preventing property destruction.)

The Justice Department now could most easily end the armed confrontation simply by withdrawing US Marshals and FBI Agents from the Pine Ridge Indian Reservation—if it could trust that no armed people in Wounded Knee would not move to another site or town for renewed confrontation; and if it did not know and expect that Indian and non-Indian people outside of Wounded Knee would likely attempt an armed and violent attack upon the people inside of Wounded Knee.

The encouragement that has been given to vigilante-type activities outside of the occupied village, or the condonation of criminal actions by Indians and non-Indians opposing the people in Wounded Knee, has left the Justice Department in the middle of a difficult situation which now has no easy remedy or appropriate response for ending it peacefully. In its basic character, the takeover of Wounded Knee did not constitute any threat to Indian residents there or to any people outside of that town—unless it were to become a staging area for increased involvement for armed confrontation elsewhere. There are but few indications, if any, that there ever existed any intentions of that nature.

The more threatening attitude which prevails on Pine Ridge is that supported by Interior and BIA officials in the actions of BIA and tribal police authorities and "citizen volunteers" that "badges are law; guns are justice."

Personally, I became greatly distressed that some lawyers and attorneys involved with the Wounded Knee matter seemed to be more staunchly opposed to any peaceful settlement than any Indian people involved—and appeared to actively pursue continuation of the occupation despite the possibilities of tragic consequences. When the April 5th Agreement had all but become the basis and form for a final agreement, a couple attorneys argued strenuously for its rejection on grounds that Wounded Knee was "surrendering" too easily and for too little. Another attorney argued that any agreement should be worded in order that it would constitute "90% of a settlement" and keep the government interested, but still leave between one and ten percent "in dispute" for continued discussions and negotiations with federal authorities. One lawyer took great pains to convince the "recognized leaders" at Wounded Knee of the propriety of virtually all their decisions (except moves toward settlement), yet privately engaged Indian security forces in divisive discussions attacking principal leaders as being totally disinterested in the people and interested only in appearances before the news media, then carried the same charges among different leaders and into private meetings outside of Wounded Knee.

On the whole—with major exceptions—Wounded Knee attorneys seemed to stand without backbone in their "ethical standards" and in their advices regarding the existing law and the actions of Wounded Knee defenders. In several instances, lawyers concerned with the developing dangers in the continued confrontation did ask myself privately to express their disagreement with certain positions and interpretations of law (including the 1868 United States and Sioux Nation Treaty), but remained reluctant or refused to address Wounded Knee Indian people regarding crucial differences of opinion or understanding—which might have had favorable affect in moving the stalemated confrontation toward a peaceful settlement and resolution. As well, although there exist critical issues of law and human rights to be resolved on the Pine Ridge Indian Reservation, the legal efforts of involved lawyers have yet to touch upon those issues and intolerable situations which preceded and arguably precipitated the occupation of Wounded Knee. Generally, the Department of the Interior and BIA also have refused to correct or change those situations, or require an equitable application of existing law at Pine Ridge. Fortunately, the Justice Department has given these matters some thought and has began to initiate some improvements through investigative and legal process. A lack of Interior Department cooperation and recognitions of major problems, however, shall probably continue to render federal actions inadequate to the real needs—or to aggravate the severity of problems.

A major segment of the non-Indian support that is evidenced through supportive activities for Wounded Knee is based upon a favoring of continued confrontation whatever the consequences, rather than peaceful settlement. A number of non-Indians, who have been retarded in their attempts, or who have failed, to "get it on" and become credibly joined in a "Third World" or "American revolution," have formed a front line of support for any Indians who will operate as their surrogate "revolutionaries." Attendance at their support-related meeting finds that no discussion is made nor thought given toward peaceful settlement and ensuring that Wounded Knee becomes a compelling impetus to proper or appropriate public policy and practices toward Indian people, nor transferring the effects of broad public support for Indian into an effective force for serving Indian purposes, aims and desires. Securing more guns and increasing firepower enters discussion as being virtually the primary, singular, and almost only discernible Indian goal.

The role of the news media in bringing about a termination or prolongation of such actions as the Wounded Knee occupation—or the BIA Building occupation—should become a matter of conscientious consideration and examination by members of its professions. It would be dishonest to state or suggest that the influence of the news media on these two activities has not been considerable and decisive in determining their conduct and durations. The "power of the press" has figured substantially in determination of what has been done. Nevertheless, while there is recognition that their great "power" must come into play in behalf of the interests of Indian people for brining about concrete and constructive change—in some sense, the BIA Building and Wounded Knee occupations are an expression of the highest contempt for the American mass communications media and its professional standards or disciplines. The actions are contemptuous, not solely because news coverage is sought or may be a motivational and a principal goal, but because they are a demonstrative counterpoint to what is sought to be revealed; they are an expression that the communications media have failed to serve the necessary betterment and required advancement for the lives of Indian people in their everyday conditions around this country—but cause the news media to become operative with some certainty or consistency to give coverage to incongruously dramatic or desperate events, which—perhaps even requiring to have an entertainment value—may be called "news." (On the other hand, once moved by whatever standards to Wounded Knee, it becomes an indictment against an "American free press" that its coverage should be limited to news handouts and press briefings by federal and tribal authorities—or vigilante groups—once blockades are set up against the press and its reporters instructed that coverage must be limited to those sources or otherwise not be given.)

Respectfully submitted,
Hank Adams, SAIA

Letter

May 7, 1973
Survival of American Indians Association
US Senator Henry M. Jackson, Chairman,
US Senate Committee on Interior & Insular Affairs,
Washington, DC 20510

Dear Senator Jackson:

I regret I must write you a letter of this nature. However, I believe the matter which is discussed to be of extreme importance to the relationship between the United States congress and the American Indian people—and what we may expect to be achieved by the present Congress.

Today I called Mr. Gerald R. Gereau of your staff respecting my current trip to Wounded Knee, South Dakota. In response to a previous offer of assistance from Mr. Gereau, I requested that he exercise his previously-claimed influence to alleviate any opposition or obstacles to my travel plans which might materialize on the part of Mr. Richard Wilson, Oglala Sioux tribal president. Specifically, his earlier offer had been to provide assistance in that particular way.

Previously, I had indicated that, unless Mr. Wilson should learn of my entry upon the reservation by other means, I would prefer to just go there without press, public, or tribal official knowledge, as the easiest method of avoiding any unnecessary or injurious disputes which might impose upon a crucial time factor related to negotiations for a settlement. Although Mr. Gereau also had expressed an adverse attitude toward its occurrence and asked questions to which he already knew the answers—which I reaffirmed.

Surprisingly, he asked who had initiated the request for me to go to Wounded Knee. I informed him again that Indian people in Wounded Knee had requested my assistance and advice for finalizing negotiations, and that Kent Frizzily, Interior Solicitor, had transmitted the request along with his personal suggestion that it might be helpful and productive for me to come. Remarkably—as indicated by clarification through a subsequent conversations with Senator Abourezk's office—Mr. Gereau appears to have contacted the Abourezk office to claim that I told him that Senator Abourezk had initiated my present activity, or been instrumental in having myself return to Wounded Knee. Rather than being a misrepresentation of fact; this would have been an outright lie by Mr. Gereau—perhaps compounded by others.

Of more critical concern, I would emphasize, are previous statements made to me by Mr. Gereau regarding his own status and the status of your Committee of Senator Abourezk. In the course of first meeting Mr. Gereau, during the recent hearings of Congressman Meeds relating to Wounded Knee, he advised me of his plans to go to South Dakota in preparation for possible Senate field hearings. He pointedly stressed that: "These will be Senator Jackson's hearings. They're hearings by the full Interior Committee; Senator Abourezk can be involved if he wants—but they're Senator Jackson's hearings."

o o o

In the course of the conversation of May 3rd, instant, in which Mr. Gereau offered to intercede with Dick Wilson, Toby Eagle Bull, Leo Vocu, and BIA Agency Superintendent Stanley Lyman to eliminate obstacles to my travel on the Pine Ridge Indian Reservation, he additionally offered the 'helpful' information that, quote: "I have more influence than Abourezk." Responding to my interjection, Mr. Gereau qualified his claim to say, "That is with the Committee and as far as Senator Jackson is concerned." Oddly, he had initiated the conversation by entering a claim that Senator Abourezk personally had just finished informing him about my proposed travel to Wounded Knee—but, on close questioning, Mr. Gereau reluctantly admitted that he only had talked with a member of Sen. Abourezk's staff. He offered the gratuitous observation that there was no difference: "It's all the same."

There is no need here to repeat or question Mr. Gereau's other extravagant claims of accomplishments on his recent South Dakota trip. Since Wounded Knee has continued, one can assume that his energies are frequently misdirected. Since an Indian, who he traveled with on his return toward Washington, was not arrested after Mr. Gereau reported him to the FBI, one can guess that he is as frequently wrong.

At the moment, I am acting as a courier between the White House and Wounded Knee, carrying a sealed letter from Leonard Garment, Special Consultant to the President of the United States, to Indian people in Wounded Knee; and, incidentally, carrying another sealed letter addressed to Kent Frizell.

I understand that the first letter provides the basis for final settlement of that dispute. The purpose for my involvement derives from the other Indian people's request for my presence; my participation and work (at Wounded Knee request) in formulating and securing the April 5th Agreement; my background in working in behalf of many Indian Tribes, their governments and people, over the years; my continued interest in working for a just, equitable and peaceful settlement; and a determination that the central concerns of Indian people in Wounded Knee shall not be disregarded or overlooked, and the common objectives and goals shared generally in the attitudes, aims and desires of Indian people throughout this country are secured with whatever immediacy warranted or necessary to Indian community life and advancement.

It is consistent with these purposes that I address you regarding Mr. Gereau. While he may find it satisfactory to state today that it would be "improper" to respond to the requests that he previously invited, I find his attitudes in his staff position and his undercutting of a United States Senator, who is Chairman of the Subcommittee on Indian Affairs, as being entirely improper; as inappropriate as it has been dishonest; and totally inimical and adverse to the genuine interest of American Indian people. Senator Jackson, I can not believe that you would knowledgeably approve or condone the actions and remarks of Mr. Gereau, while he has allegedly been acting in your behalf.

Many Indian people and organizations have become greatly impressed with Senator Abourezk's personal commitment and determination to be an effective and conscientious servant to his duties as Chairman of the Indian Affairs Subcommittee in attempting to attack and eradicate major problems confronting Indian people, in acting upon the most necessary legislative needs, and in carrying out the requirements of the constitutionally-mandated relationships between Indian people and the Congress of the United States. Indian communities have not had cause to place such high trust and hopes for accomplishment with the Indian Affairs' Chairman since the time that post was previously occupied by US Senators Frank Church and Lee Metcalf, successively, nearly a decade ago—aside from the full Committee's commendable work on the Alaska Natives Claims Settlement, under your own chairmanship.

My statements and information are not expressive of a lack of confidence in Senator Abourezk's ability to act effectively, even if he, and Indian persons having business to conduct with your Committee and Subcommittees, have to contend with the undermining nuisance factor of Mr. Gereau. Nonetheless, the double-dealing tactics of Mr. Gereau—in large part being the stuff of which the causes for "Wounded Knees" are made—can only make the tasks of meeting national Indian needs more difficult, and do betray the standards of conduct and performance which American Indian people, or any people, are entitled to expect from the Congress and the national government.

Respectfully yours,
Hank Adams, SAIA

Memorandum

May 16, 1973
To: Vine Deloria, Jr., President
Institute for Development of Indian Law (IDIL)
From: Hank Adams, National Director
Survival of American Indians Association (SAIA)
Re: Participation in Negotiations for the Wounded Knee Settlement

The following is a summary of my relationships to the occupation of Wounded Knee (WK), South Dakota, on the Pine Ridge Indian Reservation, from late February through early May, regarding involvement in negotiating processes, including the extraneous information you requested: (A complete file of my "Wounded Knee Papers" is provided herewith.)

On the first day of the WK occupation, I was at Franks Landing, Washington, where some ten days earlier we had secured a private agreement with Governor Daniel J. Evans for a moratorium upon arrests of Indian fishermen by the Washington Game Department, in consequence whereof we were able to effect disbandment of an armed encampment and a series of armed guard stations involving scores of Indian people along the Nisqually River.

In the first couple days of WK it was difficult to get any information from the federal departmental officials in Washington, DC, and the FBI and Federal Marshals Service (which had already had 100 marshals stationed at Pine Ridge for two weeks preceding the occupation) were refusing to provide information through their command post. As soon as information leaked out relating to the initial WK "demands," I began calling the offices of US Senators Edward Kennedy (Tom Susman) and James Abourezk (Mary Bergren) to urge that they or appropriate representatives travel to Wounded Knee. At the same time I attempted to communicate a message into Wounded Knee through broadcast media in South Dakota to urge that anyone who might have been held against their will or free choice be released immediately (using some phone numbers of news outlets in South Dakota provided me by Senator Abourezk). Before leaving for Washington, DC, I held a press conference in Seattle to provide information on the precipitating problems and issues represented by the occupation of Wounded Knee, including the matters which I had addressed to Administration officials about an ominous situation developing since last November.

Also in the first two days of the occupation, I recommended to the Office of the Secretary of the Interior that it could seize the initiative in the matter by immediately suspending BIA Area Director Wyman Babby and BIA Agency Superintendent Stanley Lyman (and possibly Tribal Chairman Richard Wilson, but not absolutely necessary) and placing the Aberdeen Area Office and the Pine Ridge Indian Reservation under the management of a Special Supervisor of Administrator. Other than the requested Senatorial presence, Wounded Knee "demands" had not yet been fully formulated or communicated. I argued that the Department should act on the central issues and in the manner recommended before such actions should be called for either as "unnegotiable demands" on the one side or as "demands which cannot be met under threat of guns and tactics of extortion" as a plausible method for bringing about an early or immediate settlement.

Returning to Washington, DC, I continued talks with Senate offices and with Senate Foreign Relations Committee staff members. In early March, I discussed the issues of Wounded Knee hearings of the Senate Judiciary Committee, when opposing Mr. L. Patrick Gray's nomination to become FBI Director, by detailing the everyday relationships of the FBI to Indian people and reservations (including Pine Ridge) in law enforcement activities—ranging from lack of enforcement and disregard of laws to selective interferences with or protections of tribal governments by purely discretionary investigations and audits of the uses of tribes and federal funds—or refusal to answer criminal complaints in that area of concern.

In the same time period, I wrote a three-page letter to the President urging White House involvement at Wounded Knee, offering limited background on the 1868 Sioux Treaty, suggesting several recommendations for resolving the armed confrontation, and offering any assistance I might provide for helping to bring a settlement.

On March 16th, I received a call from Russell Means and Sid Mills from inside Wounded Knee asking that I take the next plane to Rapid City, where a chartered plane would be waiting to fly me to Pine Ridge, from where the National Council of Churches (NCC) John Adams would transport me into the village to assist with negotiations and the drafting of position papers. The Justice Department, represented by Assistant to the Attorney General Harlington Wood, had made a "final" five-page, twenty-point proposal for a "resolution" of the confrontation, which was characterized as "the best that can be secured" from the US Government. On March 18th, a negotiating session was held in Wounded Knee for the purpose of reviewing the proposal paragraph by paragraph, without material progress. After the session, AIM attorneys Ramon Roubideaux and Beverly Axelrod, plus myself, went to Harlington Wood's office to meet with him and his assistant Dick Hallstern for purpose of scheduling and structuring the next day's negotiating structure. Roubideaux and the federal negotiators expressed satisfaction with the earlier session and optimism for the next. In exception, I informed them that the proposal would be rejected because it failed to give any account to the Sioux Treaty and Agreements and because it insisted upon treating the situation solely as a matter of criminal activity which must be ended by oppressive and coercive police action, although not by outright police attack. On request to propose an alternative, I drafted a suggested seven-point procedure for the dispossession of weaponry and process for dealing with substantive issues throughout the

Reservation. (We emphasized that we had no negotiation authority, but were suggesting that the 7-points might become their proposal.)

Inside Wounded Knee, members of the leadership councils and organizations had reviewed my letter to the President and extracted its several recommendations as the basis for a counter-proposal to the "best" offered by the Government. (Over the course of the weekend I had drafted several information sheets, position papers, public statements, and proposals, and typed them on stencils for mimeographing.) Although the seven-point proposal had not been drafted for Wounded Knee, members of the Oglala Sioux Council got a copy and discussed it while I was asleep, accepted it as "An Offer They Can't Refuse; A Proposal That Will Defuse," and typed it up as a Wounded Knee proposal. On March 19th, the combined "counter-proposal" was circulated to the news media and transmitted to Harlington Wood at Pine Ridge. The proposals were dismissed out-of-hand with virtually no reading or review. On that rejection, negotiations were terminated by Wounded Knee—with Russell Means characterizing the alternatives, as well as expressing the key, for a resolution in his statement: "We will deal with the President now as the Treaty prescribes, or we shall defend ourselves against his outlaw nation!"

I was requested to return to Washington, DC, to help secure a White House response and involvement with the March 19th positions and proposal. Two key provisions called for dispatch of a Sioux Indian to Wounded Knee as an "emissary" of the President (referencing treaty articles), and the appointment of a "special supervisor" to assume administration of the BIA Aberdeen Area Office and its agencies. (The demand for outright or planned removal of Richard Wilson as tribal chairman was dropped from the March 19th positions. Immediately on return, I prepared a complete statement of the final 10-point proposal from Wounded Knee. Second, I received legislative drafts of two proposed congressional Joint Resolutions which would provide for authorization and funding for (1) the presidential emissary and (2) a national commission on Indian Treaty Rights, which had been prepared for me by Georgetown University law professor William H. Rogers, Jr., which I modified slightly and duplicated for submittal to Members of Congress for consideration of sponsorship.

On Friday March 23rd, I met with Leonard Garment, Special Consultant to the President, at his offices for lunch and discussions of Wounded Knee, remaining in his offices for approximately five hours. After thorough consideration of my views, followed by extensive consultations by phone with other officials (discernibly with both Departments of Interior and Justice, as well as other persons in the White House), an arrangement was suggested whereby (being asked if I would or could return to Wounded Knee) all White House involvement would remain confidential and without public mention (for practical purposes of reaching a peaceful settlement without allowing internal disputes within the Departments to develop as an obstacle to it, and for minimizing other oppositions which might otherwise develop); I would abbreviate the 10-point proposal as a new position; it would be submitted after I returned to Wounded Knee; the Departments would accept it in principle and withdraw all their previous proposals; and the body of a final agreement and settlement would be reconstructed in negotiating sessions, having some general conformity to the March 19th proposal. Brad Patterson, assistant to Mr. Garment, made plane reservations to Rapid City for me; however, I informed them that I did not want financial assistance when asked if I needed money for the trip.

Essentially, this arrangement was to allow complete conformance with the existing demands and proposals from Wounded Knee, particularly with respect to the WK insistence that the 1868 Sioux Treaty and 1876 Agreements called for a presidential assignment of Sioux persons in matters requiring a restoration of "peace and order" on Sioux reservation. Mr. Garment emphasized that the situation was primarily the responsibility of the two departments and that the White House would make no unwarranted interventions in the matter, although it was at that moment willing to help construct the mechanics for negotiating a settlement. In Mr. Garment's outer office, I had reduced the March 19th proposal to a short nineteen lines (about one-tenth the original text) and typed it there. Mr. Garment pointedly stressed that he could make no promises respecting its development into a final agreement by negotiations with the Departments and the measures or provisions they would ultimately accept. There appeared some allowance, however, that in areas of disagreement between the Departments, or in relation to matters which would normally, legitimately and properly be submitted to White House for decisions or review, I could submit Wounded Knee viewpoints there also for consideration by the Departments. (At one point subsequently, Mr. Garment in telephone conversation to me in South Dakota remarked, "You have to realize we aren't just ventriloquists here; the Departments do have their responsibilities as well, and must make their own decisions accordingly.")

The White House had transmitted the text of the abbreviated proposal to Pine Ridge by the time I arrived there on the evening of March 24th, and where I was prepared to meet with tribal chairman Richard Wilson and Assistant to the Secretary of the Interior Marvin Franklin at that time, as well as Justice Department officials involved in negotiations, all for the purposes of discussing the parameters of a settlement and the possibilities of facilitating its being reached immediately. On objection from Mr. Wilson, Marvin Franklin disappeared and refused to meet with me, as did Mr. Wilson, who had been advised of the purposes of my coming by Hans Walker, Director of the Office of Indian Water Rights. Tribal officials and BIA agency and police personnel became extremely angered upon learning that I had walked past them to begin a meeting with Harlington Wood, Dick Hallstern and another

Assistant Attorney General of the United States Kent Frizell on an upper floor of the BIA Agency Building. (At this first moment of meeting Mr. Frizell, he asked me if I was the "emissary from the President; I told him I was not.) The meeting did not really get underway before Mr. Wood left the room for discussions with local BIA officials and officers. They returned into the office to explain that they had decided not to arrest me. BIA Superintendent Stanley Lyman introduced himself to me, then introduced Delmar Eastman, Chief of BIA Agency Police, who issued myself and my assistant Mike Hunt court orders of eviction. We were then transported beyond reservation and State lines, ten miles into Nebraska before the two of us were abandoned by the BIA Special Officers. (Later that evening, a telephone conversation with Leonard Garment indicated that he had been informed that I had met with Marvin Franklin and Richard Wilson before being forced into Nebraska. I had to advise him three times that this was not true, before he accepted the fact that he had been misinformed by his governmental sources.)

From Chadron, Nebraska, I maintained contact with Dick Hallstern, Leonard Garment, and by set-time schedulings, Wounded Knee. Russell Means had announced a "major announcement" for Monday morning (the 26th). Federal officials on the scene could still not secure entry into Wounded Knee for me. Leonard Garment asked, when I indicated that I was useless in Nebraska and should therefore return to DC, that I try to stick around a couple days to see if things might loosen up. On Sunday afternoon, Dick Hallstern and Kent Frizell came to Chadron to discuss the possible forms a settlement might take, understanding that I could not negotiate any agreements in behalf of Wounded Knee without being inside the village and in participation with Indian people there. (I became an early casualty in the meeting, when Hallstern popped open a catsup bottle and splashed big blotches of catchup on my leg, side and arm, as well as my coat and the wall four feet behind me. I told him, "Damn, it's no wonder they won't negotiate with you; you're dangerous. I hope you aren't commanding the police forces out there.") In the course of the meeting, I discussed the March 19th positions and the ten points as a probable basis for a settlement, which I would try to sell to the people once I returned into Wounded Knee. Frizell ended the session with the judgement that "They would never buy this back in Washington." Hallstern remained behind momentarily to remark, outside Frizell's hearing, that "I think they will; let's work on it."

There were calls to me on Sunday from Wounded Knee. I asked Russell Means, if he did have a "major announcement" to make, or was he expecting me to provide the basis for it from the results of my trip to Washington. He answered that he thought I would have it. I advised both he and Carter Camp about my White House meeting and arrangements, cautioning them that in no instance should there be public mention of the White House or involvement by its officials. I indicated that I would continue trying to get in, but that I would not stay around indefinitely if the Government did not take me in by their means.

No progress was made Monday respecting my WK entry. However, Dick Hallstern did complete a preliminary draft of a proposed settlement agreement, conforming in large part to the March 19th proposals from Wounded Knee, which he brought to me in Chadron in the early evening of the 26th. We reviewed them briefly together. I stressed the urgency of being able to develop a final agreement proposal with Wounded Knee people, rather than independently and with greater prospects of rejection, but indicated I would make any alterations or modifications I thought necessary in his draft and get it back to him as soon as possible—for possible transmittal into Wounded Knee. Additionally, rumors had begun to circulate about all "negotiations and decisions being taken over by the Oglala Sioux and its Civil Rights Group" and being thereafter conducted in Rapid City. I indicated to Hallstern that I believed this was incorrect, that I had as much authority as anyone outside Wounded Knee for negotiations, and that I could not negotiate outside there. Additionally, I showed him a list of more than twenty new demands, which I had just received, which purportedly were to be the basis for negotiations in Rapid City. He agreed that there were very few items on that list which could be accepted, if ever effected by the US Government. After he left, I began making slight language modifications and adding a few minor provisions, or deleting some, on his proposal draft with the assistance of four other Indians who had just come out of Wounded Knee. Later that evening, Dick Hallstern called to inform me about the shooting of a US Marshal, who had been transported to a hospital in Denver in critical condition. I asked why they continued to delay in getting me inside; couldn't they take me in by helicopter? Hallstern responded, "We'll get you in there right away somehow, even if I have to do cartwheels all the way back to Washington to do it!"

On Tuesday the 27th, a dramatic shift in governmental attitudes occurred. Interest in my participation subsided almost completely with the news that Russell Means and Dennis Banks had left, or been thrown out of, Wounded Knee. The federal negotiation hopes were transferred to Rapid City, where Aaron DeSersa had declared that he and others would negotiate an end to the Wounded Knee occupation—and that had been the "major announcement" that Russell Means had been referring to. On both Monday and Tuesday, I had declined requests to travel, or to be picked up to go, to Rapid City by Ramon Roubideaux and his representatives, in order that I would be available to enter Wounded Knee at the first opportunity. On Tuesday, I advised the White House and Justice Department negotiators (Kent Frizell by then had replaced Harlington Wood as the senior Justice representative on the scene) as well as Senator Abourezk's office that I believed that the Rapid City sessions were not authorized and would be repudiated by Wounded Knee—and would primarily be a waste of crucial time. Senator

Abourezk and Interior's Marvin Franklin both flew to South Dakota for the sessions, preceded by their public statements expressing optimism that a settlement was, if not imminent, near. (Senator Abourezk had other business there, however, relating to flood relief activities and efficiency or adequacy.) Since WK entry seemed wholly unlikely at that point, I proceeded to Rapid City for the meetings scheduled there on Wednesday. (Traveling there with three other Indians and two horses was another experience in itself. A half dozen cowboys or white red necks pulled pistols on us at a truck stop, until we were taken into custody by the local sheriff and state patrolmen; in several ensuing incidents and stops, two of the others received citations, obligating us each time to return to the jail to post bonds (total $135.00 cash); the sheriff then tailgated us for twenty miles toward Rapid City, stopping us intermittently to make checks on our travel plans and time schedule, our trailer license, our horses' brands, our brand registration, and our brand clearance for inter-state travel.)

The Wednesday meeting at the Mother Butler Center in Rapid City was well-attended—but nonetheless a fiasco. The federal representatives were immediately informed that the meeting had not been sanctioned by Wounded Knee and that no negotiations could be held, although discussions could be relating to general problems on the Pine Ridge Indian Reservation. The news media was invited in briefly to view, along with Administration officials and Senator Abourezk, a videotaped statement of Dennis Banks and Pedro Bissonette denouncing the Rapid City meetings. Picturing Russell Means and other central leaders inside Wounded Knee, the videotaped segment related the fact that both Dennis and Russell had left to go to Rosebud, but had already returned to the occupied village. Their declaration was clear that no negotiations could take place outside of Wounded Knee.

Senator Abourezk, Marvin Franklin and Kent Frizell held several private meetings to discuss the situation. Finally, I and Sid Mills broke into one of their meetings to make some suggestions, being joined shortly thereafter by Ted Means, Ramon Roubideaux, and a couple score of different Oglala Sioux coming in and out to meet with officials. Almost immediately, Ramon Roubideaux received a note from Dennis Banks in Wounded Knee, instructing Ramon to leave the meeting. Ted and Sid offered various specific advices on what the government could do to bring about a settlement—finally mentioning that the papers I had could provide the form for an agreement—if negotiated with the right Oglala Sioux Indian inside Wounded Knee (including some who had not been part of the occupation, but remained outside). I offered the revised draft that we had worked on the two previous nights, and requested that a copy be transmitted inside Wounded Knee as well as being returned to Kent Hallstern. Kent Frizell, showing extreme anger, rejected the document, saying that "the Government can't accept this!" I asked, "Why not? The Government drafted it! We've only made the slightest changes from

Hallstern's draft." Frizell exploded, "Dick Hallstern does not speak for the United States Government. He's only my assistant!" "Well, who does speak for the government," we asked. "I do!" Frizell exclaimed.

As soon as I returned to my apartment, I called, first, Dick Hallstern and then Leonard Garment. I advised them of the non-results of the meeting, the effect of the videotaped instructions carried from Wounded Knee, and of the final exchange between ourselves and Kent Frizell. I stressed that I had not come to South Dakota to waste either my time or anyone else's—and that if my working with Dick Hallstern had just been someone's idea of a game, I was going to attempt to catch the first plane scheduled back to Washington, DC. I was advised that there would be an attempt to straighten this matter out, and asked to stay around for at least a little while longer to see if something new might develop.

Later that evening, Leonard Garment called to say that he had talked with Kent Frizell; that he thought things might go a little better now; and that Frizell was going to attempt to transport me inside Wounded Knee—with the permission of the tribal chairman if possible, but otherwise if not.

About fifteen minutes afterwards, Kent Frizell called. He apologized for his anger earlier that day, the stormy session, and his statements. He expressed hope that we might be able to work together and manage to get me into Wounded Knee to have negotiations begin again.

On Thursday, Frizell and Hallstern indicated that the tribal chairman had consented to Ramon Roubideaux and my entry into Wounded Knee. Ramon had other court business so did not go; but on Friday the 30th, Wayne Colburn, Chief of US Marshals, transported me in his car from the command post in Pine Ridge past the vigilante and federal roadblocks to Wounded Knee. Mark Lane, Beverly Axelrod, and Fran Olson, non-Indian attorneys followed us in route—with considerable difficulty, searches and delay. (Federal agents carefully refrained from using my name on radioed transmissions.) I explained the content and nature of my talks at the White House and discussed subsequent events. In particular, I stressed my belief that the Government was willing to drop its previous proposals and ultimatums, and proceed with a different attitude in negotiations, with greater willingness to face up to and dealings with the issues precipitating and represented by the Wounded Knee occupation. I made available the papers we had worked on and indicated that they could probably be accepted by the government as a working proposal that could be transformed into an agreement—unless Wounded Knee felt that their basic content and development had become too remote from the Indian people there and too independent of their involvement in construction. In that case, I informed them that the government would still be willing to drop all its previous positions, and negotiations could start from scratch in the scheduled negotiations the next day. The latter course, seemed everyone's preference. I did mention that there should be no discussion or public mention (the news media had been barred from the village after the Monday night firefight) of White House involvement, but that I did retain direct telephone access to Leonard Garment and would be able to carry certain arguments to him, if first argued with the departmental negotiators and unreasonable rejected by them.

Before returning to Rapid City, I talked to various members of the Oglala Sioux Council and the central AIM leadership regarding my views on the advisability of an early settlement and what might be gained from it.

On Saturday March 31st, permission had been withdrawn for my entry upon the Pine Ridge Reservation. Federal authorities consequently arranged for Ramon Roubideaux and myself to make surreptitious entry into Wounded Knee by means of chartered helicopter. We flew to Roadblock #1, manned by FBI agents, having begun our flight five miles out on a deserted, almost impassable dried-mud road in Nebraska. On our arrival at the roadblock, we were immediately confronted by an outraged Kent Frizell. Angered because the negotiations were to begin immediately at a teepee in the DMZ (Demilitarized Zone)—and the teepee had not even then been put up—Frizell declared that Ramon and I could go down into Wounded Knee and inform the people there that he would be ready to negotiate the following day, whenever they were ready—without alternative of leaving! Frizell momentarily restored his calm and restrained his temper, then advised us that they were going back to their offices, but would be available for negotiations as soon as the teepee could be put up and a half hour notice be given that the Wounded Knee Indians were ready to meet.

A brief discussion with Dick Hallstern demonstrated the efficiency and frequent accuracy of federal informants inside Wounded Knee. He advised me that they understood that a pre-condition or unnegotiable demand was going to be offered at the outset of negotiations relating to federal action to secure court approval of free passage of food, medical services and attorneys, before any other matter could be approached or discusses. Apart from this information, an agenda which had been generally agreed upon was set for the meeting. He advised me that, if the information was true, it would be an insurmountable obstacle to any movement by the government in accommodating the people of Wounded Knee in reaching agreements on the larger permanent problems and issues involved and potentially soluble.

At our preliminary meeting in Wounded Knee, I discovered that Hallstern's information had been precisely correct. A lawyer who had been staying in the village had drafted a statement of first demand insisting that the government petition the federal district court for relief that it had previously denied to Wounded Knee. A principal AIM leader instructed us that this demand should become the first order of business—and that no other matter should be discussed until the Government accepted it. If it were rejected, then we were instructed that negotiations were to be terminated. I objected and argued against the position with the AIM leader and the legal advisor. Nonetheless, the instruction remained. (In the subsequent negotiating session, Carter Camp and Russell Means immediately disregarded the prepared statement, the position and the instruction, thereby eliminating the impasses that otherwise might have developed.)

The March 31st negotiations got underway approximately four hours late. A general discussion of issues problems, complaints and grievances ensued, with Oglala Sioux persons dominating the session and matters raised. In an eloquent statement of the simple concerns and purposes of Wounded Knee, Russell Means served a number of issues from further need of negotiations and dismissed several previously-stated positions. Finally, the Government invited Wounded Knee to prepare a list of all positions and provisions that it wanted the government to accept or act upon. Another negotiating session was set for April 1st.

I stayed overnight in Wounded Knee to draft the April 1st proposals. I was given instructions by members of the AIM leadership and the Oglala Sioux Council to rely upon the March 31st discussions for the content of the proposals—and to "write them so the Government can accept them." From memory I wrote down many of the points raised that day, then took additional notes from tape recordings of the major speeches given in the teepee. That night, there was an electrical power failure in the village and other reservation towns, which prevented my completion of the document that night. The next morning, I took the liberty of delaying the negotiating session from 10 a.m. to 1:30 by radio message to the federal command post. A copy of the proposal was forwarded to the federal representatives in Pine Ridge with the notation that most people in Wounded Knee had not yet had chance to review it. At 12:30 a "mass meeting" was held in the Trading Post, where the two-page ten-point proposal, plus half-page preface, was read to everyone and subsequently accepted. In an interesting, perhaps promising, substitution of terms, where I had written the words, "agreeable settlement," or "settlement," Russell Means substituted the term, "disarmament," in presenting it to all the people and in tape recordings to be supplied to news media outside of Wounded Knee.

In the April 1st negotiation session, the government first objected to a provision which appeared to maintain an open agenda for every meeting in presenting new issues or demands. (The provision had been included at insistence of several attorneys, and with strong urging from Community Relations Services (CRS) personnel.) Wounded Knee agreed to drop it and deal only with remaining items. Several other items were consolidated, dropped from further consideration, or adopted as statements of mutual understanding. A final six points were left, with the Government accepting four of them—relating to investigations and endorsements of existing laws, plus an unformulated procedure for the "dispossession of arms" and "surrenders to arrest"—and advising that approval of the other two—relating to a presidential treaty commission, and to positive federal actions directed toward administrative and judicial application of the 1968 Indian Bill of Rights on the Pine Ridge Reservation—would have to await consultations with Washington DC officials.

In leaving with Mike Hunt by helicopter that day, I advised Kent Frizell and Dick Hallstern that I believed that Wounded Knee was seriously and sincerely seeking a settlement—but that the minimal requirements relating to White House-level meetings on a treaty commission was the one item above all others which must be met. I also informed them of my instruction to write the proposal "so the Government can accept." After stopping in Pine Ridge to discuss several details, Ramon Roubideaux picked I and Mike up in Nebraska for return to Rapid City.

By the time I was able to contact the White House to urge their acceptance of the final points, I was advised that the two points remaining after that day's negotiations had been accepted. Regarding the White House level meetings, I was informed that the Government had decided that it might be better to name a specific time frame for scheduling meetings—the third week in May. The basic language of an agreement provision for the meetings was read to me from Washington, DC. Subsequent conversations by phone with Kent Frizell and Dick Hallstern reconfirmed the decision, as well as providing me the information that the "Indian Bill of Rights" provision had been accepted and revised with language indicating a stronger federal commitment than we had previously proposed. Indicating that I would not be attending subsequent negotiating sessions for reasons relating to their movement toward a final conclusion, I gave permission for the federal representatives to state that I had reviewed the proposed Government language for the provisions and found nothing objectionable in them, if such a statement would be useful in the next sessions.

From the press briefings held in Pine Ridge by Kent Frizell and Ramon Roubideaux, news began appearing in the press and broadcast media that a settlement was near. The prospects of a settlement were plainly disturbing and upsetting to several of the white attorneys related to Wounded Knee and working out of Rapid City, Mark Lane being the person most adverse to peaceful settlement along the lines already proposed by Wounded Knee. On late April 1st and early April 2nd, I spent about three hours arguing with about ten members of the "Wounded Knee Legal Offense/Defense Committee" in support of an early settlement and against any efforts on their part of advising against the proposed settlement and an early end to the armed confrontation. There was a noticeable shift in favor of my position, which at one point led Mark Lane to "threaten" to sever himself from the Committee ("collective"), until Beverly Axelrod chided him, "That's it; take your marbles and go home. "He quickly reinstated himself. The next morning, the three lawyers who had been most hostile to my position and philosophies—and to the proposed settlement—left early in the morning to go to wounded Knee, arriving there some four hours before the scheduled negotiations and several hours before Ramon Roubideaux could travel there. (In the negotiations that day, there were several heated exchanges between Mark Lane and Kent Frizell. Lane made several arguments against the proposed agreement and the Government's motives. At one point, Frizell was moved to call Lane "a damned liar" without apparent objection from any quarter.)

In the same period, Marlon Brando called me from his Los Angeles home to propose an early meeting to discuss his support for Indian causes. He stated that he did not want to travel to South Dakota, because his presence might attract too much attention and divert public attention away from Wounded Knee. He suggested meeting in Salt Lake City or Las Vegas, but I indicated that Denver would be more suitable in case I had to become involved again in negotiations. On the afternoon of April 2nd, Brando left a message setting up a meeting at a Denver Hotel on the evening of April 3rd.

On the evening of April 2nd, I learned that there was to be another "counter-proposal" from Wounded Knee relating to the proposed treaty commission and meetings with the White House. The legal committee at that time became embroiled in the drafting of provisions in the near-final agreement relating to procedures for the dispossession of arms and the processing of arrests. I briefly argued against any overly-complicated formulations or schemes which would become a bar to a final agreement, telling the lawyer's groups that "one of the reasons Wounded Knee has happened is that Indian people want to get away from all this bullshit; once the people are ready to come out of Wounded Knee, they will want the processes to be simple and quick as possible..." Ramon Roubideaux expressed optimism that a final agreement might be reached the next day, but did indicate some possibilities of problems and requested that I return with him to Wounded Knee the following day to help deal with any complications which might arise. He also noted some discernible hardening of Wounded Knee positions as probable result of some of the most recent non-Indian attorney advices to Indians in Wounded Knee.

Ramon, myself and Sid Mills got a very late start from Rapid City the following day. My plane scheduled to Denver was for around 5 p.m., to meet with Brando upon arrival there. We planned to leave Wounded Knee by 2:30, but did not arrive there until shortly after 1:30, again by helicopter directly into the village for continuing negotiations in a small church. We took in some cigarettes and about ten pounds of candy bars. At the start of the session, Wounded Knee presented its counter-proposal relating to the Treaty Commission, but called for an immediate White House level meeting either at the White House or in Wounded Knee, preceding any dispossession of arms and disarmament. The counter-proposal had been drafted by an attorney who had first proposed such an "immediate White House meeting as a first demonstration of good faith on the part of the federal government" in the course of the April 1 meeting. At the earlier time, Wounded Knee had been willing to accept the general commitment for a series of scheduled meetings; however, the lawyer had lobbied for the "tangible first step" in the face of other lobbying for rejection of the general package which had been developed.

The federal response to the counter-proposal was immediately unfavorable. We asked for a statement detailing what their objections were. Both sides asked for a brief recess to discuss the matter. I advised Wounded Knee that I believed the Government could accept some slightly-modified formulation of the same proposal, or that proposal with some explicit understandings relating to the dispossession of arms and its timing. Additionally, I related the substance of certain conversations I'd had with Justice and White House officials regarding possible endings to the confrontation—including prospects of covert or 'informally-arranged' abandonment of Wounded Knee in the dead of night, in event of any continuing failure to reach a negotiated settlement.

Kent Frizell declared that he could not personally accept any implementation of a final agreement prior to a dispossession of arms, or without the disarmament being a first item for implementation in an agreement—and that he did not believe that the White House could accept any meetings with Indians from Wounded Knee while the village remained an armed camp. We responded that an implementation of disarmament would begin through preparations by the respective security and police forces immediately, with the signing of an agreement. We argued that it would take a couple of days' time to plan an evacuation and displacement in Wounded Knee, including an inventorying of weaponry or whatever.

We argued that the procedure proposed was precisely the same as a previous proposal of the Government—with actual and final disarmament being scheduled to coincide or commence with the receipt of a telephone call by Wounded Knee immediately preceding the initiation of a proposed meeting outside and away from the village. We sought to meet every objection expressed by Frizell, and specifically attempted to show how each objection was met or dispelled by the proposed procedure. After consultations with Dick Hallstern, Frizell noted the effectiveness of "divide and conquer" tactics, pointing out that Hallstern was in disagreement with himself and favored seeking approval or acceptance of the basic counter-proposal. He expressed explicit doubt, however, that the White House would go along with anything like it. Attempting deliberately not to invoke any White House discussions openly, I pointed out that Alvin Josephy had just spent and afternoon at the White House, and that I had reason to believe that their attitudes had undergone substantial enlightenment or transformation in the preceding month and might well be more responsive to the proposal than Frizell was suggesting. I urged that, since there was divided opinion among Frizell and Hallstern on the proposition, in fairness to the proposal that both of them should discuss the matter with the White House in seeking the final decision. Misconstruing use of the term, "both sides," to characterize their divided opinion, Frizell instead agreed that both he and I should call the White House to argue the merits of the proposal. I clarified the point. (That was to be the only open suggestion relating to our direct contact with the White House and Leonard Garment in working toward a settlement.)

Needing to get back to Rapid City, I suggested the federal negotiators fly us back to Pine Ridge, consult with the White House, and if a proposal might be approved, that they might return to Wounded Knee that afternoon for finalizing and signing an agreement. Instead, it was determined that there remained certain technical matters relating to other portions of the proposed agreement. Consequently, it was decided that US Marshals would transport me beyond Pine Ridge and then the Community Relations Service (CRS) would attempt to get me to the airport in time to catch my flight to Denver. Sid Mills remained to accompany Ramon Roubideaux back to Rapid City (as well as to hold a brief meeting with Wounded Knee leadership, ostensibly in support of the proposed settlement). Traveling at excessive speeds to overcome a real late start, we approached the airport with some small possibility of catching my plane. Five minutes from the airport, however, the CRS vehicle ran out of gas. Brando called me later that evening from Denver to learn why I hadn't arrived. We planned to meet the next morning, but surprisingly persons working all night at my motel unit took my wake-up call and failed to wake me up to catch the Denver flight. Brando had stayed overnight at the Airport Holiday Inn under my own name. When I did arrive there 24 hours late, he had already caught a flight back to Los Angeles. From Denver, however, I maintained telephone contact with Frizell and Hallstern, Roubideaux, and Garment regarding the final terms of an Agreement at Wounded Knee.

The White House was willing to undertake an immediate meeting, although reluctant to meet with leading members of the American Indian Movement (AIM). Wounded Knee had designated Russell Means, Tom Bad Cob, Leonard Crow Dog, Ramon Roubideaux, accompanied by myself, as their representatives to a White House meeting (all five of us being Sioux Indians). The Government countered with an offer to meet in Rapid City, or possibly on the Rosebud Reservation; at first ruling out a meeting in Washington, DC, or at the White House itself, if it were to be absolutely necessary to have Russell Means in participation. Wounded Knee rejected those sites, and suggested a meeting at Syracuse, New York, hosted by the Six Nations' chiefs (Iroquois Confederacy).

I urged Justice Department to accept the Syracuse site, pointing out that the Six Nations' chiefs could exert positive influence and discipline for maintaining conformance to an agreement and its appropriate and immediate implementation. Without citing reason to Leonard Garment, I recommended the New York meeting site to him. He indicated that such a site would seem to be carrying the matter too far afield; and in our next conversation, he informed me that Washington, DC, had been accepted as a site, but under the neutral auspices or on the neutral grounds of the National Center for Dispute Settlement.

On the afternoon of April 5th, a six-point Agreement drawn from the April 1 proposal was finalized and signed at a sacred pipe ceremony in Wounded Knee. Russell Means and Leonard Crow Dog were transported by helicopter directly to Rapid City for a bond hearing, having submitted to arrest after the ceremony. The Justice Department also flew a federal magistrate from Sioux Falls to preside over the bond hearing in place of the Rapid City magistrate (Wilson) who had been demonstrably unfavorable in previous hearings. US District Judge Andrew Bogue, however, overruled the arrangements made by Justice and directed that Magistrate Wilson should conduct any and all hearing relating to Wounded Knee, unless presided over by Judge Bogue himself. A $25,000 full cash or collateral security bond was required after several hours of delay for Russell Means' hearing. (If there occurred any federal violation of the April 5 Agreement, it was at that point in time, not subsequently in Washington, DC; and by judicial actions beyond the direct control of Department of Justice and the White House. However, numerous external influences began to assert themselves on the thinking of Russell Means once he was out of Wounded Knee and exposed to them. Notably, members of the Wounded Knee Legal Offense/Defense Committee began to inform persons calling for information on the final form of the Agreement that "we have thrown in some language that can still be subject to additional interpretation and dispute.")

On the morning of April 6th, I met with Russell Means, Ramon Roubideaux, Leonard Crow Dog, and Tom Bad Cob at the Denver Airport. I had planned to fly to Los Angeles to meet with Brando to secure his help in raising bail funds, but checking with his secretary I learned he was out camping with his jeep and probably would not be back before the weekend which was fully scheduled for him. Therefore, I tried to catch Means' same plane to Washington, DC, but missed it. I caught the next plane.

Almost immediately after arriving in Washington, DC, I learned of Russell Means' statements to news media indicating a revised sequence for the telephone call to Wounded Knee, to signal the beginning of a "dispossession of arms"—conditioning such a call upon the completion of a "satisfactory" White House meeting, rather than at its beginning.

Dick Hallstern had traveled to Washington, DC, to coordinate the White House meeting with Leonard Garment, while Kent Frizell had remained at Pine Ridge to oversee the disarmament and evacuation of Wounded Knee. Hallstern, Frizell, and Garment, in separate conversations, expressed their determinations to stand by the April 5th Agreement and to meet its terms—but also not to be manipulated into a situation of new terms, wherein the

Agreement might be repudiated by Russell Means after a White House meeting with him and the other Sioux representatives. Through both Hallstern and myself, Garment offered to meet privately and informally, without public notice, with Russell Means to discuss the substance and probable results of the scheduled meeting in order that it could proceed—and in order that Russell could comfortably make the telephone call prior to its commencement as previously agreed to. Russell rejected the offers for a private, non-public preliminary meeting.

There seemed a general eagerness on the part of the press and others to blame the government for breaching the agreement, irrespective of the truth of the matter. In fact, the government was willing to bend in most areas—except for refusing to hold the White House–level meeting and hazarding the chance that Russell Means might never make the call to signal disarmament at its conclusion. At Pine Ridge, telephone communications were again opened up for Wounded Knee for outgoing and incoming calls, and for Russell to coordinate with others there the plans for procedures of disarmament and evacuation. Both Kent Frizell and Dick Hallstern were willing to accept the "truthfulness" of statements made to them by the respective Wounded Knee representatives, or to take the statements at "face value." Trying to maintain checks upon the pulse of all areas of activity and to keep all lines of communication open, I found myself knowing more than I want to know and began to question my own usefulness in the given situation.

At Wounded Knee, Kent Frizell seemed confident that he was reaching a final agreement on procedures for the scheduled disarmament. He advised the news media that about ninety percent of the final agreement had been nailed down, and that progress was being made on the remainder. Privately, he pointed out that the people in Wounded Knee had declared that they would not permit anyone then outside of Wounded Knee to prevent a settlement and final disarmament. Yet, I was aware that Mark Lane had been given assignment of helping to put together a disarmament "package that is about ninety percent complete," but which would leave "about ten percent open to further discussion"—and controlled delay.

In Washington, DC, US Representative Lloyd Meeds called me at home to privately discuss the advisability of, and my recommendations regarding, retaining Russell Means on the witness list for hearing of the House Indian Affairs Subcommittee on the Trail of Broken Treaties and Wounded Knee, in view of the breakdown of the April 5th agreement. I assured Congressman Meeds of my belief that Russell would not use the hearing as a forum for lodging new demands as condition for ending Wounded Knee confrontations, and recommended that they proceed as scheduled. Also, I advised him that I thought ultimately it might require a public isolation of those persons opposing a settlement at Wounded Knee to bring it to a conclusion, and toward those ends it was important that governmental units maintain all their commitments—indicating to him my own judgement that the Administration to that point had done this. (Russell had begun by that time to advise other Indian people that I was not in agreement with what was happening in relation to the continuation of the Wounded Knee confrontation. After listening to a portion of my own congressional testimony, he became somewhat angry at myself—but agreed with most points of rationale in discussion of matters of objection. On his final evening in Washington, DC, however, he did make a strong verbal attack against myself, although much stronger against others.)

Toward the end of their stay here, both Russell and Ramon Roubideaux began blaming Dick Hallstern for the breakdown of the April 5th Agreement. In a surprising press conference statement, Russell declared that they would have no more consecrations with Hallstern or other functionaries, but that I was being assigned to open direct talked with Leonard Garment at the White House to arrange a meeting as provided in the April 5th Agreement as interpreted by the Wounded Knee representatives.

Since Russell was fully aware that I had continuous direct contact with Garment relating to Wounded Knee, I was uncertain how best to react to Russell's statement. Finally I determined that, rather than take advantage of the arrangement which had been operative and instrumental in brining both sides to the threshold of a meaningful settlement, I should terminate further direct communications with Leonard Garment. Consequently, I advised the White House that Russell's statement created a new situation which precluded continuation of our previous arrangement and lines of communication. Therefore, I agreed that future discussions should be channeled through Garment's assistant, Brad Patterson, if there should be any. I indicated my feeling that my usefulness had greatly diminished, but advised that I would be available to both the Government and Wounded Knee, if either one or both sides might think I could be helpful in any way. (At time of my first meeting with Garment on March 23rd, I had insisted on direct lines of communication to him, rather than Mr. Patterson, noting some difficulties in communicating with any efficiency past Brad. This had been accepted, perhaps with greater efficiency than Leonard Garment had actually wanted. The White House switchboard faultlessly traced Garment down for me on call, frequently at home and once at the Kennedy Center. At one point, Garment remarked (or complained), "That switchboard is getting so they're putting you through without even announcing you or even saying who's calling.")

The May 5th Agreement

The failure to secure an end to the armed confrontation through the April 5th Agreement did not lead to its abandonment by the government. Kent Frizell declared the federal intention to stick by the agreement "until hell freezes over." Frizell returned to Washington, DC, in the second week of April for his confirmation hearings on his appointment to become Solicitor for the Department of the Interior. He was replaced in the field by Assistant Attorney General Stan Pottinger. Dick Hallstern returned to Pine Ridge when the White House–level meeting failed to occur.

I did maintain periodic contact with the federal negotiators at Pine Ridge and with the lawyers' offices and communication center for Wounded Knee in Rapid City. From Rapid City, I was requested to try to secure a replacement for Dick Hallstern as the ranking federal representative in negotiations after Pottinger returned to Washington. "Anyone but Hallstern," was the demand. Kent Frizell moved into his new Interior office and in conversations asked me if I thought he could do any good by returning to Pine Ridge and Wounded Knee. I told him that I thought it didn't matter who was out there, unless Wounded Knee wanted to end the confrontation, but also advised him of the general Rapid City and Wounded Knee sentiment of "anyone but Hallstern." (From the time of the first teepee meetings, Kent Frizell seemed to begin enjoying the negotiating processes and the less dangerous aspects of the entire situation. I had previously described his demeanor to other Indians, and federal officials as that of a Nineteenth Century cavalry officer involved in treaty negotiations with the Indians as Robert Stack would play the role in a Twentieth Century movie script—while making others of us feel like we were all part of an unfilmed re-make of "The Rogue River Massacre" in the peace-making stages.)

Meanwhile, Brad Patterson continued to express interest in the meeting with the traditional headmen and chiefs of the Teton Sioux. He plainly remained committed to the third week of May schedule, provided that the confrontation at Wounded Knee had reached a conclusion at that time. Dick Hallstern advised me that he had recommended that the entire Pine Ridge Indian Reservation and the tribal government "be taken into trusteeship" (or receivership) by the Secretary of the Interior, and asked my opinion on the results. I encouraged him in the recommendation and expressed belief that it would contribute to an early settlement. Brad Patterson confirmed that the idea had reached the White House level, but that such an action would have to rely upon the acceptance and approval of the Department of the Interior. He expressed serious doubts that the Interior Secretary would take such an action, anticipating strong objections and reactions of fear among other tribal governments and officials throughout the country.

Federal representatives had repeatedly disclaimed intentions of making a police assault against Wounded Knee since mid-March, barring situations in which the suffering of casualties or fatalities among the police forces might compel an attempt to end the confrontation by force. After breakdown of the April 5th Agreement, that general policy was maintained. However, one federal official expressed the view that decisive action would have to be taken before the general period related to the end of school terms—absent a settlement. There was a pervasive fear that college and high school students might flock to Wounded Knee after school was out and create a more unmanageable and more explosive situation. Despite numerous rumors to the contrary, I felt that the government would not plan any police assault on Wounded Knee prior to the passing of the third week in May.

Dick Hallstern related to me some of the difficulties federal investigators were experiencing in following up on criminal complaints of violence to persons and of civil rights violations. The victims of several incidents, such as rape, which had been cited during the negotiating sessions, were denying that the incidents occurred or were refusing to discuss the matters with investigators. Nonetheless, in most areas of commitment under the April 5th Agreement, the government was attempting to conform to the requirements placed upon it. One official indicated that, were it to become necessary to end the confrontation by police assault, the Government wanted to have built a clear record of conformance with the Agreement, as well as having demonstrated its willingness to reach or carry out every reasonable accommodation with Wounded Knee.

Kent Frizell returned to Pine Ridge after only being in his Interior office one day. Although the *New York Times* had erroneously pictured him as the key person in negotiation the April 5th Agreement (Hallstern had been the person most instrumental in securing federal approval for the form and substance of the agreement—and in overriding Frizell's personal objections or doubts) in one of its "Man in the News" features, Frizell definitely was the person chiefly responsible for securing the May 8th evaluation of Wounded Knee. Frizell had initially attempted to maintain "friendly and correct" relations with tribal chairman Richard Wilson, but was not constrained from arguing with him, demanding acceptance of certain governmental actions, or unleashing his temper against him. After Kent Frizell was subjected to tribal arrest (twice), and saved from being shot in the head at near-point-blank by an heroic maneuver on the part of US Chief Marshal Colburn (on the other hand, perhaps foolish had they both been shot; fortunately neither were), his relationship with the tribal chairman became less crucial to the decisions being made and less affecting upon his relationship with other Indian groups, both those in Wounded Knee and the traditional headmen and chiefs. While Hallstern appeared to become more determined to limit Wounded Knee's options to the simple choice of staying in Wounded Knee or meeting solely for the purpose of prescribing the methods of coming out, Frizell showed a greater willingness to allow them some latitude for negotiating the method of coming out.

(The Legal Committee in Rapid City later informed me that the Government, prior to Frizell's latter return, had been suspicious of even proposed sacred ceremonies for effecting disarmament. Personally, I would feel that there could be ceremonies that should be cause for fear, if not suspicion, on the part of the government—in context of making war or peace. Anyone believing in the powers at hand knows he should be certain how that power shall stand or how it should direct the people. After learning of the lawyers' disappointment that some particular ceremony did not assume control over the situation, I began to suspect that the Government's suspicions were probably not wholly without justification.)

The final groundwork for the May 8th evacuation of Wounded Knee began being set in place when Kent Frizell allowed access to Wounded Knee of the respected headmen and chiefs, led by Frank Fools Crow. Ironically, Frizell and the chiefs and principal leaders in Wounded Knee were earnestly approaching an agreement at the same time that rumors were being spread by a busy telephone network around the country that the federal police forces, assisted by a number of designated military unites, were prepared to make an assault against the village on May 4th, 5th or 6th. The rumors were given greater credence by the refusal of Dick Hallstern to make an outright denial that federal assault was imminent. In his least-frank conversation with myself, Hallstern would not convey any denial to myself either, but rather engaged in the language that he had used with the press: "We have always regarded a direct police action as a viable option which we had to consider and which we might well have to use." He was, however, amused by the number and names of the different military and guard units which were then allegedly being mobilized, maneuvering, or headed toward, (on) the Pine Ridge Indian Reservation. "I am prepared to state categorically and unequivocally," he quipped, "that John Wayne is nowhere upon this Reservation, and we have no intention of calling him in…at this time."

Around 11:30 p.m., Kent Frizell called me from Pine Ridge. He stated that he thought they had pretty much wrapped up an agreement, advising me that he had just left their talks at Wounded Knee. Briefly he outlined the proposed settlement: He was requesting a letter from Leonard Garment of the White House addressed to the Teton Sioux headmen and chiefs, verifying that a meeting of at least five presidential representatives would take place with them during the third week of May; the funeral of Lawrence (Buddy) LaMont would be held in Wounded Knee on Friday or Saturday, and the village would be opened up for Indian people to attend the funeral; the dispossession of arms would take place prior to the scheduled funeral, but there would be no federal entry into or searches of Wounded Knee for a period of seventy-two hours, although at the expiration of that time period there would occur a bilaterally-supervised "disarmament" and "pull-back" by both sides. He stated that the reason he was calling me was that Leonard Crow Dog and others in Wounded Knee had asked that I be brought back into Wounded Knee, and that I receive the letter from the White House and deliver it to the headmen and chiefs in Wounded Knee. He expressed his hope that the outline would materialize into a final resolution. He asked if I would return to South Dakota as a courier with the White House letter and to be available for any counseling to other Sioux people which might be required or requested.

Kent Frizell further indicated that time was a crucial factor in finalizing an agreement and procedure for ending the armed confrontation. He informed me that all points had not yet then been cleared with the White House and that it would still be necessary to draft a letter that would be acceptable to Leonard Garment and other officials. Frizell asked if I could be ready to catch a plane to South Dakota as soon as a letter would be ready. (He did suggest that they would reimburse me for travel, inasmuch as the time requirements would pretty much obligate a personal delivery in any instance, and my expenses should be picked up as well as anyone else's would be. I did not, nor have I, requested governmental reimbursement.) Finally, he advised me that he would be back in touch with me, and that I should maintain contact with Brad Patterson's office for purposes of receiving the letter.

Shortly after talking with Frizell, Mary Bergren called to inform me that he had called Senator Abourezk and had assured the Senator that there were no plans whatever for a police assault on the village and that all rumors to the contrary should be discounted and ignored. On a confidential basis, but not totally restricted, I advised her of the substance of my just-concluded conversation with Kent Frizell. She seemed pleased by the news and expressed a view that the Indian Affairs Subcommittee should be advised privately of the new developments and their potential promise of an end to the confrontation. I did not interpose any objections, but did suggest that perverse sidelights to the entire Wounded Knee experience, I was called within an hour after completing my talk with Kent Frizell by Mr. Gerald R. Gereau, Professional Staff Member of the Senate Interior and Insular Affairs Committee, who, purporting to have talked immediate previously with Senator Abourezk about my planned trip, made certain offers of assistance relating to the alleviation of tribal oppositions to my travel. Attempting to learn precisely what Frizell might have told the Senator, I questioned Mr. Gereau about his sources of information—only to learn that he had not talked with Senator Abourezk at all. Mr. Gereau at that time gave me his unlisted home phone number; then later lied to an inquiry of Senator Henry M. Jackson (or Jerry T. Verkler, Staff Director) to claim that he had not talked with me at all until the afternoon of May 4th, a day-and-a-half after his post-midnight call to me. On my way to South Dakota, I wrote a letter to Senator Jackson protesting Mr. Gereau's attitudes and actions of opposition and of interference with my invited or requested "mission." The Senator had the opportunity to answer after the Wounded Knee confrontation has ended. Nonetheless, I understand that Mr. Gereau wrote a lengthy denial of my allegations, a denial of his own statements to and conversations with myself, indicating that most of the content of my own letter was "absolutely false," and that his own concerns had been those of preventing myself from speaking in the name of the Senate

Committee in my efforts to overthrow the Oglala Sioux tribal government, or words to that effect. It was a thoroughly weird episode!)

The following day, I checked several times with Brad Patterson and Kent Frizell regarding the proposed letter and my availability to make delivery. Surprisingly, the drafting of the letter was only nearing completion at the end of May 3rd—and Leonard Garment had not yet been fully advised in its premises or been available long enough to give approval to content. By Friday morning, it appeared that Kent Frizell felt he had better command of the situation at Wounded Knee and greater confidence than he had expressed Tuesday night. It became obvious that I personally had become less essential to the outcome, with Frizell advising me that the final decision on whether I should deliver the letter or someone else should be utilized would be made by Brad Patterson. I had made reservations on every Rapid City flight schedule since Thursday morning—but when advised by Mr. Patterson at mid-day Friday that the letter was ready along with an explanatory note to Kent Frizell, I was caught against a fully-booked flight. I left for Rapid City on Friday evening, carrying the two sealed letters provided to me at the White House. Also, I carried a copy of each of the two, hiding them upon myself as "security copies"—against any unexpected, yet possible, attempts which might be taken to prevent their delivery.

Having unscheduled delays in plane transfer in Minneapolis, I called Kent Frizell to advise of my anticipated arrival time and to learn of the general plan of action. He informed me that Dick Wilson had learned again of my travel plans and purposes and had declared that I would not be permitted under any circumstances to arrive in Wounded Knee. He said he would check with Fools Crow to find out what he wanted to do, whether wanting me to be brought to Wounded Knee, to his home, or perhaps meet at some place off the Pine Ridge Indian Reservation. He suggested we get back in touch either later that night or after arriving in Rapid City or the following morning.

The following morning, Kent Frizell called me at the legal offices. He informed me that the headmen and chiefs had agreed to have the White House letter delivered to them at Scenic, off the reservation. We arranged to meet there at 10 a.m. I rode with Ramon Roubideaux to scenic, where a CRS agent informed us that the delivery site had been changed to the Reservation boundary. Approximately 100 Oglala Sioux, including a number of the headmen and chiefs and their interpreters were waiting at the boundary line. They had a proximate draft of the letter I carried. They asked to discuss certain questions they had about the letter—as well as certain doubts about its meaning and what they should do. Kent Frizell had not been advised of the change in plans, and so we watched his helicopter fly overhead toward Scenic. The Sioux chiefs did not want to break the seal on the letter until they could carry it into Wounded Knee. Therefore, I informed them of my extra "security copies" and gave them to the elderly men to read and discuss.

They had several questions, which I answered, and which answers seemed to satisfy them that they should proceed with the agreement and end the armed confrontation at Wounded Knee. Primarily, I distinguished between the limitations in content and promise of the White House letter—and the matters which they could raise in the context of the scheduled and future White House–level meetings. (I also showed them the copy of the private note to Kent Frizell, which essentially clarified the federal position that the date deadlines in the White House letter should not be construed as ultimatums or threats. From the private note, the chiefs determined that they had an extra week to work if they wanted to take it, but indicated that they were then satisfied with the general time schedule already set forth and informed me that they would act to conclude a settlement at Wounded Knee as quickly as possible.)

When Frizell arrived back at the border from Scenic, Fools Crow and the other chiefs were ready to receive the letter. To illustrate the wrongness of the present situations on the Sioux lands, they asked that I hand them the sealed letter across a barbed-wire fence which kept away other Indians and even the "official White House courier"—as Kent Frizell called me. I made a brief statement to Fools Crow relating to the meaning of Wounded Knee and cautioning him about the representations of the Government, declaring my belief that Indian people must look to ourselves, our own labors, our own strengths, and our own spirits, not White House letters nor white man's promises, to recreate a good Indian life upon Indian lands restored to our own control, and to save or to serve Indian people. (I expressed displeasure about a number of things, including the immediate plans to take the chiefs on pleasure rides in the government helicopter. Indian persons from Wounded Knee who had condemned the government's taking advantage of the headmen and chiefs liked my statement to the chiefs—but told me that it had not been translated at all to convey what I had said to them.) There were no television cameras at the site, but as we finished transferring the White House letter, a camera crew arrived and requested a brief "re-enactment" for their newscasts. There was no repetition of statements, although some additional ones; otherwise we briefly complied with the request.

Late that night (May 5th), Frizell informed me that Ramon Roubideaux and Dick Hallstern had finalized a draft agreement and that it had been signed, although it might have additional signatures in Wounded Knee the following day. That evening I reported to the Wounded Knee Legal Office/ Defense Committee my understanding of what was happening and what would take place over the next several days. Again it seemed obvious that various members of the legal group were greatly disappointed that a settlement was nearing. I told them: "I've never hid the fact that my central interest, apart from securing general and specific Indian objectives, had been oriented toward helping achieve a peaceful settlement."

The funeral of Buddy LaMont proceeded as scheduled on Sunday, but with persons being allowed into Wounded Knee having been limited to a list of relatives and close friends of his Oglala Sioux Nations as provided by his mother.

On Sunday the 6th, I walked into the legal offices and the midst of a meeting. The conversations were directed toward the question of whether it was already too late to prevent acceptance of the settlement which had already been reached. Almost immediately, the subject of my presence at legal defense meetings was brought up, with one of their members declaring that I should be asked to leave and not permitted to attend the "Committee" meetings. They were, in the absence of any objections, in unanimous agreement. (Later one of their members called to "explain" and express apology, informing me that they "are a collective and operate as one person"—advising me that since I did not regularly stay and work in Rapid City, that some just did not know me and so I just did not fit it.)

Just before catching a plane back to Washington, DC, shortly after Monday noon, I was called over to the legal offices to talk to one of the central Indian figures in the Wounded Knee occupation. I had already been advised by federal negotiators that they believed the evacuation would take place much more rapidly than scheduled under the seventy-two hour delay. ("It looks like we're going to get an empty bag. There's been a heavy infiltration out and it looks like most weapons are being taken out. But that's what we've more or less expected all along. We think Dennis Banks is leaving tonight, and Carter Camp seems ready to come out.") The Indian leader criticized me sharply for delivering the letter to the chiefs, and counseling them to settle. He blamed me for the agreement, alleging that there wouldn't have been a settlement if I hadn't become involved again: "You know those old people trust you!!"

As I left, Mark Lane was recording a final message from the Indian leader to the people in Wounded Knee—a last desperate effort to stop the settlement. It would be taken into Wounded Knee the next day. Fortunately, it would be taken into an empty village.

Letter

June 13, 1973
Survival of American Indians Association
Mr. Elliot Richardson
Attorney General of the United States
ATTN: Mr. William Ruckelshaus, Acting Director
US Federal Bureau of Investigation
Department of Justice
Washington, DC

Mr. Attorney General:

On January 31, 1973, a number of FBI Agents arrested myself in front of the apartment building where I live, then without invitation or warrant entered my apartment at the above address. After securing a search warrant several hours later, they removed certain properties and papers from my apartment.

In mid-March, an IBM electric typewriter and some documents and papers were returned to me by Assistant US Attorney John Rudy. These documents were from among others which belonged to myself, but which were being carried or transported on the top of boxes of other papers and properties stolen from the Bureau of Indian Affairs building last November and being returned there for delivery to agents of FBI at the time of their being seized.

To date, none of the documents or papers taken from my apartment have been returned to me by the United States Government. Nor have the remainder of the other documents, included in the several boxes seized but which were not stolen from the Department of the Interior, been returned. Additionally, the federal agents have kept the set of apartment keys which they used to gain entry, and may continue to use in gaining entry, to my apartment. As well, a movie film, "As Long As the Rivers Run," produced by myself, and a short film clip, relating to the failure of the federal government to protect treaty fishing rights of Indian people upon their reservation lands in Washington State, and depicting a large-scale, illegal and brutal police attack upon Indian men, women and children, was removed from my apartment by your Department's undercover agent John Arellano and not subsequently returned to my possession. Inasmuch as Mr. Arellano was authorized by the Attorney General's Office in late January to maintain electronic surveillance upon my conversations with recording, sound or transmitting devices, and was apparently acting under the direction and recommendations of Assistant Attorney General Henry Peterson, I regard it ludicrous that your department should disclaim all responsibility for the actions of Mr. Arellano and the taking of these films, as well as the set of apartment keys, as being matters which must be resolved by the Metropolitan Police Department of this city.

I would sincerely appreciate your office's now undertaking to return the remainder of my properties, papers and documents to me as quickly as possible. None of these items constitute the proceeds or evidence of any crime committed by myself or persons with whom I've been associated. Nor have I destroyed or stolen any such evidences, or other properties of the United States.

The documents I seek return of do, indeed, relate to actions of the Department of the Interior, its Bureau of Indian Affairs, HEW's Social Rehabilitation Services, the Office of Minority Business Enterprises (OMBE), and the Environmental Protection Agency or application of the National Environmental Policy Act (NEPA) upon actions of the Interior Department—where most these documents did originate, but from where they were not unlawfully removed or taken. None were actual file copies, nor copies which were meant, in their particular, to be actually maintained in the possession of that Department, although identical copies certainly would be and undoubtedly are. It is my understanding that most of these copies were withdrawn from a general informational distribution made to scores of offices or employees of the Bureau of Indian Affairs for maintaining the general knowledge of Bureau activities, but otherwise having a normal wastebasket destination without requirement of destruction or limitations upon additional use or external distribution.

These documents are not unlike those which, according to recent published reports, are being provided to external distribution points, such as members of congress and news outlets, by officers of the Office of Economic Opportunity of that agency's internal and public records for purposes of affecting future programming, authorizations and funding. More closely related, these documents and records are not unlike the record information and documentation which the Department of the Interior and Bureau of Indian Affairs offered to make available in quantity, without specific requests on particularized matter or documents, to a private Arizona citizen and constituent of US Representative Sam Steiger, upon the request of that Congressman, for use in writing a book. (This generous offer was made last autumn.)

On the other hand, I do believe that some of these documents clearly evidence wrongdoing and maladministration of trust responsibilities for Indian people by Department of the Interior officials. For instance, among the papers taken from me, one memorandum legal opinion and departmental briefing paper, which should have been controlling upon departmental and bureau decisions, spelled out the provisions of the National Environmental Policy Act (NEPA) shortly after its enactment and left no question but that the Act applied in its requirements to various departmentally-approved actions of Interior in the leasing or developing of, or contracting upon, certain Indian tribal and trust lands. Notwithstanding the applicability of the effective law, an official in the Secretary's Office nonetheless made a policy decision that NEPA would not apply to nor restrict tribal or departmental actions, in their government or administration, based upon a justifying rationale that "tribal leaders do not want it (applied)" and because "Indian lands are private property."

That policy decision, nationally-applied to Indian Country, preceded the subsequent legal opinion contrived for its support. Disregarding their own legal opinion that Environmental Impact Statements were required before finalizing or approving certain tribal actions, hundreds of thousands of acres of Indian tribal and trust lands were, subsequently and in consequence, subjected to contracts, leases, or otherwise opened up to mineral and mining exploration and exploitation, or other forms of industrial or resources development and capitalization by non-Indian business interests, without either tribal leaders or memberships having the benefit of minimal, much less full, knowledge and understanding of possible adverse affects and ultimate impacts on these actions and undertakings.

One effect, evolving with greater frequency, is that Indian people in different parts of the country where these large-acreage leases and contract were effected, are being called upon to draw from their manager tribal and individual or collective resources to challenge the well-financed industrial lease-holders and contractors, as well as the United States, in attempting to nullify or overturn some unwisely wrought decisions affecting their resources and rights. A fundamental deficiency in the policy pursued, besides its disregard of the NEPA law, was its total disregard of the fact that each Indian tribal member possesses legal proprietary and equity interests in tribal actions and the management of tribal resources, which interests and rights are deserving of protection—and which are not wholly surrendered at the tribal ballot boxes or elections, but which may be invoked against demonstrably wrongful and adverse decisions of tribal leaders under existing law. (Your Assistant Attorney General Stan Pottinger would do well to understand this in formulating his declared plans or intent to more fully implement the "Indian Bill of Rights" measure of the 1968 Civil Rights Act upon Indian Reservations in the immediate future. Most Indian persons do not want to haul their tribal leaders into court in search of recourse to rights having been violated already or for remedy to legal interests being denied. Rather, most want their interests protected and their rights preserved for enjoyment by conscientious application of well-constructed governmental procedures or administrative decisional processes, structured with full cognizance of these individual and collective tribal rights and interests.)

I have digressed from the basic subject of this letter. However, it seems timely and not inappropriate to express these several viewpoints related to the content of the documents taken from me by your Department and not returned to my possession, despite my continuing needs for their various information.

Additionally, I would note my hope that, under your direction, the Department of Justice would take cognizance of a fact that the trust responsibility and relationship toward and with Indian people extends to the entirety of the federal or United States' Government, particularly all of the Executive branch and its Departments, although certainly the Interior Secretary and Department is its principal agent and instrumentality as trustee, and that the Justice Department and its agencies would review its policies and practices relating to Indian people, tribes and individuals, in order that its future actions might conform more conscientiously and consistently with those trust responsibilities and relationships, as well as with existing laws placing specific obligations upon the Justice Department with respect to Indian people and our rights and reservations.

It is not simply self-serving to say that a good step to be taken would be for your Department to effect the immediate return of my house keys, papers, documents and other properties so disingenuously taken from me January 31, 1973, and previously thereto.

Respectfully yours,
Hank Adams,
National Director

Civil Rights and Termination

As a young man, Hank Adams arrived in Washington State in the 1950s during the height of the federal government's last major assimilative campaign on Native peoples—a period of forced political and legal termination, relocation to urban areas, and the delegation by the federal government, via Public Law (P.L.) 280, to several states, including Washington, of criminal and some civil jurisdiction over Indian lands and peoples in those states. This gross imposition of state law over Native peoples occurred without tribal consent.

In fact, P.L. 280 was the first major issue to attract Adams's attention, and from that time forward he kept a vigilant eye on the actions of federal, state, bureaucratic, military, and tribal officials and institutions if he believed their actions might destroy or impinge on the civil, constitutional, treaty, or human rights of Native nations and their citizens.

The selections in this section evidence some of the strategies—letters, congressional testimonies, speeches, and so forth—used by Adams to combat such assaults. In several cases, his actions had a positive effect in ameliorating the potential damage that some of these policies might have caused.

December 1964
"Let Us Not Speak of Termination"
by Hank Adams
ABC—Americans Before Columbus

(A bill to terminate federal supervision and trust status of the Shoalwater Indian Reservation* will, in all probability, be introduced in the coming session of Congress. The Shoalwater Indians are unalterably opposed to proposed termination plans. For several months of the past year, this writer aided them in their opposition and the presentation of their views. This article is based upon my involvement, research, and interpretation of the issues—and although believed to be basically reflective of the Shoalwater's views, the author assumes responsibility for all statements made. Any statement of a hypothetical, interpretative, or argumentative nature should be attributed solely to the author. H.A.)

In January, the Secretary of the Interior spoke to a national Indian organization. "Let us not speak of termination, until we have terminated poverty" he said, then waited for loud applause to subside.

Had someone from the Shoalwater Reservation of Washington State been there, he might have interrupted, "But, Kind Sir; have you not coupled heaven and hell in a single breath, naming both a goal? Bitters of position may hide in the offerings of sweet wine. We have sought the rose you speak of, only to find it between the jaws of the dragon you would not have us see. We are not blind! Let us slay the dragon, and let the rose grow free."

For the past four decades, the Shoalwater Indians have been attempting to develop the economic resources of their 334 1/2-acre reservation on the central coast of Washington. They have not only been denied every existing opportunity to do so—but have been denied the right to do so!

Ironically, the long-oppressed desire and efforts for the economic development of their reservation have given force to the Bureau of Indian Affairs' attempts to terminate federal supervision and trust status of the reservation.

The Bureau plans to have a bill introduced in the coming session of Congress to effect the termination of the Shoalwater Indian Reservation. It will be an updated version of two previous termination bills that were introduced in 1958 and 1960. It is a matter of record that the Shoalwater Indians are opposed to the current plan, as they were to the earlier ones.

The BIA's position has remained constant and unchanging throughout the past eight years, although the current Agency Superintendent indicates a

---

* The Shoalwater people were able to avoid being congressionally terminated and, in fact, responded aggressively to the threat to their political existence by adopting a constitution in 1971 and electing a governing council soon thereafter.—Ed.

willingness to listen to the Indians. Therefore, the termination plan can be considered as one concerted effort, and attempts need not be reviewed separately in terms of time.

The Shoalwater Reserve was established by Executive Order of President Andrew Jackson on September 22, 1866. In addition to stating the location of the land tract, it ordered that it be "reserved for Indian purposes, as recommended in the letter of the 18th instant." A very brief document, the Executive Order stated little more.

The interpretation of this document by the Bureau of Indian Affairs, in essence, is that it only provides Indians with the occupancy rights, and recognizes no Indian claim to land or title. By virtue of this interpretation, the Shoalwaters have not been allowed to establish businesses, nor attempt any development fo the land or natural resources.

On various occasions during the past four decades, Indians living on the Shoalwater reservation have had themselves, or had access to, the financial resources for undertaking land development or establishing business enterprises there. Repeatedly, they were refused this right.

In 1956, however, the Bureau led them to believe that they could secure this right by agreeing to a plan of calculated land division and definite land assignment. They were informed that this was the only way they could. Convincing the people that their long-standing demands would be met, and expressed desires be realized, the BIA secured the signatures of the eleven adults living on or adjacent to the reservation on a so-called Memorandum Agreement.

This signed agreement provided for the land division and land assignment—but it also stated that the signatories agreed to a removal of all their lands from federal trust status!

In truth, the signatures did not represent agreement with the words of the document; but more exactly, expressed approval of the verbal statements fo the Agency Superintendent regarding the results that would be achieved—and satisfaction with his assurances that the "Memorandum of Agreement" would not result in the termination which it was expressly designed to achieve.

When the true nature and meaning of the signed papers was fully understood by the Shoalwaters, they disavowed and repudiated the document. However, it became the basis of the termination bills. The Bureau used the so-called memorandum of Agreement to argue that the Indians favored and wanted termination. With this paper, they secured the endorsement of Governor Rosellini, the local County Commissioners, and various civic and service organizations, for the termination of federal responsibilities, supervision, services, and trust status over the reservation.

In view of the Shoalwaters' disavowal of this document, the BIA does not—for they can not—use it to support termination plans, but they continue to use the endorsements for termination that were secured by it.

The Bureau justifies their termination plans in terms of the desire of the

Shoalwaters to develop their reservation. This aspiration is one of the premises from which they derive their perverted conclusion.

However, they say, "The Executive Order of September 22, 1866, establishing the reservation merely stated" that it be "reserved for Indian purposes." The brevity and lack of elaboration in the Executive Order has created "a very complicated situation," they argue.

"Therefore," concludes the Bureau of Indian Affairs, "The only remedy" is "an effective and amiable assignment program" "with subsequent termination of trust status and of federal supervision and services." "This would free these Indians to make their own decisions on the type of economic development they desire."

Essentially, the Bureau's capsule version of the "complicated situation" is thus:

It appears the land was acquired by the government to provide homes for a number of Indian families then (1866) living in the area, who did not choose to move to the Quinault Reservation. These people were fragments of various Tribes. There is no Shoalwater Tribe, and it is doubtful that there ever was one. The reservation has been occupied at various times by different families, who seemingly moved there and always at will. It should be realized that the original occupants of this land were also allotted on the Quinault Reservation. There is no tribal entity, but the affairs of the reservation are taken care of by the adult resident of the area. Because the Executive Order spoke only that it be reserved for Indian purposes. Indian claim to land or title is not recognized, and it is the belief that only occupancy rights were secured. (Note: End of version attributed to BIA).

The Bureau's interpretation of the situation consists of both fiction and fact. Bureau personnel have asserted that, technically, any Indian in the United States could assume the same rights on the Shoalwater reservation. It has even been stated that by virtue of its authority, the Bureau could lease the entire reservation to non-Indian, if the revenue was placed in the US Treasury under the name of the, supposedly, non-existent Shoalwater Tribe.

Apparently, the BIA can read anything they want to into the words, "Indian purposes," except economic development of their reservation. Fighting poverty might be an Indian purpose; but developing his economic resources—never!

Departing from the Bureau's attitude and arguments, we acquire a different perspective.

It is my belief and contention that the "letter of the 18th instant," referred to in the Executive Order of September 22, 1866, is an integral part of that document. In examining it (actually several documents and a map), "Indian purposes takes on fuller meaning and the intent of the Executive Order becomes exceedingly clear!"

Especially relevant is the letter from Supt. W. W. Waterman, dated June

1, 1866, and the letter from Giles Ford, Indian Agent, dated May 2, 1866. The significant portions in the Superintendent's letter read:

"These Indians said to consist of some 30 or 40 families have always lived upon the Beach and subsist upon fish, clams, oysters, and sea animals. They are unwilling to abandon their former habits of life and turn their attention to agriculture. They desire a place upon the shore where they can fix their homes, without being exposed to be supplanted and driven off by white men."

"This tract which they have selected is a Sand beach yielding some grass for the pasturing of their horses but of little value for cultivation, and it is my judgement that reserving it for the use of the Indians would work no injury to white men, but would have a tendency to promote peace between them and the Indians and would secure the contentment and well-being of the latter, I therefore leave respectfully to recommend that the tract of land selected by Mr. Ford and designated upon the enclosed map be reserved for the use of the Indians." Mr. Ford wrote as follows:

"I have visited Shoalwater Bay and examined the spot that the Indians wish reserved for them. It is peculiarly adapted for a home for them; begin situated in close proximity to good fishing, hunting, and grazing grounds. And I would recommend that it be immediately reserved for sale."

It seems quite clear that "Indian purposes" meant considerably more than the strict interpretation that has been applied by the BIA. Unquestionably, Indian purposes included that of securing an adequate and sufficient livelihood from the resources available.

The Shoalwaters have been restricted in their "subsistence upon fish, clams, oysters, and sea animals," however. And they have been restricted from "securing the contentment and well-being" offered by their home.

What of the Bureau's argument that there are no Shoalwater Indians?

First, it might be realized that those were real Indians referred to in the previously quoted letters. "Reserved for Indian purposes" was not an abstraction arising from the fact that Indians exist, but related directly to a definite group of Indians.

Aboriginally, and in the mid-19th century, there were seldom large Indian populations or high concentrations of Indians in a single locality, in Western Washington. Generally, small bands, clans, or families were scattered along the rivers, beaches, other waterways, or along the forests and prairies. Some comprised political units by themselves, and others belonged to larger tribal complexes. Factors of language, geography, and self-determination, etc., figured in this determination.

Under the treaties, executive orders, and establishment of reservations, the government attempted to concentrate, centralize, and consolidate the Indians of this area wherever possible. Bounties, gifts, intimidations, and inducements were used to accomplish this, and these practices continued in some cases until some time after the General Allotment Act of 1887.

On the basis of documents of the Washington Territory Superintendency from 1853 to 1873, the existence of a district band, or bands, of Indians of Shoalwater Bay, who disassociated themselves from the Quinaults to the North, the Chehalis and Cowlitz Indians to the East, and the Chinook to the South and Southeast, can be established.

It can also be argued, quite validly, that this band, or bands, were a group, or groups, of the above named tribes who had intermarried, which was customary for this particular area.

For reasons stated in the previously quoted letters, it is understandable why the Indians did not want to be moved. A significant reason that figured in their selection of site, and staying was that their dead were "buried" there. The reservation encompasses their cemetery.

What of the Bureau's arguments that the Shoalwaters are allotted on the Quinault Reservation, and that the reservation has been occupied by different families from time to time?

Actually, the claimants to Shoalwater are enrolled members of the Quinault Tribe, and own or have interests in lands on the Quinault Reservation. However, a number of families have steadily resided on or near the Shoalwater Reservation. (My use of the words "Shoalwaters" and "Shoalwater Indians" refer to those who have sustained residence or claims upon this reservation, rather than to their Tribal membership.) The primary factor in movements away from there has been economics and the lack of means for livelihood.

Tribal membership is a crucial consideration for the Shoalwaters, and greatly influences the BIA's attitude. The federal law restricting dual-benefits, or membership in more than one tribe, seemingly presents major difficulties.

To be allowed to develop their reservation, it would be demanded that they establish a formal tribal organization and enrollment. Consequently, they would be obligated under law to surrender their membership in the Quinault Tribe. The point consistently overlooked is that their Quinault membership and claims to Shoalwater are not mutually exclusive issues.

The fact is that if claim to Shoalwater were surrendered and complete reliance placed upon Quinault membership, these people could not find residence or sustenance upon the 149,000-acre Quinault Reservation! It has been attempted in the past, and found unworkable. At present, the Quinault Reservation does not provide an adequate livelihood for the 200 families now living on it. It would be difficult to get a residential assignment and to establish a home there. It would be considered an unwelcome intrusion to draw upon already-strained resources.

On the other hand, to surrender Quinault membership and create a recognized tribe would overburden the 334 1/2-acre Shoalwater Reservation to the point where the right to develop the resources could not be implemented. For a dozen or more families to rely solely upon this tract might satisfy current residential needs, but would preclude economic development. Also, it would sacrifice and deprive their heir's potential and rightful opportunities on the Quinault Reservation, as it advances economically.

It seems frightfully unreasonable that the medicine of termination should be prescribed for the Shoalwater when all the evidence indicates that the infirmities and afflictions are actually those of the bureaucratic physician.

The original termination plan called for the 334 1/2-acre reservation to be divided into eleven approximately equal portions. The current plan will be updated to include the heirs of several of the previous number, now deceased. Subsequently, trust status and federal supervision and services would be terminated. Individual landholder, the Bureau argues, would then be able to sell or develop their land as they desired.

A resource inventory and analysis of this small tract of land would reveal that the economic potential exists primarily in the location and physical features of the reservation.

It is located on the north shore of an ocean harbor, centrally located between growing tourist centers about ten miles away. Two major highways cross, or are adjacent to it. On the south side, where one highway runs and where the present houses are, there is a half-mile stretch of beach and tidelands, additional to the 334 1/2-acre but assumed to be part of the reservation. The land runs on a level plane for several hundred yards, then rises abruptly into a high bluff. In the lowland, virgin and second-growth alder is abundant, with evergreens growing elsewhere. A tribally-owned reservoir provides the reservation with a fresh-water supply.

In the semi-natural state, Shoalwater is undeniably beautiful, and has tremendous landscaping possibilities—in addition to those for business enterprises.

However, to divide it would be to destroy it, and its value. Only in its entirety, does it comprise an economic unit. Its developmental potential exists only in its remaining intact.

It must be remembered that its total acreage is only slightly greater than two 160-acre allotments, or two similar homestead tracts. In fact, we can draw significant parallel between Shoalwater and the denial fo the Hopkins-Dukes application for homesteads in Colorado by the Secretary of the Interior. Supposedly, economic considerations prevailed in that case where 160-acres would not support one man. Yet, Shoalwater would be parceled out among a dozen, or more.

The Bureau argues that individual owners, with land out of trust, would be able to secure loans or mortgages upon their land to finance businesses. However, they have repeatedly pointed out that the value of Shoalwater is very small in its unimproved state. One point argues against the other. Realistically, loans and mortgages that might be secured would be insignificant to business development—and if too large would undoubtedly lead to the loss of the land. Nearly-applied taxes would increase, or pose, the same threat.

Granting the Shoalwaters the freedom to use and utilize their land, only by granting the individuals the freedom to lose their land, as provided by the termination plan, would have disastrous and cruel effects upon the entire community—if the latter should be exercised, intentionally or otherwise. Each segment is a vitally important key tract, which must be considered and integrated fully into considerations of the whole reservation as a single unit. It must remain intact!

Justification for termination will be attempted on the basis of the Shoalwater's enrollment and allotments on the Quinault Reservation 100 miles to the north. Restricting real benefits on the Shoalwater rather than risk a technical existence of dual-benefits—the BIA has denied these people any benefits.

It should be noted that no more than five of the 800 persons on the Quinault Reservation are living on their own allotments. They are living on tribal or private land in two different villages. The BIA would not restrict economic development there—although the fact is that feasibility dictates that it would not occur on individual allotments, but on lands secured elsewhere on the reservation, with few exceptions!

Furthermore, had it been permitted, certain Shoalwaters have had timber money from their Quinault allotments, with which they could have established businesses on the Shoalwater and been in on the ground floor of a thriving and still-growing tourist business! Sadly, they were not. This story has been communicated many times over the years. Where willingness to listen has existed, willingness to be responsive to the desires and aspirations of these people has not.

Earlier this year, communication was made with the Washington State Congressional delegation. In several instances the Shoalwater's letters were referred to the BIA for comment and reports of background material.

In a classic example of problem solving, the Portland Area Office of the BIA informed one Senator that he could expect complaints from that quarter, cautioned him that there would be more—and for all intents and purposes—advised him he should lend them a dear ear.

At a time when the Bureau of Indian Affairs is emphasizing programs "designed to promote maximum Indian economic self-sufficiency"…and has set up a Division of Economic Development for this purpose—we can critically question whether termination is the only alternative for the Shoalwater Reservation.

Actually, it offers no alternative—but presents a cruel hoax. These people have long sought the economic development of their reservation! Their claim to land rights goes unrecognized, except when final termination is being contrived. They are recognized as a de facto tribal government when a highway right-of-way is needed, when a resolution is needed to expend funds for the non-existent "Shoalwater Tribe"—but not when economic development is possible and sought!

The nature of true alternative is not in inconsistency, but in the existence of true choices. Inconsistency does not provide freedom of choice—however great the inconsistency!

Yet, above all, Shoalwater is their home. Even those forced away by economic pressures consider it their home, above all houses built elsewhere. Now, their home is threatened.

They have endured forty years of unrealized dreams. Termination will destroy that dream, divide their home, and bury their hope. Ironically, this is their fourth decade as citizens of the United States. Is this the price that must be paid? Is it a fair price—a heritage, a home, a heart?

Can Shoalwater be preserved? Against what has become the strongest nation on earth in less than 200 years? Shoalwater can not survive against strength and unquestioned power. But should this power be guided by justice, equity, purpose, and understanding—then Shoalwater finds no threat, no opposition. These people will find new promise and new opportunity.

Full hearing must be accorded these people. True alternative must be considered. If the "complicated situation" must be clarified by Congress, a distinction must be made between the complications on the reservation and those existing in the Bureau of Indian Affairs.

Necessarily, a program must be devised that will best serve the interests of everyone involved. Full observance and recognition should be given to the rights of the present occupants and homeowners of the reservation. The Shoalwaters must be given every latitude for the realistic development of reservation resources.

Such a program might give recognition to a community government, to handle the affairs of the reservation. The land should remain intact, and this would probably be best insured by retaining the land and tidelands under tribal ownership. The community government would be obligated to respect current residential assignments, and authorized to grant new ones which might be necessary. Under this type arrangement, economic and resource development could proceed in coordinated and orderly fashion. Regarding the reservation as a single economic unit, and integrating planning to that consideration, individual Indian investments could be encouraged, and cooperative or corporate business enterprises undertaken. This would be under the jurisdiction of the community government. There should be no termination of trust status or federal responsibilities, in any event!

The true spirit of the Executive Order on September 22, 1866, should prevail, tempered by the Indian aspirations of 1964, and natured by their deeds.

These are, of course, only suggestions thrown from a distance. Even these, nevertheless, are ideas to keep us from speaking or effecting termination.

Let us terminate poverty. Period! Let us not speak of termination. Period! These are two separate considerations—not two phrases to be hung on a single comma and single meaning. But perhaps the message intended for Indian people was, "Let us not speak!" Period.

Letter

May 14, 1974
Survival of American Indians Association
Dennis Banks & Russell Means
American Indian Movement
Attention: Ken Tilsen
US District Court
St. Paul, Minnesota 55103

Dear Dennis, Russell, & Ken:

Enclosed is a copy of a letter I wrote to Sen. Sam Ervin, with first intentions of preparing a summary cover statement for publications or public release. I've not had a moment to complete those plans. Also, I had planned to ask Vine Deloria to edit it down and then request some Eastern organization to print it in a full-page fund-raising ad for Wounded Knee Legal Defense/Offense Committee (WKLD/OC). Didn't do that either.

Am sending the bulk of my Wounded Knee & related politics file to you. Some things should be useful. But an attorney or legal researcher should read the whole thing, to synthesize interrelated matters for possible use. You probably have copies of much of it.

You might note the General Accounting Office (GAO) report to Senator Jackson on Pine Ridge Indian Reservation. I'm certain that he did not make it public—the level of federal expenditures ($2000-plus per capita; $11,000-almost per family) on the Pine Ridge (PR) doesn't seem quite consistent with the severity of poverty that was universally recognized and reported (even acknowledged by Dick Wilson) during news coverage of Wounded Knee. Also, if you don't already have it, the GAO Report does confirm the Interior-BIA assistance to the PR Agency Realty Officer in his unlawful acquisition of other Indians' allotments; failure to return title; failure even to re-transact purchase by paying an additional $26,000 to allottees to meet 'fair price' standards and allow the BIA to approve the conveyances; but, nonetheless, holding onto the land, taking steady promotions from the supervising BIA employer and benefactor, and enjoying the protection of Interior—which 'forgot' the matter, closed its files, and refused external examination of its investigation.

If you keep the files I'm forwarding somewhat intact, I can explain them once I'm able to break away from here and final phases of treaty rights fishing matters that need to be approved by the federal court by June 1.

The "Jackson Connection" is primarily established through the actions of his staff representative Gereau—particularly one memorandum written for Jackson as result of my own letter to Jackson. But also the Executive Session that Jackson had with Attorney General Kleindienst and Ralph Erickson—which I think must be taken in context with the content of other Justice

Department statements in the same time period from Wounded Knee to the White House, as well as with the Gereau representations at Pine Ridge and in memoranda. (Abourezk was in Colorado, not in DC, when the Executive Session occurred. It's my understanding that Abourezk had Gereau thrown off Indian Affairs Committee work in the early part of May 1973, because of his various actions and statements.)

The full eighty-five pages of the Minneapolis Field Office FBI Report on civil rights violations is not together, since I only copied selected sections. The Hurd-Clayton statements and letters were reported in its body, one as a final action in the report, and the other as an enclosure. The consistency of BIA and FBI statements (background of each interview) are so precisely slanted against a phantom "criminal element" on Pine Ridge Reservation—that it demonstrates to myself that both Bureaus were using an identical prejudice and justifying language for their decisions, which has precluded any fair investigations or lawful protections for most Oglala community people for many years. (Another reason for not copying the whole report was that everyone of nearly a dozen or more FBI interviews of officials and offenders were the same—to effect a pre-determined conclusion and result.) The file relates a constancy of attitudes at least back to early 1970...

The files I'm forwarding have been copied on both sides of paper to cut down bulk—though making more difficult reading, and causing a few items to be mixed. Shouldn't be too confusing though.

Please read the letter to Ervin in its entirety. It is somewhat confusing in parts. Incidentally, I include the part about Carlton Stoiber, both because I can verify it through witnesses and because I think the adequacy of his Indian investigations, particularly in South Dakota, has frequently been influenced by the political result sought or intended to be maintained.

How is the trial going? Did hope to fly over there last week, but got tied down—then it took me some time to sort this stuff out to take or, as now, send.

Am sending this file also to Abbie Mann in LA.

Wish there was some way to get better coverage on issues & events on your trials and activities.

Incidentally, I have not sent a copy to Judge Fred Nichol as indicated. Thought I better wait until hearing from you, or allow yourselves to give him a copy if useful to your purposes.

Hank Adams

Letter

April 19, 1974
US Senator Sam Ervin, Chairman
Senate Subcommittee on Constitutional Rights
New Senate Offices Building
Washington, DC 20510
Re: Administration of the Justice Department

Dear Senator Ervin:

Various hearings on Justice Department operations and appointments have demonstrated congressional unwillingness either to provide for basic qualitative reforms in its agencies or to insulate their operations from abusive political control and manipulation by successive Administrations—and powerful members of Congress.

My central concern arises from the apparent fact that the US Government has determined that there shall be 'no system of justice' for American Indian people and our tribal communities. This is evidenced most fully by the political prosecution of Indians involved in the 1973 Wounded Knee incident, as viewed in context with prevailing patterns of federal actions involving Indians. I shall present some facts and pose some questions pertinent to the practices of the Justice Department and relationships with other governmental units:

1. What remedy do community Indian people have when Secretary of the Interior Rogers Morton persistently joins with or directs the Justice Department and US Attorneys in the deliberate misprision and willful concealment of felony criminal actions by tribal government officials and employees?

A. Interior's auditing section sand FBI Special Agents have repeatedly furnished the Secretary's Office and Justice Department units with concrete evidence and proof of such felony crimes. US Attorneys routinely follow Interior officials' requests and rulings against prosecutions on crimes ranging from probable murders to embezzlement or unlawful conversions of large amounts of tribal and federal funds to personal use. Facts and investigative results are resolutely withheld from the complaining Indian individuals and tribal memberships....

2. What is the fundamental difference between the infamous conspiracy and actions through agents by which Tony Boyle effected the murders of members of the Jack Yablonsky family and the process by which US Senator Henry M. Jackson (March 19, 1973, Executive Session) and White House and Interior officials (Brad Patterson, John Whitaker, Marvin Franklin; March 16, 1973) gave insistent instruction and direction to the US Attorney General's Office (Richard Kleindienst and Ralph Erickson) which, in being accepted and followed at all Departmental levels, carried through to the unpunished

killing of at least four Indians and the shooting and injury of others in South Dakota during the remainder of 1973?

A. Economic and political control, as exercised by tribal and federal officials on too many Indian Reservations, has been transformed into a corrupt 'unionism' with vices as intolerable as any which have marred the grand history of the American labor movement. The Pine Ridge Reservation has been among the worst, with its system of goon squads and political protection rackets, and has allowed the people of that Indian nation to become oppressed and imprisoned in their home communities—in a sense constituting a veritable 'American gulag archipelago,' localizing there but linked with Indian communities elsewhere. The national government fosters and funds this 'corrupt unionism' and protects it from either internal or external challenge and reform—operating by deliberate design of federal officials participant in its system or those finding useful purpose in its continued operation, and relying upon the indifference of most Congressional and Executive officials for its perpetuation.

○ ○ ○

3. Do political manipulations or unlawful abuses of the Justice Department and its subordinate units cease to be objectionable, and derive sanction to continue, when the politics and attitudes of the Executive and Congressional branches of the government coincide or join in general agreement that some particular target population, however vaguely defined or haphazardly identified, is to be victimized by their powers or by deliberate denial of protections?

A. On the first day of Wounded Knee, the Senate Judiciary Committee questioned Patrick Gray about political use of the FBI in the 1972 presidential campaign. Mr. Gray advised that the FBI did respond to White House and Deputy AG Ralph Erickson's requests for reports between September 1 and 11, 1972. Indian activists who had complained of police and court abuses on the Pine Ridge Reservation were identified as a problem of "sufficient magnitude" for capitalizing on in giving the "President maximum support during the campaign trips."

○ ○ ○

4. In matter unrelated to federal criminal investigations, the Justice Department and other federal agencies have acted deliberately to deny protections to the legal rights of Indians; to injure and discredit Indian individuals and organizations or to diminish their impact, influence and effectiveness among Indian people generally and upon public policy or decisions of general government officials and units; and to mislead the public about the nature of these federal activities and motivations for them. Who can Indians look to for protections?

A. Mr. Carlton Stoiber, a senior Civil Rights Division attorney in the Justice Department and the person responsible for supervising investigation of complaints about criminal actions and civil rights violations against community Indian people on the Pine Ridge Indian Reservation in 1973 and 1974, has exercised the unauthorized and unlawful liberty of showing FBI and Justice Department files relating to myself to private citizens, having nothing to do with government or any investigative processes, and who have merely been in his office in Washington, DC, on their own personal business.

o o o

5. Although the Constitution provides clear process for dealing with presidential culpability in the commission of crimes, and Members of Congress stand liable for criminal breaches of laws passed by that body, what process protects Indian people if Congress as a unit engages in collective criminality? If such "collective criminality" has been operative, it may be seen in the genesis of Wounded Knee. It can be seen in the transformation of laws to situationally create "no system of justice for American Indians." It can lead to the systematic maladministration of programs, laws, and tribal governments, to label and punish populations of Indian people as a dangerous, "criminal element," as was done on the Pine Ridge Reservation before there existed an AIM. And, when an AIM comes into being and acts or responds to pleas from their people, it permits extension of the punitive actions and provides for indiscriminate punishment to be initiated by the general white society as a threatening lesson to all other Indians.

A. Although the Indian people being prosecuted as result of Wounded Knee 1973 claim that the 1868 Treaty between the Sioux Nations and the United States constitutes the foundation of their defense, the material relevancy of the Treaty is challenged by federal prosecutors, and has not yet been allowed or admitted by the Court. The foundations of the offenses and conspiracy charged against them has origin, in the essential elements, with laws governing Indians since 1834 and 1885—the latter being enacted for direct purpose of "implementing" provision of the 1868 Sioux Treaty.

o o o

6. What prospects are there for positive change or qualitative reform in the federal governmental units which have continuously abused their powers to control the affairs and the future of Indian people?

The Wounded Knee confrontation and preceding Trail of Broken Treaties Caravan can not be explained away simply by enlarging the numbers of Indian people who federal officials choose to categorize as "criminal elements" who must not be listened to or responded to in any way, and who—being "all tarred by the same brush," in the words of a vindictive White House aide—are deserving only of punishment and extreme deprivations. Nor can intolerable situations encompassing or devouring the lives of Indian men, women and children, and daily destroying Indian communities, be resolved or made more tolerable merely by carrying out scores of political persecutions of Indian people in South Dakota or adjacent states.

As you know, June 2, 1974, will mark but the 50th Anniversary of the Indian Citizenship Act passed by Congress on June 2, 1924! Truly the present conditions and treatment of most Indian people would seem more understandable had that US Citizenship never been conferred or imposed; and perhaps partially explains why many Indian people shall never conceptually, psychologically, nor spiritually accept or reconcile themselves to it. After nearly two centuries of American nationhood, the enforced US law does accord greater protection to psychiatrists' files and to the private papers of political parties and personages than it does, in practice, to Indian people who must rely for protection upon laws which remain unenforced and which are systematically disregarded or trampled upon—from the Constitution; through the Treaties; on down through the 1968 Indian Bill of Rights, which your office labored for nearly a decade to place on the law books. For what purpose, if application was to be denied?

What may not pass without punishment against white properties and privacy in the dead of night, can readily pass as approved actions against Indian people and properties at any time. As in the weeks of February 1973 before Wounded Knee, no questions of impropriety are raised from any official quarter—nor from the commercial American free press—when federal armed forces occupy and control Indian communities and populations; nor when the full force of the United States stands ready to kill hundreds of Indians in daylight or dark by general order on the first passable or politically acceptable excuse.

When White House officials having daily responsibility for coordinating administration of Indian Affairs make class distinctions among Indian people, and characterize "dissidents" as being "psychotic, bestial, savage and sick"—what can the families in the reservation communities—who have been administratively classified and programmatically treated as being "criminal population" expect from the government of the United States?

Is there anyone in the Congress who Indian people may look to for better attitudes and some chances for corrections and changes? When Senator Henry M. Jackson, for instance, wrote on May 9, 1973, that "the job ahead for all of us who are interested in the underlying causes of Wounded Knee is to launch the kind of effort that will seek to resolve or overcome such issues," one might initially hope that this most powerful US Senator has advanced from his negative positions in conference with the US Attorney General at an earlier date. Instead, subsequent internal memoranda in his office demonstrates his approval of wholesale prosecutions by the Government—and accepts endorsements or approves the worst governmental abuses in the reservation community. Such endorsements and abuses have become license for unpunished killings and murders of Indian people at Pine Ridge, in one extreme—and only offers a promise of worse things to come.

If things do not improve, and continue to worsen by federal design, I fully anticipate that "Wounded Knee" shall become "necessary" again—and will occur even if all Indian persons presently indicted, or at trial, are committed to the nation's prison for years. As the killing of Indians continues, without adequate investigations or any consequences attaching, other events similar to Wounded Knee become more inevitable; and inevitably a different and more tragic result threatens for both Indian people and others. Personally, I reject all notion that violence will work for anyone. However, I recognize an existing basic commitment on the part of many Indian people of all ages—both before and after Wounded Knee—that efforts must be made to end the violence and injury done against Indian communities and our most defenseless members, perennially and perpetually. Of course, not all Indian communities suffer the same injuries or the same level of governmental abuses. Among the most severely oppressed—those for whom 'no system of justice' is the imposed rule over their lives—can anyone expect that they shall be satisfied to celebrate this Nation's Second Century of Independence and to proclaim that they surrendered their last defense and hope for justice with their last major victory in the Custer Battle in 1876? As one noted author has indicated, 'There are more chapters in the Indian history to be written.'

Senator Ervin, I address you with the knowledge that you have spent major amounts of time on this issue of civil and criminal justice for Indian people. Further I recognize that, although your Judiciary Subcommittee has jurisdiction over some of the issues and situations I have referred to in this letter, that your remaining time in the Senate may largely be obligated by other major concerns and activities assigned you. Nonetheless, I am hopeful that you shall be able to find some time to examine the general failure of the Justice Department and the Department of the Interior to encourage, advance or aid the implementation of the 1968 Indian Bill of Rights—or more precisely their deliberate actions in subverting its purposes and provision, together with other civil and legal rights of Indian people, on the Pine Ridge Indian Reservation, South Dakota. Otherwise, I urge your service in interesting your colleagues remaining in the Senate in these issues of vital importance to Indian people.

Please accept our sincerest appreciation for your notable accomplishments in the Senate, and our kindest best wishes for your future.

Most Respectfully yours,
Hank Adams, SAIA

Testimonial

Hearings Before the Committee on the Judiciary. US Senate. Ninety-Third
Congress, First Session. On the Nomination of Louis Patrick Gray III, of
Connecticut, to be Director, Federal Bureau of Investigation (February
28, March 1, 6, 7, 8, 12, 20, 21, and 22, 1976)
Testimony of Hank Adams, National Director, Survival of American Indians
Association
"Statement in Opposition to the Senate Confirmation of Mr. L. Patrick Gray
III to be Director of the Federal Bureau of Investigation"

Mr. Chairman and Members of the Judiciary Committee, I respectfully
request that my statements be received into the record of these hearings. I
request opportunity to address the Committee partially to respond to FBI
Acting Director Gray's personal attack against my motives, integrity and
character by his testimony regarding my recent arrest by his agency. More
importantly and purposefully, I want to point out certain deficiencies in the
operational policies and practices of the FBI relating to American Indian
people and federal criminal statutes under the enforcement or investigative
jurisdictions of the FBI.

I oppose confirmation of Mr. L. Patrick Gray's nomination to become FBI
Director because I believe his demonstrated disinterest and failure in eliminating discriminatory and negligent investigative and enforcement practices
from his agency's operations has been harmful to the American Indian community and has denied many Indians the benefit and protections of laws
within FBI jurisdictions.

Various other levels and divisions of the US Justice Department and the
Department of the Interior may well warrant the blame for the inequities and
injuries which draw my concern, at least in greater measure than the FBI. However, I believe that Mr. Gray and the FBI have frequently betrayed whatever independence and good conscience that may be allowed them by statute and organizationally within the Justice Department—and as frequently have not been
controlled by the obligations and responsibilities imposed upon them by law.

I call your attention to Wounded Knee, South Dakota. If Justice and
the FBI might be inclined to invoke the same situation as refutation to my
charges—as within hours they may regard it as basis for reputation and their
future pride—I believe it provides essential proof to my complaints.

The FBI has gained its present high visibility at Wounded Knee for reasons arising from the fact that the Justice Department and its FBI choose to
be invisible to Oglalla Sioux Indians—seeking to preserve their personal
liberties and lives—on the Pine Ridge Reservation for months preceding the
takeover and occupation of that small town.

My time of this writing, the federal government has announced a 6 p.m.,
March 8, 1973, deadline for Indians at Wounded Knee to surrender or face

police and military action to "arrest" them. The United States has claimed that it "has gone as far as it could go" to negotiate a settlement, but could not meet an "impossible demand" that the Department of the Interior suspend two of its BIA officials, Aberdeen Area Office Director Wyman Balby and Agency Superintendent or Police Chief Stanley Lyman, and remove tribal chairman Richard Wilson from his office in the Oglalla Sioux government.

I urge this Committee to examine the FBI's experience in the maintenance or removal of Indian tribal governments. I appeal to this Committee for immediate examination of the FBI's relationship to the Oglalla Sioux people over the past five months—as well as those of other authorities and officials in the Justice and Interior Departments.

During the week of November 20, 1972, the United States Attorney and the FBI Office in Rapid City, South Dakota, refused to receive or act upon complaints and requests for assistance against actions of Chairman Richard Wilson and other Oglalla tribal authorities which were lodged by several tribal members, including tribal council Vice-Chairman David Long and Russell Means. They claimed violations of their legal and civil rights as well as continuing threats against their lives and personal safety. They and other tribal members were convinced by the Justice Department's attitudes and inaction that additional requests or complaints would be futile. Both Interior and Justice agencies refused to investigate complaints of violations of Title 18 of the US Code by tribal officials which were presented from a number of sources.

In my opinion, the deprivation of basic constitutional and human rights on the Pine Ridge Reservation is obvious. This Committee should be particularly concerned by the refusal of the Justice Department to give attention to such matters, inasmuch as these elementary rights were extended to Indian tribal members for protection against abuses of tribal governing authority only five years ago—after a near decade of persistent and conscientious work by the Honorable Senator Sam Ervin of this Committee in bringing about their enactment.

On November 22, 1972, I wrote separately to the President of the United States and to the Honorable Julia Butler Hansen, US Representative, to express my concern—upon learning that the Bureau of Indian Affairs was funneling generous amounts of new funds into the Pine Ridge Reservation to effect enforcement of these rights deprivations and denials and to equip Chairman Wilson with all the armed manpower he required to enforce his personal and court directed dictates, BIA Area Director Wyman Babby appeared to be the chief advocate of the increased spending for these purposes. Also in mid-November, Directory Babby had cut off disaster relief funds to Indians in Rapid City from a $120,000 BIA allocation for victims of the flooding in that City. My complaint to the President did not find routing to the Justice Department, but to Interior which merely affirmed that Pine Ridge and other reservations were being provided such funds. (Oddly, the President is requesting $800,000 in new funds in Fiscal Year 1974 for Interior to commit toward the "implementation" of the 1968 "Indian Bill of Rights." Federal actions on the Pine Ridge Reservation have been nothing less than a mockery of that measure.)

Mrs. Hansen responded to my letter and the general Indian situation by initiating requests by the House Appropriations Committee to its Surveys and Investigations Staff to undertake an exhaustive inquiry into such matters. The FBI on January 31, 1973, seized various of the materials that I was acting to provide that investigative unit of the House at the time I was arrested. Those documents remain in the possession of the FBI—as do keys to my apartment, a typewriter belonging to my organization (SAIA), and apparently (2) movie films belonging to organizations in the State of Washington and which are both produced between 1968 and 1971, one by myself.

Mr. Chairman: I respectfully request that this portion of my statement be accepted by the Committee at this time and that I be permitted to complete an additional statement for entry in the record relating more fully my reasons for opposing the confirmation of Mr. Gray to be FBI Director.

I would likely have completed my prepared statement on a more timely basis, or by now, but as I've indicated previously, Mr. Gray has my typewriter. There are a number of incidents which have occurred in my relationships and contacts with the FBI, which I think would be helpful to the deliberations of this Committee and the Senate in this matter.

I sincerely appreciate your every consideration.

Respectfully submitted,
Hank Adams,
SAIA

Testimonial

Hearings before the Subcommittee on Indian Affairs of the Committee on Interior and Insular Affairs. US Senate, Ninety-Fourth Congress, Second Session on S. 2801 "A bill to repeal the act terminating federal supervision over the property and members of the confederated tribes of Siletz Indians of Oregon (March 30 and 31, 1976)*
Statement of Hank Adams, National Director, Survival of American Indians Association

Mr. Adams. My name is Hank Adams and I am National Director of Survival of American Indians Association presently on leave and working with the task force for the American Indian Policy Review Commission.

Senator Hatfield. Could you speak a little louder, Mr. Adams? Just put the microphone right up close.

Mr. Adams. In reviewing S. 2801, I again regard it necessary to point out an issue which I emphasized in an early February 1976 letter to Congressman AuCoin—which I believe weighs against inclusion of Oregon Fish and Wildlife Commission's proposed amendments to S. 2801.

This issue relates to Indian persons, who except for their termination as Siletz Indians, are presently members of, or eligible for membership in other Indian treaty tribes which have never been terminated.

Under the provisions of this bill, those persons are classified as members of the Siletz tribes, if their names appeared on the final Siletz termination rolls.

In my prior work with Indian persons in Oregon and Washington as national director of Survival of American Indians Association, I have been involved with terminated Siletz Indians who have attempted enrollment in other tribes for which they possess membership entitlements.

Particularly, I have worked with Siletz Indians who are eligible for membership in the Quinault, Chehalis, Nisqually, and Muckleshoot tribes—and under the Medicine Creek, Quinault and Point Elliott Treaties, each of which vest immemorial fishing treaty rights in these tribes and their members.

Now, in the past, these Washington tribes have acted affirmatively to enroll, or otherwise to adopt, these terminated Siletz Indians into their tribal membership on the basis that they were also bloodline Quinaults, Chehalis, Muckleshoot, or Nisqually Indians.

However, the Bureau of Indian Affairs has refused to recognize these Indians' status as tribal members or Indian persons, because of their Siletz termination status.

If the neutrality of this bill is abandoned, and the proposed Oregon Fish and Wildlife Commission amendment might be adopted, I can anticipate an

---

* Within two years, Congress enacted the Siletz Restoration Act, which was signed into law by President Jimmy Carter on November 18, 1977.—Ed.

explosion of new litigation which would involve treaty tribes of Washington State against the State of Oregon—and very likely the State of Washington against individual Indians, whose membership in other tribes would no longer be blocked in any manner by their former status as terminated Siletz Indians.

Under the proposed amendment and perhaps under the present language, Washington State could readily challenge the treaty rights of ever mixed-blood Quinault, Chehalis, Nisqually, Muckleshoot and other Washington Indian tribal member—who choose their membership in those tribes, but who also were once terminated Siletz Indians.

And that would be the end of my statement.

Senator Hatfield. Thank you very much, Mr. Adams. I don't think I have any questions of either one for you. I appreciate your being here very much and your contribution to our hearing.

Essay

Indian Self-Rule: First-Hand Accounts of Indian-White Relations from Roosevelt to Reagan
Kenneth R. Philp, ed. (Salt Lake City, UT: Howe Brothers, 1986)
From the section "Activism and Red Power"

The central promises of the Indian Reorganization Act, as stated by John Collier in 1934, were complete economic independence and self-determination for Indian tribes. A half century later, Indian people remain far removed from either goal. One of the basic reasons is that we have never been talking about self-determination, but about self-administration.

As I look back at John Collier's writing, I find that his intent in the Indian Reorganization Act was to provide a mechanism for indirect administration of federal policies and programs. In the last fifty years, an unbelievable number of different policy proposals and policy objectives have been "self" hyphenated. The goal of termination was self-sufficiency. It sounded similar to John Collier's self-rule. In the last month, one of the members of the Indian Affairs Committee stated that he was going to continue his fight against Indian treaties because they violated his concepts for self-fulfillment. In recent years I have almost come to believe that it does not matter what the particulars of details of a policy are so long as you do not divest the Indian leadership of their capacity for self-congratulations.

How far have we fallen from that day in 1830 when Blackhawk was taken prisoner in chains to Washington, DC, to see President Andrew Jackson? Blackhawk told Jackson, "Even in chains, sir, I am your equal." Indians have fallen very far from that day. If there would be a return to the introspective capacities that Indian people possess in analyzing problems, there also would be a return to some measure of respect. That is really essential to have before you ever achieve self-rule, self-government, and something other than self-administration.

When you realize what the good guys have done to Indian people, then you cannot accept the way things are now and how things are moving toward the future. President Dwight D. Eisenhower has been held accountable for carrying out the termination policy, but termination was well under way before Eisenhower entered office. In 1949, the Interior Department met with its created organ, the National Congress of American Indians, to ask it to take the lead in planning termination. The NCAI, at that time, did not object to this request. The lawyers for the NCAI helped write up some of the termination bills.

The Menominee first wrote a termination bill in 1947. They consented to it at a rapid hearing schedule in 1954, when some two dozen tribes and several states were subject to termination. At that point, lawyers led the Menominee toward termination. They did not object until later when there were slight modifications in that termination bill.

I have read in a number of publications that termination ended in 1958. Termination was going strong in the 1960s under Philleo Nash, James Officer, Stewart Udall, and President John F. Kennedy. Another hated policy is the Relocation-Vocational Training Act. Relocation started in 1948 under President Harry S. Truman. It was expanded into a national program in 1950 and received its first statutory authority in 1956.

When James Officer's task force went around the country and met with Indians, it found out how much this program was hated. So the task force decided that the name of the program should be changed to Employment Assistance. Today, you can hear Indian leaders condemn the relocation policy of the 1950s under Dwight Eisenhower. But in the 1964 Democratic platform, it was proudly proclaimed that the Kennedy and Johnson administrations had doubled the enrollment in the program. Indian leaders did not object because it was call Employment Assistance. Commissioner Philleo Nash, the champion of many Indians, had the authority to stop Menominee termination when he came into office in 1961. But he did not do that until 1964 when a majority of Menominee submitted a petition against this policy to the government of the United States. In 1962 and 1963, both Philleo Nash and James Officer threatened to administratively terminate tribes in the state of Washington. And the Congress of the United States threatened to terminate every tribe that submitted a claims judgement distribution bill in 1965. It took some behind the scenes maneuvering to stop termination from being re-instituted more aggressively than it had been carried out in the 1950s.

Congressional termination ended in March 1965, when Melvin Laird, a conservative Republican from Wisconsin, and Congresswoman Julie Butler Hansen made strong floor speeches in the House of Representatives. They condemned this policy, not only for the Menominee, but for all Indians. They also worked behind the scenes to prevent the Senate from re-instituting this policy.

In 1966, Interior Secretary Stewart Udall and Commissioner Robert Bennett threatened termination in a confrontation with the NCAI at Santa Fe. It took two more years before Lyndon Johnson issued a presidential message against termination. Beyond that, Indian tribes such as the Colville supported termination.

President Richard M. Nixon proclaimed the policy of self-determination on July 8, 1970. Most of the measures that were proposed in the Nixon message grew out of the work that had already been underway through the National Council on Indian Opportunity and various Indian organizations. The good guys in the BIA created the National Tribal Chairmen's Association (NTCA). They decided that the NTCA would have ten people on its board of directors. The three members of the executive board were supposed to be the voice of the Indian people. Now that is not self-determination when you are talking about several hundred tribes.

The Nixon administration had already committed itself in favor of the

Indian Financing Act and the Self-Determination Act. So, why did they need the NTCA? One reason was that they were trying to consolidate a force against commitment to urban Indians. The Nixon administration also used the NTCA to demand an assault on the eight hundred Indians who had occupied the BIA building.

The NTCA requested a police action to "take those people out" of the BIA building. They meant to kill them, because members of the American Indian Movement and other activists were in there. Some of the good guys such as Ernie Stevens, Sandy McNabb, LaDonna Harris, and Louis Bruce were even talking about assaulting the building.

John Collier's philosophy was that all power flows to organization. He had a philosophy that the common people, the unwashed people, should look to the experts and enlist their help and assistance. One of the most scandalous things that the experts have done for Indian people in the twentieth century is the claims policy. At first, the NCAI was organized to make the IRA applicable to all tribes, even those who had rejected it. It also had a second goal: to get behind the passage of an Indian Claims Commission Act that Collier had been pushing. On October 30, 1978, the Indian Claims Commission, in its final report, stated that its problem had been a matter of giving the Indian his due while at the same time serving federal relations.

The discussion of Red Power surfaced in the 1930s when John Collier used it to subjugate Indian people. Red Power as a form of activism, was not something that the National Indian Youth Council originated in the 1960s. Every generation of Indian people has fought valiantly against what has been happening to them.

Media, Literature, and Scholarship

One of the most striking and innovative skills Hank Adams has long possessed is a deep understanding and ability to engage the broader world of the media and to effectively marshal its vast resources to facilitate positive policy changes, to end abuses, and to help shift public opinion. This was evident very early, when he wrote a number of erudite editorials for the National Indian Youth Council's newsletter and in the manner in which he strategically enlisted the aid of Hollywood personalities like Marlon Brando, Dick Gregory, and Jane Fonda to aid in the fishing rights efforts.

He also was involved, as one sees in his correspondence with Brando and others, in the writing, editing, and critiquing of documentary and movie scripts that he believed might help educate the broader public and policy makers about the status, rights, and needs of indigenous peoples. And he used his sharp pen, trusty typewriter, and quiet voice to challenge mistakes and stereotypes that frequently appeared in newscasts and news columns.

One of the last entries in this section is his stunning and successful investigative expose of Gregory Markopulos, then operating under the name Jamake Highwater. This is a brilliant piece that shows how relentless Adams was in compiling the truthful data about Markopulos, who was at that time an extremely popular fraud who had manipulated the media and the American public for many years for personal gain and literary fame.

Article

July 27, 1964
"Washington Tribes and NIYC"
by Hank Adams
ABC—Americans Before Columbus

Past issues of *ABC* have related the essence of the steady attack against Indian fishing and treaty rights in Washington State.

Armed with new court decisions and laws of their own making, of the supreme court and legislature, the state had stepped up its efforts to completely abrogate Indian treaty rights.

Tribes Face Odds

The tribes have faced tremendous odds in this ceaseless battle. In addition to the machinery of state government, the news media had been attempting to write the Indians' obituary daily.

Past years have seen the newspapers filled with the propaganda of the State's Department of Game and Fisheries in their effort to brand the Indians as deflators of the salmon runs.

Guided by so-called sports fishermen groups—who have pressured the state, the press, and the politicians with fierce demanding—the drive to completely halt Indian fishing moved closer to success.

And the Indian people? What was our strategy? How were we meeting the threats to our families' livelihood? Threats to our existence as Indian people?

For the most part, no strategy existed.

At best, individual tribes established their own lines of defense for their own tribe only.

Usually, however, a defense was made only by individual Indians who had been challenged directly by arrest or general harassment.

No Defense Made

Frequently, unfortunately, no defense was made—the consequence being that entire rivers were surrendered, in some cases, and entire tribes withdrew from their aboriginally-derived and treaty-protected fishing grounds.

In some sense, the lack of Indian action was understandable.

Many of the smaller tribes derive their only income from taxes on the fishery resource. And the livelihood of many Indian families are wholly dependent upon fishing income.

Therefore, a number of small tribes just could not afford to defend their rights—or uncertain of their rights, not sure that it would be worth it—neither could they secure the aid of other larger tribes, nor adequate voluntary legal aid.

But the saddest situation involved those tribes who thought, and think they would not be seen, that their lands and fisheries would be overlooked, if they jumped on the state-sports-fishermen bandwagon.

Actually, these tribes practiced concession for themselves and betrayal of other tribes—actually supporting nothing or no one.

Makah Are Exception

The Makah Tribe, plus a few others, stood as an exception to these general descriptions. This tribe was concerned with every threat, every infringement upon Indian rights, regardless of the tribes directly involved.

It was their victory in reasserting their rights on the Hoko River—in a court case spanning the 1930's—that had again asserted all tribes' rights for full utilization of their off-reservation usual-and-accustomed fisheries. For many tribes, these are the most important fisheries; for some tribes, the only fisheries.

Therefore, every state success was erasing the earlier court victories of the Makahs and other tribes.

Years—decades—centuries—of ceaseless battle and protection of their rights—their way of life and living—has not lessened the Makah's determination to continue fighting as long as necessary.

In January, their tribal council committed themselves to renewed action.

Their tribal chairman, Quentin Markishtum, realizing the magnitude of the battle, depicted the spirit of his tribe and the coming campaign in his statement, "We are going to fight this to the end! If we can't get the support of the other tribes—then, we'll fight it alone!"

The Makah Tribe, then requested the National Indian Youth Council (NIYC), as represented by Executive Secretary Bruce Wilkie and Hank Adams, to lend whatever assistance possible to further the Indian cause, and to protect the Indian rights.

Immediately, NIYC and the Makahs began mapping plans and strategy for the campaign.

Every tribal council in the state was contacted, and a meeting scheduled for February 15, in Seattle, Washington.

The response was overwhelming—the results historic! From more than fifty tribes in the state, representatives from forty-seven attended the meeting.

Marceline Kevis, NCAI Area Vice President represented the National Congress of American Indians (NCAI).

Also represented were the Washington State Indian Council Inc., the Northwest Affiliated Tribes, the Inter-Tribal Council of Western Washington, and the National Indian Youth Council.

Each tribe gave general and detailed accounts of the attacks and encroachments upon their rights and lives.

A press conference was arranged—the first one conducted at a meeting of Washington State Tribes.

Covered by three network stations, and major newspapers, a large portion of the public began hearing the Indian viewpoints and arguments for the first time.

Council Gives Aid

The results of the meeting were heartening to the Indian people throughout the state. Forty-seven tribes had pledged themselves to a unified fight against loss of rights retained by them in treaties with the United States.

As a part of the joint effort, it was decided that a "Campaign of Public Awareness" would be undertaken. The mechanics of this campaign were delegated to the Makah Tribe and the NIYC to determine.

The NIYC agreed to handle public relations and publicity, and to help coordinate activities and arrangements of the campaign. Various details, information, and facts were released at a press conference on February 24, 1964. The following position statement was included: "At 11 A.M., March 3rd, delegates from Indian tribes throughout the state will meet with Governor Rosellini in Olympia.

We will present him with a proclamation of protest regarding the violations of our treaties and other agreements with the United States.

Indians from throughout the state shall attend the presentation.

The presentation will be conducted in such a manner as to insure that the great pride and dignity of the Indian people shall be upheld.

Indians throughout the nation will conduct activities on their support for our endeavor.

A number of national Indian leaders shall be present in Olympia, as will a number of internationally known personalities who have become aware of the Indians' situation in the State of Washington.

It is for the purpose of making our position known, and for dispelling widely-spread misinformation and prevalent misconceptions about our tribes and people that we have arranged this meeting with the Governor.

It is the fist major step in our 'Campaign of Awareness.' This program was initiated by the Indian Tribes of this state, and will be carried out by us in a united effort.

It will be conducted under the banner of truth.

We consider it highly unjust that our country's duty and consequent power, to protect Indian treaty rights is too often measured only by our own expenses with complacency and indifference as a measure of the part played by our nation.

We have tried to resolve these differences through proper channels—winning cases in the higher courts, but losing in the lower ones.

We have depended heavily upon the "Good Faith" of our nation, only to experience favorable federal court decisions falling upon deaf ears in state courts, when Indian treaties are at issue.

We can no longer bear the strain and burden imposed upon us by 'Broken Promises.' We are keeping our part of the bargain. Now it is time for our country to uphold its end!

Our treaties with the United States were made in 1854, 1855, and 1856. No question about antiquity for them exists in the minds of the Indian people. These treaties were made with a view toward the future, and the spirit of the treaties is alive on the reservations today.

We must protest the utter disregard and unjust denial of rights retained in our treaties! These rights, that were exercised freely by our ancestors, are the mainstay of our livelihood today. They have been the essence of our survival since time immemorial.

However, it is with regard to the future that we believe it necessary to protect our treaties and preserve our rights.

As an investment in the future, Indian tribes have always been advocates and employers of conservation practices. To conserve our fish, we believe that we must first protect our streams and waterways.

We deplore the laxity of state agencies in not taking effective measure to control destructive, yet unnecessary pollution: to control improper logging and other commercial operations that clog or severely damage river beds; to protect the watersheds; to provide adequate passageways past dams; nor to regulate modern fishing equipment, such as electronic devices, which virtually allow entire schools of salmon to be caught.

In the pretense of conservation, however, the state is trampling on sovereign treaties!

It is ironic that the "original conservationists"—who practiced conservation as a way of life, long before there existed a State of Washington, or its Dept. of Fisheries, or Dept. of Game—should be made the scapegoat of a few militant non-Indian citizens who misinform the public and, as a result, deprive a people of a livelihood!

We have no other choice now, but to take our problem directly to the Governor of the State of Washington, the citizens, and the nation!

We are confident that we have the best wishes of all citizens who believe in the 'Good Faith' of our nation, and will be joined by those who are able to do so, as we congregate at the State Capitol in protest of the violations of the Supreme Law of the Land.

Meet with Governor

The initial arrangement for the meeting with the Governor had already been made, and his office has a clear understanding of its nature.

The tribal officials were meeting with Governor Rosellini as representatives of sovereign nations, no less than his equal.

It was the first time since the negotiation of the treaties with the United States that the tribes stood with such stature.

Although a protest meeting, it was also designed to be a major step in the Indians' "Campaign of Awareness." Therefore, a highly formalized and programmed schedule of Indian and non-Indian speakers was devised.

All Indian people in the state were invited for the purpose of showing a personalized vote of confidence in their leaders and support for the Indian position.

Realizing that a campaign of awareness can be successful only if conducted before the public eye, the public was invited also. These arrangements having been made, other plans for the "awareness campaign" were made.

NIYC President Mel Thom; Executive Board of Directors Clyde Warrior, Karen Rickard, Gerald Brown, John R. Winchester, and Shirley Witt; plus NIYC Executive Director Herb Blatchford arrived in Olympia to aid in the effort.

Marlon Brando was invited for the purpose of drawing national attention to the campaign, and for attracting closer coverage by the news media.

Other prominent Indians and non-Indians came from out-of-state to witness the event and to become informed about the issues.

In order to assert Indian fishing rights and to dramatize and draw national attention to the fishing issues, a series of fish-ins (as they were termed by the press) were conducted at the request of several Tribes.

On March 2, Marlon Brando, Bob Satiacum (Puyallup), and Canon John Yaryan of the Grace Cathedral Episcopal Church in San Francisco drifted the Puyallup River and caught two Steelhead—as scores of Indians cheered them from the bank, and many non-Indians looked on. Brando and Canon Yaryan were promptly arrested by the state, but later released without charge—in an obvious attempt to minimize national coverage and attention.

Another fish-in was conducted on Wednesday, March 4th, by members of the Quileute Tribe, Brando, and members of NIYC. No arrests were made on this occasion. However, at the same time on the Nisqually River, six Indian fishermen were arrested for fishing and sent to jail for thirty days for fishing in violation of a restricting order, and violating the terms of a suspension of sentence on contempt charges.

Present Issues

The mass protest meeting in Olympia was the major activity, however. With more than a thousand Indian people looking on and as many non-Indians, Indian spokesmen and our guests made a clear and impelling presentation of the Indian cause and issues.

Dancers and singers from the Makah and other tribes initiated the occasions with dances and songs emphasizing the Indians' attachment and closeness to nature.

Prior to the meeting and afterwards, Governor Rosellini invited members of the NIYC, and the representatives of tribes to engage in discussion and consultation on the issues involved and other problems. Whereas, we had originally been allocated an hour in the Governor's schedule because of his other commitments, we resulted in utilizing more than four and one-half hours to present our viewpoints.

What is significant is that we proposed a very positive and constructive approach to the solution of the various problems and issues with which we were involved.

Our proposals included a demand for a moratorium on the arrests of Indians fishing in their usual and accustomed fishing grounds; the initiation of a joint federal, state and Indian study of Washington rivers to determine actual causes of depletion, and for establishing a realistic program of salmon resource rejuvenation; the setting up of an Indian advisory board to the Governor; a program of public information on Indian problems; and the repeal of a 1953 legislative law which extended partial state jurisdiction over Indian reservations.

Governor Rosellini agreed to establish the advisory board, and promised that the sovereignty of tribes would be protected as long as he is in office— but for the most part, the demands were not met.

Editorial

1972

"A Legacy of Richard Oakes: His Spirit Remains"

The death of Richard Oakes (Mohawk) provides emphatic proof there has been no ebb in the sickness and sea of violence which White America has maintained against Indian people throughout its history to sweep away the lives of our nameless and our renowned.

The flood tide of Indian deaths and murders has swept unabated throughout all the states—repeatedly in California, New York, New Mexico, Arizona, Pennsylvania, Nebraska, South Dakota, Montana, Minnesota, and Washington—and beyond these borders in Canada, Mexico and Brazil, to cover the full expanse and breadth of the Native American continents. But in the United States, the record of late is most foul and savage.

The pastime of killing Indians has not been surrendered from the self-esteemed "pioneer spirit" of White America in the 1970's. Both policemen and private citizens, as vigilantes and as hunters, recognize no sanctions against stalking Indians and shooting them for any cause and on any occasion.

A notable national sentiment in favor of capital punishment is abandoned in favor of no punishments and no penalties when an Indian is shot by a white man. Minor charges may be brought to mitigate against the possibilities of public controversy, but the penalties fall when the charges fail to a complete defense afforded by any reason offered for the assaults and the shootings. We are now protected by a standard of "justice" whereby any reason becomes sufficient cause for the killing of an Indian.

Already the public mind is being conditioned to justify the slaying of Richard Oakes: the "ending of his stormy career"; "horse thievery"; "Indian"; "Alcatraz invader"—indiscriminately attaching unrelated facts and misleading assumptions to the justification for his murder, and for the release of his murderer.

If Richard Oakes is only to be publicly identified with Alcatraz to the public by news media, then let the public remember that Alcatraz was instrumental in placing the needs and concerns of Indian people upon the national agenda. Remember that, despite its own failure in claims, Alcatraz had direct and powerful bearing upon the final results in settlement of claims with Alaska Natives, in return of Blue Lake to Taos Pueblo, Mt. Adams to the Yakimas; the establishment of Deganawide-Quetzalcoatl University (DQU) in Davis, Calif., and the Seattle Indian involvement in the President's "Legacy of Parks" decision at Ft. Lawton, Wash.

For Indians, Alcatraz was never meant for confinement of people or of purposes, nor to constrain the ideas or dreams of any. Its impact has been felt elsewhere.

Richard Oakes' presence beyond Alcatraz and his influence upon many

Indian people shall continue to live within the body and soul of Indian experience. Born to the American soil, and responding strongly to his peoples' struggle and suffering upon it, the living spirit of Richard Oakes could not now die nor cease to be remembered upon Indian land.

Neither elegy nor eulogy can satisfy his life or death. But both can be looked to for generating within this land of legacy of protection for Indian people throughout it, a simple legacy promised Indian people during the infancy of the United States—when assuming dominion over our separate Nations, and promised again and again with each succeeding treaty.

Can fifty states and 225,000,000 people now shield themselves from their own obligations under their Constitution and their treaty contracts to deny Indian people the protections due them—or to allow their violation within any of the fifty states and by any of the more than 225,000,000 non-Indian people? They can; it is obvious, because they have done it. The question is simply whether the United States and its citizens shall continue doing so.

We are committed that such legacy of protection shall immediately find life within the public policy of the American nation.

We shall call upon the Congress and upon the President to invoke their authority to provide national protections be directed enforcement within the federal judiciary of newly defined felony offenses committed against Indian persons, wherever they might be within the territory fo the United States, and to create a permanent investigative body to assist in the prosecution of such criminal offenses upon occurrence, allegation, or request.

Certainly the President and the Congress can embrace and proclaim an enforceable policy in support of a "Legacy of Protection for Indian People" as proudly as any other "legacy" programs which might be conceived.

It would be in service of the "Tanyas of the World" by helping to initiate a standard for their protection. It would be a good first step in carrying the meaning of the phrase "Never Again" beyond the slogan of partisan causes and killing campaigns toward a universal commitment to "Never Again."

It can do nothing now for Richard Oakes. But he is survived by his family and his people—and we remain in as much need of that legacy as was Richard.

Memorandum

January 20, 1974
To: Abbie Mann, Vine Deloria, Marlon Brando, John Foreman
From: Hank Adams
Re: Possible Storylines for Movie

(Attached are excerpts from Indian statements issued in the past couple years, primarily relating to the Trail of Broken Treaties Caravan and Wounded Knee or both. The November 3rd, 1972, statement among Indian people within the BIA Building in DC is perhaps the most closely expressive of the attitude toward an integration, or unified relationship, of history and contemporary and personal experience, which I attempted to communicate last Monday in support of presenting an 'Apache Chronicle' from the perspective of a credible contemporary Front Story.)

I think an artistic and dramatically successful movie can be put together, virtually carrying the 'Apache Chronicle' from time of tribal or Apache Indian creation to a contemporary period, cohesively and comprehensibly.

Here at Franks Landing, for instance, where the oldest and youngest Nisqually Indians (four generations, spanning 1879 to 1974) live, Grandpa relates much of the Nisqually history before his time as if it were personal experience, and in, a real sense it is. And as he shares that experience, knowledge and beliefs, with his children, grandchildren and great-grandchildren, it becomes part of their bearing and personal experience. And many tribes retain concept and belief of their people's own creation, which continue to be considered valid in their minds and emotions—and which is not regarded as too temporally remote to have influence or impact on their spiritual or human relationships to the living universe.

The storyline I suggest could give continuity to Apache life from the creation to the contemporary, and rely on a contemporary human story to give cause to examine or review the past and history of white and Apache relations, and relate some of it from point of initial contacts.

My own conception would be to begin the movie with some visual representation of some version of Apache creation, without dialogue or narration, and brief, followed in fade away or transfer to the contemporary story. Reference to creation and the scenes depicting it could be made when the movie returns to relating the experiences of first white contacts, developing relationship to horses, etc., (Providing Apache beliefs or historical fact supports the supposition). Common territory and sites would give background or continuity to development of Apache life between creation and first white contact.

For the contemporary story, I propose a 1969–1970 time period centered upon a single Apache family, having ties perhaps to several of the separate Apache groups (through marriages or relations). There are two sons, having about ten years age difference (twenty and thirty), and at least a couple of sisters between twenty-one and twenty-six. The father died sometime in the early 1950s, and had been recognized among Apaches as a World War II hero (he'd suffered several serious wounds, received Purple Hearts and other medals). The mother, about age forty-seven, survives. One paternal grandmother still lives, as does a maternal great-grandfather (the mother's grandfather), at least in his late eighties, perhaps nearing 100, but able to get around himself fairly well and retaining clarity of thought, reason, and memory, while showing advanced age in appearance, voice, and some mannerisms.

The two sons have grown up with slightly different experiences. The older one was close to his father after the War until his death when that son was entering his teen years. The younger son was still a young child when the father dies. The family lived off-reservation during the War years in a medium sized town, while the father was gone, and when the mother worked in some small industry. After the War, they continued to live there for a few years since the father found a good job in the town. He lost his job about the time the mother was pregnant with the youngest son, and so they returned to the reservation where he was born. (The grandparents had never left the reservation). When the father died a couple years later, the mother got a job at a local restaurant or trading post; leaving much of the care and rearing of the younger children to various grandparents.

The older son (A) had his first contacts with white people as a child off-reservation. It wasn't a bad experience to him; he remembers being popular with the white kids from about the time he was starting or ready to start school—about the time his father came home from the War. He's never been unpopular from the time he was able to bring white kids in from all around the neighborhood to see his dad's war wounds—which the father displayed only because of his son's innocent insistence—or to be told about wounds which couldn't be seen. (A) attended high school away from home in a BIA boarding school. While in attendance, he regarded it as an earthly hell; but when coming home for summer and vacations, he related his experiences much like his father's War adventures and undefined heroism. After almost two years home on the reservation after graduation, where he tended toward harmless delinquency, he left for Dallas on a BIA vocational training program. In Dallas in 1963, he was drafted into the US Army and was routed to the infantry. In 1965, he reenlisted for a four-year tour as a paratrooper. Inevitably, he was assigned to combat in South Vietnam—and being gung-ho and Super GI Joe volunteered for three consecutive duty tours in the 'Nam.

The story picks up with (A) arriving home after discharge from the Army, and with community ceremonial awaiting to honor him (and perhaps other Indian soldiers on leave or returning home). His separation and mustering out pay is sufficient to last him the several months before he has to decide whether he shall re-enlist again—and receive an astronomical re-enlistment bonus, which he would be paid for his re-up signature. It seems a strong likelihood, his mind virtually made up, but nonetheless wanting to take advantage of the time allowance in which he could maintain his eligibility for the bonus. As well, he wants to have some time to spend with his younger brother (B), who, his mother has written to him, has been drafted into the Army too and been scheduled for induction within a couple months.

(For Presentation's sake: (A) is Allen; (B) is Billy.)

Billy and a couple of Allen's friends, about Allen's age, pick him up at the airport. He's in uniform, totally conforming to regulations. Among the four, Billy is conspicuously different because of his long hair. Almost immediately in greeting, Allen jokingly remarks about his brother being a hippy, and periodically afterward, but immediately an obvious affection between the brothers becomes apparent, and conversation sporadically becomes direct between the two in nature to demonstrate a sincere and intense interest in one another. On the way home, a quick stop is made for a half case of cold beer, which the three older guys readily share in drinking, and which Allen sort of forces on Billy in celebration of the homecoming. Conversation runs to family, Vietnam, Allen's plans while home, girlfriends (and wives), Billy's induction into the Army and what the first GI haircut is going to do to his hippy hair, Allen's time before re-enlistment and the amount of his possible bonus, they need to come back to town to pick out a car which he can buy with the bonus or which he might pay down on with his separation pay and allowances, what he might want to buy members of his family as soon as he gets it, and the plans for the community ceremonial to welcome him home and to give thanks for his safe return from combat, with perhaps some light jokes about the Gold Star mothers of four wars or about the Indian Legionaries (American) or Veteran's of Foreign Wars (VFW) perhaps moderated in mention of Indians killed in Vietnam from the reservation.

Ultimately, Allen recognizes things he's failed or refused to see or consider before. He disclaims his military uniform, in recognizing that he has allowed himself to exist or become somewhat empty while the uniform became his identity. It was his badge of pride in life and in the community, more so than the Apache man within the uniform. He reaches his decision privately with mixed and real emotion, not in public show, and quietly pack away the uniform in a permanent place in his home. He's chosen against the re-up bonus and all it could buy of what he wanted; and implicitly against any future role in VFW or American Legion and the position or status they would hold for him in the community for perhaps twenty of his later years. He has reclaimed his own life and repatriated himself with the collective experience and future of the Apache people. To inform his family what he's decided, he probably first disappears into a bedroom with his mother for a private, undisclosed talk; when they emerge before other family members, he's fully composed and still strong, while his mother might silently show tears. Allen probably makes just a simple statement to the effect that he's decided to stand with his little brother among the Apache (or tribal group) and before (or against) this nation. The mother might partially embrace both and express pride in both her sons. Allen might suggest to Billy, who has never asked Allen not to re-enlist but only that he try to understand why he couldn't serve the USA, that they take off for Alcatraz.

Credibility: Various Indian actions (Wounded Knee, Trail of Broken Treaties Caravan, Custer SD, Scottsbluff, Fort Lawton, Puyallup Encampment, and Alcatraz) each had high numbers of Indian Vietnam veteran participants. At Wounded Knee, one of the first wounded by the government was the Vietnam veteran son of former tribal chairman Enos Poor Bear ("My son should get a medal for fighting for his own people here on the reservation.")

Military resistance by Indians have produced mixed courts martial and court results: Donald Bitsuie (Navajo), convicted of willful violation of draft laws, was sentenced to either two years in federal prison or five years residence on the Navajo Reservation, and given some time to make his crucial choice, by a federal judge in San Francisco. In some cases, Indian religion has been recognized as a basis for conscientious objection (a Minnesota Chippewa) and other times not (Mike McCloud, Umatilla; Richard Williams, Paiute from Battle Mountain, Nev., also losing a treaty issue). The Selective Service System at national and local levels agreed not to draft Puyallup Indians after that tribe enacted ordinance prohibiting it.

Sid Mills was wounded severely in Vietnam, and left the Army before his enlistment was up to fight for Indian treaty rights, and was one of three enlistees (not draftees) for which we secured summary discharges without penalty when they chose Indian people over Army service. In 1968, Richard Sohappy (Yakima), who did suffer three series of wounds during three consecutive combat duty tours in Vietnam, was arrested three consecutive times on the Columbia River for fishing while home on recuperative leave. He already had several high medals. After his first arrest, I visited him in jail to ask him to keep fishing while I flew to DC to secure certain legal assistance and action by the US. In the jail, as in Vietnam, he wore his dog tag, a bearclaw necklace, and a medicine bag. As a result of his assistance, we expedited the filing or effected the prosecution of *United States v. Oregon*—although he was convicted on his illegal fishing charges, by a part-time Justice of the Peace and full-time professional barber, who ruled that the Yakima Treaty did not protect his fishing activity. His plans, however, were for an Army career, and he returned to Vietnam. But the following June (1969), he fought with one of his cousins at home over political matters; the cousin died and Sohappy was charged and convicted of manslaughter, ending his military career as well.

The 1924 Indian Citizenship Act was enacted primarily as reward to the fact that Indians volunteered for World War I in proportionately greater numbers than any other racial class (including whites), although not then subject to draft. In World War II, Korea, and Vietnam, a disproportionately high number of Indians have been in the military service, again exceeding other races.

The military uniform has become the most prized identity of many Indian men, and VFW or American Legion Halls provided them to the memberships of which they are most proud. Many will use any excuse or occasion to again wear their uniform, no matter how out-of-place. In one recent wedding ceremony, announced to be an "Indian wedding" rather than white, the groom showed up in his US Marine dress uniform—and requested that everyone stand at attention later while he cut his wedding reception cake with his marine saber! And he was serious. When a male family member dies, it's not unusual for some sympathizer to arrive early and ask the inevitable question, "Is he eligible for full military honors?"

Conclusions & Comments:

I realize, of course, there are many storylines which might be tried and which undoubtedly could be better. I suggest one here partly for purpose of pushing ourselves toward development and selection of one.

I think the Apache historical content could be integrated easily and with relevance to the contemporary theme suggested, partly because of the military flavor and internal conflict. And that historical content, which would predominate the time of the movie, would necessarily have to be persuasive to the Indian film characters as well as to any audience. I believe we are committed toward producing something more than just 'a better western movie' or a 'better treatment of Indians' than previous films. That's why I favor an integration of past and present content; and perhaps why, if accepting that premise, I urge you all to come up with an even better idea.

You know, even after Alcatraz and after all those Indian men went to Vietnam for this country, and partly because of Indians' contemporary "popularity," there was published a children's book for mass distribution in an educational series, which demonstrates that good feeling toward Indians is not enough for creating even fair understanding. That educational book was about the proper names for the children of animals. Pictured along with the cub of bear, the fawn of doe and buck deer, was an Indian "papoose" with the parent "squaw" and brave. That's 1970!

The suggested contemporary theme, or some variation of it, is related in nature to the causes for Wounded Knee & TBT and other recent occurrences and the community and movement people involved in them. It operates toward their explanation and understanding—and is related to the theme of Indian unity and unifying of forces. (The sacrifice of the re-enlistment bonus in the suggested storyline can relate to a number of things, past and present. In 1969, with six-year's service going for ten years or even nine, I'm certain would have amounted to somewhere between $6,500 and $10,000, if not more. That's more than most Indians will ever receive from per capita distribution on claims for millions and millions of acres of land wrongly taken by the US, but which many families dream about finally receiving year after year. But rejecting that incentive, and all it would buy, becomes a declaration both that there will be no more 'Apache Scouts' and 'BIA, I'm Not Your Indian Anymore.')

This isn't a proposal for an esoteric movie of limited interest or comprehension. The dialogue of the principal characters would probably be less difficult and develop more naturally, while including essential content and statements, than peripheral members of the family and community. It is almost too easy to know what they would say in a variety of circumstances and scenes. It allows considerable range for different human emotions, and would naturally incorporate an appreciation of Indian humor and its different natural uses beyond 'jokes'; from wit and 'good time' humor to uses of the right words and expression at the right time to breach or alleviate real anger threatening harm.

There is little tranquility in Indian life at this time, but there are some realms of peace and many areas of promise. I think this can be simply shown; the present and past human condition of Indian people revealed and known; the complexities of personality and character of a Clyde Warrior or a Russ Means recognized and more readily understood; and our hopes and aspirations for our children removed from the toll of overwhelming white societal resistance.

Let me know your thinking.

Let's hear some other ideas.

Best wishes,
Hank

Letter

July 17, 1974
Mr. John Foreman
Columbia Pictures
Burbank, California 91505
Mr. Abby Mann
Encino, California
Mr. Marlon Brando
Papeete, Tahiti

Gentlemen:

Have read Abby's treatment several times. I am at once impressed, yet pervasively uncomfortable with certain aspects of it. None of my own misgivings present sufficient cause to deter proceeding as rapidly as possible with further preparations and production of the movie.

I've no problem with the fictionalizations or dramatizations of the non-Indian roles. Frankly, I would have preferred that the main living Indian personalities assume fictional names (presuming that is not intended). Either a partial or an indiscriminate merger of "invariable facts" of Wounded Knee with veritable fictions gives some dimension of artificiality to some attributes of several Indian characterizations. Passing the whole off as truth leaves me with some question of whether that is a good service to either the individuals or Indian people in general.

My overall reaction is, "What the hell. Let's get on with the movie and not get caught up in details or objections." The actual situation in South Dakota, as elsewhere, and what continues to happen to Indian people justifies any effective slant, the presenting and taking of "sides"; even justifies the adoption of self-serving stereotypes or evolution of better fictions. Selling the product through the packaging deserves the priority, and immediacy, and the content actually doesn't matter that much.

Reviewing Bob Burnette's *The Road to Wounded Kneee* and the Richard Erdoes' books, I find the same extravagant revisions of 'personal role and actions' and artifice of self-serving fictions that are evident in Abby's outline. Going to Stan Steiner's *New Indians*, Earl Shorris' *Death of the Great Spirit*, and Marion Gridley's *Contemporary American Indian Leaders* and *American Indian Women*, I'm reminded that any white person's favorite Indians can be contemporary Indian heroes or heroines if they are at all presentable between hard covers. Lives are rewritten to permit that possibility. If any personal contact with the Indian subjects occurs, the writer's own 'life' is transformed and personal outlook is fundamentally changed. After the transformation is proclaimed, it's easiest then to forget Indians (Shorris); go on to the revelations of new people subject matter (Steiner); or to stop bothering with Indians and just write the books about the good and great ones (Gridley). Burnette perhaps has to be admired for having escaped being at the mercy of independently whimsical writers. He has found what he considers the ideal subject matter—Burnette himself—and then enlisted successively better co-authors to treat the subject matter in the best possible light and perspective. As with the general new media, such past efforts, when successful, has allowed part of the general Indian population to suffer some temporary relief, while finding the great permanent problems and insufferable conditions unchanged.

Abby has indeed captured the ingredients for an extraordinary movie. The basic form and outline suggests promise of such a film. Nonetheless, there seems some failing in the sense of proportion which puts the ingredients together. The writer appears to have been overwhelmed by the Indians while fully confident of their possibilities as basis of a unique and successful story. In context, he is like Cavett with Brando in their dismal interview. There a grand opportunity for revelation and education, either about Marlon or Indians, was lost to Cavett's supposition that his mass audience was hungering for interesting or proactive tidbits, and that he (Cavett) being educated to both horseshit and human lives should focus on the rumor of the former and ignore the realities of the latter to tie his show together and satisfy his bored mass audience. How can you fail in an interview with America's greatest actor? By perceiving the superficial as the essence of the moment or the whole of the reality; by regarding that superficiality possessively as self-inspired insight; and by refusing to proceed beyond the interest of first impression or superficial perception. Can a Wounded Knee Indian movie fail? By standard tests, it won't. By higher standards, while publicly adjudged a success, it can fail.

One concern or question: What is the positive content or hopeful direction communicated by the film? That some Indian people have again reacted to their oppression; have non-collectively and deeply divided gotten up off America's rug and shouted, 'Stop screwing us!' 'Sometimes, anyhow!' We see the white rancher is both good and bad. We are disappointed that Charley Barban, not transformed but mind-fucked, will not be a constant or saving force for good in the end, and we seem to address the audience asking, 'What will you be in the future?' We even see that the cop-out feds are in possession of conscience, philosophic and non-compelling, but nonetheless a verbalized conscience. But what good or possibility of redemption do we view in the goon squads and Indian opposition? What is the cause for their confusions or the motivations for their simplistic cause on the other Indian firing lines? May no real Indian hero ever emerge from their ranks, or ever help lead the divided Indian ranks together? The movie treatment doesn't tell us, and it doesn't give them any chance for change. Are we content to believe that they can be 'good' like the Indians in Wounded Knee, and let it go at that? Or, are we missing a crucial part of the story by showing them simply as a gone-bad, bought-out dark side of Indian people which should not be revealed through any close-ups or development of character or statement of viewpoint? Do they stand and end solely as the enemies of the Indian future, deserving to go on eating their lard pancakes and potato soup, or are they as much a part of the answer and needed forces as we anticipate the movie audience in variant form will be in establishing change?

I've elaborated more than I had intended. Damn, I'm not asking for an esoteric movie and never wanted one. I understand the restructuring of time and events and sequence. To many of the Indian people who were in Wounded Knee and involved in its support on the periphery, I do believe there will arise a question, "Why didn't they do it honestly?" I will not be able to explain it, because I just don't know.

Respectfully yours,
Hank Adams, SAIA

Letter

January 8, 1975
Mr. Robert McDaniel,
United Press International
Olympia, Washington 98501
Attn: National Managing Editor, UPI (NYC)

Mr. McDaniel:

Honest errors in reporting can, generally, be readily excused and ignored. It appears that in your reportage of any items relating to Indians that you are wholly unwilling to make any concessions to honesty, even in error. I simply cannot understand the basis for your continuing deliberate, prejudicial distortion of news and facts relating to Indian people. What was the use of your seeking clarification of certain points on the 'Brando story,' if you were intending to report out your original misunderstandings?

You have several times apologized for the irrationally vicious attack on local fishing Indian tribes that you were expressing to a number of Indians in Washington, DC, and which occasioned our first meeting some seven or eight years ago (when I was called in to respond to you), as being a product of your overly drunkenness and temporary lapse of control and judgement. Obviously, you have continued to nurse your biases.

A reporter's 'making the story' by giving it his own clever, personably subjective, additions and slant, can have serious consequences, and constitute an abuse of press power.

A good example can be seen in a UPI reporter's contribution to the death of Dr. Martin Luther King. The Memphis UPI Bureau's national dispatch of a report that "when the trouble started, Dr. King disappeared and ran out on his people" was the direct cause for Dr. King's returning to Memphis in order to challenge and refute the lie. I read the article in LaPush WA, and in Forks saw the ridicule the report gave rise to. In meeting with Dr. King in Atlanta on April 1st and 2nd, 1968, the Memphis incident was explained, as was the necessity for Martin to revise his schedule and return to Memphis and counter the force of the unfounded UPI report.

Another reporter had just left an interview with myself in DC when the report of the Memphis shooting came in. He didn't file his story because he was dispatched to Memphis for a bigger one. With myself, he had attempted to get me to confirm his opinions of Dr. King as being "undemocratic, dictatorial, arrogant, and actually isolated from and uncaring of the masses of poor black people"—which I strenuously disagreed with. That reporter had the audacity several months later to belittle the Rev. Ralph Abernathy in a national magazine for failing to meet or possess the enumerated 'faultless' qualities and character of Dr. King as adjudged by the reporter. You remind me of that journalist.

There are a lot of good reporters, and I'm thankful that I've had opportunity to work with some of the best in the nation. Norman Kempster has advanced to that level. It's unfortunate that you have moved into his former office only to besmirch the trade and profession.

Hank Adams
SAIA

Op. Ed.

Seattle Post-Intelligencer
May 17, 1975
"Indian Voices"
By Hank Adams
Survival for American Indians

During a lengthy talk with Senator Edward M. Kennedy a few years ago, the Massachusetts Democrat began reciting the familiar phrases.

"The problem is that the Indian people have not come to us with unified positions," the Senator remarked. "If the Indians could only agree on what they want, then I'm certain the Congress would be willing to act and get something done."

I responded, "Senator, your own career and procession is based upon divisions of opinion among the state population you now represent. I have never understood why uniform or unanimous thought has always been expected or demanded of Indian people."

The exchange illustrates some general political and social problems which commonly have afflicted Indian communities.

For most of the past century, the US Congress has enacted its Indian legislation upon the principle that it possessed the unquestionable power to act in the manner of its choosing—irrespective of what was wanted or not wanted, advocated or opposed by Native Americans. Reliance upon the doctrine of arrogance has subsided only in the past decade.

The classic question, "Who speaks for Indians," usually is asked with anticipation that no acceptable answer can be given. It is a useful device for disregarding Indian voices and for failing to listen to or hear the expressions of competent native spokesmen and tribal representatives.

Near unanimity of majority Indian viewpoints frequently has been most obvious in instances when they were nonetheless ignored by the Congress.

Hated legislation of the past quarter century—which terminated Indian tribes; abrogated treaty provisions; nationalized lands and other economic resources, with either no compensations or unjust compensation; and transferred civil and criminal jurisdiction from the federal and tribal governments to various states—passed despite overwhelming objections from a justifiably fearful Indian population.

Personally, I've felt that too often there has been an almost disgusting lack of diverse opinions and political viewpoints within the respective tribes and general Indian community. I regard this condition also to be at fault or design of national policies and programming affecting Native Americans.

Individual freedom of thought and expression is essential to the dynamics of self-determination for any community. That vital freedom has been quieted or oppressed within many Indian tribes.

Traditionally, most Indian societies did value and encourage independent and creative individual thought, action, and expression. An inviolate sovereignty of the individual was recognized as a source of community strength and growth in harmony with the collective sovereignty of the tribe.

Federally-imposed governmental systems on most reservations have redefined "sovereignty" to promote total submission of Indian populations to the unrestrained powers of a few office holders, who might no longer be compelled to countenance or tolerate any dissent.

A commendable national policy of 'Indian Self-Determination' has been proclaimed by recent administrations. Unfortunately, the policy has been interpreted immaturely by federal officials to hold that tribal officials embody all Indian authority, and that the general Indian body politic, or populations, possesses none.

This reading has favored dictatorial rule by some tribal chairmen who are inclined to disregard the personal and political rights of tribal members. It has allowed tribal constitutions to be set aside or effectually trampled upon, controlling the actions of neither tribal nor federal officials.

Expressions of political dissent or opposition have been equated as criminal activities—and police agencies of both tribal and federal governments been mobilized to arrest or control it.

Results of the irresponsibility and abuses have ranged from the Nisqually Indian Community—where constitutional government and personal rights have been vacated—to the Pine Ridge Reservation of South Dakota, where domestic civil war is producing a homicide rate exceeding those of Detroit and Chicago.

Fortunately, many tribes have rejected, the sterile conditioning of uniform controlled political thought and have reverted to their former standards of tribal self-government.

Tribes like the Quinault, Puyallup, and Colville have recognized again that official position is but an instrument of service to their Indian communities. They do not fear new ideas and creative thought evolving among their own members, but invite their contribution to the good of the people.

Their governments have sent their elderly and their young students to Washington, DC, without reluctance of saying. "They speak for us and Indian aspirations." "They are proud to invite others into their school programs for their youngest Indian children—and don't want anyone to deny that they represent Indian people."

Poem

September 1982
The Death of Pain

un - re - spon - sive,
un - re - spon - sive,
it simply read,
like - a - heart beat,
like - a - heart beat,
the chart, lying on
an antiseptic
stainless steel or
aluminum table
and night stand with
folding wings or leaves,
traversed by tubes,
taking fluids,
from or to,
the body;
un - re - spon - sive;
un - re - spon - sive,
to stimulus
and pain.
Encephalography?
negative,
unresponsive to pain
stimuli;
Is this an Indian?
Dead.
Defined by an
absence of pain.
Oh, Life!
Oh, God!
Oh, Pain!
How Great Thou Art!
The Trinity
I have known
as One,
Hath left me together,
at once;
Dead.

Letter

November 22, 1982
Ms. Sandra Osawa,
Upstream Productions
Seattle, Washington 98125

Dear Sandy:

Your *Dakah* script is a magnificent work. Even in this first draft it qualifies as the best presentation of contemporary Indian life that I've seen written for movies or television.

Dakah is perhaps the first true expression of the internalized experiences which bring forth an independent Indian life or existence, within a modern context, that has been produced from within the Indian community by an Indian writer. Non-Indian writers routinely have failed to provide realistic depictions of Indian characters and reservation life; and, unfortunately, most Indian written scripts have followed the patterns established by white writers.

Your characters stand their own as Indians, at once intelligent human beings in diversity and in relation or in reaction to one another. Their humanity does not rely centrally upon being placed in a white milieu or in their being embraced by the hostile environment of the general society—to which, in the usual dramatic forms, they are obliged to always react, usually unnaturally, often comically or with a standard stupidity reflective of a progressive regression in intellect subsequent to birth. (One gets impression that such "Indian" characters must have been absolute geniuses while still in the womb. Nothing can arrest the ensuing intellectual devolution in the outer world—except, scripturally, the onset of a decrepit old age. The ancient "Indian" of film is spared senility and the class stupidity of his younger tribe and own earlier life; he acquires a miraculous beneficial utility in his dying years and words, damned simply with all the wisdom of the ages—too late to have done himself any good in his own life.) You do not prove the humanity, validity, or realities of your Indian characters by engaging in a reverse stereotypical disparagement or denial of the human and humane qualities of your non-Indian characters; and that is good, also, because it avoids artificial proofs.

Dakah can establish some new standards for realistic cinematic treatment of Indian people, experience and emotion. It will be a grave misfortune, a true injustice to a world audience seeking knowledge and understanding of American Indians and expecting emergence of honest and revealing portrayals from a maturing film industry, if *Dakah* does not succeed to production and completion. You have our solid support in this vital endeavor.

Most respectfully yours,
Hank Adams, SAIA

Letter

Mr. Marlon Brando
Beverly Hills, California 90210
Mr. Vine V. Deloria, Jr.,
Tucson, Arizona 85710

Dear Marlon & Vine:

Please read the enclosed first-draft script, *Dakah*, written by Sandy (Johnson) Osawa this October. It absolutely warrants movement into a film production—and, hopefully, will attract your active support toward that end. (I'm forwarding your support letters from SAIA and Russell Barsh to Sandy; plus my scathing review of a prior Osawa script undertaken by Sandy and myself for the former PBS *Vision* series at KCET initially in 1975, but worked on by Sandy periodically since.)

The main character, Dak (short for Dakah, which means "East Wind" in the Makah language), has reminiscent parallels to the life of Bruce Wilkie, which you will probably recognize. Clyde Warrior appears in the character, "Bill Dancer." Several other characters are based, undoubtedly, upon real life figures. (Dick Gregory, Jane Fonda, and Marlon Brando make brief appearances in the script.)

This project could be a real breakthrough for Indian script writers, but more importantly for Indian storylines or contemporary dramas about Indian life—which do not focus centrally upon Indian white conflicts, or find the hackneyed "conflict of cultures" as the only drama assignable to Indians. Most reservation Indians draw their character definitions from one another in the first instance. Like a tree crashing thunderously in the forest with no one there to hear it, Indians do live and exist even without the presence of white people there to affirm it. The human dramas among Indian people, thus, do not require a necessary white base or association to occur in their own right or being.

You both know that I've insistently opposed some fairly bad scripts about Indians—and even some marginally good ones marred by fundamental dishonesties. Although my judgement in those instances might even have been off-base—I'm totally confident in my judgement that Sandy's *Dakah* can be developed into an important and impressive film production which would be marketable, and well received by mass audiences.

Please, again, read it. And, call or write me with your own reviews or reactions. Best Wishes.

Respectfully yours,
Hank Adams, SAIA

Letter

October 12, 1983
Mr. Marlon Brando,
Beverly Hills, California

Dear Marlon:

I sincerely urge you to consider doing something to help Mike Lowry in his campaign for election to the US Senate, in the position formerly held by the late Senator Henry M. (Scoop) Jackson. Mike yesterday won an upset bid for the Democratic nomination, and will now face former Washington Governor Dan Evans in the special general election on November 8th. (Evans was appointed interim Senator.)

The enclosed *Wall Street Journal* and *Seattle Times* articles on the extensive national Indian budget cuts by the Reagan Administration emphasize the real need for both ousting Reagan next year, and for returning the US Senate to Democratic control. Beyond budget questions, the recent trends in the US Supreme Court on basic Indian issues, such as water rights adjudications, make it imperative that a new Administration be elected before Reagan has a chance to add any more Rehnquist-types to its numbers.

On the issues and in courage and character of heart, Mike Lowry is the one political figure in America who most closely approaches the Robert F. Kennedy of 1968. His personal philosophies and legislative actions and initiatives as a Congressman have been consistently aligned with the pursuits for "Peace, Jobs, and Freedom," given renewed emphasis by the Twentieth Anniversary of the 1963 March on Washington and Dr. Martin Luther King's "I Have A Dream" oration.

Mike entered Congress in 1979, by defeating the notorious Jack Cunningham, whose Indian treaty abrogation bills had prompted 1978's "The Longest Walk," initiated in California with Dennis Banks. In the Congress, Mike has formed coalitions to prevent passage of other anti-Indian measure under sponsorship of other Northwest congressmen—most notably in securing some seventeen proxy votes in merchant marine and Fisheries Committee actions to eliminate provisions for condemning and purchasing Indian fishing rights, while rewriting the measure into a pro-Indian law elevating tribes to a status equal with the States of Washington and Oregon. Ramona Bennett and I first started working with Mike when he was a key staff member in the Washington Legislature, where he mobilized leadership and member opposition to State bills, designed to impose taxes on tribes and Indians generally, and to restrict tribal revenue-producing trade. He would be an able advocate for Indian interests, and for protecting Indian rights, in the US Senate.

Mike believes that peace is the overriding issue of our time—along with justice and economic equity and opportunities for all people.

Mike has been a leading advocate for issuing a national apology and reasonable reparations for Japanese Americans who were interned in concentration camps during World War II—helping to bring the investigative commission into being, then sponsoring the bill in Congress which would effect the just outcome.

Mike is one of the original sponsors in the US House for a mutually verifiable freeze on nuclear armaments between the Soviet Union and United States and its allies (better known as the Kennedy-Hatfield Amendment, after its chief Senate sponsors); and opposes the Western European deployment of Pershing II Cruise Missiles, as well as funding for the first-strike MX missiles. He wants real arms reductions, not the heightened instability and global insecurity that his opponents are pushing through the jingoistic canard "Peace through Strength," or through the equally deceptive build-down build-up of destabilizing first-strike weaponry which would tighten both Soviet and American grips on hair-trigger "defenses."

Lowry proposes a new Central American policy for the United States, initiated by ending CIA covert war activities, in Nicaragua, and by exercising effective US influences for ending the slaughter of civilian populations by right-wing death squads from El Salvador through Guatemala. He speaks knowledgeably on the problems of that region, and has been there; and has correctly forecast developing difficulties in the Philippines, arising from this nation's willingness to trade off a historic relationship with the people of the Philippines—kept promises for independence, freedom and liberty—in exchange for the personal amity of the Shah-like, dictatorial regime of Ferdinand and Imelda Marcos.

In wanting "an American foreign policy our nation can be proud of," in brief, Mike wants a first reliance upon the powerful moral authority this country can exert by, first, keeping faith with its own democratic ideals in human rights and dignity, and reaching out with that moral authority to other peoples of the world—"who want to be our friends." He wants America to stop forcing its friends into the arms of its enemies; to give renewed strength to such agencies as the Peace Corps, while restricting the counter-productive destructiveness of a near-universally hated CIA.

In Mike, we can hear the voices of a Thomas Paine, a Thomas Jefferson, a James Madison, echoing across the ages in renewed pleas for the "rights of man," and womankind, and human dignity, world-wide. He knows the Constitution does not restrict the duties and responsibilities of the Congress of the United States to its "water's edge"; but rather vests it with the highest of duties in the maintenance of peace and favorable relations with other nations, and—wholly apart from its power for "declaring war"—is vested with obligations of "enforcing...the law of nations" upon ourselves as a nation as much as upon any other.

Domestically, Mike Lowry has gained support from a range of environmental, labor, women, racial minority, and other broad interest groups, not only because of his support for a majority of their positions—but mainly because of his effectiveness in advancing his positions and their causes. The last Democrat (with Al Swift) into the Washington congressional delegation, he quickly established a record and reputation as being its most effective, while remaining its most independent. Labor unions, environmentalists, and such organizations as the League of Women's Voters, have given him 100% correct voting ratings—but everyone knows that he is no one's captive. He earns respect because he works hard, learns and listens, and is willing to give leadership on issues. His able advocacy needs to be evaluated to the more powerful posture afforded by membership in the United States Senate.

He has fought Reaganomics from the outset, and has not abandoned that fight after others have shied away. He is one of the few who is offering realistic plans for attacking the burgeoning Reaga-Mega-Deficits which will choke the American economy for the rest of this century, if not curtailed, and which will be funded by increased deprivations to the poor and minority peoples of this country for more than another generation.

Marlon, Mike Lowry needs your help! He has an opportunity to advance the causes that you have worked on for more than a quarter-century; that the Ed Asner's, Jane Fonda's, Sally Struther's, Robert Redford's, Alan Alda's, Joan Baezes, Buffy St. Maries, Jerry Brown's, Tony Franciosa's, Tony Bennett's, Paul Newman's, Joann Woodward's, Jack Nicholson's—as well as the Russell Means,' Vine Deloria's, Darcy McNickle's—and other compatriots have devoted so much time and energy. He needs endorsement and fund-raising support.

I've given all my telephone money to his campaign—so you can't reach me by phone for a couple more months. But I do wish you would call Ramona Bennett, who's now working on social services programs (which Reaganomics has robbed of funding) at the Seattle Indian Center, and Ramona can tell you how important it is that Mike Lowry be elected to the Senate.

There's only about three weeks left for doing the things that need to be done for his campaign. Dan Evans has had no shortage of money support, since the Reagan Administration and its party and business support are so fully committed with their pocketbooks and treasury to hold onto this Senate seat for the Republicans, as an edge in controlling the US Senate for another five years.

I would hope you would consider a quick attempt at sponsoring a fundraiser or two for Mike Lowry in Los Angeles or elsewhere in California—and trying to call some of your friends for joining in that, or helping independently.

I respectfully ask you as well to call Mike Lowry at the Congress in Washington, DC, or at his Seattle headquarters, and talk to him personally about his candidacy for the United States Senate.

Please, Marlon, try to do something on this.

Best wishes as ever, I remain
Your elusive friend,
Hank Adams

Letter

April 11, 1984
The Honorable United States Attorney,
Office of the US Attorney,
Washington, DC 20001
Attn: Assistant Attorney General of the United States,
Criminal Division,
Washington, DC 20530
Re: "Jamake Highwater's" Multi-Million Dollar Fraud.

Dear Mr. US Attorney:

In little more, if not less, than a year's time during 1982 and 1983, "Jamake Highwater" has received more than $825,000.00 in grants and grant offers to his Primal Mind Foundation from the Corporation for Public Broadcasting (CPB) for the production of television programs and broadcast by the Public Broadcasting Service (PBS). The $600,000+ CPB grant offer made in the early days of the current Fiscal Year, conditions the federal funding on acquisition of a multiple amount from other sources, public and private. The effect, in this case, is to guarantee that an already intolerable fraud shall assume multi-million dollar dimensions!

I am referred to you, presumably, by US Senator Mark Andrews who, when this matter was addressed to his office, advised that it is a federal offense to "misrepresent any material fact in applying for federal grant" funds. "Jamake Highwater" has secured his CPB federal grants on basis of his false claim that (1) he is an "American Indian" (Blackfeet & Cherokee), and (2) that he is—by personal experience and advanced educational study—an "expert" on Native American cultures.

Mr. Highwater's major writing, a book titled *The Primal Mind: Vision & Reality in Indian America* (Harper & Row, 1981), became a subject for funding by CPB ($225,000) as a television production, which is completed and scheduled for broadcast via PBS on April 18, 1984, under "The Primal Mind" title.

On January 13, 1984, Mr. Ron Hull, Director, CPB Program Fund, responded to an acknowledged "challenge to Jamake Highwater's background" with a CPB letter, stating:

> Mr. Highwater has submitted to us a legal affidavit concerning this background that bears out his statements concerning his Indian heritage.

We have reviewed all the material that Mr. Highwater and the Primal Mind Foundation have submitted to us in support of the series proposal, and have no reason to believe that he has misrepresented himself in any way to the Corporation for Public Broadcasting.

One presumes that it was not "a legal affidavit," but rather the "extracts" from a purported affidavit which Mr. Highwater's attorney, Mr. Jonathan W. Lubell of New York City, has circulated in behalf of Mr. Highwater in support of his false claims. These "extracts" were taken from an Affidavit in the name of Marcia Marks and the extract notes: "Original Signed and Notarized 1974...."

The most significant information contained in the "Affidavit" is the statement of Marcia Marks, "foster mother of J. Marks," declaring that "... in 1947 my husband, Alexander Marks and I legally adopted Jamake Highwater, requesting that all records of the adoption be kept confidential. His name was legally change by this adoption to Marks."

It is significant because it would mean that, if an adoption, in fact, had taken place, there would be a legal record of that proceeding on file in some court somewhere. Without breaching "confidentiality" at least his attorneys could affirm and verify that an "adoption" had occurred—through a best evidence form—which should have been required by legal counsel for the CPB, rather than allowing CPB to be satisfied by an "affidavit" which is itself suspect, and which has an overriding design of furthering a fraud. Beyond the "Indian identity" support it contains, the "affidavit" also seeks to lend credence to a substantial "age change" for Mr. Highwater; and to "foster" an ostensible reason ("the adoption"), cloaked in "confidentiality," why the matter—reliant upon fraud and false statements—should not be inquired into further. The whole matter is absurd!

Under separate cover, I am forwarding a copy of my own study into the "true identity" of "Jamake Highwater," with its concordant study into the nature of his major "non-fiction" writings, relative to their purported "Indian content"—which, almost surprisingly, is virtually non-existent, except in the most meager and immaterial respects. (The study is in excess of 325 pages.)

With this letter, I am sending photographic evidence of Mr. Highwater's "identities," and other documents in evidence of his frauds and misrepresentations. (Unless he travels under his "true identity," there is a likelihood also that he has committed offenses with respect to passport applications and use. If his passport has been secured under his true identity, then it is all the more evident that his fraudulent applications for federal funding from CPB and PBS has been "willful and knowing" and in support of an "intent to deceive.") In addition, there is substantial evidence in the present custody of the United States Government relative to his "true identity" and frauds, which I would urgently suggest—because some may remain under his nominal control for removal—should be "secured" in an appropriate manner by your office. I will identify these later in this letter.

First, I would note that I had to attempt to discover whether "Jamake Highwater" was borrowing the "identity" of another person, and plagiarizing much of his "derivative" works—or whether two identities were being maintained by one person. It has proven to be the latter case, in effect, although it appears that "one person" has maintained additional identities as well—and very deliberately in "staggered simultaneity." The series of photos which I secured from throughout the United States also, at first, suggested that perhaps two different peoples were "switching" identities—but the final complement of photos, and some of the last received, showed that they readily could have been—and are—photos of a solitary person.

Persons who know "Jamake Highwater" in his "true identity"—some of whom themselves subsist on federal funding and operational grants from the National Endowment for the Arts—were uniformly unhelpful, except for maintaining a uniformly incredible "cover story" for him, and in supplying enough provably untruthful information that one could soon discount their attempts to mislead.

Second, "Jamake Highwater" has lived continuously under the successive identities of "J Marks" and "Jamake Highwater" for the past thirty (30) years. Although, as J Marks and Jamake Highwater he has hidden his "true identity"; he nonetheless has maintained his true identity at the same time, sometimes (1960–68) as a living present person—and elsewise as a person whose absence has been accounted for by various devices. In the *International* and *American Who's Who*, he lives under both his true identity and that of Jamake Highwater—one, an artist lost in Europe; the other, a very public figure in the United States.

The attached copy of birth certificate for George John Markopulos; dated birth, March 12, 1928, at Toledo, Ohio, is the birth certificate of Jamake Highwater. They are "one being."

Jamake Highwater is the eldest son of John Markopulos and Maria Paras Kavopulu, both of whom were born in Greece.

In the past decade, Gregory Markopulos has acted, or threatened legal action, to restrict availability of writing which discuss him—most notably the books of P. Adams Sitney; particularly *Visionary Film*, but also *Film Culture Reader*. These books, from 1974 and 1970 respectively, provide substantial evidence that "Jamake Highwater's" conceptualizations for his "primal mentality" found formation in the "culture" of "experimental film-makers," and, of course, that Jamake is Gregory Markopulos.

To preserve and protect his true identity, he has sought to totally restrict the availability and viewing of several films which might tend to identify him—particularly those in which he appears as Gregory Markopulos, film maker or protagonist, both in the 1940s and early 1950s, then finally in the mid-1960s; plus, those in which his voice provides the "soundtrack." In the 1980s, he has written to the Library of Congress for purposes of maintaining restrictions and personal control. One cannot know without seeing those films—which have received appreciable critical acclaim—if there is any identifying content.

The Maria Markopulos Film Collection of Gregory Markopulos works and writing—together with Markopulos' correspondence files with the

Library of Congress, which possesses them—should be secured against tampering or any destruction, and for any evidence of "identity" and "motive or intent" which the collection and the files may contain.

There is something wrong at PBS and CPB! It apparently requires criminal investigations as the remedy. I know that Jamake Highwater has absolutely no relationship in blood, upbringing or ancestry, to the Blackfeet, Piegan, or Blood Indians of Montana, Alberta, The United States, or Canada. Yet, as a "Native American," he has received substantially more funding and other available support from both PBS and CPB than any actual Native American who has been a funding applicant or recipient. The person who, perhaps and likely, has received the next most to Jamake Highwater (whatever the form or whoever the formal applicant) has been Chris Spotted Eagle, who, when I first met him nearly fifteen years ago in New York City while he was under another name, initially had made no pretension of "being Indian."

Notwithstanding the above, an executive program officer at CPB advised me that CPB, from a practical standpoint, had limited its funding support "to traditionalists" or "traditional Indians." A listing of Indian film makers was cited to me of those who had received CPB funding. I challenged that information on the basis of one film maker known to me, and asked the CPB representative to tell me when the particular film maker had received funds. The CPB officer then admitted that the particular Indian, a reputable professional film maker, had actually not received any program funds, but that CPB had "considered" funding "a couple" of that person's applications.

Another example of the absurdities prevailing in this matter is that officers and officials of the Bureau of Indian Affairs have invoked that agency's support in behalf of funding applications of Jamake Highwater to PBS (and CPB by virtue of repeated use of the BIA endorsements). One attached BIA letter stresses the federal "Indian Preference Act" in its support—and expounds upon the philosophy that it is time "Indians should speak for Indians."

My own first determination that Jamake Highwater was not what, nor who he claimed to be, came with my initial reading of articles about and by him—after being asked to look into the matter last September or October. The impossibilities in his claims were immediately obvious—and, because they were impossible, did not require being dis-affirmed. The "Indian childhood" he described could not have existed in time with time nor the world. A proof that he was not Blackfeet was evident in his repeated use of the term, "Blackfoot," as applied to himself and "his tribe." He predicates the entire myth of Jamake Highwater—his intellectual pursuits, his understanding, and his "very life and survival"—on his life-and-experiential response to a traumatic "mind-screw" as a child, when he is told that his favorite, "wonderful creature" was "called duck. 'Duck'?"—by a "white teacher" he acquired following the tragic death of his "father." This had totally shaken his world, supposedly, inasmuch as the Blackfeet have called this bird, "Meksikatsi," for "thousands of years"—its "ideal" and "perfect name," since the word meant, "bright pink-colored feet"; and "it really did have bright pink feet." The blatant incongruity of Highwater's repeated use of the erroneous and offensive term, "Blackfoot," was revealed in his proper recognition that "meksikatsi" would not translate perfectly nor ideally, much less descriptively, into "bright pink-colored foot!" In short, after several years as a "Blackfoot" and "Indian," Jamake Highwater had learned what the Blackfeet may call a duck—but he did not know, or carelessly forgot, what the Blackfeet call themselves.

Representatives of PBS have informed me that they and CPB lawyers have "investigated" this matter thoroughly and have no reason "not to believe" that "Jamake Highwater is an Indian." It's fairly obvious that they did not even need the "legal affidavit" to sustain their "belief" in the "impossible." They were fully prepared "to believe only what they want to believe," apparently. That affidavit satisfies "no standards" of "proof."

The amount of federal funds committed to this single individual, plus his partner in "The Primal Mind Foundation," in one year's time, exceeds considerably the approximate three-quarter of a million dollars the US Government is now demanding in repayment after expenditure in behalf of thousands of poverty-level minority citizens served by *Push for Excellence in Chicago*. I cannot understand how the US Government could, on the other hand, determine that no system of accountability exists for halting or redressing the fraud and the designed "mis-education" which Mr. Highwater is scheduled to perpetrate upon millions of American television viewers on April 18, 1984—courtesy of a quarter million federal dollars channeled through CPB and PBS; and which the January 13, 1984, letter of CPB Program Fund Director Ron Hull would indicate is but a preliminary to what is offered next: a multi-million dollar series fraud, perhaps already committed to contract.

I trust this matter will receive your consideration and sincere attention—and that any "investigations" which your office may undertake will not be of the same "mythical" character as the one alluded to by CPB and PBS.

Respectfully yours,
Hank Adams

P.S. Recognizing the unusual nature of the information and "incredible" assertions which, by their nature, invite doubt; I would suggest that you might want to contact the US Attorney for the Western District of Washington in Seattle, The Hon. Eugene Anderson, relative to my own credibility and reputation. His office can attest to my own credibility and reputation. His office can attest to my integrity as a researcher and analyst of documentary evidence in support of valid conclusions.

Trust, Land Issues, and Indian Claims

This triumvirate of interrelated issues have been and remain a constant focus for Hank Adams. It is in the retention and, in some cases, reclamation of aboriginal lands (and the resources appurtenant to those lands, waters, fish, timber, and so forth); the struggle to hold the federal and state governments accountable to historic diplomatic accords and specific and reserved rights retained in those accords; and the recognition of that vital force known as the trust doctrine—which generally means that the US has both legal and moral obligation to respect and protect the remaining rights, resources, and territories of Native nations—that Adams has labored tirelessly over the years.

The following selections vividly demonstrate how he has engaged these topics in a manner that has had lasting benefit for not only indigenous peoples, but also their treaty and trust partners, the federal government, and the states as well. In the process, we see Adams at his best when he is reminding the states of their limited rights in Indian Country, while at the same time showing the states and federal officials more just ways of dealing with aboriginal rights.

Testimonial

Hearing before the Subcommittee on Indian Affairs of the Committee on Interior and Insular Affairs. US Senate. Ninetieth Congress, First Session on S. 307. A Bill to Amend the Indian Claims Commission Act of 1946, as Amended (February 15, 1967)
Statement of Hank Adams, Member, Board of Directors, National Indian Youth Council

Mr. Adams. Mr. Chairman, my name is Hank Adams. I am a member of the board of directors of the National Indian Youth Council.

I respectfully request permission to offer this statement into the record of these hearing in behalf of the National Indian Youth Council (NIYC) and in support of extension of the life of the Indian Claims Commission for an indefinite period,* but with qualification relating to need for change in its operations and need for change in the policies which have applied to the disposition of awards.

Much has been said and written about the Claims Commission since its inception almost twenty years ago, which tend either to support or oppose it in nature and in purpose. Most have agreed that the Commission is preferable to individual authorizations by Congress to Indian tribes for bringing such suits against the United States.

But others, such as *Reader's Digest's* Blake Clark in the latter 1950's have maintained, in effect, that if the Indians should have material need, this Nation should respond to its own sense of morality and meet such need. But in no case should this nation subject itself to the humiliation of bringing forth the remnants of a defeated people to make judicial demand upon the public for wrongs inflicted by one's ancestors upon the other's. In this line, humiliation becomes a one-way street.

Others assert that the Indian is entitled to his day in court in any case, win or lose, because that is the American way. America sustained in principle, interest does not extend beyond expression. Whether America may die in process or resulting action is of little concern to the expressor.

Some are even surprised in learning that the Commission exists, such surprise having extended even to a former US Attorney General in learning that the Justice Department at that time had twenty-three lawyers hidden away in its bureaus, arduously working in defense of the United States in denying the skeletons in the country's closet.

---

* The I.C.C. was established by Congress in 1946, initially for a ten-year period, to hear what would eventually become hundreds of Native claims dating back to the 1800s for treaty violations, wrongful seizure of lands, failure to fulfill trust obligations, and the like. The commission's life was extended several times because of the adversarial and time-consuming manner in which the federal government adjudicated the claims. The I.C.C. was formally dissolved in 1978 and the remaining cases were transferred to the US Court of Claims.—Ed.

Then come forth the lawyers and law firms, asserting that no money can be had by working with the Indians, but that money is less scarce in working with the Government. Nominal retainers from tribes for incidental advices may be tolerated, if, at the end of the rainbow, lies the pot of gold. Not many make a million dollars in a single whack—but some do, and some several times over—but ten percent is a slim price for the expense of waiting, and smaller yet in having been the ones to tolerate the clients for the duration.

Additional are those who humorously note that "we're buying it back from the Indians." They become alarmed, however, in learning that if all judgments were sustained in the claimed amount, it would approach in total the several billions spent in all the years since 1813 on the contingencies of this Nation's "Indian policy."

The Commission has demonstrated the fallacy of such notion, however, and it sometimes becomes confusing as to who is paying whom. The United States trying to regain any portion of those past several billion that it might, the Indians find themselves paying for such items as education they did not receive, schools they do not then own, or lands they did not surrender.

The public should be aware that claims are no great boon to the Indians, and that the approximately $200 million awarded, thus far has been of benefit to a limited number of Indians. The public should be aware that an excessive percent of these awards go to a selected band of lawyers and law firms; in amount, equaling almost double the $12 million for which this nation saw fit to spend on community action programs nationally this year on Indian reservations.

On the other hand, many tribes will benefit more each year, financially, under the nation's War on Poverty, than they shall ever benefit from awards made through the Indian Claims Commission.

Perhaps the central issue involved in considering termination or extension of the life of the Commission is consideration of how Indians shall benefit from such awards and what these benefits shall be.

For some tribes claims judgments perhaps aren't too meaningful in amount. Yet, for some of them, as well as others, these awards can provide the only gleam of hope in a bleak future, as created and sustained by a bitter past.

But in practice, this hope has gone the way of prior hopes and previous destroyed dreams. Tribes have found too often that the award is there in name only—at best a bookkeeping device and at worst the price of what remains theirs in the way of resources, community life, land base, and federal services.

The Kalispels of eastern Washington State and Idaho may well have continued to survive on an average per capita income of $96 per year, had they not received a $2.7 million judgment. The Bureau of Indian Affairs then discovered there were Kalispel Indians, and a new tribal name began appearing in proceedings of this Senate committee. No program has been or was offered previously for these people from either source. The bureau learned that the

Kalispels could now afford to benefit, and the Senate subcommittee learned then that the Kalispels could now afford to be free.

Few people in America would permit themselves to be bought out with their own resources, but for the Indian it has come to be expected as a matter of course. And should the awards of the Indian Claims Commission continue to be used as the government's money, merely as supplemental appropriations to the BIA's budget, or even displacement, to sustain the proven failures, or failure-ridden programs, then perhaps the commission should be terminated.

Indians have been programed through a poverty program for the past 130 years, and the most obvious manifestation of this nation's efforts is that they have failed. Permit the Indian communities to now stand as Indian communities, in large part to plan for themselves, but also to take advantage of the genius this Nation could bring to bear on the many problems confronting us in a mutual-help effort at finding solutions. Utilize the Claims Commission that the Indian may benefit from this nation's strengths, and not forever be the lasting victim of its unwitting weaknesses.

Mr. Chairman, I would like to make a couple of statements on specific issues of the legislation.

Senator McGovern. We would appreciate having your statement.

Mr. Adams. First of all, we feel if there was any justification for having these claims entered against the United States in the first place, or that the United States agreed to consider them, they should not be dismissed without appropriate hearing and without some definite conclusion on an arbitrary date.

We see on the other hand, a need to expedite the action before the Claims Commission. We feel that it has been too slow perhaps, for understandable reasons in many cases, and in some cases not.

Senator McGovern. I am sure the members of this committee share your concern about protecting fully the interests of the Indian claimants. That is really the purpose, as I understand it, of this legislation. It is to see that these claims are not delayed interminably, that they are brought to trial and a judgment made, so that the Indians are not left waiting forever on claims that may have real validity.

Mr. Adams. Well, we think that there perhaps is need for some modification in functioning of the Claims Committee.

In consideration of them, we feel it is a very tough burden on a few men on the Commission, and that other means could be employed to perhaps speed this up; perhaps a lower level of consideration as a clearinghouse to bring them before the commission in final form, or in a more final form, so that the commission itself is not involved with so many of the things that are not necessarily a part of the final decision.

We feel that for the most part Indians are not being kept informed on their claims cases; that, in fact, frequently lawyers employed by the tribe or retained by the tribe lead tribes and Indian people on perhaps with undue optimism, and in fact sometimes false information as to time and amount of claims they might expect, and the working processes that are involved.

Second, we would think that there is a need for the Indians themselves to know the status of these claims. In listening to the testimony here today, I get the impression that few people know the status of all the claims at any given moment. I think in just a common course that the plaintiff would generally know what action is being carried on in his claim or court action—in this case the Commission action—and whether it is dormant, or whether it is in some stage or process.

We think there is then a poor, very poor, lack of communication, and this is perhaps largely on the part of the lawyers, but if others, such as even the commissioner, perhaps, himself, is not fully aware at any given moment of what the status of all claims are, it might be difficult for the lawyers to know also.

Relative to the element of needed additional power, I think it is a general feeling among many Indian organizations and Indian tribes that perhaps too much power has been consolidated in the hands of one or three men, the commissioner and his Associate Commissioners, and that to have all determinations made at that level or through that point has created some animosity toward the commission on the part of the Indians, generally speaking, I would say.

Additionally—relative to dismissing these claims—we do not think that should be done. We are aware also of continuing causes for claims that are evolving today. Although we would hope that there should not be such cases evolving—because when such cases evolve, it means that we are losing something—it appears at the present time, on the present basis that every once in a while you are going to have to set up one of these Claims Commissions for Indians: Washington State fishing rights, Alaskan claims, land claims. And in the Indian's mind, for the most part, just compensation is a poor device for taking what is theirs.

Senator McGovern. Well, thank you very much, Mr. Adams. We appreciate your prepared statement and also your additional observations, and they are now part of the record.

Mr. Adams. Thank you.

Letter

February 28, 1971
The Hon. John N. Mitchell,
Attorney General of the United States
Attn: Messrs. Jerris Leonard & Carlton Stoiber
Department of Justice
Washington, DC

Mr. Attorney General:

Various officials of the Puyallup Indian Tribe, as well as ourselves, have requested of your Department and the Interior Department that a federal suit be initiated immediately to enjoin further state prosecutions of Indian persons arrested last September 9th on Puyallup Indian Reservation lands held in trust by the United States and subject to federal control and protections.

Even aware of possible difficulties in successfully prosecuting such an action, we are nevertheless extremely disturbed that your Department would consider the February 23rd rulings of the United States Supreme Court restricting federal interventions of enjoinder against state prosecutions under a doctrine of "Our Federalism" as having general application to the dependent Indian peoples, further as presenting insurmountable obstacle to success in such action as we've requested, and as foreclosing the possibility of favorable departmental action upon our request.

Although it is clear that Indian people have not been the object of federal concern in seeking to enjoin state prosecutions in recent times, it is as well clear that this has been result, generally, of a failure by the federal government to sustain its responsibilities and obligations to Indian people in a manner neither inconsistent with nor contrary to the recurrent doctrine of "Our Federalism," at least not as embraced by the Constitution of the United States.

The relationship of Indian tribes, nations or people, to a 'doctrine of our federalism' has always differed from that of other people or citizens under the federal Constitution—as explicitly determined by the Commerce Clause and Supremacy Clause of the US Constitution.

Interestingly, the Treaty of Medicine Creek of 1854, with which this nation contracted Puyallup Indians, in its language distinguishes between the United States as a union of equal states making the treaty for each and all the states (in Article IV) and "the government of the United States" upon which the Indian Tribes agreed to "acknowledge their dependence," an explicit provision of Article VIII.

We are appalled by the continuing attempts of the federal government to abdicate or abandon its obligations for providing protections to Indian people, and the attempts to absolve itself of its responsibilities by a basic failure to make frequent recurrence to fundamental principles inherent to the federal-Indian relationship and essential to the security of Indian rights.

The inapplicability of the recent supreme court decisions upon the federal-Indian relationship and the federal obligations inherent thereto is certainly not denied by any previous holding by that Court. Several landmark Indian jurisdiction cases decided by the US Supreme Court are instructive to the understanding that both in the infancy of this nation and at the present date Indian people require and are legally deserving and entitled to energetic federal protections. So you may understand our disposition and attitudes, we include several citations.

United States v. Kagama, (1886):

Because of the local ill feeling, the people of the States where they (the Indian tribes) are found are often their deadliest enemies. From their very weakness and helplessness, so largely due to the course of dealing of the Federal Government with them, and the treaties in which it has been promised, there arises the duty of protection, and with it the power. This has always been recognized by the Executive and by Congress and by this court, whenever the question has arisen.

United States v. Pelican, (1914):

Nor does the territorial jurisdiction of the United States depend upon the size of the particular areas which are held for federal purposes. It must be remembered that the fundamental consideration is the protection of a dependent people.

United States v. Getzelman, (1937):

The power of Congress to impose, extend, or reimpose restrictions on property of an Indian ward is plenary and not open to doubt.

The basic judicial regard for the relationship between the federal government and Indian tribes and Indians, and particularly for the character of jurisdiction arising therefrom and adhering to Indian people and their lands, was drawn by the US Supreme Court in *Worcester v. Georgia*, (1832). The late Felix Cohen, who was perhaps the greatest legal expert on federal Indian law this century, discussed the result and effects of that case on page 123 of his *Handbook of Federal Indian Law* (1942), as follows:

> John Marshall's analysis of the basis of Indian self-government in the law of nations has been consistently followed by the courts for more than a hundred years. The doctrine set forth in this opinion has been applied to an unfolding series of new problems in scores of cases that have come before the Supreme Court and the inferior federal courts. The doctrine has not always been so highly respected in state courts and by administrative authorities.

The present Puyallup Indian situation evidences an incredible departure by the federal government from its traditional and obligatory role as protector of a dependent Indian people and an absolute disregard of its trust responsibilities.

The US Departments of Justice and Interior, acting through US Attorney Stan Pitkin and Assistant Regional Solicitor George Dysart, oddly, have effectively reduced their responsibilities to that of protecting Puyallup Indians "from themselves" and "from each other" while proceeding to give extravagant exercise to that limited "responsibility." The results have ranged from the ridiculous to the ludicrous.

It should be noted that prior to the arrest action against sixty-two persons, mostly on Indian trust lands, last September 9th—both the City of Tacoma and the State of Washington were agreed upon the position that if the lands were in fact Indian trust lands, or lands held in trust by the United States for Puyallup Indians, that state and local authorities would lack jurisdiction over the subject matter of fishing rights as well as lacking jurisdiction over the locus. The action of September 9 was taken, however, under an assertion of knowledge and understanding that the lands were neither held in trust nor owned by Indians.

The prosecution of Indians arrested upon the Puyallup's trust lands occurs in violation of the Washington statehood Enabling Act, and its irrevocable ordinance and compact with the United States as incorporated in Article XXVI of the Constitution of the State of Washington, which, in pertinent part, provides:

The following ordinance shall be irrevocable without the consent of the United States and the people of this state:

...That the people inhabiting this state do agree and declare that they forever disclaim all right and title to...all lands lying within said limits owned or held by any Indian or Indian tribes; and that until the title thereto shall have been extinguished by the United States, the same shall be and remain subject to the disposition of the United States, and said Indian lands shall remain under the absolute jurisdiction and control of the congress of the United States.

Yet there remain basic and insurmountable difficulties associated with the defense of Indian lands and the character of their federal-Indian jurisdiction within the local courts of the State. Particularly, Pierce County judges have repeatedly refused to accept any notion or proof that there remain Puyallup Indian lands other than those bounded within the cemetery. The absence of any positive federal presence within the courts to support Puyallup Indian and tribal claims have always proven fatal to their cause at the local level.

The difficulties confronting Puyallup Indians are compounded when other federally-related Indians, not Puyallups, appear in court and attempt to raise jurisdiction issues. Yet the landmark ruling of *Kagama* clearly recognizes that the obligation of federal protection is one of national application wherever a federally-related Indian may go within Indian country. 18 U.S.C. 1151, 1152 and 1153 reflect a general application of federal jurisdiction over Indians, as is likewise asserted over any federally-related Indian by the various Courts of Indian Offenses—there has never been a localized application of the federal obligation of protection to limit it only to the local Indians, or to subject Indians from other states or areas to an exercise of state jurisdiction, when upon other Indians' federally-protected lands.

Again, we believe that the power, duty, and obligation to provide protection to dependent Indian people places our situation outside the scope and limitations of the recent US Supreme Court rulings restricting federal intervention in state prosecutions. Furthermore, the situation of Puyallup Indians and the Puyallup Tribe has been made more difficult, complicated, extraordinary and extreme by improper actions and failures to act by federal authorities. It is time that the federal government now act properly and appropriately, as is its duty and obligation, to prevent further prosecutions of Indians arrested upon Indian trust lands last September.

Respectfully yours,
Hank Adams, SAIA

Memorandum
1976–1977
Trust Responsibility Issue (Proposed Study)
Issue: BIA Forest Management & Logging Practices (Quinault)

Background: Since 1921, the BIA has collected ten percent of all Indian timber sales receipts as reimbursement for their management of Indian forests and individual allotments in trust status, and in their performance of BIA trust responsibilities to Indians with timbered lands.

The heavily-forested Quinault Reservation, having 98% of its 150,000 acre reservation allotted to individuals, presents an excellent case for study of the BIA's management of their trust responsibilities, to both tribal interests and individual interests—and where the BIA activity is Indian-financed. (The study has added implications for the common illusion that Indians are constant beneficiary of, or drain on, the public dole.)

Problems & Issues: For more than a half century, Quinault tribal members and congressional committees have questioned the timber management practices and purposes on the Quinault Reservation. A succession of national administrations have promised forthcoming changes or corrections in practices, but then acted to formulate new rationales for not changing in event that subsequent inquiries might be made or questions asked. Few improvements have ever been instituted, and the damages to water, fish, and forest resources have compounded through the years—at a damages cost of some unknown multiple of the more than ten million dollars. Quinaults have paid to BIA for their forest management and exercise of 'trust responsibilities'. Among the issues to be studied are:

(a) The BIA's processes in contracting timber sales; enforcement of contract provisions; and the issue of forced sales of lands as condition of logging scheduling;

(b) Improper methods of logging, as relate to concerns for reforestation, tribal interests in preservation of watersheds, fish resources and in-stream habitats, and stream quality;

(c) Scaling practices and revisions, and methods of determining market values of timber and prices paid to Indian allottees;

(d) The consideration of competing tribal interests and the benefits for individual timber owners in controlling BIA actions under claim of the proper exercise of trust obligations.

Both the US Forest Service and US Fish & Wildlife Service's Northwest Fisheries Program have concluded highly-critical reports on BIA Forest Management on Quinault—showing massive destruction of natural resources, including new forests. Their reports have been limited, however, to their particular interest. A broader study would be useful, and might involve Task Forces Nos. 7, 2 & 3.

Letter

February 22, 1989
The Honorable Mark O. Hatfield,
United States Senator
The Honorable Sidney R. Yates,
United States Representative,
Chairman, House Appropriations

Dear Senator Hatfield and Congressman Yates:

I take the liberty, respectfully, of addressing you jointly, having formerly had the high personal privilege and honor of working in service with both of you during your tenure with the American Indian Policy Review Commission and my year's employment as chairman of its Task Force on Trust Responsibilities and the Federal-Indian Relationship, including Treaty Review (1975–76).

I write to urge and request your active support and expeditious actions within the respective House and Senate Appropriations Committees for securing approval this year of the $77.25 million designated federal share for concluding the "Puyallup Tribe Indian Land Claim Settlement Agreement," as accepted by a tribal vote on August 27, 1988.*

A 'Settlement Act' to authorize appropriations is the subject of hearings this week before the House Interior Committee and the Senate Select Committee on Indian Affairs. One must anticipate favorable actions on the measure by those Committees and, hopefully, early passage by both bodies of the Congress.

The total valuation of the Settlement Agreement is $161,844,000—the non-federal share of assigned costs and contributions totals some $84,594,000 in new expenditures and specific land title transfers. This includes a State of Washington contribution of $21 million which, thus far, has been receiving remarkable support in the state legislature. (The responsible state House committee recommended its immediate appropriation by a unanimous bipartisan vote of 26–0, already. The lead sponsor is in the one-vote majority party of the Senate, where passage is virtually certain, but where timing in process is vulnerable to partisan bids at leveraging to affect other unrelated matters, unfortunately.) The remaining private sector ($11,460,000) and local government ($52,134,000) settlement contributions, in lands and funds and project costs, have each been approved and committed for consummation with the combined state and federal enactments. The valuation of direct benefits to

---

* In June 1989, President George H. W. Bush signed the settlement agreement into law. The act had been under negotiation for more than six years and along with the Puyallup people the other parties were thirteen municipalities, the state, and the federal government. This was the second largest land settlement case—the 1971 Alaska Native Claims Settlement Act, which cost over $960 million and involved 40 million acres, was the largest.—Ed.

the Puyallup Tribe and its members in specific funding and properties is roughly some $111+ million from the $162 million settlement total.

The Settlement Act prepared by Congressman Norm Dicks' office, and introduced for himself and The Honorable US Representatives Foley, Miller, Unsoeld, Chandler, Morrison, McDermott and Swift of Washington's congressional delegation, is very judicious in the selection of principal and salient terms to be given expression in the federal statute as distinguished from matters generally given force by incorporation of the negotiated agreement and the related technical documents. Continuing rights and protections for the Puyallup Tribe are made clear, and the miscellaneous provisions provides both clarification and certainty to certain points which might otherwise have become a new basis for needless contests or contentious disputes which the agreement should not have intended to engender. In short, it is a well-crafted Act—and dispels such possibilities.

It was 100 years ago this date that the Enabling Act for Statehood of Washington, North Dakota, South Dakota, and my own birth state of Montana was passed into law. On November 11, 1889, Washington's admission into the Union was proclaimed by the President of the United States. Thus, a number of states celebrate their Centennials this year. The Puyallup Settlement Act presents itself at a most propitious historical moment—both for ending what has often been the most embittering of experiences, and for marking the promise and hopes and opportunities which may arise with utmost good faith and new beginnings.

A full fifty years of total prohibition against a harvesting of salmon on the Puyallup River and Reservation by tribal members preceded a five-year period of state court protected fishing after 1957, for example. The prohibition was reinstated in 1962 and continued, with only limited exceptions, until the Boldt decision was issued February 12, 1974. Even then, appeals and applications in the remand cases producing the Puyallup trilogy of decisions by the Supreme Court of the United States (1968,1973,1977), with-held substantial benefits of the Boldt decision from the Puyallup Tribe until after the court affirmed the basic holding of US Judge George H. Boldt in its opinion of July 2, 1979. Ironically, the court's decision, authored by Justice William O. Douglas in the 1968 *Puyallup I*, directly has provided the basis for the *Belloni* decision of 1969 in the *Sohappy* Case on the Columbia River (*United States v. Oregon*)—which, in turn, had established a "fair share doctrine" that became the remedy or result sought by federal attorneys in filing the case of *United States v. Washington* before Judge Boldt in September 1970. (That filing, too, was instigated by actions of Puyallup Indians attempting to assert their treaty reservation and fishing rights on the river within the city limits of Tacoma.) Thus, while these cases were restoring significant resources to the benefit of the other treaty tribes, machinations in the state and county courts continued the deprivations to the Puyallups almost to the very end of the 1970's. Pierce County's Judge William Brown produced a formulation allowing a total tribal harvest of far less than one fish (steelhead) a piece per tribal member—not even one fish per family, given current enrollment numbers. In point, the vindicated treaty rights and valued fish resources were last restored to the Puyallups—from among the federally recognized tribes—whose members had already suffered the longest and most complete deprivation. And, although the Puyallup Tribe might have been entitled to the greatest amounts in assessed damages for losses accounted to the prior denial of their treaty rights, claims for damages were waived in the *Boldt* case proceedings, in part as a price for the United States agreeing to pursue the habitat protection and related environmental issues embraced by the still pending Phase II proceedings of the *United States v. Washington* civil case.

My own direct and continuing involvement with Puyallup and Nisqually Indians and the Franks Landing Indian Community began twenty-five years ago this month, when I was organizing the beginnings of a national Campaign of Awareness on Indian Rights for the National Indian Youth Council, in association with the National Congress of American Indians and with the formal participation of more than fifty tribal governments. And it was eighteen years ago this month—in February 1971—that I hand carried title documents and other records into the offices of US Indian Commissioner Louis R. Bruce and Associate Commissioners Helen Peterson and Art Gajarsa, for several days requesting a determination of the status of the Puyallup Indian Reservation and its continuing existence. With the assistance of related inquiries entered by Senator Edward Kennedy's Judiciary Subcommittee on Administrative Practices—and by columnist Jack Anderson's associate Les Whitten—an immediate review was concluded and again the original external boundaries of the Puyallup Reservation were restored their formal recognition as having never been extinguished. (That determination was immediately communicated to Washington Governor Dan Evans, and formal Solicitor's Opinions were issued in march and April 1971, preceding a federal lawsuit which fully settled the reservation existence question in favor of the Tribe.)

Favorable consideration for the Puyallup Settlement appropriations might also take into account the selfless and admirable character of tribal actions displayed in the period of re-establishing and developing its capacities of institutional self-government and services over the past two decades. Beginning in the early 1970's, the tribe acted as a service agency in behalf of many non-Puyallup Indians from among the sizeable urban native American population of Tacoma and Pierce County, in addition to its own members. (In one instance beyond that, the Puyallup Tribe used its federal applicant eligibility status to secure program funds for an independent Asian American community organization in Tacoma, until that body established its won eligibility status.) Although budget restrictions have imposed some periodic limitations upon service beneficiaries in recent years, the inclusion of non-Puyallup Indians in programs continues—most notably in its highly-praised independent contract day schools and in its long-acclaimed alcohol and substance abuse in-patient and out-patient care facilities or program.

Perhaps one caution carrying to the present agreement is found in the Puyallup Agreement of 1876 reported by chairman Vine Deloria, Jr. and executive director Kirke Kickingbird in the Institute for the Development of Indian Law's treaty and agreements series of the early 1970's. In that congressionally-ratified agreement, the granting of a lengthy, reservation railroad right-of-way was made with promises of preference hiring of Puyallup Indians over both "whites and Chinese laborers," and for the separate building of a tribally-owned railway spur and depot at which the Puyallups might ticket passengers and freight for transport throughout the rapidly developing United States. (Congress ratified the 1876 deal, or taking, in February 1893.) Nothing came to Puyallup Indians beyond a proclaimed perception of a most 'lucrative' promise or deal. And soon it was the Puyallup Indians themselves who were forcibly transported from the area of their lands, reservation, the non-existent depot and warehouse spur, and the negotiated right-of-way.

The agreement should foster an accelerated economic integration of the Puyallup Indians into the increasing wealth and investment or developmental potential of the area immediately surrounding them. Yet, certain aspects of the negotiations—particularly related to rejection of several tribal property siting or acquisition proposals—gave some portents of an unspoken commitment among non-tribal parties toward the imposition—perhaps, rather, the maintenance—of an economic and territorial apartheid or designed redlining against Puyallup Indians to restrict their movement or entry into various choice development, ownership, and rights utilization, sites.

For the non-Indian parties, economic projections and valuations have been made, publicly issued, and submitted to the federal and state legislative bodies, showing the expected gains and economic growth, returns and revenues, which can be anticipated as result of the settlement. The measurable economic return, in both short and long terms, is projected to be a sizeable multiplier to the immediate Settlement costs of $162 million—with a multiplier perceived for each constituent share. (For example, the State recoups its $21 million cost in as quick as two years.) These promising projections are, doubtlessly, realistic. One assumes that it is the stark forces of realism, also which explains why no one perceives a need to supply a work-up on perceived or anticipated multipliers in values to accurate to the Puyallup Tribe and its members in result of the Settlement.

This settlement, in fact, could provide opportunities for breaching the sad history where Indian monetary resources—particularly Claims Settlement Funds or Judgement Awards—are quickly expended or otherwise dissipated and diminished, are simply passed through to non-Indians, or are corruptly reduced when attracting the involvement of a nefarious range of unscrupulous political figures, lawyers, consultants, confidence artists, and businessmen. Examples are found from the Alaskan Native North Slope corporation at Barrow to the highest echelon of the Navajo Nation at Window Rock. A US Senate Office and the Office of Commissioner of Indian Affairs were in euphoric state at time of introducing $8 million of Sisseton-Wahpeton monies to a St. Elizabeth's alumnus once tagged "criminally insane," partly for his adeptness at confidence games.

The point of the preceding, in part, is to indicate that the Settlement does not stand in total isolation from other events, processes, and considerations. It is of considerable importance that state officials who possess the conscience and political courage to be something other than anti-Indian receive the necessary federal support to succeed in some of those efforts undertaken for the benefit of both non-Indians and Indians, or for all citizens. (And, it occasions also my appeal for your consideration of lending support to the continuing actions by US Representatives Norm Dicks and John Miller to have Puget Sound added to the bodies of water granted line item budgeting status for OMB and the Congress in requests and appropriations for clean up or clean water funding.)

Congressional policy of recent years has enabled Indian tribes to assume a greater institutional role relating to a number of public policy issues. But also because of the emergent—involved and quality—Indian leadership being demonstrated in numerous instances on these issues, that Indian tribal role is beginning to become institutionalized in the processes of government in the Pacific Northwest and enjoys an increasingly favorable public acceptance.

Not a century after Washington statehood commenced, the Puyallup Indian Settlement Act affords an opportunity to begin writing an uncharacteristically new or different chapter in relations between Indians and others in the region, a chapter of clear promise and more than marginal hope. Also, it can begin to eradicate remaining residues of bitterness born in unkind histories of thoughtlessness and racism's political collectivism, while giving rebirth to the spirit in public policy that George Washington, as first President—and for whom the nation's forty-second state endures as namesake—invoked as standard, or espoused toward Indian people, for "reflecting an undecaying luster on the national character."

Thus, I urge your support for the Act's immediate and full funding in the coming fiscal year.

Respectfully yours,
Hank Adams, SAIA

American Indian Policy Review Commission

In the wake of the Alcatraz takeover, the Trail of Broken Treaties, Wounded Knee II, and the many other demonstrations and protests, the Congress in 1975 opted to establish this bipartisan panel to address how and why the Red Power movement had arisen, to study the contemporary status of Native peoples, and to provide a blueprint for improving socioeconomic conditions for Native nations, urban Indians, and unrecognized Native groups as well. Additionally, the hope was that the panel's recommendations would lead to better intergovernmental relations.

This was certainly not the first Congress engaged in such a study, but it was one of the largest and most comprehensive efforts since the Senate had conducted a similar national study in the 1930s and 1940s, and this one featured several Native commissioners, not a common feature in past endeavors. Hank Adams was tapped to head Task Force I, Trust Responsibilities and the Federal-Indian Relationship, arguably the most important of the eleven organized task forces, which included such topics as tribal governments, Indian education, urban and rural non-reservation Indians, and Indian health, among others.

Adams's own words best encapsulate what he saw as his task force's principle objectives: "to analyze and study treaties, statutes, court decisions for one; to clarify and perhaps better define the unique status and relationship of Indian tribes to the people or to the United States; to clarify just what was the character and the nature of the Federal-Indian relationship; to clarify and define just what is the nature and character of trust responsibilities; and to review treaties for the purpose of communicating just what is the standing and viability of treaties with Indian tribes in the life of Indians as well as the life of this Nation."

The commission's work lasted for two years, culminating in a two-volume final report in 1977 that featured over two hundred recommendations, only a few of which were enacted into law.

Memorandum

July 23, 1975
Task Force Memorandum
To: John Echohawk & Doug Nash
From: Hank Adams
SUBJECTS: (1) Definition of Task Force Work;
               (2) Task Force Plan of Operations;
               (3) Selection of Task Force Specialist

I. We definitely must progress and make decisions on the above subjects at our Task Force (TF) meeting. Commission staff projections on schedules set an August 1st deadline on Item (1), and an August 15th deadline on Item (2). Although we will have brief delay on finalizing (1), we should be able to get ahead and mainly complete (2) at our early August meeting. Some modifications will stem from exchanges and feedback from other Task Forces.

Our primary investigative task is to study basic and broad issues of "trust responsibilities" and Federal-Indian relations, through "analysis of the Constitution, treaties, statutes, judicial interpretations, and executive orders to determine the attributes of the unique relationship between the Federal Government and Indian tribes and the land and other resources they possess"—as that relationship has developed, or particularly been impacted or affected by "policies and practices of the Federal Agencies charged with protecting Indian Resources and providing services to Indians," in the past and presently...

The following pages present some of my own ideas on our Task Force's workload and approaches, plus activities I will start work on.

II. General Approach

Files & Information Development: Task Force #1 will maintain certain study files, probably segregated from those of other Task Forces in Commission offices, but available for their general use.

(People & Documents): A general file system will be oriented toward the inclusion of all identifiable Indian tribes or groups in the United States—with each having a separate file set developed.

The respective files will develop by addition of documents, information, and materials that specially or particularly relate to the specific Indian people, and pertinent proceedings involving them. Completely as possible, and when appropriate, these will include treaties, statutes, court decisions, executive and administrative orders, and tribal (organic) governing documents—in chronological sequence of issuance or enactment.

Notes and summaries of document content, by subject matter and special issues raised or dealt with, will be maintained with the file. Informational summaries, notes, or references, in some instances may substitute for actual documents, copies, or volume complications. (Example: A summary of each claims case carried by Indian tribes of people to the US Court of Claims and to the Indian Claims Commission will be entered in the appropriate Indian file, identifying its basis or character specifics and final dispositions on issues. Copies of the summaries would also be maintained in a single file relating to Indian claims to aid analysis of the general subject matter.)

(Subject matters & Issues): Separately, files will be developed for specific subject matters, issues, or problems—within the categories subject to Commission review; of particular interest to our Task Force #1, or identified from our analytical research; or which reflects the interest, concern or requests from other Indian and non-Indian sources or governmental units favoring further study.

Subject matter or issue-oriented file sets will include copies of statutes, court decisions, orders, opinions, or other documents particularly dealing with the matter or issue; or will include approximate extracts, excerpts, or summaries from basic documents. (Example: (1) All different treaty provisions relating to "hunting" and "fishing" rights should be extracted verbatim from the identified treaties for filing by that subject matter. (2) Where uniform or identical treaty provision language recurs in a multiplicity of treaties, the provision can be stated once and an enumerated listing be included to show all treaties where the common language appears.)

The full range of subject matter identified by treaty provisions, negotiations, or purposes in contracting them, will be reviewed by the Task Force. Relevance or implications to contemporary application, if any, will have significance to our final report and recommendations for the future.

III. Central Topics for Study and Report:

Our study of the development of, and changes in, relations between Indians and the United States will focus heavily upon principles of law and legal doctrines, together with valid explanations of their origins and applications. Our analysis will identify the varied effects upon the lives of Indians and their relations with the United States, evolving either from adherence to such principles and doctrines, or arising from misapplications or deviations from them.

1. Genesis of Relations: The political status and sovereign character of Indian nations prior to the birth of the United States will be reviewed, with particular emphasis given toward showing the governing direction these had upon the developing relations with the new nation. This is fundamental to our treaty review.

2. US Constitutional Provisions: The entire history of Federal-Indian relations, up to the present date, has turned with frequent reference to the US Constitution. Our study will examine significant effects of:

(a) The Commerce Clause—with its assignment of certain regulatory powers to Congress;

(b) The Supremacy Clause—declaring the standing of treaties and treaty obligations within the nation;

(c) The Fourteenth Amendment's exclusion of "Indians not taxed" from congressional representation apportionments;

(d) The President's qualified treaty-making powers;

(e) The Congress' control of appropriations; and

(f) The Congress' power to make war.

2-A. Applied Doctrines: Application of authorities under the cited provisions have had substantial impact upon Indian Affairs. Their exercise has given realm to, or taken guidance from, a number of related or inter-related level doctrines—often considered in judicial proceedings—which we will also examine; including:

(g) Federal Instrumentality Doctrines and extensions of rights or authorities for carrying out general Federal purposes, policies, or specific national obligations;

(h) The Congress' "plenary power over Indian Affairs";

(I) Federal preemption of State Power or actions in the governance of certain Indian activities and rights;

(j) Congressional immunities to Indian challenges of an 'unassailable,' 'conclusive' presumption that Congress 'acts always for the best interests of the Indians'.

3. Treaty Relations: The Parties & The Provisions: Setting forth recognized principles and purposes of treaty-making settles few issues arising in Federal-Indian relations, when the ensuing development of that relationship is reviewed. Contradictions and inconsistencies can appear to rule the relationship, if not to vacate the vital principles of its foundation. Our treaty review will examine both principles and questions of contradiction, either to reconcile their application or to evaluate the validity and significance of application within the temporal development of Federal Indian relations.

Among the propositions we will examine, or pose as questions to be answered, are the following:

(a) The Federal-Indian relationship has its roots firmly established in international law

(b) Treaties are contracts between nations reflective of bi-lateral decision-making powers and are expressive of a mutuality of interests and a view toward the future.

(c) What attributes of "power," and what attributes of "rights," are reflected in the treaty-making processes as relate to the respective contracting parties?

(d) What actual role did a "Doctrine of Conquest" play in the treaty-making processes or in any process of treaty violations or breaches?

(e) Which attributes of "Federal Trust Responsibility" evolve directly from treaty provisions or treaty-making processes?

(f) Where do the doctrines of "guardian-ward"; domestic dependent nations; "trustee-and-protectorate"; and other such terms used to character-ize the Federal-Indian relationship factually evolve from?

(g) What were the legal nature of executive order actions and the charac-ter of presidential authority exercised (e.g., treaty-making powers)?

(h) In what manner and forms did the "plenary power" of Congress over Indian Affairs find expression prior to the 1871 termination of "further con-tracting by treaty?"

(I) What factors caused deterioration of bi-lateral decision-making pro-cesses, and what were the stages of decline?

(j) What processes were employed to cause extinguishment or diminu-tion of any attributes of Indian sovereignty prior to 1900; and what attributes of sovereignty remain for Indian exercise today?

4. Treaty Subjects and Issue Identification: The treaties deal extensively with varied transaction, authorities, obligations and considerations, which will be reviewed in both historical and contemporary application. These include:

A. INDIAN LANDS; PROPERTIES; AND RIGHTS
(1) Indian land cessions by treaty;
(2) Retention of Land Reserves and Related Resources, (including min-eral and water rights);
(3) Loss of treaty lands reserved against cession;
(4) Executive actions or failures in implementing treaties;
(5) Allotments of reservations authorized by some treaties;
(6) Restrictions & allowances on land use or holdings;
(7) Hunting & Fishing rights;
(8) Trade rights and allowances or restrictions;

B. TRIBAL GOVERNMENTS AND PEOPLE
(1) Levels of tribal autonomy;
(2) Relationships to Agencies & Federal Government;
(3) Extent or limitations of civil & criminal jurisdiction;
(4) Character of "dependence on US" proclaimed by treaty;
(5) Control of community social, economic & education processes;

C. FEDERAL OBLIGATIONS AND CONSIDERATIONS
(1) Payments & considerations for land cessions;
(2) Purposes of rations policies & related provisions;
(3) Commitments to economic security and sustenance;
(4) Provisions for Indian education & community services;
(5) Any provisions for homes or community facilities;

D. PROHIBITIONS OR REQUIREMENTS PLACED ON INDIANS
(1) Relating to Indian mobility or travel;

(2) Relating to highways, railroads and other transportation (and communications) systems;

(3) Relating to war-making powers and hostilities;

(4) Relating to religious and cultural ways or practices;

(5) Relating to use of alcohol and liquor;

E. EFFECTS OF UNRATIFIED TREATIES

5. Statutory Impacts; Congressional & Administration Policies:

Relations between Indians and the United States have undergone dramatic transformations with time's passage. Evaluating the character of federal trust responsibilities and obligations requires review of major congressional actions, legislative histories and national policies affecting the Indian relationship and condition; We may examine:

(a) Early Indian Trade and Intercourse Acts, governing non-Indian relations with Indians;

(b) Northwest Ordinance; and statutory creation or instructing of treaty commissions;

(c) Fourteenth Amendment provisions; the 1871 termination of treaty-making; and the 1924 Indian Citizenship Act;

(d) General Allotment (and Homestead) Acts and amendments;

(e) Indian Removal Acts; & development of the Indian Territory

(f) Statehood Enabling Acts and conditions on Statehood;

(g) Land lease and sale authorizations and restrictions;

(h) Indian Reorganization Act and Implementation;

(I) The so-called "Buy Indian" and "Snyder" Acts;

(j) Johnson-O'Malley Act and transfers of education responsibility and governmental jurisdiction to certain States;

(k) Major and Assimilative Crimes Acts; & Indian liquor laws;

(l) Indian Claims Commission Act and purposes;

(m) Termination Policies and Acts;

(n) Public Law 280's qualified transfers of jurisdiction to States;

(o) Policies of Relocation and vocational training policies

(p) Development of separate Indian health agency;

(q) Indian Appropriations Acts; their character and identifications of purpose in the national history;

(r) The nature of Indian legislation in the 1961–1975 period;

(s) The effects of reasoning of including Indians specially or distinctly in general national programs, dating back to CCCs and WPA; through federal impact school funds; OEO; Accelerated Works Programs; and the education and other social legislation of the 1970s, plus some earlier laws.

6. Judicial Decisions and Structures: The nature and scope of Indian relations with the Federal Government and the States have been given voluminous interpretation and definition by the courts.

Many decisions relating to land status, the character of Indian rights, and the extent of federal powers or State limitations, have evolved from criminal prosecutions—often murder charges and liquor violations; frequently state actions against claimed treaty rights—habeas corpus proceedings, and taxation cases.

Numerous civil suits brought by Indian tribes and individuals have been against Interior Department officials, ranging from local BIA Agents to the Secretary, relating to their exercise of claimed trust authority or to claimed violations of trust responsibilities.

After review, our report will consider the adequacy of both administrative and judicial structures and provisions for securing remedy to violations or abuses of trust authorities; and recommend standards for their exercise; as well as for providing protections to the exercise of affirmatively established treaty or Indian-related federal rights.

7. Justice Department: The role and policies of the Justice Department and US Attorneys in acting to sustain federal trust responsibilities, to carry out federal treaty obligations, or to protect established federal treaty or tribal rights in their exercise will be reviewed for report.

8. Trust Counsel Authority: The issues of "conflict of interest" as the basis for such an independent agency, as proposed, will be examined.

9. Trust Responsibilities in Interior and BIA: The term 'trust' 'responsibility' has become a code for many actions and inactions in the Federal Government, and is perceived in numerous varied ways outside that realm. Our report will give definitive statement to supportable conclusions specifying 'what it is' or what it should be; 'who has it' or 'where is actually resides.' And, 'how does it, or how should it, manifest itself in application or exercise as an authority, duty, or obligation?'

Much investigative work of Task Force #1 will center upon the federal trust relationship to Indian lands, exploitable natural resources, and certain funds and other properties, of both tribes and Indian individuals. Leasing, selling, and contract policies and practices warrant careful scrutiny and evaluation.

Controlling involvement or excessive interventions by BIA and Interior officials in various tribal political or defined governmental processes, compared with other declinations to act in similar situations—ranging from matters of tribal membership to recognition of election results; and from actions on audit findings to enforcement of tribal constitutional standards—will be reviewed in relation to claimed justifications for determining existence of any unjustifiable contradictions or patterns of discrimination. This also addresses the issues of discretionary and obligatory authority, and their delineation.

At the beginning of the Nixon Administration, less than ten percent of Indian-owned lands (reservation) in use for agricultural and dry farm production was being leased by non-Indians. Yet, non-Indians were delivering substantially more than 50% of the farm income earned from all such Indian lands. The ratio of return on agricultural investment dollars prevalently was much higher for non-Indians only because, in most instances, the best farm lands were being leased, while Indian farmers were investing in the worst of the dry farm lands.

A general review of such BIA 'realty' actions relating to both dry and irrigated agricultural lands, as well as range, should include several instructive concentrated studies of selected areas and some different reservations.

The population demographics of Indian land ownership and non-ownership; residency patterns of land owners, and of Indian non-owners on reservations, could also provide some interesting points for consideration and report.

We need to examine the different categories of reservations and Indian land status, and formulate recommendations regarding consistent provisions in policy or law governing their status. As part of that, we will review development and legitimacy of the 'restrictive elements' of the 'trust relationship'; any causes of retardation in the 'beneficial' purposes of the relationship; factors of 'incompetence' and 'competence' and their affects;' and recommend revisions or alternatives in sustaining the trust responsibilities and relationships.

'Trust Responsibilities' do entail legal obligations. Whether these obligations are altered or set aside by policy declarations—such as a 'Policy of Self-Determination'—which may have indeterminate or abstract meaning, or which may be whimsically, discriminately, or indiscriminately applied, likewise deserves our study.

10. Taxability and Tax Immunities: These issues most appropriately come under the matters of treaty rights and trust responsibilities or relations, although Task Force #4 on Jurisdiction will likely review some States' claims to taxing authority over certain Indian properties, activities, or persons, as incident to jurisdictional transfers under P.L. 83-280.

Affirmative rights to certain tax immunities were maintained or directly vested by some treaty provisions. Continuing statutory extensions of the trust status of certain allotted lands have controlled the matter of taxation and exemptions on them, and the termination of trust status has been the threshold factor on Indian land taxation.

Our Task Force could best conclude a comprehensive report on these issues, addressing all inherent implications, while advising other Task Forces of ramifications for consideration under their subject matters.

(Example: Education of Indians is a recurrent treaty theme—although some tribes protested ceding their children along with their lands. Then federal governmental jurisdiction was transferred to several States in the 1930s for educating Indian children, the tax base support for a number of school districts was derived entirely from within some reservations. The (Quinault Tribe) Taholah District #77 has had a community-controlled, all-Indian school board for these four decades, although it has been a 'state public school,' with the county and state acting as 'tax collector', but obliged to return the funds and levies back to the Indian community school. Effectually, the school system has been an institution and instrument of tribal self-government and self-development. Could not the education jurisdiction and taxing authority have been transferred directly to the Quinault Tribe originally; or now? Comparative studies on tax authorities and revenues within specific reservation areas could help other Task Forces to explore such questions and alternatives.)

IV. General Comments and Consideration

The preceding 'suggestion outline' relates primarily to our general scope of work, and is intended only to provide a substantive basis for our August 4th–6th Task Force meeting and decision-making. I plan to make it available to other Task Force or Commission members to invite their comments and viewpoints for consideration when we meet.

Although I've not tried to define extensively the inter-relationships and demarcations of assignments with other Task Forces, I do not think there will be any problems of our usurping, displacing, or duplicating any of their work or obligations. Coordination will, of course, be necessary and some joint hearings will be extremely helpful.

I anticipate we will be providing findings in the course of our work, or upon others' requests for our inquires, particularly where our studies or authorities or relations and federal obligations may provide a background or conclusion that is but a departure or starting point for consideration in the handling of their respective Task Force subject matters and studies.

Attached to this memorandum are two background statements indicating some forms and focus we may utilize in particular cases for concentrated studies for approaching the broader national issues on the same or similar subject matters. The one on BIA forest management would rely mainly on study of past information; while the one on treaty rights fish resources would involve hearings and be oriented toward determining future applications and impact probabilities.

Another point we will be involved with is the matter of treaties affecting Indians, although contracted between other international bodies (eg., Treaty of Guadalupe Hidalgo; The Jay Treaty; Alaska Cession Treaty; Canadian-American Treaties on Fish Resources; Migratory Birds.) Brief attention might also be given to comparisons between the United States and other American Nations, and what has been the relationships and status of other Indian populations. The positive attributes of US actions, policies, or attempts to uphold a legal standard in dealings with Native people has not been all bad, and where the US may have reasons to be 'proud' of its Indian relations can be an important part of our review.

Testimonial

US Senate Select Committee on Indian Affairs. Meetings
of the American Indian Policy Review Commission.
Washington, DC and Portland, Oregon (June 4, August 10,
and September
25, 1976)
Statement of Hank Adams, Chairman, Task Force No.1,
Accompanied by Kevin Gover

Mr. Adams. I am Hank Adams, chairman of Task Force No. 1; Trust Responsibility and the Federal-Indian Relationship, including treaty review.

Congressman Yates. Mr. Chairman, we all want to hear what he is saying. He is talking only to you.

Mr. Adams. With me is Kevin Gover, specialist with the task force. Since the chairman stated that opening statements have been dispensed with, I have no opening statement.

Chairman Abourezk. First of all, how far along are you on your final report to be submitted to the Commission?

Mr. Adams. We are just going into the drafting on the final report at this point. We have virtually, I would say ninety-five percent-well, 100 percent of all direct research done. There are details we are still trying to get from Government agencies and answers to specific questions or some specific detailed information. Other than that, we are proceeding to the drafting and writing of the final report.

Chairman Abourezk. When will you complete that draft?

Mr. Adams. We will be completed with our final report on the date of expiration of the task force.

Chairman Abourezk. When is that?

Mr. Adams. July 20th.

Chairman Abourezk. You will have your report submitted to the Commission on or before July 20th?

Mr. Adams. Yes.

Chairman Abourezk. What was the objective of your task force?

Mr. Adams. The basic objective was to analyze and study treaties, statutes, court decisions for one; to clarify and perhaps better define the unique status and relationship of Indian tribes to the people or to the United States; to clarify just what was the character and the nature of the Federal-Indian relationship; to clarify and define just what is the nature and character of trust responsibilities; and to review treaties for the purpose of communicating just what is the standing and viability of treaties with Indian tribes in the life of Indians as well as the life of this Nation.

Congressman Yates. May I ask a question, Mr. Chairman?

Chairman Abourezk. Yes.

Congressman Yates. What is the conclusion about the trust responsibility to the off-reservation Indians? I look at your task force report and I didn't get a precise answer there. Let me read the paragraph.

Extensive documentation of the trust relationship with Indians would be provided to verify that the relationship embraces the sovereign entities of Indian tribes and that the trust responsibilities relate directly to Indian people, property and rights.

Per tribe: What happens to the individual when he leaves the tribe? Does the Government's trust responsibility cease to exist? As for example, during the Eisenhower administration the national policy was to try to persuade Indians to leave reservation and go to the cities and get good jobs there.

Mr. Adams. Essentially, what we are indicating is a person does not leave his tribe just by physical mobility. The fact is, there are only a few methods of separation from ones tribe and from the Federal trust responsibility and that is by expatriation of some form or another.

In fact, the Federal obligation carries with it an individual person as long as he is in tribal relations, whether he goes to Los Angeles or comes here to the District of Columbia.

Just one of the Alaskan Native corporations, the North Slope Alaskan Corporation, has native people in fifty-six different counties of the United States and we do not see a severance of responsibility, either by the Native corporation or the United States, to those Eskimo people just because they are not located right now on the North Slope.

Congressman Yates. When you say you don't see it: Is your contention sustained by the law?

Mr. Adams. Our contention is sustained by the law and we do feel there has been a misapplication or administrative voidance of a law by the failure to recognize the code of Federal responsibilities and the full application of the law from a standpoint of eligibility.

We have now looked at a number of tribes just to see where their populations are, like the Yakima Tribe. It has twenty-five percent of its population off the reservation and the tribe recognizes the responsibility to those members, but the Federal Government does not. However, there are a comparable number of Indians from other reservations on the Yakima Reservation and the federal government recognizes eligibility for those non-Yakimas just because they are on the Yakima Reservation.

It has seen a severance of responsibility for those Yakimas who have gone away, if they have gone away to a non-reservation area, but it picks them up if they go to Quinault, an Oregon reservation. That mobility has been misapplied and has been a real unnecessary problem for Indians.

Congressman Yates. The term mobility, as you use it: Does that apply to movement from one reservation to another or does it apply as well to a movement from the reservation to the city?

Mr. Adams. It applies under the law as we see it. Byron Ellis' going from, say, Yakima to Los Angeles or Yakima to Chicago. However that is not the application that has been given.

Congressman Yates. Do the tribes recognize that? In conversations with Mr. Sinnett of the BIA, he indicates the tribes themselves are opposed to recognizing the responsibility of the Government to the Indian people who leave the reservation. What has been your experience in talking to the tribesmen?

Mr. Adams. In directly asking the tribes and tribal witnesses in hearings on this question: the tribes have been saying that the Federal responsibility and the Federal obligations carry with our people when they leave the reservation.

I would acknowledge that the framing of questions perhaps leads, in some parts, to the result. We did not ask Yakimas if they felt the same way about other tribes as they do about their members. They may think that is great for Yakimas but they may not have the same concern about a Navajo going from Window Rock to Los Angeles.

Congressman Yates. To summarize then, what you propose to recommend finally, as we see it now, is the recognition of the trust responsibility by the Federal Government for Indian people, whether they are on the reservation or not. Is that correct?

Mr. Adams. Yes, that is correct. One of the things I think we are going to be able to demonstrate very well is the whole question of eligibility and this was mentioned at the last Commission meeting.

It is that although if there has been a general denial of eligibility of persons off the reservation from numerous Federal services, the fact is most Indians on reservations who have every eligibility are not getting the services, even though they have every entitlement to eligibility recognized by the United States.

Congressman Meeds. In that case then: How do you define "Indian peoples" if the recognitions runs to them whether they are on or off a reservation? Who defines who are "Indian people?"

Mr. Adams. This is another element of defining the trust responsibility. We are saying it can be well demonstrated, well proven by history and by law. Legal analysis that the basic trust responsibility goes from the United States to an Indian tribe rather than a person of individual Indians.

The basic definition of who is an Indian and who is eligible for that relationship is determined, or should be determined, in the first instance by the tribe.

Congressman Yates. By each tribe?

Mr. Adams. By each tribe for itself.

Congressman Yates. You are suggesting, in administering a trust relationship, the Government is to be bound by the interpretation given by each tribe as to what is an Indian for purposes of membership in that tribe?

Mr. Adams. That is correct. There are some problems in just accepting the current status of all Indians because there has been substantial federal administration intervention in membership in the past that has created some problems for a number of tribes. We are indicating there should be some period of realignment for membership before anything gets set solidly on who constitutes membership of tribes.

You do have situations where persons of, say, fractional one-hundredths of Indian blood are automatically members of tribes by federal law. You have federal law determining, say in the case of terminated Utes, where any of the terminated Utes less than half-blood cease to be Indians.

In the cases of some of the other terminated tribes like the Klamaths, you have full-bloods who have ceased to be Indians.

Congressman Yates. Under what conditions would your full-bloods cease to be Indians?

Mr. Adams. Under explicit termination legislation, plus some of the Indian Reorganization Act constitutional governments. You have a number of things that were essentially imposed by the federal government. The Indian Reorganization Act constitutions were rarely motivated by the judgments of an Indian tribe and what was best for themselves. They pretty much sold on this.

You have a number of provisions in constitutions that can disallow memberships for Indian tribes. You have many that have a residency at birth provisions, so if a full-blood Indian couple are living, say in Los Angeles, when their child is born, that full-blood Indian may not be entitled to membership, except by adoption, in its tribe.

You have a number of fractionated bloodline provisions. You have it frequently easier, that you be entitled to membership, if you have one non-Indian parent that if you have two parents who are members and are full-blood Indians from different tribes or full-blood Indians from several tribes.

Congressman Yates. Hank, is it the responsibility of your task force to define who is an Indian?

Mr. Adams. No; it is more our responsibility to characterize what are the rights of the tribes to define membership.

Congressman Yates. Mr. Chairman, may I ask staff which task force has the responsibility of defining who or what is an Indian?

Mr. Adams. We do have the responsibility of addressing that question in just the category of Federal-Indian relations.

Congressman Yates. I would assume the definition itself, if not yours, would be somebody's. Who has that?

Chairman Abourezk. I think it ought to be given to somebody. Somebody ought to have that responsibility.

Mr. Adams. I think a number of task forces are addressing it.

Commissioner Dial. This wasn't given to any one task force to define. This would not be the responsibility of Mr. Adams alone. Neither would it be the work of Task Force 10, along with some other task forces, because they may very well disagree on what an Indian is.

Chairman Abourezk. Congressman Meeds just pointed out something that I think is very accurate. We will have a recommendation from a number of task forces. It will probably be the Commission's responsibility to make a final definition of it if we possibly can. I think it is going to be one of the most important things we can do. What procedural changes does the task force intend to recommend?

Mr. Adams. We expect to recommend that: A new Department of Indian Affairs or whatever it is called or whatever its name, and more clearly to clarify or define, in law, what the Federal obligations are.

Chairman Abourezk. That is policy, I have got a question on policy. In terms of procedure, what kind of things are you going to recommend?

Mr. Adams. Whose procedure?

Chairman Abourezk. Procedure on the part of the US Government. What procedural changes will you recommend the US Government undertake to fulfill a treaty responsibility?

Mr. Adams. We are going to recommend a basic restructuring of the relationship of the tribes with the administration or the executive body and we are going to recommend some procedural changes in consideration of Congress on these issues.

We are going to essentially propose a system of restored bilateral relationships.

Chairman Abourezk. What does that mean?

Mr. Adams. To involve Indian tribes in the decision making processes, both with the Congress and with the executive branch. So that some of the powers taken away from the tribes and invested with the administrative branches—and in the past, churches, the Board of Indian control that was in existence from 1869 to 1934—to give some of this decision making power directly back to the tribes.

Again, to work on some basis of equality, both with the Congress in making its decisions relating to Indians, as well as the executive branch.

The powers that have been bested by Congress with other people— whether it be a Secretary of Interior, whether it be a Commissioner of Indian Affairs—we are going to recommend some of those powers be vested directly with the tribes again, so that there will be a reality to self-determination and involvement of Indians in decision making processes.

What we see now is not self-determination but self-administration. The tribes administering themselves along the lines of procedural and rules, guidelines and regulations, that somebody else makes up for them.

Chairman Abourezk. Hank, I think what is important in this, not only for your task force but all of the task forces, you are all going to make policy recommendations of some kind or another and I know you have them and I know the other forces have them.

It is up to you to give us specific ways of how those policies can be altered one way or the other. It is good to talk in general terms, as you have been talking, but a general intellectual discussion of what might be done or what is to be done is not enough. We are going to have to have it laid out just like a roadmap, so we can take the recommendations, if we adopt them, and present them to the legislative drafting service and put them right into bill form and try to move them through Congress.

What I am saying is that the Commission will not have the time and will not be able to expend the effort to take a general intellectual framework and transpose that into legislation. That is up to you, that is up to all of the task forces. I hope you will all keep in mind that is exactly what we need as you start writing your reports.

Mr. Adams. One of the things, also cognizant of our own time limitations, we are going to spell out all of the alternatives for future actions. We are going to discuss different options, different alternatives, but without saying a step-by-step reform or we are not going to take one, say, component of BIA and say this is what should be done to change that, to reform.

We will try first, to spell out a complete new policy structural framework in the standards of how that new structure would best be able to fulfill responsibilities that the existing structure is not doing, rather than saying what minor or major changes should be made in the existing structure to do that.

So, we are not going step-by-step, just giving a slightly different character to the existing structure.

Commissioner Bruce. Hank, you are going to spell out the definition of trust responsibility and its execution?

Mr. Adams. Yes; we are.

Commissioner Bruce. I don't find it in your report, that is why I asked.

Mr. Adams. Yes; we are going to. But even at this late date, we are still directing questions to the Interior Department relating to what they consider to be trust responsibility. They are giving it a different application almost daily over there and they have statements, legal analyses written in the solicitor's office that are being rejected at the Secretary's level.

Legal analyses of trust responsibilities are still being adjudged for their political acceptability or non-acceptability by the political elements in the political department as well as the White House and Office of Management and Budget.

We are trying to get some clarification of where they are standing on their definitions or lack of definitions. We will give a clear-cut, straightforward statement of what we see as being both the nature of trust responsibilities as well as the standards that need to be upheld, some of the procedures that need to be followed, and both the administrative and judicial enforceability or liabilities attached to trust responsibilities.

Congressman Meeds. Mr. Chairman, first, Hank, I would like to compliment you on your report. I think it is a workmanlike job and obviously you have put in a lot of time. I would like to ask some questions with regard to the methodology and procedure first, rather than policy questions.

The first question asked by the gentlemen from Illinois indicates what I am really looking for here—the question of jurisdiction.

A question of trust responsibility, also has roots in other task forces. What kind of communication and work have you done with other task forces on that issue of who is an Indian? Task Forces 3, 4, and 8 are also asking that question. What kind of communication do you have with them with regard to questions like that?

Mr. Adams. We have had consultations and discussions, particularly with Task Force No. 2, on tribal government. The other member of our task force, John Echohawk, was with us at a meeting in Denver.

We have had discussions since the quarterly report on just these types of issues. I have had discussions with the education task force briefly, just on the question of how we were going to define or touch upon these questions with respect to, say, education, eligibility for services. We have had these discussions.

Congressman Meeds. Have you had any formal discussions or meeting with other task forces?

Mr. Gover. Task Forces 1, 2, 3, 3, and 9, in Denver. A coordination of issues meeting.

Congressman Meeds. How many of your task force members are active in your task force procedures, hearings, preparation of reports and so on?

Mr. Adams. All three task force members have been active in the discussion of how we are going to treat issues. We had a meeting two weeks ago, after the quarterly report.

The meeting in Denver with the other task forces was prior to the development of the quarterly report. Our task force met with John Echohawk and Doug Nash, and we met also with the Director of the Commission....

Congressman Meeds. Who are the other task force members?

Mr. Adams. Doug Nash and John Echohawk.

Congressman Meeds. Are they working full-time?

Mr. Adams. Both are working in their respective offices in Boulder, Colorado, and in Pendleton, Oregon, on draft reports relating to trust responsibilities, treaties, and some of the things like water rights.

Congressman Meeds. Did they help you in the preparation of this report?

Mr. Adams. Only from a discussion basis, then I formulated it.

Chairman Abourezk. What about the research? Did they help with the research?

Mr. Adams. In part. They are, more or less, going to be moving into Washington for this final drafting portion of the report. They have not had the same opportunity to review all of our resource materials that are mostly centered here in the Washington office, but they have done independent research, as well as major documents that we have sent to them.

Chairman Abourezk. The question is, "What will be your specific legislative recommendations?"

Mr. Adams. We are doing a draft bill on an organized new department, at the Secretary or Cabinet level, entitled the "Department of Indian Affairs."

Chairman Abourezk. Does that have a trust council authority concept included in it?

Mr. Adams. The trust council authority concept will be tied into that organizational plan, but our judgement is the Bureau of Indian Affairs in the Department of Interior cannot carry out its obligations.

Chairman Abourezk. You are suggesting it should be removed from the Interior Department?

Mr. Adams. Yes.

Chairman Abourezk. How about congressional committees? Should they be separate committees? The Indian Affairs Subcommittee should be out the Interior Committee?

Mr. Adams. Yes; it should be. There should be some way of divorcing the dealings of Indians at the congressional level from the committee structure of Congress.

There are several ways the Congress operates out of committee and subcommittee jurisdictions; the Economic Committee, the Budget Committees of the House and Senate. We are going to ask for something different on the part of Congress in dealing with the tribes.

Chairman Abourezk. What will that consist of?

Mr. Adams. I am not certain of the final form right now. We are discussing this with a number of people. We are reporting on a number of things we see as problems in the relationship between Indian tribes and the Congress.

Some very recent activities we will be reporting on, for instance, is the introduction into the Senate of the United States of the Arizona tribe's water bill. We have statements from two Senators of the United States, who have made public statements to the effect these are our Indians, they aren't any other Senator's Indians.

In trying to localize problems when you are dealing with national obligations, the area Indians don't belong to Senator Goldwater or Senator Fannin and it is a problem. If a Senator can control what happens to Indians in his State, the same as Senators can control who gets on the Federal bench in the Judiciary, we think there is something wrong in that relationship and we are going to be reporting on some of these type of things in building this case for a new relationship with Congress.

Commissioner Jake Whitecrow. Mr. Chairman, I have had about a week to review a lot of these reports. I have tried to go through yours because I think your particular report is going to have a great responsibility in the entire Commission report.

As an Indian—who for some forty-seven years has lived under the blanket of being what we have been told all of our many years that we are a ward of the United States and that we are, in effect, subject to the rules and interpretations of one particular department of the government—I was very interested in your approach to the subject of sovereignty, insofar as the trust responsibilities of the federal government are concerned.

Can you tell me at the present time, whether or not your task force has gotten into the subject of sovereignty and what type of sovereignty or what quantity of sovereignty do you see coming out of your task force? Are you recommending a return of this form of sovereignty to the tribes?

Mr. Adams. As a primary base, we have reviewed colonial treaties and relationships that existed between Indian tribes and the governments of England, Spain, France, and the Netherlands.

We have reviewed how that relationship developed to see what the character of sovereignty for Indian tribes was at the time the United States came into being.

The best expressions of that character of sovereignty, we find, are in the volumes, the *Law of Nations* by Emmerich de Vattel and these are the authorities John Marshall looked to in deciding the first Indian cases. These are the authorities that Thomas Jefferson and John Adams and George Washington looked to in trying to structure just what the relationship with tribes would be.

So we're beginning at that point, to see just what the character of sovereignty was acknowledged or recognized for Indian tribes at the beginning of the United States, and looking to the principles involved in the initial relationship, say, as opposed to going to the 1934 Solicitor's opinion—the Margold opinion—on what are the rights of self-government.

We are going back to the base point to see what were the principles of self-government, the principles of relationship in the beginning of the relationship with the United States.

We do find in our analysis that the basic relationship is one of between sovereign entities or between two governments, rather than, say, the United States to individual Indians and the trust relationship initially was acknowledged to be more in the form of a protectorate relationship between nations, rather than an all-consuming power vested in the United States, to control all elements of Indian existence for Indian's benefits.

Then we reviewed the end of treaty-making in seeing what was the basis for any treaty-making and what was the effect of that 1871 act of Indian treaty-making. We have a tentative judgment that although the 1871 act was a restriction that the United States could impose upon itself to stop recognizing tribes as independent nations who might be contracted by treaty, but that act did not create new powers for the United States to legislate completely over Indians.

Commissioner Whitecrow. In your comments here you brought up Justice Marshall's opinion that Indian tribes might best be denominated as being domestic, dependent nations.

.... However, it does worry me when Dr. Blue Spruce, at Tahlequah, Oklahoma, said the Office of American Indian programs had identified over 800 Indian tribes with populations from two through 90,000.

That particular statement really gave me some concern. How do we return any form of sovereignty to a domestic, dependent nation with a population of two?

Mr. Adams. We are not asserting that domestic, dependent nations exist, irrespective of the factual situations. When Justice Marshall was speaking in the 1830's, there had been, at that point, some tribes who were more or less regarded as extinct because they were only a handful of people left and they were not categorized in the same way Justice Marshall categorized the Cherokees.

Congressman Yates. We were discussing before the definition of an "Indian." Do we have to move into definition of a "tribe" now? You raise the question of a two-member tribe.

Commissioner Whitecrow. I think we have to face this issue head-on as a Commission. I think the Commission's responsibility is to get into the definition of who is an Indian and who is an Indian tribe. I think this is most important from the Commission's standpoint.

Chairman Abourezk. I would personally tend to agree with that. I think we have to deal with what is a tribe as well as what is an Indian.

As usual, we are always cramped for time. In order to get this room, because we have votes on both sides today, we have agreed to give it up at 11:30 and come back at 1:30. They have another meeting scheduled here.

Some of these task forces will take longer than others and Hank will take longer because he gives convoluted answers to every question we ask him.

Mr. Adams. That is because in all of the other Commission meetings no one has asked me any questions.

Testimonial

August 10, 1976

Meetings of the American Indian Policy Review Commission:

The first report that we are going to take up this morning is that of Task Force No. 1. Hank Adams, you are here to present that?

Statement of Hank Adams, Chairman, Task Force No. 1, Accompanied by
Kevin Gover

Mr. Adams. Yes; I am here. The task force report was submitted to the Commission a little over a week ago.

Chairman Abourezk. Did everybody in the Commission get a copy of that report in sufficient time to go over it?

Then I guess we will open up with Commission members who might want to ask questions or make comments about it.

Congressman Meeds. Mr. Chairman, and members of the Commission, first let me say that I have not had an opportunity to read the full task force report. I have only had access to the summary prepared by the staff.

It is not signed so I don't know who did it. I am well aware of the hard work of the chairman of this task force, Hank Adams, and of his capability, but I must say from the limited resources that I have had available to me and have had the time to take advantage of, that I am very, very chagrined with the task force No. 1 report and the summaries that I have seen of it.

First of all, I think that task force No. 1 went far beyond the original charge—which was a study and analysis of the Constitution, treaties, statutes, judicial interpretations, and executive orders to determine the attributes of the legal relationship between the Federal Government and Indian tribes, and the lands and other resources that they possess.

They got into the field of other task forces. One of their major recommendations is that of a new structure for dealing with Indian matters, which I think was the primary function of the other task forces.

I find the suggestions and recommendations of the task force at the threshold totally unrealistic in today's world, and the kind of thing which will, if adopted by this Commission, make our task force reports and our Commission report and recommendations almost totally impossible to enact into legislation.

I see no way personally to establish complete economic independence of the tribes. I see no way to return the Black Hills to Indian ownership. I see no way to restructure, as they have set forth, an independent agency at super Cabinet level, a Department of Indian Affairs, or whatever you want to call it.

I see no thorough discussion, at least in the summary, of what the trust responsibility is with regard to tribes, with regard to resources, with regard to individuals. I see no discussion of the trust responsibility with regard to individual allottees as opposed to tribes.

Mr. Adams. Just in brief response, I would say that the summary is not a fair review of the report either with respect to trust responsibility, treaties, and discussion of the law either as is or what anyone might hope it to be or wish it to be.

Commissioner Whitecrow. What I am questioning here, frankly, I have been hearing all around the country with people I have been visiting and have been confronted with in the past. I have noticed that most people feel, particularly, that the federal government has a trust responsibility of assuring the protection of lands, whether it be individual or tribal-owned lands.

Also they have pretty well indicated to me that opinion of the trust responsibility also gets into the protection of mineral resources in addition to the absolute certainty that treaty rights are protected.

I don't find in the report here any place when it actually defines trust responsibility. Do you have that in your report somewhere?

Mr. Adams. Yes. There is one section that deals with it exclusively from legal standpoints. There is one section that deals with it exclusively from legal standpoints. There are two sections that deal with it from historical development and construction and trust responsibilities going back to the early 1500's.

Commissioner Whitecrow. Can you tell me where, in your report, you refer to any recommendation with regard to the continuation of trust responsibility?

Mr. Adams. In section seven, the analysis of trust law, and in section three, which also shows some of the difficulties of just saying that the trust responsibility should be continued forever.

That is implicit on page three in both items one and two as well as three. The question of permanency as tribal entities—distinct as political communities.

Commissioner Whitecrow. Did you, in your report, at any place look into the policies that we have experienced in the past with regard to determination and also the new, current policy of self-determination? Did you look at anything with regard to perpetuity of trust responsibility of the Federal Government in regard to self-determination?

How did you approach this?

Mr. Adams. Yes. We approached it probably in four separate places: One, in the discussion or analysis of the law; two, the section that relates to the state of confusion in which the trust responsibility has been as a result of failure to clearly define trust responsibility in the past, and a ready refusal on the part of the Department of the Interior to define trust responsibility in an y formal opinion or statement that would then set some standards for itself or set some rules that would have to be imposed on, say, the Department of Interior and all its agencies.

Commissioner Whitecrow. Let me ask you another question. Then I will be finished.

In regard to sovereignty: We keep hearing this constantly every place we go, that some tribes have sovereignty to a degree, and in other cases that tribes have very small or slight amounts of sovereignty.

When we complete our work on the Commission, if we do determine that a tribe does have some sort of sovereignty to a certain extent, whatever that extent might be: How have you covered this particular fact of activity insofar as trust relationships?

For instance, if it is determined that a tribe does have the sovereignty as an independent nation, I think that possibly would be very difficult to achieve, but in the event it should have sovereignty as an independent separate nation: How have you covered trust relationship or did you?

Mr. Adams. First of all, through our historical analysis of trusteeship and treaties, we indicated the formation of the relationships generally was formation of a protectorate or trusteeship relation. In exchange for that relationship and the obligations it carried with it—both to the United States and to the tribes, the Indian people—that a surrender of some portions of sovereignty is a legitimate price to exact for that relationship of trusteeship and the obligations assumed by the US support.

So we do not claim an external international sovereignty for the separate tribes. Virtually every treaty—not eighty-five percent of them—particularly declare the dependence of the tribes involved on the United States of America or on the US Government or on the Government of the United States.

And in doing that, in framing or forming that relationship, there is a surrender of some elements of sovereignty, particularly in the first instance, the surrender of external sovereignty.

But it comes with a price to both parties to the relationship. It comes with an assumption of obligations on the part of the United States and it comes with some responsibilities on the part of Indian people or of the tribes.

Also, in our analysis and historical review, we show authority where the trusteeship between the United States and an Indian tribe also is protective of that tribe's retained level of sovereignty or self-governing character or his tribal autonomy as a distinct political society or group.

Commissioner Whitecrow. Let me ask you this question. Perhaps Kevin will get involved in this also. I see the report has no stated actual definition of trust responsibility.

However, it is implied in a few places. The report implies trust responsibility includes a duty of the federal government to provide services. In regard to this, particularly in your charge of task force No. 1 with treaty review: When we began taking a look at the return of some powers to tribal government, when we start looking at treaty boundary areas, if we take a look at this particular aspect that is a return of some semblance of a system of government and a reestablishment of some system of tribal governments particularly with jurisdiction over some areas. How have you looked at this in regard to private government relationships, with regard to county governments within the State?

Mr. Adams. Pretty much on the jurisdictional question, we were saying we have deferred to task force No. 4. However, we do imply—not particularly stated in our report—that there has to be a greater level of accommodation between Indian tribes and State and local governments as well as the United States, and get out of the realm of dispute that has a single finish, and that is the extinction or extermination either of some rights or the complete elimination of their interests.

There has to be a greater level of accommodation between the varying interests, particularly at local levels, but it has to have a different outcome than has been the case when these disputes have come up in the past.

The Cherokees going from North Carolina to Oklahoma and having no place to go beyond that, but having a lot of injuries done to all their lives where they ended up, or a good share of them.

Commissioner Whitecrow. One of the things, Hank, I believe we have to consider here is the fact of local relationships. You know that possibly is one of the ways, as I understand this, of local politics and local pressures being applied for the abrogation of treaties.

I think we still have the same attitude, that we have got to look out for at the standpoint of this Commission. If we recommend something that is just too far out, local politics are going to become deeply imbedded, and there is a very good possibility that we could bring about a great amount of turmoil and a great amount of personal problems within a community.

I think our trust relationship here has to enter into this aspect and make it very clear to the entire community what the trust relationships are. To give you a general idea of what I am referring to here: I have had many people come to me and ask me, "Well, what happens in the event this Commission comes out with the fact that the tribal government actually does have taxation authority and to what extent, what kind of taxation are we talking about? Personal property, sales, taxation on land, etc.?" If a tribe should have that kind of authority and it imposed that type of authority on its tribal members, or if it should try to impose that type of authority on all persons living within the original treaty boundary area for that particular tribe: What kind of fight will we have on our hands and what type of problems will the federal government have insofar as its trust relationship to that tribe in protecting that tribal government's rights to apply this?

Mr. Adams. If you look at the reservations around the country today, you have very few tribes asserting tax authority generally over their own members, and certainly not over the trust lands.

You have them asserting tax authority only in rare instances against non-Indian, and yet you have that intensive fight trying to get that taxing authority into the hands of State and local governments.

That fight exists now, the fight you referred to. It is going on in virtually every State legislature in the West every year or biennial session of their legislatures. One of the problems is that Indians have been overtaxed. I think we show that in some strong ways in our report, and we show that it is not Indian people who are on the federal dole.

There are three million white people in the State of Washington. In four States—Washington, California, Arizona, and New Mexico—there is a $15 billion drain on the US Treasury.

That is how much they get in federal funds beyond the taxes that they pay into the US Treasury from all their personal incomes, business incomes, whatever the federal source of taxation.

That would finance ten years of federal programming at the present level. That is what the United States has paid out to the white populations of those States. The states that are furnishing that $15 million are Illinois, Michigan, and Pennsylvania alone. Those three states are asking the federal government to extend their responsibilities to their Indian citizens, and the federal government is saying, "No."

They are delivering $15 million more than they are getting back from the government, but that doesn't go to the Indians. It is picked up by Washington, California, Arizona, and New Mexico alone.

Nobody denies that Washington, DC, has a right to exist as a distinct community, whether or not it is self-governing, but the population of Washington, DC, today is roughly equal to the national Indian population by census.

Yet people are questioning Indian communities' rights to exist. That is what those treaties were all about—saying that Indian communities would exist forever. This report does not substitute for any on of those treaties.

It does not deny the voice of any one of those treaties. Every one of those treaties assumes some obligations. Most of them surrender much, but most of them promise that the Indian communities have the right to exist forever.

Chairman Abourezk. How do you respond to the statement of position by Indian traditionalists? I am thinking specifically now of some of the traditionalists on the Pine Ridge reservations in South Dakota who say that, "We don't want government social services. We don't want the government interfering with us in any way."

I don't know what percentage of the population they may comprise but nevertheless, there is a substantial number who say that. They just want the government to leave them alone.

How do you reconcile that attitude on the part of a lot of traditionalists around the country who say that? I am sure you talked with them more than I have?

Mr. Adams. I would have no problem with that either as an individual or as a government of the United States. I think that there are a lot of people who have had some real feelings about even more traditional people in Latin America or South America or even this satellite television program to put a television in every Eskimo house throughout the Arctic, in Canada, or Greenland.

I have some personal questions about the morality of imposing that impact upon all those traditional people who in their own way were probably doing fine.

Chairman Abourezk. You don't have any personal problem. My question is: How do you reconcile it with a strong advocacy position of what we call a trust relationship?

Obviously, one part of a trust relationship is that the United States should defend Indian rights on land, hunting, fishing, and so on. The other part of it is trust rights to social services, health, welfare, education, and so on.

How do you reconcile it? Not whether or not you have any problems with it, but how do you do both at the same time? How do you satisfy both demands?

Mr. Adams. On a single reservation you can have essentially a pluralistic or a small pluralism within an Indian community.

Chairman Abourezk. What does that mean?

Mr. Adams. You can have Indians divided on other bases than the political division that have come to be accepted among the tribes. You can have different lifestyles.

Chairman Abourezk. You can or cannot?

Mr. Adams. You can on a single reservation. Another problem is dealing with Indians as a singular group—either nationally or at a local level.

Chairman Abourezk. Let's take Pine Ridge as a microcosm of what might be happening nationally in a lot of places. You say you can have both lifestyles. Now my question is: How do you do so without intertwining the political aspects?

Let me give you an example. The Wounded Knee takeover in 1973, as you know better than I do, arose directly because the traditionalists said the Pine Ridge government, the political system that exists on this reservation, is ignoring us.

We want to be left alone. They are leaving us alone. In a way they are also depriving us of our rights out here, so that political fight resulted in a lot of violence, as you know, and more political division.

Mr. Adams. There are some other elements on the "leave us alone" concepts that generally also relate not just to "leave us alone in our most depressed state" or the lowest state that we have been driven, allow us just the minimum chance of recovery so that our "leave us alone" posture is viable, not saying return the Black Hills but that there are some necessities for at least partial recovery for many of the people, before they can, say, have the freedom that they want or require to more or less have that "leave us alone" situation again.

Chairman Abourezk. That is not precisely what they said to me. I don't know if you attended the hearings held in 1973 following the Wounded Knee event. Were you there?

Mr. Adams. No; I wasn't there.

Chairman Abourezk. The thrust of what most of the witnesses said was: We are going to manage if you can make Pine Ridge leave us alone, and if you can make the BIA leave us alone, and the FBI and the government. We will manage somehow.

We would much rather be deprived that way then we would the way we are deprived at this point under these conditions. But they didn't say, we want a lot of things to change before you leave us alone. They just said leave us alone.

Mr. Adams. They don't want to be frozen in the static situation that exists right now. I am absolutely certain of that. I am meeting with some of their treaty council tomorrow in Wisconsin.

They are asking the White House for some things again. That is not because they want to be frozen in a static situation that now exists. They do need some breathing space before a "leave us alone" situation becomes viable again...

Taxation, Economic Development, and Socioeconomic Issues

In these documents, Hank Adams displays a relentless and yet accomplished understanding of three complicated topics. These selections include a broad socioeconomic overview of the pressing needs in Indian Country, a brilliant analysis debunking Washington State's asserted right to impose elements of its taxing authority over tribal lands and resources, and a critical response to Senator George McGovern's diatribe against the Native nations in South Dakota.

While each of these documents is thoroughly researched and revealing, his outstanding report to Ramona Bennett of the Puyallup Nation shows the breadth and depth of his self-taught knowledge in the complicated area of taxation, especially as it was then playing out in tribal-state conflicts, with increasing numbers of states, in clear violation of a federal statutory law, treaty law, case law, and state constitutional law, attempting to extend their jurisdictional reach ever deeper into Indian lands.

Testimonial

Hearing Before the Subcommittee on Employment, Manpower, and Poverty of the Committee on Labor and Public Welfare. US Senate. Ninetieth Congress, First Session. Examining the War on Poverty, Part 14. Sparta, Wisconsin (May 26, 1967)

Prepared Statement of Hank Adams, Chairman. Washington State Project of the National Indian Youth Council, (NIYC), Taholah, Wash., Member, NIYC Board of Directors, Schurz, Nev.

Mr. Chairman and Members of the Committee: I respectfully request that our statement be entered in the official records of testimony in your Committee's current hearings on the conditions of poverty in the United States and the needs in government and other programming for eradicating such conditions and their causes.

The relevance of such concerns as related to the American Indians and Alaskan Natives is, unfortunately, usually ignored or given but perfunctory pass-over in consideration by the Congress.

It is not difficult to disregard 1/400th the American population—the number of Indians being but a few more than the total 525,000 elementary and secondary school students in New York City proper, or roughly comparable to the American population cycled to Vietnam in the past year.

Perhaps basic cause for lack of appropriate attention, however, arises in the thought that the American Indians are fully taken care of. This is not the case.

Certainly America has no official racial policy by race other than its "Indian policy."

And more than a third of a billion dollars ($355,514,176) was appropriated in fiscal year 1967, (exclusive of supplementals) is now being spent each year to handle the policy's economic, education, health and related contingencies by just the Bureau of Indian Affairs (BIA), US Public Health Service (PHS), and the Office of Economic Opportunity (OEO)!

Yet the Indians remain collectively the worst clad, most poorly fed, least educated, poorest housed, most diseased, fastest growing yet fastest dying, group in America (If we were but a minority bloc of citizens of any country in Africa, Eastern Europe, or Southeast Asia—very few of us could even qualify for immigration into the United States of America!)

If we may overlook these facts about the first citizens of this land, surely we must find some compulsion to inquire into what is being—and not being—accomplished with the more than billion dollars in federal funds that are now expended in the Indians' name every three years.

Such inquiry should take form of an exhaustive national investigation!

Demands National Investigation

This requires much more than a review of programs and results under OEO's $32,000,000 additive Indian budget (FY-67), but also of programming and results under BIA's $241,570,000 and PHS's $97,733,000 Indian budgets as requested for Fiscal Year 1968.

We believe the fact that this nation's "100 Years' War on Indian Poverty" has escalated to such levels without materially affecting the basic causes of poverty in most areas demands a national investigation of all Indian programming, results, related policy objectives—and the overriding failures that become unmistakenly evident.

Essential human services and assistance should not be viewed as merely a condition of a federal trust relationship and consequent geography. Even if so regarded, then our protectorate government can be found but in criminal violation of its trustee responsibilities and guilty of gross negligence in the related assistance role—both to those less than twenty-five percent of Indian people that it does serve, in some degree, and to the more than seventy-five percent of Indian people that it does not serve at all.

People of OEO Programs

OEO provided grants to approximately sixty Indian Community Action Agencies (CAA) last year, comprising a service population of 291,301 persons in seventeen states, of which 235,303 fell below the national poverty index, according to OEO figures.

Unserved Poverty Areas

News releases originating in OEO have stated that ninety percent of Indian people below the poverty level are now being served under OEO and related poverty programs. These figures, first, seem to follow the fallacious figures of the Bureau of Indian Affairs—and at the outset ignore the calculated 47% of Indian people no longer living on the reservation—irrespective of their economic standings.

A most flagrant oversight, however, appears to exist relative to the 53,000 Alaska Natives (Eskimos, Indians, and Inuits)—among whom some of the most critical and severe problems of poverty in the nation exist by standard definitions.

More than ninety percent of these people have not qualified for major programs of OEO and its Special Field CAP section and Indian Desk, whether or not ostensibly eligible—primarily because most Alaskan Natives are not in conformance with the reservation system in the Continental United States.

In testimony before the House Appropriations Committee earlier this year, the Federal Development Planning Committees for Alaska cited an unemployment rate among Alaskan Natives of eighty percent.

Yet the Civil Service Commission reported a total of 666 American

Indians (including those from other states) among the 14,104 Federal employees in Alaska in 1966. The Department of Defense report of State population employed by the military in Alaska cited seventy-one Indians as compared to 6,627 non-Indian citizens. Alaska Natives comprise one-third the permanent resident population of the State!

The Selected Vital Statistics for Indian, Alaskan Natives, and All Races for Calendar Year 1964 lists an infant death rate per 1,000 registered live births of 54.8 among Alaskan Natives compared to 24.8 among All Races—and a comparative 24.6% and 5.5% of deaths, respectively, which occur before 1 year of age. Moreover, the birth rate of Alaskan Natives is 45.7 for registered live births per 1,000 population, while only 21.0 for all Races.

The average age of death for Alaskan Natives is 34.8 years, whereas the life expectancy at birth for all races is 70.2 years.

Notwithstanding all the claimed program advances in the past decade among the Alaskan Native population—very much remains to be done. Yet too little is being done by all agencies concerned. OEO is scarcely involved.

A comparable situation exists in Western Washington State, as in others, where in the past federal activities (service and assistance) have been confined primarily to five of the larger and more financially stable Indian communities—while thirteen others have been almost completely ignored. The OEO appears to be following the long-standing patterns set by both the Bureau of Indian Affairs and the Public Health Service.

General View of OEO

Although the foregoing comments have generally taken a critical vein toward OEO, our basic belief is that it has done a great deal for the amount of funds available through it. However, we do not believe it should be viewed as something that it actually is not—nor credited with doing things that it has not done, nor serving people it has not served.

Its most positive points are that it provides capital directly to the Indian communities, and that it has stimulated better service activity and regard for responsibilities among other agencies.

It has been restricted most fully, however, in funding activities where it can be most useful, such as creating employment on permanent basis for heads of families, and in precluding its funds act as investment capital.

Few of OEO's overall accomplishments would survive a termination of the program.

The failure to bring balance between structural or improvement materials and paid labor under Neighborhood Youth Corps, for instance, has resulted in many of these programs engaging in little more than meaningless activities or time-clock leisure. Otherwise it could be one of the most promising government programs available for its particular age group.

National Indian Program—BIA

There can scarcely be favorable accounting by accomplishment for the several billion dollars expended in the Indians' name in the national history. After being programmed through a poverty program of sorts for the past 150 years, the American Indian finds himself yet at the lowest levels of national living standards and conditions. We approach the future with the most negative economic, education and employment rates in the nation.

Whereas fault must be shared by all, on the part of all there has been great reluctance to examine into the bases and cause for failure. As result, the federal government has always found itself committed most fully to errors of the past and primarily engaged in carrying forth the burdensome foundations for continuing failure.

Even now the basic causes of poverty and its related conditions remain virtually untouched and unaffected by federal programming. The long history of costly "palliative" federal expenditures has been unbroken by OEO and is continued by the Bureau of Indian Affairs. A program of "curative" aid has never been adopted.

Now is the time to recognize the overall federal program as the gigantic placebo that it is—inefficient, ineffective and degrading—perhaps placating a few Indians and misleading the American public into thinking the Indians are being taken care of—but doing little to bring forth the actual solutions required and doing less to eradicate conditions of poverty, misery and despair.

Income and Employment

The annual federal expenditures for the BIA, PHS, and OEO together would now amount to incomes of $4,685 for average families of five, if paid directly to 400,000 Indians.

The average annual Indian family income is, in fact, but one-third that amount ($1,000)—and is largely gained from sources other than federal expenditures!

Indian tribes themselves provided 57.6 million dollars in development capital in 1966. There are few statistics for determining the amount of States' expenditures directed toward Indian people. The primary source of Indian income, in any case, is in private and self employment.

There is an abominable fifty-eight percent of unemployment, underemployment, and seasonal unemployment among the Indian labor force nationally. It has been estimated by several university and private surveys that approximately 40,000 jobs are now needed by Indian adults.

The creation of new jobs is not keeping pace with Indian population growth, and has been without impact in providing the 40,000 permanent jobs that are needed.

Education and Employment

The BIA's Education Branch estimates that by 1969 there will be an annual output of 5,400 Indian high school graduates and in excess of 5,000 dropouts. The federal program will not accommodate the employment and additional educational education needs of these few numbers, nor deal with them as influx into the Indian labor force—let alone an increasing amount following annually and those of older age groups now in need of assistance.

Although it may readily be assumed that the high school graduates are in best position for helping themselves, a BIA study in 1966 indicates that the bulk of their Employment Assistance, Relocation and Adult Vocational Training programs are directed to this group.

High school graduates and college dropouts comprised sixty-eight percent of the recipients of adult vocational training, whereas persons with less than nine years of school comprised only nine percent of recipients. The graduates were recipients of thirty-six percent of assistance in securing direct employment and thirty-one percent of those receiving on-the-job training, as compared to thirty-one percent and twenty-eight percent respectively afforded these services among persons with less than nine years of school. Persons having attended between nine and eleven years of school comprised the remainder of recipients.

Yet the average schooling of young adults on reservations is only eight years—this average lowering progressively with older age groups.

Relocation and Vocational Training

If past patterns are continued, high school graduates will continue to command "practical priorities" under the BIA's Relocation Services and Adult Vocational Training, for which the Bureau requested $7,267,000 and $15,000,000 respectively for Fiscal Year 1968.

As estimated 4,186 units (10,085 persons) participant in this year's program can be projected to return to the reservations, if the relatively constant ratio of returnees indicated in studies for Fiscal Years 1953 through 1961 remain applicable. One-third the relocatees and trainees were found to return to the reservations.

The dubious success of the overall program is reflected in another sample study of the Bureau comparing annual earnings for a eight-year period prior to and after services were given.

Persons in the survey receiving direct employment assistance were earning $1,039 prior to services and $2,694 afterwards—an increase of 159%. On-the-job trainees were earning $1,264 prior to training and $2,119 afterward—an increase of sixty-eight percent. Adult vocational (institutional) trainees were earning $681 before training and an average of $3,120 afterwards—an increase of 358%.

BIA sheepishly noted that, "Most of the institutional trainees were single and under twenty-four years of age when they entered training. Income before receiving services, therefore, reflects earning capacity while still in high school. The Bureau does not infer that training alone increased the earning capacity of these younger adults by 358 percent."

Profile of Indian Education

Many of the problems the federal program purports to be alleviating among the adult Indian population are now being perpetuated in the education systems "serving" the Indian children.

Two-thirds the 161,694 Indian elementary and secondary student population are attending state-supported public schools. The 254 Bureau operated schools in seventeen States had 49,834 students enrolled in 1966.

As previously noted, more than 95,000 of the 162,000 Indian students are now projected to drop out before completion of high school. Also, more than 5,400 high school graduates and more than 6,000 dropouts are expected annually by 1969. The dropout rate is about ten percent higher in the public schools.

Not all Indians are suited to, nor capable of, attending college. Until a few years ago, it was the attitude of the Bureau that none were. Emphasis has not changed in programming, although one more reality was finally recognized.

Yet the levels of American higher education remains a moot question to more than eighty percent of Indian students—almost sixty percent not even completing high school—and with more than half having completed little more than a twelve years attendance record and a paper or plaque of substantially higher quality than the education to which it refers.*

Although pre-school is being given greatest emphasis presently, the report of Dr. James S. Coleman last year, "Equality of Educational Opportunity Report" indicated that the Indian child was closest to the non-Indian in aptitude at first grade level—but fell further behind the longer he stayed in school. Isolated studies have further shown that many Indian children with the higher IQs are the first to drop out of school.

The native Indian languages have never been considered a critical factor in the education process—the only concern that it not be spoken. More than forty-five tribes have more than a thousand persons continuing to speak their own language—this ranging up to the more than 100,000 combined Sioux and Navajo who speak their respective languages almost exclusively in their homes and communities.

If education policy is served by failing to use native languages as teaching media and prohibiting their use as communication media among students,

* Indian education was also being closely examined in 1967 by Senator Robert Kennedy, who chaired a Special Subcommittee on the subject during this time. After Kennedy's assassination, his brother, Edward, became cochair of the subcommittee. A two-year investigation culminated in a report, *Indian Education: A National Tragedy—A National Challenge*, that called for major reforms. Congress responded in 1972 when it enacted the Indian Education Act, the most comprehensive piece of legislation on Indian education to that time.—Ed.

we may question what objectives are accomplished when the students nevertheless drop out of school and then proceed to speak their own language almost exclusively the rest of their lives.

If education is regarded as a primary means of overcoming many of the problems confronting Indian people, much change is required in all quarters. As objectives have fallen victim to policies and prevailing attitudes, "education" has served but as destructive process for the Indian—not one of development.

Indian Housing Health

Under present pattern and pace, current housing needs shall not be met in another thirty years, and without provision for needs developing in the interim.

The BIA has estimated that 57,000 Indian homes are below standards and that 45,000 of these are in need of replacement at the present date. Notwithstanding the effort to remove as many as ten percent of Indian people to the cites each year, the estimate seems conservative.

The housing sewage and sanitation and water needs (seventy-five percent of the Indians are reported to secure their drinking water from unsafe sources or to haul their water from sources in excess of twenty miles away).

This has crucial implications toward overcoming abominable health conditions and disease rates, now featuring such indices as an infant and child mortality exceeding in rate and in number the American casualty counts in Vietnam as of last January 1st.

Conclusion

American Indians approach the future with the most negative economic, education and employment rates in the nation.

That this should be so is nothing less than a national scandal of ineffectiveness and failure—of short-sightedness and simple-minded solutions.

Indians have had and yet possess many resources that have not been at advantage and command of the millions of people in the urban slums and ghettos and other rural poor. And although 'the Indians' problems compare with theirs in nature and severity or degree, ours is without their magnitude and dimension. Comparatively, Indians' poverty is but a 'small' problem— but one with which the federal government has long dealt.

Congressional concern should not be focused upon how Indians are faring in the present "war" with the ally OEO—but should review in close examination the entire scope of federal Indian programming.

The need for change is too obvious to be denied, and too critical in nature to be betrayed. Requirements of change fall not solely upon the Indian, but extend to the structural elements that have administered only too fully upon Indian lives and given little more than misguided direction to Indian destiny.

Any forthcoming change must, in any case, be free from the "termination" concepts that have gained so frightfully in influence and proven so destructive in effect—and carried some to new depths of poverty.

It seems inconceivable that our country can rightfully encourage or insist upon needed government and social reforms among nations of Central and South America in serving their populations, which totally include forty million Indian people—yet resist and ignore the necessary reform in our government for serving the needs of half a million here.

I respectfully request that the accompanying materials be included in the record as appendages to this statement.

Thank you most respectfully.

Letter

February 14, 1972.
Ms. Ramona Bennett
(Member, Puyallup Tribal Council)
Re: Unconstitutionality of State Tax

Dear Ramona:

I have discussed the matter of Washington State impositions of excise or other taxes upon cigarettes held or sold by Indians upon Indian reservations with Vine Deloria's new law firm, and with Mr. Hans Walker, formerly Interior Department Office of the Solicitor's specialist on taxation prior to becoming director of its Water Rights Office. There is uniformity of opinion that the state tax against Indian properties and Indian trade is patently illegal. It is hoped that Mr. Deloria can enlist the active involvement of the several new law firms specializing in litigation of Indian rights in proceeding in court challenges against the existing state laws—and the chances that the federal government shall join in support of the Indian positions has improved in the wake of the current activities and attitudes of the Washington legislature.

Since I have successfully argued the issues of law and secured restraining order against the Washington Revenue Department in the US District Court of Oregon, Mr. Deloria suggests that I outline the judicial doctrines and specific constitutional, statutory and treaty law which vest Washington Indians with impregnable immunities to state taxation. Although it is summary in nature, I hope you may find it useful.

1. An illegal tax, passing by any name, remains an illegal tax.

The United States Supreme Court has consistently looked beyond the labels attached to taxes to test their legality in application to Indians and our various immunities to state taxation:

Where a federal right is concerned we are not bound by the characterization given to a state tax by state courts or legislatures, or relieved by it from the duty of considering the real nature of the tax and its effect upon the federal right asserted. (*Carpenter v. Shaw* (1930); *United States v. Allegheny County* (1944); *United States v. City of Detroit* (1958).

The present measure before the Washington Legislature in providing for a 'possession' tax merely attempts to affix a respectable label to an illegal tax. The measure is more repugnant than prior enactments inasmuch as it, in effect, attempts to tax 'Indian immunities to taxation' and use such immunities as a source of State revenue. The enforcement provisions of the bill, taken with the proposed tax, appear to carry the State directly into new violations of the Constitution of the United States, which in Article I, Section 10, provides: "No State shall, without the consent of the Congress, lay any impost or duties on imports or exports…(nor) shall pass…law impairing the obligation of contract…"

The taxing measure attempts to "lay an impost" or to effect an embargo against the importation of untaxed cigarettes for resale by Indians, and as well impairs the contractual provisions of treaties between the United States and Indian tribes. The question is not what violation of the US Constitution is made, but rather, which provision of the federal Constitution is being violated most grievously: its Commerce Clause (Article I, Section 8); its Supremacy Clause (Article IV, Section 2); its Prohibitions Against the States, (Article I, Section 10); or its Fourteenth Amendment, Section 2, which preserves the unique and sovereign status of "Indians not taxed" in relation to the federal and state governments?

2. The Medicine Creek Treaty of 1854, 10 Stat. 1132, provides for absolute immunity to State taxation for Indian people and their properties and their trade with anyone within "the dominions of the United States."

The Medicine Creek Treaty, which became the model for other treaties with Washington Indians, provided in Article 2 that Indian lands should be held for "their exclusive use." Article 8 declares: "The aforesaid tribes and bands acknowledge their dependence on the government of the United States..."; and Article 12 provides: "The said tribes and bands finally agree not to trade at Vancouver's Island, or elsewhere out of the dominions of the United States..."; andArticle 13 proclaims: "This treaty shall be obligatory on the contracting parties as soon as the same shall be ratified by the President and Senate of the United States."

In the landmark case of *Squire v. Capoeman* (1955), the foregoing treaty provisions, coupled with statutory authorization for allotment of lands to individuals under the General Allotment Act of 1887, were interpreted by the United States Supreme Court to provide exemption to a federal capital gains tax for the timber sales of a Quinault Indian. Mr. Chief Justice Warren, in writing the Court's unanimous decision, ruled:

...exemptions to tax laws should be clearly expressed. But we cannot agree that taxability of respondents (Indians) in these circumstances is unaffected by the treaty, the trust patent or the Allotment Act....Although this statutory provision is not couched in terms of non-taxability, this Court has said that "Doubtful expressions are to be resolved in favor of the weak and defenseless people who are the wards of the nation, dependent upon its protection and good faith." Hence, in the words of Chief Justice Marshall, "The language used in treaties with the Indians should never be construed to their prejudice." *Worcester v. Georgia* (1832); *Carpenter v. Shaw* (1930).

2. The Medicine Creak Treaty, however, was more explicit than the Allotment Act in its terms of non-taxability of Indians and their properties. Article 6 provided that treaty reserved lands would be assigned to "individuals or families" "on the same terms and subject to the same regulations as are provided in the sixth article of the treaty with the Omahas." These terms and regulations, stated in the Omaha Treaty, 10 Stat. 1043, provide:

"...And the President may, at any time, in his discretion, after such person or family has made a location on the land assigned for a permanent home, issue a patent to such person or family for such assigned land, conditioned that the tract shall not be aligned or leased for a longer term than two years; and shall be exempt from levy, sale, or forfeiture, which conditions shall continue in force, until a State constitution, embracing such lands within its boundaries, shall have been formed, and the legislature of the State shall remove the restrictions...No State legislature shall remove the restrictions herein provided for, without the consent of Congress."

The treaty terms and regulations additionally provided that Indians might lose their lands, or their assignment be canceled, and federal financial aid be withheld from them, if they did not remain upon their lands or reservations, or if they refused to return to them and "resume the pursuits of industry." The Medicine Creek Treaty provisions are expressed explicitly in "terms of non-taxability"—and placed explicit restrictions upon the State legislature, which the treaty clearly anticipated with statehood.

3. Washington State accepted her admission into the family of States on condition that the Indian rights should remain unimpaired.

The Enabling Act for Washington Statehood expressly conditioned Washington's entry into the Union of States by provision that Indians and Indian properties should remain immune to State taxation. The condition was incorporated into the Washington State Constitution, Article XXVI, as an irrevocable ordinance between the citizens of Washington and the people of the United States. Considerable weight has been attached these ordinances and provisions of Statehood Enabling Acts, conditioning state entry into the United States, by the US Supreme Court. The case of *Squire v. Capoeman* (1955) construed the immunity against state taxation as evidencing an intended invulnerability against general federal taxing measures, which might defeat the purpose of Indian tax immunity. The Supreme Court relied upon the enabling act prohibitions against state taxation, and the federal control over Indian trade and commerce, to affirm tax exemptions to non-Indians trading with Indians in *Warren Trading Post v. Arizona State Tax Commission* (1965). And the landmark case of *United States v. Rickert* (1903), proceeded from the affirmation of continued tax immunities under provision of restrictive statehood enabling acts, to rule that Indians' general tax exemptions must be given contemporaneous application and modern usage in order to extend to new types of business enterprises, properties and industries, in order to contribute to the economic and social advancement of Indian people consistent with federal policy. The Washington Supreme Court has consistently embraced the *Rickert* doctrine.

The US Supreme Court rendered its clearest decision relating to the effects upon Enabling Act taxation restrictions when applied to Indians subject to terms and regulations of treaty provisions identical to the Medicine Creek Treaty Indians in the case of *The Kansas Indians* (1866). It deserves emphasis that the

Congress, the State of Washington, and Indian people were fully aware of the significance of these restrictions in the Enabling Act and the Washington Constitution's Article XXVI irrevocable ordinance with the United States. In spelling out the relationship between Indians and the State government, the Court ruled:

If under the control of Congress, from necessity, there can be no divided authority. If they have outlived many things, they have not outlived the protection afforded by the Constitution, treaties, and laws of Congress. It may be said that they cannot exist much longer as a distinct people in the presence of the civilization of Kansas, "but until they are clothed with the rights and bound to all the duties of citizens" they enjoy the privilege of total immunity from state taxation. There can be no question of state sovereignty in the case, as Kansas accepted her admission into the family of States on condition that the Indian rights should remain unimpaired and the general government at liberty to make any regulation respecting them, their lands, property, or other rights... The Treaty of 1854 left the Shawnee people a united tribe, with a declaration of their dependence on the national government for protection and the vindication of their rights...This people have their own customs and laws by which they are governed. Because some of those customs have been abandoned, owing to the proximity of their white neighbors, may be an evidence of the superior influence of our race, but does not tend to prove that their tribal organization is not preserved...(Kansas) accepted this status when she accepted the Act admitting her into the Union. Conferring rights and privileges on these Indians cannot affect their situation, which can only be changed by treaty stipulation, or a voluntary abandonment of their tribal organization. As long as the United States recognize their national character they are under the protection of treaties and the laws of Congress, and their property is withdrawn from the operation of state laws.

Even after Indian lands had been assigned under the Medicine Creek Treaty to Nisqually and other Indians, and prior to Washington Statehood, the US Supreme Court rendered another decision which turned upon the constitutional bases for Indians' immunity to State taxation. Incidental to ruling that the Fourteenth Amendment did not confer United States citizenship upon Indians in the case of *Elk v. Wilkins* (1884), the Supreme Court effectively ruled that the Fourteenth Amendment continued Indian immunities to State taxation. In pertinent parts, the Court decided:

Under the Constitution of the United States, as originally established, "Indians not taxed" were excluded from the persons according to whose numbers representatives and direct taxes were apportioned among the several States; and Congress had and exercised the power to regulate commerce with the Indian tribes, and the members thereof, whether within or without the boundaries of one of the States of the Union...Indians and their property, exempt from taxation by treaty or statute of the United States, could not be taxed by any state.

The US Supreme Court in *Elk* concluded that the rule of Indian immunity to State taxation "is confirmed by the second section of the Fourteenth

Amendment," with its explicit reference to "Indians not taxed."

4. The United States or Congress has not consented to taxation of Indian properties nor to interference with Indian trade and commerce by the State of Washington by device of taxation.

The real and personal properties, as well as the trade and commerce of Indians, have been uniformly protected by the federal courts in their exemptions to state and local taxation. The federal responsibility to act for the benefit of Indian people, and even the federal policy to provide for the social and economic advancement of Indian tribes and individuals on fair and favorable, or competitive, terms with non-Indians, have been judicially confirmed as lawful instrumentalities of the United States government which are to remain free from the devastating or destructive effects of state taxation. (*Squire* (1955); *Warren Trading Post* (1965); *Rickert* (1903); and *Agua Caliente Band of Mission Indians v. County of Riverside* (1971). The applicable doctrine is aptly presented in the case of *United States v. Thurston County* (1906), which stated:

...Every instrumentality lawfully employed by the United States to execute its constitutional laws and to exercise its lawful governing authority is necessarily exempt from state taxation and interference...The lands and their proceeds...are alike instrumentalities employed by it in the lawful exercise of its powers of government to protect, support, and instruct the Indians, for whose benefit the complainant hold them, and they are not subject to taxation by any state or county...No change of form of property divests it of a trust. The substitute takes the nature of the original and stands charged with the same trust...

The courts have proceeded beyond the "federal instrumentality doctrine" in affirming protections to Indian exemptions and immunities to state taxation, however—declaring them to be "vested property rights" which may not be extinguished against the will of Indians possessing them. The most explicit ruling on this point is stated in *Morrow v. United States* (1917), holding:

...There is no question that the government may, in its dealings with the Indians, create property rights which, once vested, even it cannot alter. *Williams v. Johnson* (1915); *Sizemore v. Brady* (1914); *Choate v. Trapp* (1912); *English v. Richardson* (1912); *Jones v. Meehan* (1899); *Chase v. United States* (1915). Such property rights may result from agreements between the government and the Indian. Whether the transaction takes the form of a treaty or of a statute is immaterial; the important considerations are that there should be the essentials of a binding agreement between the government and the Indian and the resultant vesting of a property right in the Indian.

Noting that the decision was based upon contractual relationship of trusteeship rather than upon governmental wardship, *Morrow* strengthened its own ruling, thus:

That exemption of land from taxation is a property right is established. *Choate*, supra...if this exemption came to him as a legal right, it has fully vested. It came as such legal right if it rested on the solid basis of a binding agreement...

If there were any doubt as to the status of this matter, the understanding of the Indians as to the agreement would control...His rights are vested and are impervious to alteration against his will except through the sovereign power of eminent domain. One of these rights was freedom from state and local taxation.

The completeness of the federal protections for Indian immunities to unconsented taxation is such that even federal taxing measure have been held not to apply to Indians, unless an express intent to include Indians is manifest in explicit terms, or consent provided for. See *Squire* (1955); *United States v. Daney* (1966); *United States v. Wright* (1931)...Even the federal statute, *Title 28, United States Code*, section 1341, which otherwise prohibits the federal courts from enjoining or restraining the "assessment, levy or collection of any tax under State law," has been held to not apply to cases involving Indian immunities or exemptions to state taxation. See *Agua Caliente* (1971)...

5. Public Law 83-280 (1953), does not constitute a consent from the United States or the Congress to the State of Washington to tax the properties, commerce or trade of Indians, nor to regulate their commerce or trade in properties; Public Law 280 vests no taxing authority with the State, nor does it create any new tax immunities for Indians.

The Washington Legislature ought to closely examine the decisions of the Washington Supreme Court relating to Indians' cigarette sales in the cases of *Makah Indian Tribe v. Tax Commission*, and of *Tonasket v. State of Washington*, filed September 2, 1971, before basing the funding for new programs on such cigarette sales. The *Makah* case simply decided that the untaxed cigarettes had never been introduced into Indian or interstate commerce, but assumed a taxability or tax liability in Port Angeles which was not lost or vacated by transferring the cigarettes to Neah Bay on the Makah Indian Reservation.

The *Tonasket* case is more unique, and divorced from the general trade of cigarettes by Indians, inasmuch as both Tonasket claimed that Public Law 280 of 1953 created his immunity to state taxation—while the State of Washington erroneously claimed that Public Law 280 created its authority to tax Indians, and Indian properties and trade. A critical first distinction which must be drawn has reference to the fact that, unlike most Indian Reservations in the State, the Colville Reservation and lands were not established or reserved by specific treaty provision, and therefore not restricted, controlled or regulated by such treaty terms as provided in the Treaty of Medicine Creek and other such treaties. Although I would not deny the existence of a valid tax immunity upon the Colville Reservation, I would contend that such immunity does not have origin in treaty provisions or agreement, nor in Public Law 280.

(The two decisions disclaimed the applicability of the US Supreme Court decision in *Warren Trading Post* (1965), on the basis that the federal government had not maintained any system of Traders' Licensing in the State of Washington. The high court decision had ruled that a non-Indian "Trader" possessed a tax advantage and exemption against state authority on the

Navajo Reservation because the non-Indian was acting in furtherance of federal policy and programming, and was protected from state taxation as a federal instrumentality fully subject to the near-complete control of the Congress and the United States under implementation of "Commerce Clause" constitutional authority. The State Supreme Court apparently adopted a queer and unsustainable position that the United States Constitution fails by default in the State of Washington—ignoring, in the first instance, that Traders Licenses have not traditionally been required of Indians themselves in any area of the country, but only of non-Indians; and secondly, that the Indians' tax immunities have remained insuperable, even when non-Indians have had their Indian-based tax shields removed or eliminated.)

(The State of California, and its State Board of Equalization, has based its taxing policies in recent years upon the *Warren Trading Post* decision, and the limitations imposed by Congress upon the authorizations of Public Law 280 for extending civil and criminal jurisdiction over Indian lands to exclude taxing authority, as well as *Solicitor's Opinion,* 58 I.D. 562 (1943) and 57 I.D. 124, thereupon determining that the fields of regulating, licensing, or taxing Indian business operations or properties used in trade is closed to state action. In rulings dated July 23, 1969, and May 1, 1970,...J. Kenneth McManigal, tax counsel for the California State Board of Equalization, ruled that "groups of or individual Indians or both which are making sales and purchases on Indian reservation would be subject to Federal Trading Laws and would not be subject to" State taxing laws and authority. In accordance with the rulings, the State Board did not require the Indians to secure federal Traders Licenses, but instead merely acted to rescind State licenses and permits previously issued, as it were, improperly in not being lawfully required of Indians on Indian reservations.)

(California has held the afore-stated position even though "all Indian country within the State" was subjected to state civil and criminal jurisdiction by the explicit provisions of Public Law 83-280. Consent of the United States to assume an equal measure of civil and criminal jurisdiction was authorized to both Arizona and Washington, but in measure and effect, no greater than that level of jurisdiction conferred upon California by the Act itself. The Act conferred taxing authority upon neither California, Arizona, nor Washington.)

Both the Colville Indian, Leonard Tonasket, and the State of Washington have embraced the qualification, limitation and restriction upon Public Law 280, included there-within, as basis for their respective tax immunities and taxing authorities. A brief background dispels the legitimacy of either position.

Public Law 280 limited any transfer of civil and criminal jurisdiction to States by the following qualification:

Nothing in this section shall authorize the alienation, encumbrance, or taxation of any real or personal property, including water rights, belonging to any Indian or any Indian tribe, band, or community that is held in trust by the United States or is subject to a restriction against alienation imposed by the United States; or shall authorize regulation of the use of such property in a manner inconsistent with any Federal treaty, agreement, or statute or with any regulation made pursuant thereto....

This proviso was intended as a basic limitation and restriction upon the authority extended to sates under the Act, and to prevent any misconstruction of it as being a taxing measure or conferring any taxing authority upon the states. The qualification was made necessary by a statutory suspension of the provisions of Statehood Enabling Acts, which otherwise would have precluded any number of states from assuming any measure of civil and criminal jurisdiction over Indians. The Enabling Acts affected, but not repealed, drew distinction between "civil and criminal jurisdiction" and "state taxing authority"—but the authorization to states to assume jurisdiction over Indian territory was prefaced by the statement, "Notwithstanding the provisions of any enabling Act for the admission of a State, the consent of the United States is hereby given..." Accordingly, a reservation of Indian tax immunities was necessary in order to confine the operation of the Act to a transfer of civil and criminal jurisdiction and to prevent its extension to taxing authority, maintained in the Enabling Act provisions.

Public Law 280 simply preserves and protects Indian tax immunities in existence prior to its enactment; it creates no new exemptions, but exempts all taxing authority from an operation of its jurisdictional law and authorized transfer.

The Washington Supreme Court has erroneously construed the qualifying provision as being "an enumeration" of tax exemptions and created a "taxing authority" over all matters, properties, persons, and activities "not enumerated." That Court has simply ignored the fact and prevailing judicial doctrine that "the 'ordinary' rules of taxation" do not apply to Indians in tribal relations. *Daney* (1966). Also see *Squire* (1955); *Wright* (1931); *Morrow* (1917); *Rickert* (1903); and *Agua Caliente* (1971). The 1966 *Daney* case, with strong reference to the *Squire* case, most explicitly pronounced the doctrine: "Congress did accord a different set of rules of taxation." In abbreviated discussion, the Court stated:

The government makes much of the fact that, under the Act, an Indian... shall be taxed the same as...other citizens of the State of Oklahoma...This misses the mark. We are not dealing with an ordinary citizen. We are dealing with a non-competent Choctaw Indian...This Indian's lease bonus is taxable if and only if the Act of 1928 says it is....The government also says...it is not fairly to be assumed that Congress thereafter intended one set of tax rules for the Indians and another...for ordinary citizens." We do not agree. Congress did accord a different set of rules of taxation.

The *Daney* case also reiterated the limitations upon the courts and states in Indian taxing 'disputes,' which doctrine has repeatedly been cited by the

Washington Supreme Court, simply stating: "It may be said that there no longer exists any need to give the restricted Indian a tax advantage, that he has
become an independent, qualified member of the modern body politic, and,
indeed, that all the 'ordinary' tax principles should be applicable to him. It is for
Congress to make that determination and change the Act...This court cannot."

The judicial and statutory history of Indians relationship with the federal
government provides additional proof that a transfer of civil and criminal
jurisdiction has not carried taxing authority as incident to the transfer. From
the time of *Worcester* (1832), until the passage of the Assimilated Crimes
Act in 1898, Indians were largely outside the civil and criminal jurisdiction of the United States. The assumption of such jurisdiction over Indians
did not subject the Indian people and properties to federal jurisdiction as
incident of the assumption—indeed, most Indian immunities to State and
local taxation prevail as well against general federal taxing measures, unless
specific provision is made to include particular Indians and properties, or
unless the measures are applied in such universal terms as to extinguish all
exemptions and immunities otherwise held by Indians. In relation to general
taxing austerities of state and federal governments, as well as in a certain
remoteness to provisions of the Constitution of the United States, Indian
tribes and members thereof "have a status higher than that of states. They
are subordinate and dependent nations possessed of all powers as such only
to the extent that they have expressly been required to surrender them by
the superior sovereign, the United States" *Native American Church v. Navajo
Tribal Council* (1959).

Mr. Justice Douglas' decision for the United States Supreme Court in
Menominee Tribe v. United States (1968), interpreting the scope of protections
intended in the qualifying provision of Public Law 280 against the operation
of State authority, declared, with reference to the language and related matters: "...That provision on its face contains no limitation; it protects any...
rights granted by a federal treaty..."

Public Law 280 is definitely not a taxing measure, nor does it extend
any taxing authority to the States not previously possessed by them. That
the State of Washington, its agencies and its courts, have misconstrued the
nature and application of Public Law 280 is further evidenced in a 1971 ruling of the Ninth Circuit Court of Appeals in *United States v. Burland* (1971).
The Court ruled that "the language of Public Law 280 indicates that Congress
intended no more" than an extension of state civil and criminal jurisdiction
"on a geographic and subject matter basis rather than in terms of persons."

The federal court further noted that "separate legislation was contemplated to free individual tribes and the members of those tribes, as such,
from 'disabilities and limitations specially applicable to Indians.' Many such
statutes were subsequently enacted. Each contained detailed provisions for
distribution or management of affected property, removal of restrictions on

property transfers, termination of trusts and tax exemptions...and other matters." "Obviously, therefore," the Court concluded, "Congress was aware of the difference between ceding jurisdiction to the states in terms of subject matter and territory and ceding such jurisdiction in terms of persons. When Congress provided for the latter it did so subject to a variety of specific conditions not present in Public Law 280. If Congress had intended by Public Law 280 to do both, as appellant suggests, the provisions quoted and others like it would have been surplusage as to tribes to which Public Law 280 applied."

Implicitly, the Congress was aware of the difference between taxing authority and general civil and criminal jurisdiction. The Court rejected a position that an Indian whose tribe has consented to an extension of State jurisdiction became a "definitional non-Indian" when traveling to another Indian reservation where State jurisdiction had not extended, both in Montana. The agencies of Washington State, incidentally, treat this as an unsettled issue and persist in embracing the "definitional non-Indian" position, already rejected by the federal courts.

Finally, Public Law 280 may not be construed to extinguish any tax immunities possessed by Indians under applicable treaties, nor to equip any state with taxing authority not previously held by it—unless that Act specifically and expressly provides for such extinguishment or equipping. It does not. Different rules of taxation do apply to Indians, their properties and trade. The US Supreme Court has consistently held that "the intention to abrogate or modify a treaty is not to be lightly imputed to the Congress." See *Pigeon River Co. v. Cox Co.* (1934); *Squire* (1955); *Warren Trading Post*, (1965); and *Menominee Tribe* (1968), which held that treaty rights shall "not, by implication, be abolished."

The Supreme Court's 1906 decision, *United States v. Celestine* (1906), held that Indians and Indian properties, subject to provisions of both the Point Elliott Treaty (and identically, Medicine Creek Treaty provisions) and the General Allotment Act, were controlled by the superior protection of the treaty contract, particularly the Omaha Treaty "exemption from levy, sale, or forfeiture, not to be disturbed by the state without the consent of Congress," brings us to the present point.

While "bearing in mind the rule that the legislation of Congress is to be constructed in the interest of the Indian" *Celestine* maintained the absolute Indian protections on the basis that "it is for Congress to determine when and how that relationship of guardianship shall be abandoned. It is not within the power of the courts to overrule the judgement of Congress. It is true... courts may wisely insist that the purpose of Congress be made clear by its legislation, but when that purpose is made clear, the question is at an end...."

Respectfully submitted,
Hank Adams, Special Tax Consultant

Letter

September 6, 1973
US Senator George McGovern
Washington, DC 20510

Sir:

Your indiscriminate, intemperate remarks of last week, condemning American Indian persons and groups as "rip-off artists," contribute virtually nothing toward creating a climate of racial justice, and even less for diminishing the incidence of violence, either in South Dakota or elsewhere in the Unites States.

Your demonstrated inclination to selectively disregard the violence constantly committed against, and injuries done to, Indian communities and the daily lives of Indian people is not unrelated to the present turmoil evidenced among the Sioux Nations on the respective Reservations.

If one wants to detail "an anatomy of an attempted rip-off," comparable to many having common occurrence in non-Indian attempts to take advantage of Indian people and resources, one needs only examine the relationships of your Senate Office and personal associates to the $5.87 million claims judgement awarded to the Sisseton-Wahpeton Sioux Indians of the Lake Traverse Reservation in your State.

Anatomy of a Rip-Off:

As you know, a $5,870,000 land claims settlement was awarded to the Sisseton-Wahpeton Sioux Indians in 1967 and was appropriated by the Congress in 1968. However, absent a congressional authorization for distribution of the judgement, the funds were frozen in trust by the United States—some in the US Treasury and others deposited in interest-bearing accounts with several different banks, and were not available for use by the tribes.

Among the reservation's 2,350 resident Indian population, many of the Sisseton-Wahpeton families earn or receive less than $1000.00 annual income, from all available sources, to live on. Last year, sixty-seven percent of the male labor force was reported to experience chronic unemployment, while forty-seven percent of women workers remained without jobs. The tribe consequently has been eagerly seeking industrial development opportunities and, lacking other resources, has been heavily reliant upon the claims monies to begin meeting some of their desperate economic needs.

As US Senator from South Dakota, you undoubtedly have been aware of general tribal desires in these respects, when you routinely sponsored the measure to authorize distribution of their funds, and in your dealings with the matter as Chairman of the Indian Affairs unit. I assume that Mr. Owen Donley, your Indian Affairs specialist prior to his leaving your staff in 1969, also worked on these matters. Whatever legislation authorizing the distribution of funds did not reach the President's desk for routine approval and passage into law until latter October 1972.

Since the bills earmarked a minimum thirty percent of the award and interest to be used for "industrial development purposes," that portion of the amount was worth around $2,000,000.00 by time of the final action. This is not an insubstantial amount—it could be quite attractive to 'con men' and 'rip-off artists.' The attraction became operative when the monies were appropriated in 1968, notwithstanding their continued unavailability to the Sisseton-Wahpeton Tribes.

In a series of proposed joint white-tribal business ventures, a number of non-Indians attempted to place their designs upon this new Indian capital. (Previously I have related some of these incidents in an uncompleted report issued at the end of 1972. The completed report is enclosed, with the added portions being the subject of this statement.)

Washington, DC, attorney Owen Donley had a most persuasive approach and influence in representing "Larklain Products, Ltd." in selling business 'opportunities' to the tribe in 1972. (Last December, your office informed me that Mr. Donley had left his Senate staff position in 1969, but that "he's never stopped working for the Senator" indicating that he remained an important aide in your two-year US presidential campaign. In any case, his continued association with yourself was well-known.)

In 1972, four years after having their judgement appropriated, and five years after having won their claims case, the Sisseton-Wahpeton's were faced with a dual task of developing viable business and industrial enterprises— and yet securing authorization from the Congress and the related communities for making any of their funds, then increased to about $7,000,000.00, available to them.

Likewise, the "Larklain Products, Ltd." proposal for a "pet carrier" and plastics molding company on the Lake Traverse Reservation was dependent upon Senate and House action on the authorization for distribution of the Sisseton-Wahpeton funds for coming into being. The proposal provided that "no private funds" would be required from Larklain, but that the industrial plant would rely upon the capital investment from the tribes, plus various federal grants and loans. Coincident to Larklain's involvement with the Tribes, the Congress began moving toward the necessary actions on the final authorization.

Unsurprisingly, the private consultant firm, Booz-Allen, retained by EDA Technical Assistance funds, produced an evaluation report early in 1972 that was wholly "negative in nature and recommended that the Sisseton-Wahpeton Tribe not invest in the project."

Facing rejection of the project, Owen Donley, in behalf of his client "Larklain," met with tribal representatives and federal technical assistance personnel in Chicago on March 12th and 13th, 1972, to secure rejection of the "Booz-Allen" feasibility report instead. The general nature of the arguments were that the original proposal had been drawn on too small a scale and that a more grand design, calling for higher investments, would meet the objections of the negative evaluation. A narrative summary of the meeting states: "Mr. Donley said he has been in touch with the acting head of GSA (US General Services Administration) and has been assured that GSA would be interested in purchasing many different plastic products from a plant at Sisseton."

Owen Donley was accompanied to the meeting by Larklain's own consultant, a Mr. Art Chapman, to offer advice in favor of a substantial investment from the tribe's funds. Larklain's president, Mr. Jim Payne, claimed that if Mr. Chapman became directly involved in the project, Chapman's involvement itself would attract an additional $350,000.00 in credit and investment funds from private and corporate sources to aid the industry.

By the end of the meetings, the tribal representatives were convinced that they should proceed with Larklain: "It would be good business judgement for the Lake Traverse Development Corporation to go ahead." They were encouraged in that view by BIA Agency Superintendent Dennis Peterson, who "by virtue of his personal experience with the Mowbridge Plastic operation had some valuable comments to make and to add to the overall programs."

The non-Indian unwillingness to contribute any of their own funds to the project became obvious when evidenced in a letter of May 31, 1972 to Owen Donley from EDA Executive Planner Gideon Raile, responding to Donley's request that the Economic Development Administration and BIA "compensate Mr. Chapman as a consultant." EDA replied, "I realize a man of his caliber and experience wouldn't be cheap, but most valuable in coordinating the project."

Had the rip-off succeeded, the Sisseton-Wahpeton Sioux Indians would have expended a significant percentage, or hundreds of thousands of dollars, of their available "industrial development" funds to this project. The project was abandoned as apparent result of unrelated actions of tribal members to secure federal and state investigations of a white man, who was acting as tribal business manager during that same time, and who was found to have a decades'-long record of fraud, confidence, and other criminal arrests and convictions. When the investigations of this questionable character were sought, the various "respected" and "respectable" business interests, who had been trying to sell their projects to the tribe, also scattered from the scene.

I have little doubt that the principle attractive feature of the "Larklain Proposal" for the tribal business managers was the involvement of Mr. Owen Donley, because of his known association and closeness to yourself—then a US Senator crucial to certain legislative action, as well as then being a US presidential candidate. The latter capacity might well have influenced certain questionable judgements of EDA personnel, given its then vulnerable position under the Administration.

The largest rip-offs in this country are occurring within the limits of the law—where wrongful actions, abuses of influence and position, can yet be legal. Some good examples arise where parent corporations have found it profitable, under the nation's tax system, to use subsidiary companies to fail with losing business propositions in "partnerships" with Indian tribes, using mostly tribal and federal funding to undertake their profitable "failures."

Sincerely yours,
Hank Adams, SAIA

Critiques of Federal
and Native Agencies

Hank Adams's concerns about fairness, justice, and equality sometimes compelled him to turn a critical eye on institutions, organizations, and individual policy makers—be they Native or non-Native—when he believed they were violating the rights of Natives or their own organic charters.

In the documents that ensue, we witness Adams challenging and criticizing Native organizations like the National Congress of the American Indian, the now defunct National Tribal Chairman's Association, and even one that he worked for in his early days, the National Indian Youth Council. And, of course, he continued to confront entrenched federal organizations like the Bureau of Indian Affairs, the Federal Bureau of Investigation, and others for some of their practices.

He was also willing to focus his attention on the actions of specific tribal nations if he discovered that their constitutions, membership requirements, or voting practices were in need of vital sunlight so that necessary reforms could be put into place. Importantly, his appraisals and critiques were also well researched and fully documented, as his attention to detail has always been one of the hallmarks of his modus operandi.

Essay

1970

Approaching a "Third Century of Dishonor"
by Hank Adams

The latest White House message on American Indians may create a new sense of accomplishment. It almost assures that nothing substantive will be done to alter conditions of life which the presidential statement properly ranks 'at the bottom' on 'virtually every scale of measurement.' Its policy rejection of termination of federal relationships is noteworthy; in context, it hardly matters. The old programs remain, threatened in proposal only be limited transfusion of 'red control' at local levels. Apparently no effective Indian political force exists to provide more. More organizations develop to consume Indian lives and to maintain distance from the issues and critical problems which have devoured too many such lives.

The National Congress of American Indians (NCAI), which repeatedly has credited itself with "killing the termination issue" while seeming preoccupied with the 'dead issue' most of its quarter-century existence, is already under contract to Spiro Agnew's National Council on Indian Opportunity (NCIO) for $80,000 to begin "implementing the President's plan" by holding sixteen $5,000 meetings. Another grant from Commerce's Economic Development Administration is expiring. Additional to receipts from its 183 member tribes, NCAI is otherwise largely dependent upon a $200,000 grant from OEO's Indian Division, Office of Operations, running two years from June 1, 1970. The grant is for "encouraging economic development on Indian reservations"; it also helps maintain their seventeen-member staff in dignified headquarters in Washington, DC, and Albuquerque, NM.

NCIO, whose white director Robert Robertson competes with the Indian members for credit as the "moving force" behind the presidential proposals, is itself product of Lyndon Johnson's Executive Order and Indian message of March 6, 1968. Its contract payment to NCAI will come out of its congressionally authorized $300,000 budget, as will funds for a number of Indian consultants being selected for task assignments from approximately fifty resumes volunteered to them.

The National Indian Youth Council (NIYC), once a politically sophisticated group of activists, ends its first decade of operations in Washington, DC, entrenched for the summer under an iron-clad contract with the Bureau of Indian Affairs (BIA). Their short-term $72,000 contract, mainly from BIA employment assistance funds, sustains forty college-age interns in shuffling between federal agencies, congressional offices and private organizations to learn how their government operates. Some are learning difference between sham and sustenance; others experiencing development of misplaced loyalties at $100 per week; with high take paying out at a hard-earned $1,500 per month. The interns move for a final two weeks of community and university program orientation in Gallup and Albuquerque, NM, where NIYC maintains headquarters and where a concentration of Indian organizations has built up under church and federal funding. In that area, besides NCAI and NIYC, are Southwest Indian Development (SID); Organization of Native American Students (ONAS); and the multi-purpose Gallup Indian Center.

A new Indian unit recently opened office in the Nation's capitol under a six-month $72,400 grant from OEO's Legal Services Division to provide a director, staff counsel, secretary and consultant to the American Indian Task Force, Administrative Services Corporation (AITF) (ASC). AITF is the by-product of the $120,000 project concluded by the white Citizens Advocate Center (CAC) to produce the well publicized, decimally-precise, sometimes-accurate report, *Our Brothers Keeper: The Indian in White America* (New Community Press, 1969), as edited by CAC Director Edgar S. Cahn with accompaniment of an Indian editorial board or listing. The new monies, in category of research and development (R&D), expire with the calendar; the corporate (recipient) status of ASC does not. ATTF director Judge Charles Lohah, Osage from Oklahoma, readily refers to their R&D designation when questioned on their purpose, which appears to be formulation of recommendations based on field inquiries and familiarizations now being undertaken; and to further capitalize on the impact of the $120,000 CAC report...

Another national organization has evolved from the resignation of LaDonna Harris from her expiring NCIO term, resulting in the spin-off creation of Americans for Indian Opportunity (AIO) and celebrated fundraising parties at the expensive New York Plaza and in Southampton, Long Island, NY, in June and July. Mrs. Harris has shunned government funds for her myth-dispelling program, relying instead upon foundation support and the drawing power of celebrities like Barbra Streisand, Candice Bergen, and her own husband Fred, the US Senator from Oklahoma. So far, foundations have responded meagerly with a "couple small grants to get AIO started" in a Washington, DC office.

American Indians United (AIU), which fumbled around under restricted Ford Foundation funding for a year attempting to develop the first credible coalition of Indian-controlled urban centers and organizations, has momentarily dropped from view. Indian activists in Minneapolis, Chicago, Seattle, Denver, New York, San Francisco and Los Angeles have gained public visibility and some accommodation from news media, but remain lost in orientation to local issues and limited concerns.

Promising moments do occur; and fade. The newly-formed All Indians Coalition, comprised of groups which spearheaded the confrontations at Alcatraz and Pitt River in California, on Fort Lawton and salmon-producing rivers in Washington, in the Alaska land and revenue settlement issue, and at Ellis Island and the island chain in the St. Lawrence Seaway of New York and

Canada, raised questions of national strategies and objectives at a meeting of convenience on July 1st. The next day, the groups marched on the Ford Foundation to demand examination of their Indian aid programs, particularly in area of legal assistance. Finding nothing objectionable in the eighteenth-month $155,000 supplemental grant to the California Legal Services (CLSI) disclosed to them, the groups backed off. An FF program officer later referred to them as "Panthers without a punch." The All Indians Coalition settled down for the moment to organize a mutual assistance communications network.

The point for focus in the preceding and in the President's message was perhaps most clearly stated at the coalition meeting by Dave Matheson, action director for Survival of American Indians Association (SAIA) of Washington. Matheson, who is turning down Selective Service deferments in favor of testing his claim to draft exemption under a Treaty of Medicine Creek provision and an April 25th Puyallup tribal ordinance prohibiting military service by tribal members in foreign or domestic actions under US command, declared: "It's time we stopped America's wasting taxpayer dollars in the Indian's name and stop America from destroying Indian people in the taxpayers' name. We must expose the irrationality of federal programing and the Bureau of Indian Affairs; and we must eliminate the irrationality of Indians betraying one another in that structure!"

Mr. Nixon does not propose rational programming for Indians, nor even offer minor reform for controlling the $626,000 federal expenditure obligated to be spent, ostensibly in Indians' behalf, in Fiscal Year 1971. The $626 million allegedly serves 462,000 reservation Indians; there's speculation that the new census will have found about half "America's Indians" off the reservations, excluded from the federal programs, and spending.

The fictional character of service populations can be seen in a look at the education allocation of 221,000 Indian children of school age: slightly over 50,000 attend federal Indian schools; 89,000 attend state public schools with federal aid currently budgeted at the $20 million level under the 1934 Johnson-O'Malley Act; the others are absorbed in local state and church schools without special federal aid, with many not in school at all.

The cruelest implications for the Indian future comes in the President's plan to "develop their economic infrastructure" with an Indian Financing Act of 1970, supplemented by continuation of the BIA's Industrial Development Program. In noting that seventy-one commercial and industrial enterprises have come into operation in the last two years, Mr. Nixon dishonestly fails to inform the Congress that the 6,000 new jobs he mentions are the total established under IDP in the fourteen year life of the program, not just the past two. The BIA itself is continuing under a schedule that will add 6,252 additional employees to its employment structure by 1973 over the 16,177 it counted in 1968.

Other figures developed in 1968 showed non-Indians securing 56.6% of gross income from Indians' non-irrigated agriculture lands; grossing $52,400,000 in lease of just 2.13 million acres of select Indian agricultural lands out of the total 44.2 million acres in use for range and dry farming. Now the government is asking general authorization for ninety-nine-year leases to encourage non-Indian industries to settle on the reservations, while treating the needs of an extraordinary number of Indian jobless with financial aids to white interests and non-Indian businesses.

By advocating return of 48,000 acres to Taos Pueblo in a non-economic move, Mr. Nixon could afford to remain silent on the question of an equitable claims settlement with the natives of Alaska, where the potential to totally eliminate poverty is readily possible. The July 16th measure passed by the Senate, even with a ten million land acres selection and billion dollars revenue provision, it is not directed toward that aim. Probably the best the natives can hope for in the House is action on the measure and a shortening of the cash payment schedule.

Most active support of the Alaskans was the New York based, Association of American Indian Affairs (AAIA), a white organization in the business since 1922 and now operating on a budget anticipating income of $522,000 in their current fiscal year which began in February. The federally-funded Indian organizations in the lower forty-eight states were noticeably inaudible and grossly underfunded.

In lieu of granting Indians command and functional control over their existing economic and monetary resources and fifty-five million acres of reservation lands, Mr. Nixon offers unit control over some lowest levels of the Bureau of Indian Affairs. Funds could even be contracted to Indians to hire the bureaucrats now holding the jobs; the incentive for attracting quality personnel to such lowly undertaking: their federal civil service standing will remain intact.

In short, the government is advocating a general spread of the 'Quileute Plan.' There the BIA has tried to convince the Quileute Tribe of the seacoast town of LaPush, Washington, to sink the major portion of a $130,000 claims award into development of new freshwater sources to serve the thirty-seven white businesses to whom the Bureau has leased all the tribe's shoreline and waterfront, including a river mouth boat harbor servicing hundreds of ocean-going charter fishing boats. The whites gross more than seven million in a six-month season while the tribe realizes a mere $8,000 in lease income and another $3,000 in landing levies per year. The BIA argues for the new water sources, which the Quileutes themselves do not need, with a promise to help the tribe establish and operate the first Indian business: a parking lot. The Bureau, in their wisdom, has advised, "If you control the parking, you control the economy!"

Memorandum

June 22, 1973
Memorandum Regarding the Nisqually Indian Community & Reservation
To: US Senator James Abourezk, Chairman
Senate Indian Affairs Subcommittee; et al.

I respectfully offer this informational memorandum to your offices for assisting in responding to requests recently addressed to you by numbers of Nisqually Indians from that Washington State reservation, and for raising the most pertinent questions with the Interior Department and BIA in helping to resolve the crucial matters at issue.

Nisqually Indians v. Interior Secretary Rogers Morton, Filed June 8, 1973, in DC Federal District Court by thirteen enrolled and non-enrolled Nisqually Indians, this lawsuit presents the fundamental issues and problems of concern:

A. Rights to Membership in the Nisqually Tribe of Indians;

(1) Under existing Constitution & Bylaws (September 9, 1946);

(2) As vested by the 1854 Treaty of Medicine Creek;

(3) As vested by the 1884 Nisqually Schedule of Allotments;

(4) As altered or preserved by 1934 Indian Reorganization Act;

(5) As affected by 1918 Condemnation of Nisqually Lands;

(6) As permanently denied by exclusion from 1965 Membership Roll;

(7) As extinguished by recent Constitution, Adopted July 9, 1973.

B. Dispossession of Individual and Tribal Rights as Nisqually Indians by wrongful construction of incomplete enrollments, and adoption of the new Constitution, through abuses of Administrative authority and approvals in "final" actions disregarding the controlling Tribal Constitution and Federal Laws and Regulations.

C. Denial of Treaty Protections to off-reservation "Lieu Lands";

(1) Contrary to Articles 2 & 6, Treaty of Medicine Creek;

(2) Contrary to Article 6 of the 1854 Omaha Treaty;

(3) As wrongful consequence to dispossession and displacement of Nisqually families by 1918 Condemnation Proceedings.

D. Denial of Treaty Trade & Commerce Rights and Tax Immunities.

E. Surrendering to Washington State the Nisqually sovereign tribal rights to manage fisheries and control the taking of fish by, treaty Indians throughout its customary fishing domain as secured by Article 3, Treaty of Medicine Creek; and totally dispossessing numerous treaty Indians of all their treaty fishing rights.

F. Designed Derivational Irregularities in Constitutional Election.

II. The adoption of a new tribal constitution on June 9, 1973, is the matter of most immediate concern. Specific new provisions relating to present and future membership in the Nisqually Tribe, as well as those relating to the form of the day-to-day "governing body," are the principal issues in dispute.

However, the irregularities in the conduct of the federal election are challenged as issues representing abuses of federal administrative authorities having regular occurrence or frequency.

The Nisqually constitutional election—to revoke the 1946 Constitution and Bylaws, and to adopt a completely new constitution—was authorized by the Office of the Interior Secretary on February 26, 1973. As pointed out for attention in the letter of authorization, under 25 CFR 52.5 such authorizations become void after 90 days. Nonetheless, the election was held 104 days after the issuance of authorization.

o o o

III. Rights to Membership and Entitlements to Vote: The Secretary's Election Board considered only those Indian persons whose name appear upon a "Revised Membership Roll," approved by the Associate Indian Commissioner on November 3, 1965, as being qualified Nisqually voters who could be registered.

The sixty-three Indian persons whose applications for voting registration were disallowed by the Election Board claimed their entitlements to vote under the explicit provisions for membership in the Nisqually Indian Community contained in the Nisqually "Constitution & Bylaws," approved September 9, 1946, by the Office of the Secretary of the Interior.

o o o

The Secretary's approval form for the 1946 Constitution declares: "All officers and employees of the Interior Department are ordered to abide by the provisions of said Constitution and Bylaws." Yet it is plain by the facts that neither the development of the 1965 "Revised Membership Roll" nor the June 9, 1973, secretarial election were controlled by the provisions of the present tribal constitution.

o o o

It begs credibility to think that a tribal constitution formulated by the Indian Service and approved by the Secretary of the Interior in 1946 would define and determine the Indian people who were to be governed by it and who would give it application with reliance upon a census document which did not exist, or which could not be reasonably or correctly constructed. Also, the non-existence of the 1945 census roll, referred as the basis for declared membership and future membership, raises the question of how the 1965 revised membership roll could have been developed from a non-existent base.

o o o

IV. Development & Use of the 1965 Revised Nisqually Enrollment: The Nisqually Indian complainants, some being included on the 1965 enrollment and some being excluded from it—but all being persons who unquestionably qualify for membership under the 1946 tribal Constitution, argued with the BIA and Interior Department that the central questions of rights to membership and entitlements to vote should be decided prior to an election on, or imposition of, a new constitution for the Nisqually Indians. If possessing tribal political rights before the election, by right or entitlement to membership, they reasoned that they should be permitted to vote in the election which would determine how their political rights were to be controlled or governed after, or as result of, the election.

Since 1965, federal and tribal actions relating to Nisqually Indians have been governed more fully, perhaps controlled completely, by the 1965 Revised Nisqually Enrollment, constructed under the direction of the BIA, than by the provisions of the 1946 tribal constitution.

The 1965 enrollment, in controlling governmental actions and relationships at all levels of government, effectually dispossessed numerous Nisqually Indians of their legal rights as Nisqually Indians, or as federally recognized Indians entitled to benefit from a range of federal programs.

o o o

V. Subversion & Violation of the Purposes & Provisions of the Indian Reorganization Act of 1934:

The Nisqually Indian Community or Tribe was organized under Section 16 of the 1934 Indian Reorganization Act. Although, surprisingly, the Nisqually Indians did not become organized under an approved IRA constitution until September 1946—it was among the first tribes in the nation to vote in favor of becoming organized under its provisions.

The Nisqually Tribe voted on October 27, 1934, to organize under an IRA constitution. For that election, no absentee ballots were issued or allowed.

o o o

The general reason given for not allowing absentee voting was that the available time between the election and its initial authorization and scheduling was too brief to allow either a clear determination of who should be eligible to vote or the issuance of absentee ballots. Although there was a first determination that the Nisqually Indians should "organize as a Tribe," the failure to allow absentee voting was inconsistent with that determination under the provisions of the IRA law. (The Quinault Tribe in the same jurisdiction vehemently opposed absentee voting in deciding whether to be excluded from IRA organization. In their election, non-resident absentees overwhelmingly favored IRA organization and won the majority by a margin of less than a dozen votes of more than 600 cast. Withstanding tremendous federal pressure, the Quinaults subsequently never did organize and adopt a constitution under IRA.)

o o o

VI. Misapplication of Secretarial Enrollments: In pursuit of its policy and plan to reduce the number of Nisqually Indians who might claim treaty rights as fishermen for the harvest of salmon and other fish resource, the Interior Department used its authority under 25 U.S.C. 163—a law authorizing the Secretary to establish and approve tribal enrollments to be used for the limited purpose of "segregating tribal funds" for division or distribution—to formulate the 1965 Nisqually enrollment. The 25 U.S.C. 163 law can only be considered to be tangentially related to the Indian Reorganization Act and its purposes, if at all related. While the law allows for such enrollments' usage in distributing tribal funds to tribal members listed upon the, and under that law are declared to be legally conclusive as to the age and blood quantum of Indian persons listed, it is well-established that such enrollments are not necessarily to be regarded as being conclusive as to the rights of Indian persons not listed or named to be included in such enrollments.

o o o

The Interior Department has misapplied or abused its enrollment authorities to deny Nisqually Indians their rights under their tribal constitution, including membership rights for many. This has been clearly volatile of the congressional mandates under the Indian Reorganization Act and of the standing which the Congress assigned to tribal constitutions.

Summary of Nisqually Issues & Aims:
The several score of Nisqually Indians actively seeking resolution of issues discussed in this paper and raised in the lawsuit against Secretary Morton do not seek to take anything away from other Indian persons. They only seek the small justice of ensuring that a number of Nisqually Indians themselves are not deprived or dispossessed of their rights as Nisqually Indians.

The Interior Department in the past decade has wrongfully applied or abused the existing law which should be controlling upon its relations with the Nisqually Indians. A basic fault in its actions and deficiency in its considerations has been the general failure or refusal to review pervious federal actions affecting the Nisqually Tribe or Indian community to determine their intended effects and impact upon future or succeeding federal actions.

In the Nisqually lawsuit against the Interior Secretary, both the unqualified issuance of absentee ballots—and the extension of voting rights to eighteen-year-olds under the Twenty-Sixth Amendment to the US Constitution, contrary to provisions of the Nisqually constitution—are challenged in regards to the June 9th election. The absentee voting issue relates to conformance to the IRA. More significantly, the other issue questions (1) what constitutional standards are controlling upon the Interior Secretary's relations with or actions affecting Indians, or conversely (2) what constitutional protections may Indians invoke as Indians against actions of the Secretary; and (3) to what extent may the US Constitution intrude upon tribal actions and decisions in the exercise of the powers of autonomous self-government?

o o o

The succeeding questions, on separate page, are questions which need to be asked of the Interior Department, if the Nisqually complaints are to be adequately responded to.

Questions Which May Appropriately be Addressed to the Secretary of the Interior for Answering the Complaints and Understanding the Issues Affecting Nisqually Indians:

1. How soon is it expected that the newly-adopted Nisqually tribal constitution will be approved by the Office of the Secretary of the Interior?

2. Is there any likelihood that the new constitution will be disapproved?

3. Does your department or the BIA have knowledge of any Nisqually Indians who are entitled to Nisqually enrollment or membership under the 1946, or present, constitution who are not listed on the 1965 tribal enrollment?

4. Does the department or BIA have knowledge of any such persons whose application for registration to vote in the June 9th election was denied or disallowed by the federal election board?

5. For the constitutional election on June 9th, did the federal election board consider registration applicants who claimed entitlement to vote under the membership provisions of the 1946 constitution, or solely those applicants whose name appear on the 1965 revised enrollment? Did it register any Nisqually Indians not listed on the 1965 roll?

6. In organizing under the Indian Reorganization Act and constitution in 1946, did the Nisqually Indians organize "as a tribe" or as "Indian residents of a reservation"?

o o o

10. Does not 25 CFR 52.5 require that constitutional elections be held within ninety days after the issuance of authorization by the Office of the Secretary, or otherwise that authorization becomes void? How long after the date of issuance of authorization from the Secretary's office was the Nisqually election held?

o o o

12. Inasmuch as the political rights of all persons entitled to be enrolled as Nisqually Indians shall be controlled by any new constitution, when approved, would there not be any merit or advisability in an action of disapproving the constitution adoption until after the central issues of tribal membership are resolved and all persons entitled to be members are added to the tribal enrollment?

o o o

15. Would there not be merit or advisability in the Secretary's rescinding the 1965 revised Nisqually enrollment, or its approval, in favor of developing a complete, accurate as possible, up to date, Nisqually enrollment prior to acting upon or approving any major constitutional action by the Nisqually community?

16. Did the major dispute over Indians' treaty fishing rights in the Nisqually or Puget Sound are, or departmental attempts to alleviate that problem, play any significant part in the development of the 1965 enrollment? Have any Indians suffered State criminal prosecution for fishing by reason of not being listed upon that enrollment, while claiming Nisqually treaty rights? Has the department or United States acted to give judicial protection to any persons it recognizes to be of predominant Nisqually Indian blood who has been arrested for fishing under claim of Nisqually treaty rights?

17. In lieu lands were secured for Nisqually Indians in consequence of the 1918 condemnations, why has the department not sought to protect the rights provided to such good lands under the Medicine Creek and Omaha Treaties of 1854?

Letter

March 19, 1974
The President of the United States
Attn: Mr. Leonard Garment,
 Special Assistant to the President
The White House
Washington, DC
US Vice-President Gerald Ford,
Chairman, National Council on
Indian Opportunity (NCIO)
The Hon. Rogers C.B. Morton,
US Secretary of the Interior,
Department of the Interior
Re: Federal Agencies Relationship with the NTCA & NTCFI.

Sirs:

Having reviewed the January 18, 1974, GAO Report (B-114868) regarding operation of the National Tribal Chairmen's Association (NTCA), as well as its establishment and funding by federal agencies, we have no doubt but that the NTCA exists as an instrument of the federal government fully covered by the provisions and requirements of the October 6, 1972, "Federal Advisory Committee Act,"(86 Stat. 770)....

In the organizational chart for NTCA, as prepared for it by the Bureau of Indian Affairs and Interior Department officials, the advisory relationships are drawn to the White House and to the respective executive agencies or Departments. The narrative states:

NTCA will relate to the White House and Executive Agencies through its Board, Officers, and Executive Director. Initially, White House and Executive Agency contacts will be with the aid of NCIO and needs to consider the White House Counselors on Community Development, Human Resources, and Natural Resources.

Subsequent NTCA activities have demonstrated that, in varying degree and extent, each of your agencies or offices has worked with the NTCA officials as an "advisory committee" or comparable entity. Consequently, we herewith request various items of information, including designated transcripts of agency meetings with NTCA, under the provisions of the "Federal Advisory Committee Act." Additionally, we respectfully request that your respective offices and agencies detail for us the procedures which are being followed by each for conforming to the federal Act when utilizing NTCA (or National Tribal Chairman's Fund Incorporated—NTCAI) as an advisory committee or "resource." We request:

(1) A listing from each of your Offices or Agencies of all meetings with

NTCA Board, Officers, or Executive Director for securing advice, recommendation, or for promising commitments, with respect to governmental policies, actions, or appointments to federal positions; including information on the availability of minutes, transcripts or agency notes taken at or resulting from each such meeting;

o o o

(5) The transcripts and minutes of meetings between NTCA officers and representative Agency officials, including Messrs. Leonard Garment and Frank Carlucci, of the "Special Federal Inter-agency Task Force on Indian Affairs," as established November 6, 1972, during the period December 5, 1972, through January 8, 1973;

(6) The transcripts and minutes of agency and advisory proceedings for the January 18–19, 1973, meetings between Interior, HEW, NCIO and other agency officials with NTCA Board members and officers;

o o o

As a separate listing of requests, under the Freedom of Information Act, we would appreciate the designated offices or agencies providing us:

(1) From the Justice Department:

a. A copy of the September 1, 1972, White House Memorandum from Geoff Sheppard to Deputy Attorney General Ralph Erickson, requesting information for use of the President or John Ehrlichman in 1972 presidential Campaign Trips and for capitalizing on "criminal justice" issues;

b. A copy of Deputy Attorney General Ralph Erickson's September 8, 1972, Memorandum to Acting FBI Director Patrick Gray, requesting the FBI to secure the political information requested on September 1, 1972, by the White House;

o o o

d. A copy of the US Government Memorandum of September 11, 1972, containing the political information gathered by the FBI for Deputy Attorney General Erickson to transfer to the White House for use by the President or John Ehrlichman, and particularly all documents relating to or explanatory of the September 11, 1972, statement by the FBI that:

Militant Indian groups on Pine Ridge and Rosebud reservations (South Dakota) contend favoritism shown the non-Indian in criminal matters from the standpoint of investigation and prosecution. They also contend politics controls law enforcement within the Bureau of Indian Affairs (BIA).

e. A copy of the memorandum or statement of Assistant US Attorney R.

D. Hurd, Sioux Falls, South Dakota, between the dates of September 17th and 23rd, 1971, citing reasons why he desired no additional investigation of civil rights violation complaints made in regards to Indians and BIA or tribal police on the Pine Ridge Indian Reservation;

o o o

Available records reveal that NTCA, and an associated dummy corporation, or National Tribal Chairmen's Fund Incorporated (NTCFI), were established by the Department of the Interior and its Bureau of Indian Affairs, aided by the National Council on Indian Opportunity (NCIO), in a deliberately designed fraud upon Indian people. Since its inception in 1971, and through its expenditures of more than $875,158.00, NTCA has not escaped from that basic design. It has, consequently, been costly to both Indian people and other American taxpayers, while harming the general Indian welfare immensely.

My own questioning of a number of elected tribal chairmen in the Pacific Northwest supports a conclusion that most tribal officials are not even aware that there are two separate, although related, organizations: NTCA and the NTCFI. The GAO report does not indicate which, unless solely NTCA, has been recipient of their considerable federal advisory grant funds.

As indicated in the attached letter to OMB Director Roy Ash, the flow of federal monies to NTCA's Board of Directors began with an October 12, 1971, directive designating them a "consultive or advisory group." Prior to that, during the days of July 27–29, 1971, the Indian Commissioner's Office and aides established and structured both NTCA and NTCFI for its own select purposes—and retained Mr. Marvin Franklin, along with Associate Commissioner Arthur Gajarsa, to control that development.

o o o

BIA officials declined to become a "registered agent" for NTCA and NTCFI for the simple reason that "BIA wished to stay out of the picture as much as possible." Marvin Franklin immediately accepted appointment as legal counsel to NTCA, and there seems no evidence that he has formally relinquished that relationship at any subsequent time—through all the funding and lobbying enjoyed subsequently by NTCA/NTCFI, and through the period of subsequent federal and private employment of Mr. Franklin.

Both NTCA's status as a lobbying group and as an advisory group was stressed in a September 20, 1971, meeting with the Secretary of the Interior; resulting in a commitment that "yes, we should give them all the help we can"; and where Interior both asked the question, "Who speaks for the Indians?" and answered with its own declared hope, if not determination, that "NTCA will become the voice!" The directive for "advisory group" funding followed, citing the secretarial decisions of September 20, 1971.

We recognize that the "Federal Advisory Committee Act" was not enacted until almost a year later—nonetheless, its provisions extended for application to advisory groups already in existence or being utilized.

The initial development and succeeding actions of NTCA or NTCFI leaves some questions which should be answered for Indian tribes and people. Which group or organ has been funded by each respective federal grant?? Given the intense concern over construction of a tax-exempt, non-lobbying organization, has NTCA/NTCFI maintained clear separation of functions in its activities, including its reportage to the Internal Revenue Service, and particularly with respect to its uninvited congressional lobbying activity?

During the past two years, a number of elected tribal chairmen have been denied entrance to a number of meeting of NTCA, particularly when occurring in the security-tight Executive Office Building. This is not permissible under the Advisory Committee Act; is it consistent with the provisions of grants, contracts or other federal funding NTCA/NTCFI?

Subsequent to its December 1973 annual Convention in Phoenix, Arizona, NTCA's Board of Directors and Executive Director passed all political resolutions—misrepresenting their authorization for acting upon resolutions and the body which acted upon them. Such deliberate misrepresentation has permitted NTCA's executive officers and partial board to become the strongest lobbying group in favor of Administration legislative proposals, while disallowing question or examination of their merits. For instance, NTCA supports the Administration's plan for transfusing federal BI employees into the employment structure of the tribes while maintaining full Civil Service credits, protections or control. In the name of virtually all tribes, it also misrepresents positions to remain the strongest advocate for eliminating civil rights protections for Indian groups and individuals in reservation communities, and for denying them all recourse to abuses of tribal governing officials, power or authority!

It's downright pitiful that a few Indian people in official positions would allow themselves to be manipulated and misused so abusively as the handful of NTCA officials who have sold themselves to the Administration for these past few years. The relationship between NTCA/NTCFI and the various federal agencies epitomizes the gross artificiality of the Administration's policy of so-called "self-determination" for Indian people. Personally, I fully believe that both the President and Indian people have been betrayed by those policy-makers and decision-makers who have had free rein and acted in the field of Indian Affairs for the Administration since 1969. From the White House to the Indian Affairs for the Administration since 1969. From the White House to the Indian Agencies, the only remarkable "new dimension" evidenced among the personnel with the power in this Administration has been an almost-incomprehensible smallness.

We shall appreciate your most immediate response to this letter and its several requests for documents and information.

Sincerely yours,
Hank Adams, National Director

Letter

February 2, 1978
The Hon. James O. Eastland,
United States Senator,
Washington, DC 20510
Re: Opposition to Confirmation of Mr. Jack Tanner, Nominee for US Judge-
ship for Washington State

Dear Senator Eastland:

I respectfully request that this statement be entered into the record of hearing on the nomination of Mr. Jack Tanner of Tacoma, Washington, to be
appointed as a US Judge in the Western District of Washington.

o o o

I have been acquainted with Mr. Tanner since 1964, and had periodic personal contacts with him during the first decade after first meeting him. In
1964, he was acting as legal counsel for various Nisqually and Puyallup, plus
other, Indians who I was working with and with whom I've worked with
continuously since then. In fact, Mr. Tanner in 1964 acted to incorporate
the organization I now work for, and which I've directed since 1968, minus
several leaves of absence.

I have not previously stated opposition to Mr. Tanner's nomination, nor
provided information for consideration by any agency in pre-nomination
periods. My decision to not speak on this matter previously was premised
partly upon the possibility that this nomination would not be made; but
more so upon a disinclination to merely aid in the elimination of one potential nominee in favor of another who would be selected totally outside "merit
system" processes in this judicial district.

o o o

I call upon the Senate Judiciary Committee to delay action on this nomination and to refer it back to the Justice Department for additional investigative
review under the personal direction of FBI Director-designate William Web-
ster, whose own experience as a federal judge would lend greater understanding to the significance and importance of questions raised relating to this
nomination and to the qualifying of judgeship nominees.

I would note for the record that my last appearance before the Judiciary
Committee was in 1973 for the purpose of opposing the nomination of Mr.
L. Patrick Gray to become FBI Director. I have since appeared before other
Committees relating to nominees, and have provided counsel to the Interior

Department in the evaluation of potential or actual appointees for high positions in the Carter Administration.

Today, I am thoroughly convinced that this nominee, Mr. Tanner, is even more extremely less qualified for the position, a federal judgeship, than has been any other nominee for any position that I have been compelled, in this case by conscience, to testify upon or to evaluate.

I question Mr. Tanner's competence and qualifications. And I question Mr. Tanner's integrity.

I regard Mr. Tanner as a master of deceit and deliberate deceptions. I recognize that Mr. Tanner has a disarming personality, colorful language and accomplished verbal abilities, which gain him the confidence of many people and has probably made him effective with juries. My association with his work has primarily been in civil matters, or otherwise outside the courtrooms altogether. However, to refer to his "work," is to use that term loosely. His propensity for losing civil cases for Indian clients throughout the past fifteen years rests with his invalid assumption that competence can come without work—that cleverness and cunning is the equivalent of competence.

o   o   o

In the last meeting held between Jack Tanner and the Survival of American Indians Association, probably in 1969 in Fife, Washington, when I was present, as were several members and government officers of the Puyallup Indian Tribe, I recall Mr. Tanner's advising the group on courses of action for the election and the operation of a tribal government. He told them that they should "Do what you want; declare the results you need; and destroy the records. Ain't no way anyone's gonna prove what happened if there are no records." He informed us that's the way things are done in politics, business, and labor unions all the time, adding a question in proof of his statements: "You've heard of burning the ballots, haven't you? It's done all the time."

o   o   o

Dean Edgar Cahn of Antioch Law School can verify for the Committee that by early 1969 I had formed judgement that Jack Tanner was incompetent and inept as an attorney in civil cases, if for no other reason than Tanner's aversion to research and case development work. Beyond questioning his abilities, I had lost confidence fully in his integrity. Edgar can verify this because he called me from Washington, DC, to accuse me of being against Jack, and refusing to allow him to handle the case of an Indian police shooting victim, for the sole reason that Jack Tanner is a black man. I explained at length to Mr. Cahn at that time that Mr. Tanner's color was wholly immaterial to my judgement on his lack of competence and inability to provide quality representation in civil cases, or in criminal cases where investigative work might be crucial to the outcome.

Parenthetically, I would note that Mr. Cahn has been the only person I know of who has ever accused me at any time of being against black people. Throughout my adult life, I have acted to help break down barriers between Indian people and black people, even to the point of filing complaints with federal agencies against other federal agencies who have actively sought to maintain or intensify an antipathy or hatred against blacks among many Indian people. Just hours before his fatal trip to Memphis in 1968, I recall explaining to the late Dr. Martin Luther King about this "white-imposed racism or racial prejudice," and the importance of Indians joining with Blacks in the national Poor People's Campaign of that year. From that period to the present, our organization has maintained working alliances with a number of Black, Chicano, and other racial and economic class minorities, on a number of concerns. In the matter of Mr. Tanner's nomination, I do not believe that his race or color should be used as a shield against inquiry into his qualifications or competence. It is patently unfair to other opponents of this nomination that a general accusation has arisen as standard response to the opposition that "they are just opposed to having a black judge." It is more grossly unfair to those black attorneys in Washington State who would warrant consideration for appointment to a federal judgeship on the basis of merit and unquestionable qualifications.

Although I have read in the newspapers of latter 1977 that various charges have been made and investigated by the FBI regarding Jack Tanner's relationships to Mr. Bob Satiacum, a Puyallup Indian engaged in various past and present business enterprises on the Puyallup Indian Reservation, the specifics or nature of any allegations have not been stated in the news accounts. Inasmuch as Mr. Tanner's nomination has actually been made, I cannot believe that a complete investigation has been made of his involvements on the Puyallup Reservation, or of his relationships with Bob Satiacum beyond the attorney-client one.

The political involvements of members of the Washington congressional delegation with Mr. Tanner, Mr. Satiacum, and the Puyallup Indian Reservation or other members of the Puyallup Tribe over the past three years provides an odd inter-mix of relationships that can only be extremely difficult for anyone to comprehend.

o o o

In the first days of January 1976, however Jack Tanner met with members of the Puyallup Tribal Council in his capacity as alter ego and business associate of Bob Satiacum, if not his slave master. The Tribal Council and Bob had agreed to hold a meeting among themselves in order to formulate an agreement for his use of the property consistent with the tribal referendum, for curtailing any illegal activities, and for eliminating the problems getting out of hand under the administration of the businesses by Satiacum's management employees.

Instead, Jack Tanner stormed into the meeting and, among other abusive and threatening statements, declared that: "We don't have to deal with you at all!" "We don't have to pay you anything whatsoever!" "We can do anything we want to on that property, and there's nothing anyone can do about it!" "We don't have to pay taxes to anyone; nobody has jurisdiction over that land. The Tribe doesn't have anything to say there!"

The attempts by Ms. Ramona Bennett, tribal chairwoman, to discuss the problems with Bob Satiacum and to tell Mr. Tanner that, "We are trying to talk to Bob....", were cut off by Tanner's angry interruptions. Bob's own attempts to speak for himself similarly were halted by Mr. Tanner's outbursts and tirade. The meeting was abbreviated and adjourned without any satisfactory response to the community problems outlined by Ms. Bennett.

o o o

Another curious sidelight to this nomination is that, since the Puyallup Tribe succeeded in removing Bob Satiacum and Jack Tanner from the tribal lands—which were converted for tribal income generation for governmental operations, tribal employment opportunities, and community services—several members of the Washington congressional delegation have ganged up against the Puyallup Tribe to deny it federal funding assistance and to restrict its opportunities.

o o o

The methods and reasons for hiding interests, income, or ownership, in business activities on the Puyallup Reservation are matters better known to Mr. Tanner than to myself. One good ancillary effect of Mr. Tanner's being considered for a federal judgeship, however, has been that, during the period his name has been under consideration, Bob Satiacum has been regularly and faithfully paying his taxes—at least to the Tribe. And, at least on those businesses he is known to own or have partial interest in.

Finally and briefly, there are two other aspects about this nomination which have disturbing implications in my mind.

One again relates to actions of members of the Washington congressional delegation, both Senators and Representatives. The frequency of letter and private telephonic communication between members of the delegation to federal judges, including Justices of the US Supreme Court, regarding Indian treaty issues and related proceedings, has increased in recent years. I have no judgements on the propriety of these actions, although I would prefer that any such communications be offered in a record form or from a formal status standing, as with *amicus* or intervener, in order that the content at least may be know publicly. I have no doubt in the integrity and abilities of US Judges George Boldt or Walter McGovern to withstand undue influence from any source whatsoever. I do not here charge that any undue influence has been attempted through these communications. However, I have no faith whatever that Jack Tanner can maintain the independence and integrity for remaining free from undue influence, even when no influence is intended. If confirmed, Mr. Tanner will have a lot to be beholden for to his sponsors and supporters.

Lastly, with reference to charges previously reported in the press against Jack Tanner, particularly relating to the Smokey Metcalf conviction and appeal, I am again extremely distressed by the implications I see. I am not so concerned about a matter of forgery and not centrally, although more so, about a question of perjury. Often I have signed other people's names with their permission or knowledge; and have authorized others to sign my own name. I am not surprised that Jack's hometown newspaper, the *Tacoma News Tribune*, did a technically-precise word usage analysis of his testimony to declare that, technically, he did not lie on the witness stand and could not be accused of perjury in that instance. However, the truth was not revealed in the, technically responsive, answers. There was design of concealment and caginess in the confusion rendered. I've not questioned Mr. Tanner's abilities as a criminal lawyer. But in that case he had another role—as witness. His mastery of the legal art of slipping and sliding around the truth to hide parts of it could only be envied by such persons as Richard Nixon. It was not a judgement to be made upon his agility of mind or adeptness which was at stake in that matter; but rather another man's liberty. When that precious value is not appreciated in the courts of this land, then I am offended—as an American citizen and as a human being.

Your vote should record that the nomination of Mr. Jack Tanner was not confirmed.

Respectfully submitted,
Hank Adams

Testimonial

Hearing Before the Select Committee on Small Business. US Senate. 96th
Congress, 1st Session. On Nomination of Paul R. Boucher to be Inspector General of the US Small Business Administration. (May 16, 1979).

The Honorable Lowell Weicker,
United States Senator,
Washington, DC 20510
Attn: Mr. Stan Twardy, Minority Counsel, Small Business Committee
Re: Nomination of Mr. Paul Boucher as Inspector General, SBA

Dear Senator Weicker:

I understand hearings are to be held on the confirmation of the nomination of Mr. Paul Boucher to become Inspector General for the Small Business
Administration. Also, I'm informed that a question of whether Mr. Boucher
may have acted improperly in the course of a trial of three Indians (Keever
and Dock Locklear, and Bill Sargent) for felony possession of stolen government property in Wilmington, North Carolina, in December of 1973, might
be raised as an issue on confirmation.

Let me affirm, first, that I do not believe that any aspect of Mr. Boucher's
conduct or participation in the Wilmington trial would constitute his dis-
qualification for appointment as SBA Inspector General, or as a practicing
attorney for that matter.

I've reviewed Jack Anderson's column after the trial in which it is stated
that: "For an attorney knowingly to present false testimony before a court is
a disbarment offense." The column centers upon the fact that Mr. Boucher
failed to act to correct or strike testimony that Jack Anderson had offered to
"pay $20,000 plus....one hundred free stories" in his column in exchange for
access to stolen documents—after I had personally informed Mr. Boucher
that the testimony was false. An additional point was that Mr. Boucher did
not simply have to rely upon my word on the matter, but that the Justice
Department in Washington, DC, was fully aware of its falseness, because—
as I had informed Mr. Boucher—the fact that neither Jack Anderson nor Les
Whitten had traveled to North Carolina, nor at any time offered money for
documents or stories, was expressed in sworn testimony before grand jury
proceedings and probable other forms.

Here are several background facts: (1) I was subpoenaed as a defense
witness for the trial and attended it through conclusion; (2) I informed
Jack Anderson and Les Whitten about the offensive testimony entered; (3)
I was present in Les Whitten's office while he made various telephone calls
in development of the story, including some to federal attorneys involved,
and defense attorneys. This latter point has import because there was disagreement on what the Larry Blacksmith testimony had actually been. The

US Attorney and his Assistant in North Carolina differed in recollections from Whitten's "source" on what the actual testimony, and its nature or substance, had been. Whitten advised them that if the transcript of testimony conformed to the federal attorneys' recollection, he would do no story on the matter. They agreed to aid in designating the relevant portion of testimony in order that Anderson's office could order or purchase its transcription. When the transcript arrived, it conformed in detail with the "sources" statements, and indicated either error of recollection on the part of the State federal attorneys, or a continuing reluctance to admit the offensiveness of the testimony and to be forthright and truthful. Mr. Boucher himself had not disagreed with information supplied Mr. Whitten; had affirmed most of it; was apologetic; and admitted that the matter probably should have been handled differently and rectified before the case went to the jury.

o o o

In North Carolina, Oklahoma, and South Dakota, I was asked to testify, or subpoenaed to testify, on matters relating to properties missing from the BIA, and regarding Wounded Knee (for which I had acted as a White House intermediary with twenty-four hour access to presidential assistant and then counsel, Leonard Garment, in helping negotiate an end to the confrontation). In the one instance where I was able to take the witness stand briefly—in South Dakota—it was again apparent that the US Attorney's Office had been supplied FBI files ostensibly relating to my background, as a means of attacking my character and credibility. Another US Attorney's Office later informed me of these files, characterizing them as "the most ludicrous and derogatory hate-file" which that attorney had ever seen. A private attorney, having no association to myself, was shown these files and was prepared to use them against me—as was the apparent situation in South Dakota. If that had been the case, in the event that I had not been kept off the witness stand in Wilmington, then I would have clear questions about Mr. Boucher's integrity. However, there was no hint of that in the North Carolina trial—and although I was aware of the shoddy briefings given Senators Cook and Hruska by the FBI and possibly Justice Department—I only became aware of the derogatory briefings and Justice Department information supply or dissemination regarding myself in the course of, and after, the Wounded Knee proceedings. (As recently as this past year, I have been advised, my picture and background statement was circulated and posted with security stations in a number of governmental buildings in Washington, DC, with warnings to watch for my entry—at a time when I was neither in DC, nor planning to come there.)

I have learned that it is possible for moral men to operate among vipers in the American government, and not be infected by their colleagues malice or venom. For instance, Leonard Garment has seemed one of the most honorable men I've been privileged to know, in or out of government. It is possible that Mr. Boucher has been untainted while in the employ of the Justice Department during a most nefarious period of its history. My own inquiries on his background—since being contacted by your office on this matter a month ago—would indicate that he, indeed, is a conscientious and dedicated person, whose integrity is intact. Most praiseworthy, I've been informed, has been his work on the investigation of criminal acts and coverups at the highest levels of the FBI earlier in this past decade.

I consider it gravely unfortunate that the Congress and its committees have never examined into the issues of wrongdoing against various Indian people, communities and organizations, by the various levels and divisions of the Justice Department. I am certain, however, that such an investigation would clearly show wrongdoing, although of both criminal and noncriminal nature. I'm certain, also, that—apart from the internal designs of Justice agencies, and directives from the White House and its Executive Offices— questionable actions have resulted from demands made upon the Department and its Attorneys General by powerful members of the Congress itself.

In closing, I would want to commend yourself and your staff for the apparent thoroughness with which you are looking at this nomination. Only a year ago, I was thoroughly distressed by the closed-eyes approach by which the Judiciary Committee, after failing to instigate serious charges against a nominee for a federal judgship—whom I was actively opposing—routinely recommended a confirmation. There were aspects of that nomination which touched upon the operation of the minority-set aside in federal contracting under the Small Business Administration, which I had intended to raise at this time as a matter which should warrant close attention by any SBA Inspector General. However, that would probably be better presented in a separate communication to your Committee, inasmuch as it does not bear upon Mr. Boucher's qualifications in any particular.

I hope this letter may be helpful to your consideration and to your review of the point raised with respect to Mr. Boucher's actions in 1973. I know of nothing which should disqualify him for the SBA position; and all that I have been able to learn would indicate that he is worthy of confirmation.

Most sincerely yours,
Hank Adams, SAIA

Letter

February 23, 1988
The Honorable John Miller,
US Representative
Washington, DC 20515
Attn: Mr. Jay Suchan, Staff Member
Re: "Misrepresentation as a Native American" (draft bill)

Dear Congressman Miller:

I've received the draft bill on unlawful misrepresentation. It would be sufficient, except that there are extraordinary problems and troublesome implications arising with the classification at:

> (a)...the term 'Native American' means an individual enrolled as a member in
> a Federally recognized Indian tribe.
>
> This should be modified to include working to such effect as:
>
> (b)...the term 'Native American' means an individual enrolled as a mem-
> ber in a Federally recognized Indian tribe, and any individual who is the
> natural child or direct lineal descendant of an enrolled member in a Federally
> recognized Indian tribe.
>
> Or, in the alternative, modified by adding:
>
> (c)...The provision of this section shall not apply to any individual who
> is the natural child or direct lineal descendant of an enrolled member in a
> Federally recognized Indian tribe.

The primary purpose of the bill should be directed against those non-
Indian persons who make a totally false claim of Indian identity or ancestry.
The draft essentially makes the bill a proposed criminal enforcement of all
tribal enrollment actions. It could compound the wrongs and injury too frequently inflicted upon numerous Indian persons by way of defective enrollment processes and requirements that have too frequently been misapplied
by federal or tribal agencies in the past.

The present draft bill would be unacceptable "termination" legislation—
and would be terribly unjust. There is no doubt but that, if the bill became
law as drafted, its primary use would be made against Indian persons who
descend from enrolled tribal members, but who are not themselves now
enrolled in tribal membership for a range of reasons.

The facts are that the federal government has had an overbearingly
intrusive impact upon membership actions of the tribes in an accommodation of its own policy, or varying political, designs of different moments. By
statutes, the Congress has "terminated" the Indian status of full-bloods (Oregon tribes, for example: Klamath, Cellos); Ute Indians of less than "one-half

of Indian blood"; and Yakimas of less than "one-fourth" of bands allotted on that Reservation. It ended enrollments or distinguished between Alaskan Natives born before and after the effective date of the Lands Claims Settlement Act. In Oklahoma, to accommodate the marginal Indian blood quantum of Phillips Petroleum's W.W. Keeler, Congress set Cherokee enrollment eligibilities at 1/16th or 1/32nd of Indian blood in federal laws.

Administrative applications of membership provisions of tribal constitutions have produced notorious abuses by both federal and tribal agencies. The writing of constitutions after the Indian Reorganization Act of 1934 created some of the problems of arbitrariness and senseless requirements, particularly relating to "place of birth" and "residency" at time of birth. Going to the wrong hospital in the wrong town could provide a birth record that disqualified an Indian person from membership in his or her ancestral tribe.

I was centrally involved in prosecuting litigation in *Frank v. Morton* in the District of Columbia federal court and in the Western District of Washington, from 1973 through 1977, to restore Nisqually Indian enrollment rights. That tribe had been reduced to forty-eight members, including families of the least Indian blood and excluding persons of predominant Indian bloodlines and parentage, due to wrongful federal and tribal actions. The membership increased about tenfold when the membership criteria was properly applied in consequence of the litigation.

It is important that the proposed bill be directed against non-Indians making false claims, rather than toward Indians who are already suffering injury.

I appreciate your assistance and consideration.

Respectfully yours,
Hank Adams, SAIA

Index

310 The Hank Adams Reader

About the Editor

Professor David E. Wilkins holds the McKnight Presidential Professorship in American Indian Studies at the University of Minnesota. He has adjunct appointments in political science, law, and American studies. He received his PhD in political science from the University of North Carolina–Chapel Hill in 1990. Wilkins's research and teaching interests include indigenous politics and governance, federal Indian policy and law, comparative politics, and diplomacy and constitutional development.